FROM PABLO TO OSAMA

MICHAEL KENNEY

FROM **PABLO** TO **OSAMA**

Trafficking and Terrorist Networks, Government Bureaucracies, and Competitive Adaptation

THE PENNSYLVANIA STATE UNIVERSITY PRESS
UNIVERSITY PARK, PENNSYLVANIA

Library of Congress Cataloging-in-Publication Data

Kenney, Michael, 1967–
    From Pablo to Osama : trafficking and terrorist networks,
    government bureaucracies, and competitive adaptation /
    Michael Kenney.
            p.   cm.
        Includes bibliographical references and index.
    ISBN-13: 987–0-271–02931–3 (cloth : alk. paper)
    ISBN-10: 0–271–02931–5 (cloth : alk. paper)
    1. Terrorism—Prevention.
    2. Terrorism—Government policy.
    3. Drug traffic—Prevention.
    I. Title.

HV6431.K423 2007
363.325—dc22
2006037198

Contents

Ten years ago, while researching this book in Colombia, I met Joaquin Buitrago, a young officer with the Colombian National Police. While it had been years since the U.S. government transformed Colombia into a central front in the war on drugs, cocaine production was increasingly dramatically. Contrary to popular misperception, the failure of Colombian and American authorities to substantially reduce, let alone eliminate, the cocaine trade was not due to a lack of effort. In the two years preceding our meeting, Buitrago's agency, with substantial support from Washington, spearheaded an intensive law enforcement crackdown, targeting the leaders of Colombia's drug "cartels." In spite of capturing many cocaine "kingpins" and disrupting their smuggling networks, the illicit drug trade in Colombia continued to flourish, and I was hoping the good captain could help me understand why.

Following a hackneyed Power Point presentation, designed for American policymakers making their obligatory tour stop on the front lines of Colombia's war on drugs, we turned to the questions that brought me to Buitrago. As we talked, rehearsed formality giving way to candid expression, it became increasingly clear how troubled Buitrago was by the precarious situation in which he and his countrymen found themselves. When I asked him why he risked his life for such dangerous and seemingly futile work, he paraphrased a sentiment expressed by Colombia's most notorious drug traffickers, the so-called "Extraditables," who famously declared their preference for a tomb in Colombia to a jail cell in the United States. "I would rather my son see me dead in a tomb," he said, his voice rising, "than say that I was corrupt, or that I turned my country over to the traffickers!"[1] It was a dramatic moment, a spontaneous admission by a foot soldier in the war on drugs that, while things were not going particularly well, he was determined to continue the fight. I encountered Captain Buitrago's dedication, if not always his eloquence, repeatedly among the dozens of U.S. and Colombian law enforcers I interviewed in subsequent years.

Three years after meeting Buitrago, I sat down with "Homero," a former drug courier from Colombia who had worked his way up his illicit network's "queer ladder" to become a wholesale cocaine distributor in the United States, prior to his arrest and incarceration for drug-related offenses. "It's a war on drugs," he conceded in our prison interview in central Florida. "I'm not saying that we're prisoners due to an injustice. No. We were, the majority of us, involved in drug trafficking. . . . But I tell you sincerely that this business will not end, because when you close one door, the drug traffickers open three or four more."[2]

If Captain Buitrago gives passionate expression to his and, by symbolic extension, his government's determination to continue the struggle, Homero provides an important clue as to why Colombia and the United States are not likely to win the war on drugs through supply-control strategies that privilege law enforcement, drug interdiction, and crop eradication. Acknowledging the insight in Homero's comment, this book sets out to explain it. I argue that the persistence of Colombia's drug trade comes in part from the ability of people like Homero, and the criminal enterprises they work for, to create multiple entryways for every path blocked by their government adversaries. What facilitates this metaphorical revolving door are the organizational learning capacities of drug traffickers and law enforcers, who change their activities in response to information and experience, store their knowledge in practices and institutional memories, and select routines that produce satisfactory results.

Five years after my encounter with Homero, I traveled to Israel with a group of American scholars to learn more about the counterterrorism challenges facing Israeli authorities. It was an intense and sobering experience. One day we visited Gilboa Security Prison, a maximum-security facility for political prisoners near Armageddon. Gilboa confines 852 of Palestine's toughest militants, including fighters from Hamas, the Palestine Islamic Jihad, and the Al-Aqsa Martyrs Brigade. "There are no stone throwers here," we were told. Following another Power Point presentation, this one apparently designed for American journalists, policymakers, and academics making their obligatory tour stop on the frontlines of Israel's war on terror, the prison commander entertained our questions. As he listened to my question about information sharing and learning among detainees, the colonel gave a knowing smile. He readily admitted that this was a problem. The prisoners, he said, gather information about their Israeli captors. They share ideas with their fellow militants and plot operations, including escape attempts and terrorist attacks. But the colonel quickly pointed out that the prison authorities also learn from the detainees. The authorities cultivate informants in the prison population, whom they use to gather information about detainees' plans and aspirations. The colonel emphasized that on numerous occasions they have used this intelligence to disrupt impending attacks.

After the briefing the colonel escorted us to the commons area in the Israeli Arab section of the prison, where we spoke face to face with several militants. One detainee I talked with vented his frustration at what he called the Israeli occupation of Palestine. While he expressed regret for killing an Israeli soldier, he complained about his treatment in the jail and suggested that the struggle for Palestinian statehood was far from over.

The visit to Gilboa prison and several other military facilities in Israel confirmed my suspicion that drug traffickers and law enforcers are not the only ones who learn. Secular and religious extremists and the governments they fight also learn from experience. As suggested in the colonel's remarks, terrorists and counterterrorists not only learn, they learn from each other, through complex interactions in shared social systems, a phenomenon I refer to in this book as "competitive adaptation." And, as the jailed detainee implies, he and his colleagues are prepared to continue the struggle, no matter how many militants the Israelis incarcerate, no matter how many informants they turn, no matter how many security walls they build. Like Homero and Captain Buitrago, the Israeli colonel and the Palestinian prisoner symbolize this co-evolutionary dynamic, a struggle that, as I show in this book, favors the traffickers and terrorists in significant, if not inevitably superior, ways.

Colombia's tragedy is not of its own making, at least not entirely. After all, millions of Americans regularly consume its illicit wares while tacitly supporting a drug-prohibition regime that artificially inflates the value of these commodities, allowing people like Homero to reap the financial rewards of our "debauchery" and complacence. Like many Americans, my own initiation to the drug trade's manifold complexities came on the demand side of the policy continuum: youthful experimentation with marijuana and alcohol produced a psychological dependence of sorts, and at the worldly age of eighteen I found myself sharing group therapy sessions in idyllic rural New Hampshire with assorted other "alkies" and addicts, all of us struggling to come to terms with our substance abuse. Following treatment, I returned to school and eventually twelve-stepped my way to Project Rebound, an in-patient rehabilitation center in Boston. At Rebound I worked closely with adolescent drug addicts, many of whom were dependent on crack cocaine and heroin. After college I became a drug-prevention specialist at the Center for Drug-Free Living in Orlando, Florida, where I worked with "high-risk" youths in community outreach. As part of an improvisational theater troupe called the Prevention Players, I educated local teenagers on the perils of drug abuse and the promise of peer resistance.

Following my VISTA service in Orlando, I joined the Peace Corps and became an agricultural extensionist in Ecuador. For two years I worked with farmers who faced many of the dilemmas of Andean drug cultivators, even if they didn't grow illicit crops themselves. In Ecuador I took advantage of my proximity to Colombia by traveling repeatedly to Pasto during my service and throughout Colombia at the end of my term. When I returned to school as a graduate student following this South American adventure, I began to formally pursue my research interest in Colombia's cocaine trade, an interest that led me back to the country several times to carry out the fieldwork that forms the empirical core of this book.

As the original incarnation of this study was nearing completion, I began to wonder whether the concepts I was using to understand the drug trade and U.S.-Colombian law enforcement could be applied to other types of criminal nonstate actors and government security agencies. Then Mohammed Atta and his colleagues carried out the devastating 9/11 attacks, and I decided to pursue my hunch by expanding my research to include a second set of players in competitive adaptation, terrorists and the state security agencies that seek to destroy them. When given an opportunity to see firsthand the difficulties facing Israeli authorities in their own long-standing struggle against terrorism, I readily agreed.

This book is the result of a long intellectual journey, and an even longer personal one. In the chapters that follow I analyze the wars on drugs and terror from a critical standpoint, reflecting not just my formal training but sundry real-world personal experiences. My aim is not to point fingers but to steer attention away from drug enforcement and counterterrorism efforts that, owing to the malleable nature of the illicit enterprises they confront, have not worked well in the past and are not likely to work much better in the future. While I suggest potentially superior alternatives, I am content to leave specific policy prescriptions to others.[3] To paraphrase Michael Ignatieff, my central question in this study is less "What must we do?" than "Who are our adversaries, and how does what we do influence what they become?"[4] My hope is that those who are entrusted with the authority to amend such policies, and the rest of us who are responsible for holding our decision makers accountable for the policies they choose, will find this effort worthwhile.

I have acquired many intellectual and personal debts while working on this book, far too many to list here (for which I beg the indulgence of friends and colleagues who find their names omitted). Numerous institutions supported my research. The National Science Foundation provided substantial support, which allowed me to carry out extensive fieldwork in Colombia. The University of Florida, the Tinker Foundation, the Pennsylvania State University, and the Foundation for the Defense of Democracies provided additional assistance for my research in Colombia, the United States, and Israel.

Transforming my dissertation into a book involved a great deal more work than I initially anticipated; indeed, sometimes I feel like I have written three books in order to create this one. Fortunately, my writing and analysis were greatly assisted by two vibrant learning communities, the Center for International Security and Cooperation (cisac), Freeman Spogli Institute, at Stanford University and the Center for International Studies at the University of Southern California. cisac deserves a special nod, not just for its unique strengths in organization theory and the stimulating interdisciplinary environment created by Scott Sagan and his colleagues, but because the center generously supported my work at both the pre- and postdoctoral levels.

Institutions are important; the people that give them life even more so. At Stanford I was extremely fortunate to work with Lynn Eden. Serving as both mentor and muse, Lynn read many chapters in this book as they appeared at different stages of gestation, always encouraging me with her infectious enthusiasm and perceptive commentary. Martha Feldman, then of the University of Michigan, now at the University of California, Irvine, inspired me with her own work and pushed me to deepen my analysis in meaningful ways. This book and my own intellectual development have benefited enormously from my association with Lynn and Martha.

At the University of Florida, Philip Williams, Terry McCoy, Leann Brown, Larry Dodd, and Joseph Spillane read the earliest draft of this study and provided critical feedback. While conducting field research in Colombia, William Ramírez and his colleagues in the Institute of Political Studies and International Relations at the National University shared their deep knowledge of Colombia and gave me a place to hang my hat between interviews. At Stanford and USC, I met many fascinating people who enriched my understanding of organization theory and international relations. My colleagues in the School of Public Affairs at Penn State Capital College have been models of collegiality and support.

I could not have undertaken, let alone completed, this study without the cooperation of several dozen American, Colombian, and Israeli government officials who took time out of their busy schedules to share their expertise with me. I owe a similar debt of gratitude to the former drug smugglers who allowed me to interview them, even when they stood to gain little by doing so. To protect the confidentiality of my informants, many of whom wouldn't mind seeing their names in print, I refrain from identifying them here. Their anonymity in no way lessens their impact on this book. Archivists at the Drug Enforcement Administration library and the National Archives in Washington, D.C., and *El Tiempo, El Espectador,* and *Semana* in Bogotá helped me track down numerous leads. Gabriela Rovillon Acosta, Maxine Downs, and Amy Weik transcribed dozens of interviews.

Toiling away in relative obscurity at a research project that at times seems never-ending has a way of exacerbating one's sense of personal and intellectual isolation from the world. Over the years, the many individuals who have listened to or read portions of this study have greatly relieved my own reclusion. I have been fortunate to present my research findings at seminars, workshops, and conferences sponsored by the Pacific Northwest Colloquia in International Security at the University of Washington, the Munk Centre for International Studies at the University of Toronto, the Institute on Global Conflict and Cooperation at the University of California, San Diego, the International Forum at Southern Polytechnic State University, the Center for International Security and Cooperation at Stanford, and the Center for International Studies at USC. I have also benefited from publishing parts of this book in the following books and journals: "The Rules of Drug Trafficking: Decision-Making in Colombian Smuggling Enterprises," in *Handbook of Decision-Making* (New York: Taylor and Francis, 2006); "Organizational Learning Processes in Colombian Drug Trafficking Networks," in *Organizational Learning in the Global Context* (London: Ashgate,

2006); "How Terrorists Learn," in *Teaching Terror: Knowledge Transfer in the Terrorist World* (Lanham, Md.: Rowman & Littlefield, 2006); "Drug Traffickers, Terrorist Networks, and Ill-Fated Government Strategies," in *New Threats and New Actors in International Security* (New York: Palgrave Macmillan, 2005); "From Pablo to Osama: Counter-terrorism Lessons from the War on Drugs," *Survival* 45, no. 3 (2003): 187–206; "Intelligence Games: A Comparative Analysis of the Intelligence Capabilities of the Drug Enforcement Agencies and Drug Trafficking Enterprises," *International Journal of Intelligence and CounterIntelligence* 16, no. 2 (2003): 212–43; and "When Criminals Outsmart the State: Understanding the Learning Capacity of Colombian Drug Trafficking Organizations," *Transnational Organized Crime* 5, no. 1 (1999): 97–119.

When I was still a postdoctoral fellow at USC, Carol Wise suggested that I contact Sanford Thatcher, director of the Pennsylvania State University Press, about publishing my manuscript. Whether because of Carol's kind intervention or because Sandy saw some promise in an early version of this book, his interest and support have been instrumental. Penn State Press's three anonymous readers provided valuable feedback, helping me improve this study immeasurably. The editorial team did a remarkable job of shepherding the manuscript through the review and production process, correcting for numerous deficiencies along the way.

Of all the people I thank here, none are more important than my family. Margaret and Chris Kenney have always blessed me with their unconditional love, as only mothers can. My father, Peter Kenney, encouraged me to think for myself at an early age, continually supported my unorthodox career choices, and read the entire manuscript and offered numerous helpful suggestions. This book is much better for his care and encouragement. My deepest debt of gratitude goes to two magnificent individuals: my wife, Emilia, and our daughter, Caroline, to whom I dedicate this book and whose love, devotion, and good humor often remind me that there's more to life than drugs and terrorism.

After months of frustrating near misses, the elite enforcement unit finally tracked its prey to a nondescript two-story row house on the outskirts of Medellín, Colombia. Within minutes, a team of commandos stormed the building, killing Pablo Escobar, the notorious leader of the Medellín "cartel," as he fled barefoot across the Spanish-tiled rooftop. Nine years later, U.S. and Pakistani intelligence officials tracked their prey to a nondescript two-story house on the outskirts of Faisalabad. Again a team of commandos stormed the building, this time shooting Abu Zubaydah, Al Qaeda's notorious operations director, several times as he fled across the rooftop.[1]

Both missions, designed to immobilize drug-trafficking and terrorist networks by eliminating their leaders, represent a central component in U.S. drug-control and counterterrorism programs. While local commandos carried out the raids, they received extensive support from their American colleagues, including intelligence, training, equipment, even reward money for informers. Organizationally, the missions used a task force approach, combining select law enforcement and military personnel from different agencies into small, rapid-reaction strike forces designed to mimic the stealth and mobility of their illicit adversaries.

These similarities are not coincidental. As members of the U.S. intelligence community acknowledge, drug enforcement raids in Colombia during the 1990s serve as models for today's counterterrorism missions in Afghanistan, Pakistan, Yemen, and elsewhere.[2] Other institutional vestiges of the Reagan era of drug control, such as the Organized Crime Drug Enforcement Task Force (OCDETF), have been resurrected by Bush administration officials as paragons of the interagency cooperation necessary to dismantle terrorist networks.[3] But if the decades-old "war on drugs," with its leadership interdiction, militarized law enforcement, and interagency task forces, is to serve as a prototype for Washington's "war on terror," policymakers and citizens must understand the lessons that can properly be extrapolated from the model. This study offers such an appraisal, highlighting the protean character of drug-trafficking and terrorist networks and the resolute, if less nimble, nature of the state enforcement bureaucracies that seek to destroy them.

Over the past quarter-century, U.S. and Colombian officials have implemented a string of drug-control programs in Colombia. While the names periodically change—from Operation Stopgap to Operation Snowcap, from the Andean Strategy to the Kingpin Strategy, from Plan Colombia to Plan Patriota—the basic strategy remains the same: to reduce the consumption of illegal drugs in the United States by eliminating their supply in Colombia.[4] In demonstration of the enormous military, law enforcement, and intelligence resources devoted to these efforts, government officials have eradicated several hundred thousand hectares of drug crops, confiscated thousands of transportation vessels, destroyed tens of thousands of drug-processing labs, seized hundreds of tons of illegal drugs, frozen millions of dollars in illicit profits and financial assets, captured thousands of suspected traffickers, and extradited hundreds of high-level traffickers to the United States to face justice in American courts.

Despite these apparent successes, Plan Colombia and other initiatives have not significantly reduced the supply of illegal drugs in the United States, as reflected in relatively stable drug price and purity levels. At their best, supply-reduction programs have produced temporary ripples that quickly settle as traffickers establish alternative sources of supply, move their drug plantings and processing labs, invent new production methods, and create fresh transportation routes. Indeed, no sooner were the original "cocaine kingpins," including Escobar, Gonzalo Rodríguez Gacha, José Santacruz Londono, and the Rodríguez-Orejuela brothers, imprisoned or killed than replacements emerged, eager to pick up where their predecessors left off. Notwithstanding record drug seizures and crop eradication in recent years, evidence of frenzied attempts by law enforcers to demonstrate Plan Colombia's effectiveness as it neared the end of its original life cycle, the country remains the primary source of cocaine and a major source of heroin for American drug markets, according to estimates produced by the U.S. government and the United Nations.[5] Law enforcers may be capturing hundreds of metric tons of cocaine and heroin per year, but drug traffickers still "crown," or successfully complete, enough shipments to satisfy drug users throughout the United States, where millions of Americans continue to consume these and other illegal drugs.[6]

What accounts for these disappointing results? Why have Washington and Bogotá been unable to eliminate the Colombian drug trade, or at least reduce it to manageable proportions? Drawing on extensive field research, including interviews with more than one hundred key informants, and organizational learning theory, I argue that the resilience of Colombia's drug trade stems in part from the ability of smuggling enterprises to alter their activities in response to information and experience, store this knowledge in practices and procedures, and select and retain routines that produce satisfactory, if not necessarily optimal, results. In short, *narcos* learn, building skills and changing practices in simple but effective ways that make it difficult for law enforcers to stop them.

Organizational Learning

Social scientists have produced a large body of literature on organizational learning in recent decades.[7] While scholars have long debated the prospect and constitutive elements of learning, a consensus has emerged among theorists and practitioners that many organizations modify existing practices in response to knowledge and experience. To date, however, much of the theoretical and empirical work on organizational learning has focused on legally sanctioned organizations, such as government bureaucracies, business firms, international organizations, and universities. Although this body of work has deepened our understanding of how organizations learn—and fail to learn—it largely ignores the "dark" side of organizational life, where people acting on behalf of organizations learn for less than benevolent purposes. After 1960, U.S. cigarette manufacturers knew there was a direct and causal linkage between cigarette smoking and lung cancer; yet, as Lynn Eden notes, "the industry both denied the state of knowledge and suppressed and twisted evidence" demonstrating the connection.[8] During World War II, the Nazi bureaucracy led by Adolph Eichmann learned to murder millions of human beings more effectively over time, devising numerous innovations that allowed them to overcome logistical challenges to genocide.[9] And, more recently, scientists from the Aum Shinrikiyo cult learned the intricate physical processes involved in developing and dispersing sarin and other chemical agents for use in violent attacks against their fellow Japanese.[10] As these examples suggest, some organizations learn to cause great harm and suffering, undermining facile assumptions that learning is inherently "good," whether as an outcome of collective action or as an ideal to which all organizations should aspire.

In fact, organizations good and bad learn to complete tasks, address problems, and create identities. In a basic sense, organizations learn when their participants learn for them: acquiring, interpreting, and applying knowledge and experience. Yet organizational learning is more than the sum of the information-processing activities of its members. Learning does not become organizational until knowledge is embedded in routines and stored in artifacts. Routines include rules, practices, and procedures that transform individual action into collective behavior, allowing organizations to perform work, make decisions, build cultures, communicate knowledge, and solve problems. Knowledge-based artifacts, also called organizational memories, include files, manuals, databases, and financial accounts that record and store information and experience.[11] While organizations differ in the degree to which they formalize their rules and artifacts, both informal and formal routines embody knowledge and experience, allowing participants to learn from organizational history even when they have not experienced that history themselves.[12]

Mētis vs. Techne

Organizational knowledge is transmitted to participants through training, apprenticeships, socialization, even stories. The method of diffusion depends on the type of knowledge being shared. Abstract technical knowledge, what ancient Greek poets and philosophers referred to as *techne,* lends itself to codification in knowledge-based artifacts and can be readily taught through formal instruction. Experiential, intuitive knowledge, what the Greeks called *mētis,* often resists simplification into formal artifacts. Mētis encompasses a variety of skills—including ingenuity, elusiveness, even cunning and deceit—that athletes, statesmen, and others use to adapt to continually changing environments.[13] Practitioners develop mētis by doing, engaging in the activity itself, rather than by abstraction. They share mētis by participating in "communities of practice" where veterans and novices communicate, swap stories, and improvise, generating "knowledge-in-practice" through everyday interaction.[14] Whether embedded in formal artifacts or informal practices, organizational knowledge changes over time as participants make sense of ongoing experience and modify existing routines based on their interpretations. Irrespective of routine change, much organizational learning occurs tacitly, through interactions among participants that create intersubjective understandings of "the way things are done around here."[15]

Learning Disabilities

Like other organizations, Colombian trafficking networks confront numerous obstacles to learning.[16] Several decades of research on organizational behavior suggest that many of these difficulties are an unavoidable by-product of the way human beings, be they lawmakers or lawbreakers, think, act, and organize. Others are more specific to the manner in which these illicit enterprises organize their operations and perform their activities. To protect themselves from the police, trafficking enterprises often compartment their participants into loosely coupled networks and limit communication between "nodes." Such practices reduce network connectivity, making information sharing, which is critical to organizational learning, more difficult. More broadly, participants in trafficking networks are only what Herbert Simon calls "boundedly" rational: they face significant computational limitations in their ability to analyze feedback from incoming stimuli.[17] To distinguish meaningful signals from extraneous noise, they create cognitive shortcuts and frames of reference based on prior experience and beliefs. These mental models bias interpretation in subtle ways, causing participants to filter out certain signals and miss others.[18] While organizations seek to learn from experience, experience is often dimly perceived. Participants may not understand what happened, why it happened, and whether what happened is beneficial or harmful to the organization. Even when participants interpret experience correctly, satisfaction with current practices, investments in established technologies, and conflict may prevent the organization from modifying its practices in response to feedback. In recognizing these limitations to organizational learning, I, like James March and others, relax the assumption that experience automatically produces organizational wisdom and increased productivity.[19] Traffickers may gather, interpret, share, and apply knowledge and experience, or they may not; but even when they do learn, their adaptations do not inevitably make them smarter or more efficient. Organizational learning is a theory of process, not of progress.

Competitive Adaptation

Drug traffickers are not the only learners of interest in this study. Like their illicit counterparts, law enforcement "narcs" (short for narcotics agents) address problems, change practices, and create identities in response to knowledge and experience, sometimes improving their performance and aiding their bureaucratic survival. Since the 1980s federal law enforcers have reacted to pressure from external critics and to changes in the international drug trade by making greater use of electronic surveillance technologies and developing innovations in their undercover operations. The Drug Enforcement Administration (DEA) and other agencies have also created massive organizational memories containing millions of records on known and suspected traffickers.

While these changes have allowed law enforcers to exploit existing drug-control strategies and technologies to greater effect, they have not led officials to explore novel routines that may yield better results. Such learning, variously referred to in the literature as "exploitation," "single-loop" learning, "tactical" learning, and "first-order" learning, is restricted to adjusting established practices and procedures in response to experience, without considering broader changes in organizational goals.[20] By failing to experiment with other, potentially superior strategies, counterdrug policymakers and practitioners have fallen into a "competency trap" of epic proportions—a critical mistake that officials now threaten to repeat in the war on terror (I explore this theme in the conclusion). Nor has exploitation allowed the DEA, the Colombian National Police, and other law enforcement agencies to adapt their practices and procedures as quickly as their criminal adversaries.

Building on theoretical literature in learning ecologies, institutional isomorphism, and complexity, I introduce the concept of competitive adaptation to explain why.[21] Narcs and narcos learn not in isolation but within complex adaptive systems, where both sets of imperfectly informed, interdependent players gather and analyze information to change practices and outmaneuver their opponents. Counterdrug agents use their adaptations to learn more about traffickers they seek to eliminate, while narcos use theirs to avoid or suborn law enforcers, allowing them to continue their activities unchecked. These interactions are fundamentally dynamic. Players who fail to respond quickly to adverse circumstances, relying on intuition and cunning intelligence—in a word, mētis—to outsmart their adversaries, do not perform particularly well in these spirited learning races.

Law enforcement agencies confront a number of disadvantages in competitive adaptation. Their participants are organized into large, centralized bureaucracies marked by multiple layers of decision-making authority and administrative oversight. They confront complex task environments, numerous interagency coordination challenges, and high information costs in conducting multijurisdictional investigations against transnational smuggling enterprises. And, as "sovereignty-bound" institutions, they follow legal and bureaucratic regulations that protect citizens' political rights and civil liberties while holding government authorities accountable to the rule of law. These protections, which are indispensable to liberal democratic states, slow decision cycles and restrain collective action in law enforcement agencies.

Trafficking networks, in contrast, are "light on their feet."[22] They are smaller and organizationally "flatter"; they enjoy simple task environments, fewer coordination challenges, and low information costs; they operate outside the rule of law; and they have clear incentives to adapt: their immediate survival often depends on it. Given these advantages, it is not surprising that smuggling networks often process information, make decisions, coordinate behavior, and change practices faster than the cumbersome bureaucracies that confront them. But rather than merely asserting that government bureaucracies are slower than criminal networks, competitive adaptation provides a comparative framework for understanding how traffickers and terrorists organize their activities, how they process information and experience, and how they draw on knowledge and experience to learn in hostile environments where their adversaries also learn from them.

From Traffickers to Terrorists

During the late 1980s, as the Colombian National Police tracked down and killed its first cocaine "kingpins," veteran *mujaheddin*, fresh from their resistance campaign against Soviet occupation forces in Afghanistan, formed a multinational network of Islamic militants ready to expand their holy war against the United States and its allies in the Middle East. While more than a decade would pass before Al Qaeda carried out the devastating attacks that made Osama bin Laden a household name, in the intervening years bin Laden's training and logistics network was involved in several assaults against American interests, including the simultaneous bombings of the U.S. embassies in Nairobi and Dar-es-Salaam in 1998 and the amphibious attack on the *U.S.S. Cole* in Yemen in 2000. Indeed, several years before the tragic events of September 11, 2001, the U.S. intelligence community identified Al Qaeda as the most formidable terrorist adversary facing the United States, initiating several ultimately unsuccessful operations to capture bin Laden and dismantle his network.[23]

Al Qaeda shares numerous similarities with drug-trafficking enterprises that have frustrated U.S. and Colombian law enforcers in recent years, including flat decision-making hierarchies, compartmented networks, and the ability to gather information and change practices in response to experience. Interesting parallels also abound between counterdrug operations in Colombia and counterterrorism missions in Afghanistan and Pakistan. These include a reliance on human and electronic intelligence sources to identify clandestine targets, the use of American-trained local forces to conduct "leadership interdiction" missions against trafficking and terrorist kingpins, and interagency enforcement networks to coordinate complex operations within and across government bureaucracies. In view of these similarities and the growing conviction among politicians and policymakers that the United States is engaged in a "long war" against terrorism, a comparison of drug-trafficking and terrorist enterprises, along with government efforts to destroy them, is in order.

This book provides such an analysis, extending the competitive adaptation framework to terrorist networks and counterterrorism bureaucracies. Like narcs and narcos, terrorists and counterterrorists engage in repeated interactions through which law enforcers attempt to identify, apprehend, and dismantle militant groups, while terrorists aim to elude, co-opt, and assault their state adversaries. In the wake of the single most devastating terrorist attack in history, it is not surprising that counterterrorism agencies such as the FBI and the Department of Homeland Security enjoy greater resources and broader public support than drug enforcement bureaus have in recent decades, even during the heyday of the most recent war on drugs (from 1986 through 1992).

While no extremist network, not even those underwritten by the fantastic oil-driven wealth of the Arabian Peninsula, can match the technological capabilities of Western states, the speed and reliability of decision cycles and information flows still matter in counterterrorism competitive adaptation, shaping—if not necessarily determining—outcomes in these contests.

Pursuing Profit or Jihad?

Comparisons of similar phenomena are bound to highlight the parallels between them, and in this study I emphasize the numerous ways in which Colombian trafficking enterprises and Islamic terrorist networks resemble one another, organizationally and operationally. Trafficking groups and terrorist networks differ in basic and profound ways, however, and it is important to remain attentive to these distinctions, particularly when analyzing them in comparative context.

Trafficking enterprises are business organizations: they exist to smuggle illegal drugs that enjoy strong demand among consumers in the United States and other countries. Terrorist networks, in contrast, are political organizations: they exist to terrorize target audiences through violence and intimidation undertaken in pursuit of political aims. While in the past some Colombian traffickers, including Pablo Escobar and Carlos Lehder, had personal ambitions extending well beyond criminal deviance, including the desire to serve in Colombia's national congress, the organizations they led were essentially economic in orientation. The raison d'etre of trafficking networks is to produce, process, and transport illicit drugs in pursuit of satisfactory profits, while minimizing their exposure to unnecessary risks. Unlike terrorist groups, trafficking enterprises generally do not seek to instill fear and dread in civilian populations, or to implement political change. To the extent that so-called narco-terrorists such as Escobar sought to intimidate the Colombian government in the late 1980s and early 1990s through bombing campaigns and kidnappings, they did so to protect their narrow economic interests and keep themselves out of jail—and their families out of harm's way.[24] Secular and religious extremists, on the other hand, use violence to change the political situation in a manner favorable to their cause, whether to overthrow existing governments, create political or religious orders to their liking, or enforce obedience to government authority among the disenfranchised and malcontented.[25]

Unlike drug trafficking, there is no economic "demand" for terrorism.[26] Although widespread antipathy toward U.S. foreign policy in the Middle East provides considerable grist for extremist mills, apart from suicide bombers (no minor exception given recent trends in terrorism), few people presumably want to experience the violence and dread that accompanies terrorist attacks. Nor is the creation of wealth central to the motivation of extremists, as it is for drug traffickers. When militants engage in credit card fraud, check forgery, cigarette smuggling, and other crimes, their purpose is to raise money for the cause rather than to make money for its own sake. But even Islamic extremists live in a material world, and some radicals are influenced by financial considerations. After one Al Qaeda associate became dissatisfied with his relatively low salary, as compared with the salaries of other, less experienced members, he reportedly embezzled $110,000 dollars from the network and became an important government informant.[27] The personal motivations of disaffected individuals notwithstanding, terrorists are inspired by a variety of political, ideological, or religious considerations. In the case of Al Qaeda, these motivations include the establishment of a pan-Islamic caliphate, removal of the U.S. military presence from the Middle East, and the elimination of the state of Israel.[28] Whereas the motivations of drug traffickers may wax or wane according to the pecuniary bottom line, terrorists are true believers whose religious imperatives and political convictions are largely—but not entirely—unaffected by worldly considerations.

These differences have implications, albeit limited ones, for law enforcement and counterterrorism. When governments succeed in capturing leading drug traffickers and disrupting their networks, they create an opportunity for other criminal enterprises that seek to capture market share. Strong demand in drug markets ensures these upstarts healthy profits, encouraging them to transact, grow, and rebuild the market. Terrorism lacks a demand-driven mechanism that routinely replaces militants in the same manner in which the market replaces drug traffickers. When extremist networks replace fallen comrades, as they often do, they rely more on the uncertain supply of new militants to the cause than on the promise of lucrative earnings driven by robust demand in drug markets. Hence the phoenix effect may be more subdued in terrorist networks disrupted by government authorities than it is in trafficking enterprises, at least in the short run. The charisma, elusiveness, and presumed survival of Osama bin Laden and Ayman al-Zawahiri continue to enhance Al Qaeda's allure among supporters. Removing these leaders may have a greater influence on reducing, but not eliminating, Al Qaeda's trade name appeal among would-be militants and on undermining the network's collective identity than the neutralization of leading drug traffickers has had on smuggling networks.[29]

On balance, however, capturing or killing bin Laden and al-Zawahiri is not likely to destroy whatever remains of "Al Qaeda," let alone the broader phenomenon of Salafi extremism, in part because both have already adapted to the post-9/11 counterterrorism environment. Since the war on terror began in 2001, Al Qaeda has responded to increased counterterrorism pressure by dispersing its operations, establishing loose ties with like-minded local militants, and relentlessly broadcasting its extremist ideology through Internet-based communications technologies. Along the way it has evolved from a relatively stable, if decentralized, network form of organization into an amorphous social movement composed of dozens, perhaps hundreds, of self-organizing homegrown extremist groups for which "Al Qaeda" represents more of an ideology than a locus of decision-making authority. Within this diffuse ideological movement other militants have arisen, eager to inherit the mantle of leadership from bin Laden and al-Zawahiri and appropriate what has become, in part thanks to strategic miscalculations in the war on terror, an unmatched brand name. In undergoing these changes, "Al Qaeda" and other terrorist networks have demonstrated that the long-term resilience of religious and ideological convictions arguably exceeds, and at least equals, that of profit. Whether inspired by god or mammon, terrorists and traffickers seek to survive hostile environments, and they organize in ways that allow them to do so, while pursuing other objectives, be it terrorizing "infidels" or smuggling illicit drugs.

Beyond Balloons

This is not the first study to emphasize the adaptability of drug-trafficking enterprises and terrorist networks. Researchers on organized crime have long recognized that volatile black markets, characterized by fluid market opportunities and shifting regulatory constraints, encourage the formation of "flexible, adaptive networks that readily expand and contract to deal with the uncertainties of the criminal enterprise."[30] Hence in Progressive-era New York, according to historian Alan Block, cocaine trafficking was organized by different networks of "criminal entrepreneurs who formed, re-formed, split, and came together again as opportunity arose and when they were able."[31] Similarly, Kathryn Meyer and Terry Parsinnen argue that after Chinese authorities outlawed the country's opium trade early in the twentieth century, smuggling networks adapted to the new, more hostile environment by creating clandestine delivery systems, developing different sources of supply, and co-opting politicians and warlords who could provide political protection and resolve "business difficulties."[32] In recent years several scholars have highlighted the flexibility of immigrant trafficking networks in Germany, Mexico, and China that have adapted to increased law enforcement pressure by changing their smuggling routes, professionalizing their services, and corrupting government officials.[33] Finally, in the voluminous literature on drug trafficking, references to the "Hydra effect" and the "balloon effect," metaphors that suggest that as states "squeeze" enterprises and areas known for drug production, smugglers adapt by shifting their activities to other areas that face less law enforcement pressure, are common.[34]

The literature on terrorism includes numerous references to the adaptability of political extremists. In the late 1970s and early 1980s many scholars analyzed the diffusion or "contagion" of terrorist methods and tactics among geographically dispersed extremists through imitation and training.[35] Since 9/11 government officials and researchers have called attention to the adaptability of terrorist networks and their ability to learn from experience. During his unclassified 2004 threat briefing before the U.S. Senate, CIA director George Tenet characterized Al Qaeda as "a learning organization that remains committed to attacking the United States, its friends and allies."[36] Jessica Stern, a terrorism expert at Harvard University's Kennedy School of Government, uses the same "learning organization" phrase to describe Al Qaeda's umbrella network, the International Islamic Front, in her recent book on religious extremism.[37] In separate studies on suicide terrorism, Mia Bloom and Robert Pape argue that this violent tactic has proliferated since the early 1980s because secular and religious extremists alike have learned that it is an effective method for achieving their political objectives.[38] Other researchers have recently offered insight into how numerous militant groups, including the Provisional Irish Republican Army, Jemaah Islamiyah, Hizballah, and Hamas, train their members and develop technological innovations.[39] To the extent that these studies, statements, and similes highlight the malleability of drug-trafficking and terrorist networks, they are helpful. My own research confirms, and extends, their findings.

Unfortunately, many government officials, policy analysts, and even researchers gloss over how traffickers, terrorists, and state agencies actually *learn,* in the sense of acquiring, analyzing, and applying knowledge and experience. Since, as described above, organizational learning is sensitive to a variety of individual and institutional impediments, this intricate process is better explained, with reference to specific cases, than assumed *a priori.* It is not enough simply to claim, as many do, that traffickers and terrorists learn. We need to deepen our understanding of *how* criminal and extremist groups adapt their practices and procedures in response to experience. After all, given the compartmented, clandestine nature of illicit networks, where robust information sharing across network nodes can be problematic, there are compelling reasons to believe that traffickers and terrorists do not learn and may be condemned to commit the same mistakes repeatedly.

In this volume I demonstrate otherwise. Using case study methods and organizational analysis, I open the black box of clandestine enterprises and, to a lesser extent, government agencies, revealing how they learn in spite of impediments. In comparing the institutional structures and information-processing capabilities of these organizations, this study highlights the dynamics of change in complex adaptive systems, showing how different rates of adaptation tend to favor the latter—but not deterministically so. This explanation, steeped in organization theory, enriches our understanding of how drug-trafficking and terrorist networks persist in the face of hostile government efforts to destroy them.

Trafficking and Terrorist Systems

Cops, criminals, and terrorists belong to different groups and organizations that engage in specific pursuits, follow norms and rules for making decisions, employ roles and practices for performing activities, and create social identities that distinguish their enterprises from the surrounding environment. Each in its own way, these actors coordinate their behavior within distinct social collectives. As sovereignty-bound bureaucracies, government agencies are embedded in legal and institutional settings that demand accountability, transparency, and respect for the rule of law. "Sovereignty-free" trafficking enterprises and terrorist networks lack equivalent constraints, which allows them greater flexibility in carrying out their activities.[40] Yet both types of networks contain rule-bearing, role-wearing participants who organize their operations in pursuit of collective aims.

Their dissimilar missions and objectives notwithstanding, drug traffickers and terrorists seek to reduce their exposure to risk and uncertainty, including government enforcement efforts. Meanwhile, drug-control and counterterrorism agencies seek to identify, apprehend, and ultimately dismantle trafficking and terrorist groups, reaffirming the state's ability to enforce law and order. These diametrically opposed aims expose a paradox in narco-narc and terrorist-counterterrorist interactions that is essential to understanding competitive adaptation. To paraphrase Peter Andreas, just as traffickers—and terrorists—depend on the state, so too may the state, or at least certain organizations within the state, depend on traffickers and terrorists.[41] Drug prohibition and those who enforce it provide criminal entrepreneurs with the opportunity to reap substantial profits by trafficking in illicit commodities that enjoy robust demand in the United States and other countries. Smugglers rely on the state to sustain the profitability of their activities through law enforcement operations that, ideally, remove their competitors while avoiding them (which they seek to achieve by corrupting public officials). Islamic extremists depend on Western states to sustain the political viability of their violent attacks by implementing policies that are tremendously unpopular in the Muslim world, such as the perceived American disregard for Palestinian concerns in the Arab-Israeli conflict and the U.S. invasion of Iraq in 2003. Conversely, drug trafficking and terrorism provide elite enforcement units and interagency task forces opportunities to put their training, technologies, and resources to use. State security agencies also rely on the perceived threat of drug smuggling and terrorism to sustain their institutional identities and funding. Indeed, twenty-five years of expanding drug-control and counterterrorism budgets in an era of government deregulation and fiscal austerity suggest that, to amend Charles Tilly's evocative phrase, wars on drugs and terror make the contemporary state.[42]

Bound as they are in webs of mutual dependence, narcs and narcos, terrorists and counterterrorists form distinctive social systems characterized by complexity, adaptability, and hostility. Trafficking and terrorist systems are complex because they contain large numbers of actors who interact with each other. The Colombian trafficking system contains hundreds of smuggling enterprises and law enforcement agencies in the United States, Colombia, and other countries. These are the principal actors in this system and the primary focus of my study. However, the Colombian trafficking system contains numerous other actors, including guerrilla and paramilitary groups that tax drug producers, protect trafficking routes, process drugs themselves, and trade drugs for weapons; law firms, money launderers, and other professionals who provide specialized services to traffickers; policymakers and politicians who create drug-control policies and oversee enforcement programs; and—ultimately—millions of consumers in the United States and elsewhere who purchase Colombian drugs.[43]

Terrorist systems contain hundreds of extremist networks that plan and carry out violent attacks for an assortment of political, ideological, and religious causes, and hundreds of government security agencies from dozens of countries, including the United States, Israel, Great Britain, and Pakistan, among others, that seek to penetrate and destroy terrorist groups. Secondary actors in terrorist systems include sympathizers who provide logistical support to sleeper cells without becoming directly involved in attacks themselves; war profiteers who sell guns and munitions to extremists; money launderers, financiers, and criminals who raise funds and move them through formal and informal banking systems; charitable organizations that wittingly or unwittingly provide money to terrorist groups; fundamentalist mosques, bookstores, gyms, and *madrasas* (religious schools) that provide fertile recruiting grounds for extremist networks; and the thousands of men, women, and children victimized each year by terrorist attacks.

Trafficking and terrorist systems are adaptive because principal actors change their practices in response to information and experience, including the tactics and strategies of other actors in the system. Traffickers, for example, respond to law enforcement crackdowns by moving their smuggling routes and drug-processing labs and developing new ways of hiding and transporting their contraband. Terrorists respond to counterterrorism efforts and press reports by changing their methods of attack and means of communication. Many of these adaptations are fairly simple but surprisingly effective, allowing illicit actors to continue their activities even in the most hostile environments. Law enforcers and counterterrorists reorganize their administrative structures and develop new strategies in response to pressure from other government institutions and the perception that existing approaches are not working. Over time and repeated interaction, traffickers, terrorists, and law enforcers accumulate information about the system and their chief rivals, knowledge they use to change their practices, sometimes improving their performance, sometimes not—but always affirming their identities as social actors operating in competitive environments.

Finally, trafficking and terrorist systems are hostile because some participants seek to destroy others. Smugglers who repeatedly ship large quantities of drugs and extremists who repeatedly engage in spectacular terrorist attacks face considerable pressure from enforcement agencies that seek to terminate their activities. Hostility provides the most vulnerable actors in the system with a compelling motive to change their practices: their organizational survival demands it. Targeted groups that fail to change phone numbers, safe houses, and other elements of their operational "signatures" may find themselves selected out of the system, courtesy of the enforcement networks that exploit their knowledge of existing practices to track them down and eliminate them. Given the capacity of smugglers and extremists to recruit new supporters and rebuild their operations, however, even the most successful crackdowns have a modest impact on larger trafficking and terrorist systems. For this reason, efforts by government agencies to mimic their illicit adversaries, creating flatter network structures with quicker decision cycles, will ultimately fail (I discuss this further in the conclusion).

Research as Paleontology

Those with the temerity—or foolhardiness—to study drug trafficking and terrorism confront serious methodological challenges. The secretive nature of criminal and extremist networks and the politically charged nature of law enforcement and counterterrorism complicate researchers' efforts to acquire, let alone analyze, valid and reliable data. In fact, there are few "hard data" available on drug trafficking and terrorism. For obvious reasons traffickers and terrorists avoid publishing annual reports detailing the scope and profitability of their activities, nor do they maintain statistical information quantifying their quarterly outputs. Members of these enterprises are not easily accessible to reporters and social scientists, and on the rare occasions when leading criminals or terrorists, such as Pablo Escobar and Osama bin Laden, grant interviews to the press, they are usually more interested in justifying their actions to the public than explaining how their clandestine networks operate. These "well-orchestrated propaganda exercises," as terrorism scholar Marc Sageman calls them, contain little evidentiary value.[44]

While law enforcement and counterterrorism agencies produce a variety of reports and documents, some more useful than others, their primary intelligence function is to gather information they can use to identify, disrupt, and dismantle their adversaries, rather than to generate data for social scientists. The questions law enforcers ask and the analytical categories they use are often different from those favored by scholars.[45] Although many government officials I interviewed possessed an intuitive sense of how narcs and narcos learn, they were not well versed in such concepts as "sensemaking" and "communities of practice," undoubtedly to their credit. Even when practitioners and academics use the same terms, such as drug "cartels," they often mean different things, which can lead to significant misunderstandings about the nature of the drug trade and the appropriate policy response. When law enforcers and scholars use the same research techniques, like social network analysis, they do so for different reasons: the former to identify links between specific perpetrators in criminal and terrorist conspiracies, the latter to search for broader patterns in network formation and performance while participating in ongoing academic debates.[46] Although senior officials from law enforcement and counterterrorism agencies regularly appear before congressional oversight and appropriations committees to testify about their latest efforts in wars on drugs and terrorism, the need to justify their actions to external stakeholders and to protect the integrity of ongoing operations encourages them to be congratulatory and circumspect. In sum, not only is it difficult for researchers to collect valid and reliable data on drug trafficking and terrorism, but the data they do gather must be treated with caution.

Indeed, the challenge of studying drug trafficking and terrorism evokes a parallel to paleontology, the scientific study of life in the geologic past.[47] Paleontologists piece together coherent scientific narratives to explain the origin and evolution of organic life by analyzing an incomplete record of plant and animal fossils preserved in the earth's crust. Similarly, social scientists provide coherent narratives of drug trafficking and terrorism by examining a sketchy empirical record. In my own excavations this record includes government documents (some of which I obtained under the Freedom of Information Act), congressional hearings, academic studies and press reports, testimony and court records from criminal trials involving alleged traffickers and terrorists, and interviews with more than one hundred key informants in the United States, Colombia, and Israel.

Drawing on these diverse sources of information, particularly my interviews, I generated a unique dataset based on the analytical categories of organizational learning and competitive adaptation. Mindful of the ethnographer's dictum to choose respondents for their competence rather their representativeness, I sought informants with substantial knowledge of drug trafficking or terrorism, preferably gained from their own professional experience.[48] By identifying prospective informants using snowball sampling techniques, I gradually constructed a diverse sample containing upper-level administrators, midlevel managers, and lower-level field agents and analysts from different law enforcement and counterterrorism agencies, journalists and scholars who have written extensively on drug trafficking or terrorism, and several former drug traffickers, all of whom worked for Colombian enterprises.[49] In the United States I interviewed dozens of current and former officials from numerous agencies, including the Drug Enforcement Administration, the Central Intelligence Agency, the Federal Bureau of Investigation, the Office of National Drug Control Policy, the Defense Intelligence Agency, the Department of Homeland Security, and the Counter-Terrorism Section of the Justice Department. I also interviewed staffers and analysts from the Senate Caucus on International Narcotics Control, the Senate Select Committee on Intelligence, and the Congressional Research Service. In Colombia I interviewed officials from the DEA, the State Department's Narcotics Assistance Section, the defense attaché's office, and an American ambassador to Colombia. I also interviewed dozens of Colombian officials, including administrators and agents from specialized counterdrug units and task forces in the Colombian National Police and the Department of Administrative Security (Colombia's version of the FBI). I interviewed other active and retired Colombian officials from the National Prosecutor's Office, the army, the National Directorate of Dangerous Drugs, and the president's office. In Israel I spoke with current and former officials from counterterrorism units in the Israeli Defense Forces, the Israeli Border Police, and Shin Bet (the internal Israeli intelligence agency). Officials from all of these government agencies provided valuable primary source data for this research. Agents and intelligence analysts from the DEA and the Colombian National Police, with their extensive knowledge of Colombian trafficking networks and U.S.-Colombian drug enforcement efforts, were my most useful sources of information, at least on the government side, and I interviewed them wherever I could, in Washington, D.C., Miami, Los Angeles, and Bogotá.

As illuminating as my discussions with American and Colombian narcs were, my most important interviews were with the former narcos who agreed to speak with me. All of these informants were convicted in the U.S. criminal justice system for various drug-trafficking offenses, and several were still serving time in a federal prison at the moment of our encounter. I located most of these respondents while conducting archival research on criminal trials at the U.S. District Court in Miami (where I also obtained written transcripts of court testimony from former members of the Cali "cartel"). After receiving permission from three different institutional review boards,[50] a convoluted process that took more than a year to complete, I interviewed each respondent separately for one to two hours in his language of choice (Spanish or English), using a semistructured questionnaire.[51] No officials or guards were present during these in-depth interviews, which took place in the privacy of the prison social worker's vacant office, nor were there any glass partitions or other physical barriers impeding face-to-face communication between the former traffickers and myself. I interviewed another former trafficker in the privacy of his home near Atlanta, and a former coca paste processor from southern Colombia (Putumayo province) in Bogotá.

All of my trafficker-informants worked for different smuggling enterprises, including the Medellín and Cali "cartels" and independent groups, generally in a mid- or low-level capacity. I interviewed no "kingpins" seeking to protect their legacy or rationalize their violent actions to the (presumably) few people who would eventually read this study. All of my informants understood the purpose of my visit, carefully explained to them in numerous letters we exchanged in the months leading up to the interview. They knew that I was an aspiring social scientist pursuing a research agenda, not a government official with the power to change their future—or the audacity to judge their past. As appropriate for this research, my questions were general and theoretical. I asked my informants how they organized their activities, how they gathered information, and whether they learned from experience—not whether they had ever killed anyone or were in cahoots with the Rodríguez-Orejuela brothers. Whether owing to my relative powerlessness, the nature of my questions, the private setting of our interviews, or their own desire to infuse some novelty into dreary prison routines and reaffirm their identities as once successful criminals, all of the informants were eager to talk about their past transgressions.[52] They admitted they had engaged in drug trafficking, which they viewed primarily as an economic activity, a way for them to make money and satisfy their acquisitive lifestyles. Like some of the government officials I interviewed, the former traffickers seemed eager to get "their side" of the story across to an independent, potentially sympathetic listener. Although they were free to decline, all of the trafficker-informants allowed me to audio-tape their interviews, as did most, but not all, of my government informants. Professional assistants transcribed all the interview tapes, creating an extensive documentary record that facilitated my subsequent analysis. Many respondents, both narcs and narcos, were understandably reluctant to be identified as sources of information for this research. To protect their privacy and security, occupational and otherwise, I cite these interviews anonymously or, in the case of the traffickers, using pseudonyms. I am aware that I have thus made it difficult, if not impossible, for others to validate the reliability of my findings. I regret this tradeoff as a necessary precaution in persuading these expert informants to share sensitive information that they otherwise would not have given me.

Of course, I cannot discount the possibility that some informants, narcs and narcos, may have tried to mislead me—or were themselves misled by flawed and biased memories.[53] Since some of my data come from government officials and journalists, one source of bias is particularly germane: the tendency of some officials and reporters to inflate the magnitude of the problem—and the sophistication of drug traffickers and terrorists—in order to generate resources for law enforcement efforts and readers for their publications. To what extent are my own findings "contaminated" by such accounts? While I have been painfully aware of this latent bias while researching and writing this study, I cannot in all intellectual honesty claim that I have completely eliminated it from my analysis.

I have, however, taken careful steps to diminish its impact. I selected many government informants for their expertise on the "ground level" of counterdrug law enforcement and counterterrorism rather than limit my sample to higher-ranking officials who are more sensitive to the budgetary needs of their departments. The former traffickers I interviewed provided useful ballast to the interpretations of their government adversaries. I interviewed only a handful of reporters, all of them seasoned journalists who have written extensively on drug trafficking and whose work appears in highly respected publications, including the *Washington Post*, the *Miami Herald*, and *Semana*, a prominent Colombian weekly. To counter inadvertent memory malfunctions and deliberate deception, I validated my interview data whenever possible through additional sources, including other informants, court documents, government reports, academic studies, and media accounts. When cross-checking for data reliability, I sought to confirm that the original informant was not also the source of the corroborating information. On those occasions when informants made seemingly extravagant, if theoretically useful, assertions I could not verify, I chose to err on the side of caution by not including their claims in my findings.[54] Whenever I was confronted with seemingly contradictory or confusing accounts, I returned to the data, reexamining the documentary record in light of what I knew about the veracity of my informants and the nature of drug trafficking and terrorism.

This study employs a comparative organizational approach: organizational because it focuses on the routines, decision-making hierarchies, and information-processing practices of identifiable collectives that pursue specific tasks; comparative because it examines variations among an array of organizations that seek to learn from each other.[55] In gathering my evidentiary "fossils" I have been guided by the methods of structured, focused comparison and process tracing, as developed by Alexander George and his colleagues.[56] I "structured" my research design around theoretical questions pertaining to organizational learning. I "focused" my analysis by emphasizing the institutional attributes and organizational processes that facilitate, and impede, learning in government bureaucracies and illicit networks. And I "traced" my analysis by exploring the connection between organizational learning, changes in practices and routines, and the ability of trafficking and terrorist groups to survive even the most hostile environments.

As numerous scholars concede, the data requirements for these methods are considerable, even more so when the subjects of analysis conceal themselves from the prying inquiries of social scientists. To overcome this challenge, Alexander George and Timothy McKeown suggest that "the researcher may need to expend considerable time and resources to locate historical data via archival search or interviews."[57] In collecting and analyzing data from hundreds of sources in three different countries over the better part of a decade, this is precisely what I have aspired to do. The extent to which I have succeeded is ultimately for my readers to decide. Following Clifford Geertz, I understand my pursuit "not as an experimental science in search of law but an interpretive one in search of meaning."[58] In the following pages I do not pretend to uncover universal laws applicable to drug traffickers and terrorists everywhere, nor do I provide a comprehensive account of Colombia's long-standing civil insurgency or international terrorism. My aim is more modest, and yet—I hope—equally significant: to understand how some criminal networks and law enforcement agencies learn from knowledge and experience. In doing so, I offer a novel interpretation that goes beyond labeling and metaphors to reveal meaning. Yet my search for meaning embraces the rules of scientific inference. Throughout the study I ground my interpretations in the observable implications of my data.[59] Like paleontologists who analyze carbonized impressions etched in slabs of shale to theorize about the form and function of multicellular organisms from the Cambrian period, I interpret a surprisingly rich documentary record to present an illuminating—if inevitably incomplete—rendition of drug trafficking and terrorism.

It is one thing to claim that traffickers, terrorists, and law enforcers learn; it is another to show how this process actually unfolds, or fails to, in real organizations. In the chapters that follow, I illustrate how illicit networks and government agencies acquire and analyze knowledge and experience to adapt their organizations and operations in response to feedback.

To understand how Colombian trafficking enterprises learn, we must first understand how they are organized. Contrary to popular misconceptions about the Colombian drug trade, Chapter 1 argues that the country's illegal industry contains hundreds of intergroup networks, rather than a handful of monolithic "cartels" that dominate drug production and set prices in overseas markets. To protect their operations from unwanted penetration by law enforcers, traffickers develop intricate yet supple routines for conducting their activities, and compartment participants into different "cells" that maintain sporadic communication with other network nodes.

Chapter 2 shows how the organizational structures of Colombian trafficking networks allow them to process information and adapt their activities in response to knowledge and experience. To illustrate how smugglers learn their tradecraft, I incorporate the concepts of mētis and techne into my analysis. Traffickers draw on both forms of knowledge to change their practices and procedures at every stage of the production, transportation, and distribution of illicit drugs. Many adaptations occur in response to perceived threats from law enforcers. By compelling traffickers to develop new innovations, law enforcers encourage them to diversify their experiential knowledge and cunning intelligence while developing linkages with paramilitary and guerrilla groups in Colombia and trafficking networks in other countries.

Like their antagonists, law enforcement agencies have also demonstrated their adaptability in the face of environmental pressure. Chapter 3 shows how U.S. and Colombian narcs adjust their practices in response to political demands and changes in the international drug trade. Agents supplement their formal training with the practical know-how and experience that come from performing their activities in local settings. Like drug traffickers, law enforcers develop their mētis by using it, exploiting electronic surveillance technologies and developing cunning innovations in undercover operations to penetrate smuggling networks.

If Chapters 2 and 3 illustrate how drug traffickers and law enforcers, respectively, learn, Chapter 4 develops the concept of competitive adaptation to highlight the interactive nature of narco-narc adaptation and the challenges facing both players as they seek to learn from experience. Narcs and narcos alike confront numerous impediments to organizational adaptation. The tendency of some trafficking networks to maintain meticulous records of their activities and compartment their participants into loosely coupled cells provides vulnerabilities that law enforcers can and do exploit. For their part, law enforcers are subject to a profusion of legal and administrative regulations that, while necessary to protect citizens from overzealous criminal investigations, limit the ability of undercover agents to use cunning, deception, and other mētis-laden skills to capture their illicit rivals.

Like drug traffickers and law enforcers, terrorists require specialized knowledge and practical skills to carry out their activities. Chapters 5 and 6 broaden the comparative scope of this study by incorporating terrorist networks and counterterrorism bureaucracies into the analysis. Chapter 5 shows how militants learn their tradecraft through training programs, apprenticeships, and actual combat. Like drug traffickers, political extremists supplement their formal training with the local knowledge and cunning intuition that come from practical experience, including planning and executing terrorist attacks.

If it is true, as many organization theorists suggest, that "failure is the ultimate teacher," then the tragic events of 9/11 offer a panoply of lessons for American policymakers.[60] But in spite of a proliferation of bipartisan commissions, government conferences, administrative reorganizations, and intelligence reforms designed to improve homeland security, the post-9/11 counterterrorism landscape continues to be characterized by tall management hierarchies, unwieldy bureaucratic procedures, and competing institutional interests. The size and organizational complexity of this apparatus, detailed in Chapter 6, suggest that government officials will continue to face significant challenges to information sharing and policy coordination.

In the conclusion I revisit the knowledge involved in drug trafficking and terrorism, arguing that the ability of illicit networks to endure hostile systems depends in no small measure on remaining more crafty, supple, and polymorphic than the state enforcement networks that seek their destruction. The conclusion also explores some of the implications of my findings for drug enforcement and counterterrorism policies. My tone is solemn, but not funereal. Ultimately I suggest that success in wars on drugs and terror will depend less on fighting drug-trafficking and terrorist networks with intelligence networks, and more on conquering the "competency traps" that compel policymakers to exploit the same militarized enforcement strategies repeatedly, without questioning whether these policies are capable of producing the intended results.

The Architecture of Drug Trafficking

To understand how Colombian trafficking enterprises learn, we must first understand how they, and the illegal industry they coordinate, are organized. This requires dispelling a long-standing illusion about the country's drug trade. For much of the past twenty-five years, the U.S.-led war on drugs has been premised on a fundamental misunderstanding of Colombia's illicit industry. Beginning in the early 1980s, as numerous trafficking enterprises extended their reach into American drug markets, a misconception developed that the Colombian cocaine trade was run by a handful of massive, vertically integrated "cartels" that restricted production and set international prices. Much of this mythical monopoly of power was attributed to smuggling groups based in the cities of Medellín and Cali, where cocaine "kingpins" such as Pablo Escobar, Jorge Ochoa, and Gilberto Rodríguez-Orejuela were credited with directing production in the Andes and dividing up lucrative American and European markets among themselves. The cartel myth achieved remarkable staying power in American popular culture, in part because the vivid imagery it conveyed was plausible—and useful—to politicians eager to pass drug-control legislation, law enforcers hoping for greater drug war resources, investigative journalists searching for profitable news copy, and citizens fearful of the harmful effects of drug abuse and addiction. In press releases, media reports, and Hollywood films, the cocaine "cartels" were often depicted as super-criminal associations bent on destroying American values in their single-minded pursuit of illegal profits. But irrespective of its political and moral expedience, as a description of the Colombian drug trade, the cartel metaphor left much to be desired.

"The cartels never existed until they were created by the media and the U.S. government," explains "Néstor," an experienced marijuana and cocaine broker with ties to the so-called Medellín cartel. Sitting in a medium-security federal prison in Florida, he elaborates:

> Pablo Escobar was a big smuggler, the Ochoas, all these guys were independent, like everyone else. When the government of Colombia and the Americans came after them, they had to

> react to the action to the government. But the cartels never
> happened naturally where guys sat down and said, "Okay, I'm
> going to control this and this, and you're controlling that." This
> never happened. . . . It was simply lots of small, independent
> groups: small clans, friends, relatives, family . . . people were
> trafficking through contacts. They networked to get the job
> done.[1]

Néstor is not alone in his assessment: other former traffickers I interviewed echoed his observations, juxtaposing the social construction
of Colombian "cartels" with the drug industry's tangible lack of a cartel
structure. In recent years the cartel myth has been debunked by several
scholars who argue that the Colombian drug trade was never dominated by a single organization or association that controlled enough
cocaine to limit production and fix prices in overseas markets.[2] Unfortunately, many researchers continue to use the 'cartel' nomenclature,
sacrificing conceptual and empirical clarity for stylistic convention. But
even during the heyday of the Medellín and Cali "cartels," cocaine production and exportation in Colombia was highly competitive, as independent traffickers in more than a dozen cities smuggled substantial
amounts of cocaine to American and European drug markets. While
some of these enterprises transacted with Pablo Escobar, the Ochoa
brothers, and other prominent traffickers, their business relations more
closely resembled informal producer-export syndicates than monolithic
cartels that controlled prices and monopolized markets. Although different groups occasionally pooled their resources to complete large-
scale drug shipments while reducing their exposure to government authorities, they steadfastly maintained their own sources of supply, financing, and clientele. "Driving this resilient structure," writes Sidney
Zabludoff, a former government economist and the author of an important study on the Colombian trade, was "an intricate network of
contacts and subcontracts built upon experience and family ties and
motivated by the potential for high profits."[3]

Like other forms of organized criminality, including weapons trafficking, immigrant smuggling, and prostitution, drug trafficking in Colombia occurs in fluid social systems where flexible exchange networks
expand and contract according to market opportunities and regulatory
constraints.[4] This durable, elastic structure did not emerge overnight
but developed over many years, as entrepreneurs built their enterprises

through personal contacts, resources, and repeated exchanges while drawing on social traditions, such as contraband smuggling, that extend far back into Colombia's colonial past.[5]

Colombian Trafficking Networks

Whether they transact in illegal drugs, antiquities, human beings, weapons, or any number of commodities that command robust demand in black markets, organized criminals confront a fundamental dilemma based on their competing needs for concealment and coordination.[6] To protect their operations from unwanted depredations by law enforcers and their illicit competitors, criminals must conduct their activities in secret. The need for concealment encourages participants to minimize personal contact between conspirators and limit information sharing to a need-to-know basis. Yet, to make decisions, perform tasks, distribute resources, and resolve disputes, criminals must communicate with each other and coordinate their activities. The need for coordination encourages participants to communicate regularly and share sensitive information that exposes the enterprise to risk and uncertainty.

Network forms of organization, when effectively exploited by criminal entrepreneurs, provide a number of advantages over markets and hierarchies in managing this dilemma. In contrast to centralized hierarchies that feature tight coupling between units and formal decision-making hierarchies, such as would be found in drug "cartels" if they existed, criminal entrepreneurs use networks to segment workers into loosely organized, functionally specific compartments, minimizing potentially destabilizing contact between participants. Entrepreneurs also exploit network forms of organization to decentralize their decision-making authority and rely on brokers and intermediaries to buffer themselves from direct complicity in criminal activity. Yet, in contrast to atomistic markets, entrepreneurs exploit embedded social ties and interpersonal networks, often based on participants' family and friendship connections, to recruit conspirators, generate trust, and discourage malfeasance among participants.[7]

Colombian traffickers have found network forms of organization to be useful in coordinating clandestine activities in hostile law enforcement environments. Traffickers coordinate commercial transactions through transnational commodity networks that produce, transport, and distribute cocaine, heroin, and other illegal drugs. Each trafficking group represents a node within a larger intergroup network that connects with other nodes through common objectives, shared experiences, and communication. Tasks among different groups vary, according to their function in the larger network, which is often spread out in numerous countries. Purchasing groups buy cocaine base or opium gum from farmers or intermediaries in Colombia, Bolivia, or Peru and transport these substances to processing laboratories, often located in Colombia, where they are further refined into cocaine hydrochloride and heroin by specialized processing labs. Exportation specialists then send these finished products to international transshipment points in Mexico, Central America, or the Caribbean, where transportation rings often change the shipping method before moving the product on to consumer markets in the United States and Europe. Distribution groups or cells in overseas markets receive shipments of cocaine and heroin and distribute them to wholesalers, who in turn distribute them to retailers. Brokers provide critical linkages between these nodes by making introductions between participants from different groups, such as exporters and transportation rings or distributors and wholesalers, and arranging transactions between them. Money launderers receive illicit proceeds from wholesale or retail transactions and "clean" them through the international banking system. Within each node of this transnational commodity network, participants perform specific tasks in support of group objectives, which include attaining satisfactory profits and minimizing unnecessary risks.

Embedded within these intergroup networks are interpersonal networks, based on participants' family, friendship, geographic, and professional ties. Social networks play important roles in Colombian trafficking enterprises. They generate trust and reciprocity among wary criminals who are often reluctant to transact with people they haven't known for extended periods. They help entrepreneurs recruit new workers based on the personal recommendations of trusted participants. They increase the costs of deviant behavior by allowing entrepreneurs and their enforcers to hold family members and friends accountable for the actions of errant employees. And they facilitate knowledge sharing and learning by communicating information within and between compartmented intergroup networks, an important theme to which I return later in the study.

Wheel and Chain Networks

From an organizational level of analysis, the Colombian trafficking system contains two basic types of networks, although in practice a variety of hybrids obscure crisp distinctions. Wheel networks, also called hub or star networks, contain a core group that manages the overall enterprise and peripheral nodes that perform specific tasks, sometimes for different core groups. In wheel networks, capabilities are not evenly distributed: core groups, as Phil Williams points out, enjoy a preponderance of "power, influence, and status within the network."[8] Core groups exploit their resources to contract the services of different peripheral nodes that perform the same task, including multiple transportation rings, distribution groups, and money launderers. Core groups are led by veteran traffickers who have the contacts, capital, and knowledge to coordinate large-scale drug shipments.

Core nodes, as befitting their central location in wheel networks, are multitask enterprises. They organize transactions among different nodes; they supply money, equipment, and other resources to complete transactions; they provide security and resolve disputes among participants; they arrange financing for multiton cocaine shipments from private investors; they suborn police, prosecutors, politicians, and military personnel; and they gather intelligence about law enforcement activities and their illicit competitors. In short, core nodes serve as the steering mechanism for wheel networks, facilitating communication and coordinating relations among peripheral groups. If something goes wrong with a transaction, relations of informal accountability ensure that participating nodes will answer to the core, protecting leaders and investors from theft and other uncertainties (see Fig. 1).

The ability to conduct sensitive transactions safely is essential for illegal enterprises, and Colombian trafficking networks place great importance on risk management, even at the expense of reducing the profitability and efficiency of their enterprises. Core groups rely on a variety of practices and arrangements to shield themselves from the vagaries and vicissitudes of counterdrug law enforcement. They coordinate potentially incriminating transactions through brokers in order to buffer leaders from direct complicity in drug violations. They use intimidation and violence to remind participants of the dangers they face should they betray the enterprise and cooperate with law enforcers. They segment their operations into separate groups that are largely, but

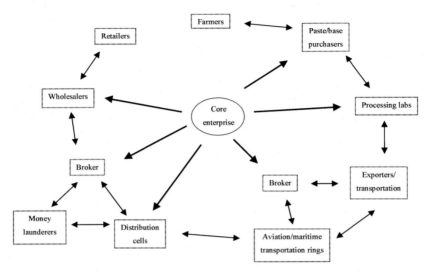

Single-headed arrows suggest relations based on vertical accountability; double-headed arrows indicate horizontal accountability. For each task, core groups often rely on multiple peripheral nodes simultaneously.

Fig. 1   Drug-trafficking wheel network

not entirely, isolated from other network nodes (more on this below). They use multiple suppliers for international transportation, wholesale distribution, and money laundering, building redundancy into their networks and preventing law enforcers from immobilizing the entire operation by dismantling a single node.[9] And they corrupt government officials, paying them to disregard smuggling activities in their jurisdictions, provide information about law enforcement efforts, become directly involved in trafficking or money laundering themselves, or influence public policy on issues of importance to network leaders, such as the extradition of Colombian nationals to the United States.

In spite of these precautions, wheel networks remain vulnerable to head-hunting approaches to drug control, particularly when core-group leaders concentrate decision-making authority in their hands and organizational knowledge in their heads, making themselves virtually irreplaceable. A related vulnerability develops when networks rely on a single node to supply a critical service, such as international transportation or wholesale distribution. The existence of nonredundant nodes creates what University of Chicago sociologist Ronald Burt calls "structural holes" in the network that are not easily filled.[10] Law enforcers can severely disrupt networks that contain structural holes and excessive centralization by dismantling nonredundant nodes and capturing core-group leaders.

Chain networks coordinate transnational drug flows sans the synchronization provided by core groups. Chain networks are decentralized and "self organizing": they contain independent nodes that perform specific tasks and transact directly with other nodes without mediation and oversight by core groups. While some nodes may contain influential leaders, relations among different groups are characterized by horizontal rather than vertical accountability. Drug shipments proceed through a series of arms-length transactions among independent nodes that often coordinate their activities on an ad hoc basis. Over time and repeat exchange, reciprocity and trust develop between interacting groups, distinguishing social relations in chain networks from pure markets. Like wheel networks, interpersonal relations are often based on underlying kinship and friendship networks that crisscross nodes and networks, facilitating trust and exchange among cagey participants. Also like wheels, chains rely on government corruption to assist drug shipments, but they direct the bulk of their bribes to local officials who have jurisdiction in their area of operations, rather than to national-level politicians and administrators.[11] Unlike wheels, chains often lack mechanisms for sharing risks and resolving disputes among different nodes, which increases their vulnerability to government interdiction and theft. The lack of a central coordinating body also means that chain networks may require more time to recover from law enforcement disruptions to individual nodes. Yet chain networks are more resistant to head-hunting approaches to drug control: there are no "high value" core-group leaders for law enforcers to capture, and those participants who are detained are generally easy to replace (see Fig. 2).

Loosely Coupled Networks

The need to conceal their enterprises from law enforcers and illicit competitors while coordinating their activities among numerous participants has led many narcos to segment their operations into separate working groups, sometimes called cells. Working groups are frequently small in size, with fewer than a dozen members who carry out much

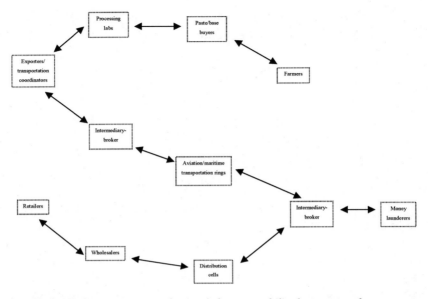

Double-headed arrows suggest horizontal accountability between nodes.

Fig. 2 Drug-trafficking chain network

of the day-to-day work of the enterprise. Cell managers match participants to roles, often multiple ones, that informally define the division
of labor within the group. Typical distribution cells contain numerous
roles, including a manager who coordinates the group's activities, logistics people who purchase motor vehicles and other equipment, deliver
money, and punish errant employees, and lower-level workers who
transport drugs, manage stash houses, and run errands for their supervisors. "Arturo," the head of a U.S. distribution cell for a Colombian
wheel network, identified five distinct roles in his operation, apart from
his own position: transportation, storage, distribution, pickup and delivery, and money laundering.[12] Another trafficking enterprise based in
Colombia relied on a network of human couriers to smuggle multikilo-
gram quantities of cocaine and heroin to the United States and Spain.
This enterprise contained approximately twenty members who performed a variety of roles, as detailed in Table 1.

To protect the enterprise from penetration by law enforcers and
other adversaries, and to limit the damage of infiltration when it does
occur, trafficking cells may be compartmented from other nodes in the
network. Within wheel networks, cell managers maintain regular com-

Table 1 Role specialization in small trafficking network

Role	Task(s)
Leader	Oversaw entire operation, providing managerial assistance as needed (based in Colombia, but previous trafficking experience in the United States). Contrary to gender stereotypes about the drug trade, the leader of this enterprise was a woman.
Investors	Invested money in the enterprise's drug shipments (at least two individuals filled this role).
Buyer	Purchased cocaine and heroin from processing labs (this enterprise did not process illicit drugs, preferring to buy them fully refined).
Recruiter	Enlisted human couriers and provided them with travel documentation, including passports and visas.
Packer	Compressed cocaine and heroin into digestible capsules using a hydraulic press.
Enforcer	Used intimidation and violence to enforce transactions and resolve disputes, including coercing people who owed money for drugs to pay their debts to the enterprise.
Trainer	Prepared human drug couriers in swallowing capsules, dealing with law enforcement, and avoiding problems in airport security.
Couriers	Transported small amounts of drugs from Colombia to the United States or Spain, sometimes by way of Aruba or Venezuela; most couriers ingested drug-filled capsules and hid narcotics in their personal luggage.
Receiver/ Wholesale distributor	Received couriers in the United States or Spain, transported them to stash houses where they could "expel" their cargo. Receiver was also responsible for selling drugs to independent wholesalers.

munication with core leaders or their intermediaries based in Colombia but limit their interaction with other peripheral nodes. Cells managers often separate workers who perform different functions and give them the minimal information they need to perform their tasks. "Freddy," a former maritime smuggler in a transportation cell for a large Cali wheel network, observes: "they don't need to know nothing about nothing, just what they need to produce."[13] The reason, explains Arturo in a separate interview, is that "if you cross over the jobs, then people will know each other."[14] By compartmenting workers into separate cells, network managers hope to reduce the potential damage to their operation caused by the betrayal of a delinquent employee.

The degree of compartmentation varies among trafficking networks; some enterprises permit workers from different cells to share experiences, while others segment their participants into fairly isolated groups. Preexisting social networks that cross cell boundaries tend to offset compartmentation, as workers from different cells communicate with each other when they share overlapping family or friendship ties. However, it is not uncommon for low-level workers to be unfamiliar with participants in other peripheral nodes and core-group leaders. Freddy insists that he never met the core-group bosses in his transnational wheel network and that he knew only two people in his transportation cell: the person who coordinated the activities of the group and the colleague who recruited him to join his *oficinita* (little office).[15] While loosely coupling workers into separate groups helps protect traffickers against infiltration by law enforcers, highly compartmented smuggling networks have difficulty learning from experience, as cells are prevented from communicating with other nodes. I explore the implications of the trade-off between secrecy and information sharing for organizational learning in Chapter 4.

Flat Networks

Smuggling enterprises are organizationally "flat": relatively few management layers separate network leaders from cell workers. In chain networks, individual nodes often contain only a single level of management: the manager or boss who gives orders—and the workers who carry them out. Some chain networks rely on intermediaries that buffer leaders from workers. When these go-betweens possess discretionary authority to make decisions or manage workers' activities, they add a second management layer to the group.

Even large cocaine "cartels," the stuff of journalistic lore, typically contain no more than three or four management levels. From top to bottom, the typical wheel network includes core-group leaders, cell managers, assistant managers, and cell workers. Some wheel networks lack assistant managers, reducing the number of administrative layers to two: network leaders and cell managers. In these operations cell workers report directly to the cell manager, who in turn reports to core-group leaders, often through a trusted intermediary acting as a buffer for the kingpins. Some networks contain an "exportation manager" who supervises different cells, adding a third management layer to the enterprise. Core-group leaders occasionally surround themselves with trusted advisors or investors with considerable smuggling experience, including former traffickers who have officially "retired" from the trade. These figures serve in an advisory capacity, sharing their extensive knowledge and contacts on request, usually in exchange for a cut of the profits or the opportunity to invest in shipments (see Fig. 3).

In many wheel networks, core-group leaders exercise ultimate decision-making authority, but management styles among different leaders vary. Some leaders not only make long-term strategic decisions regarding product development, market diversification, and group security, they involve themselves in the most mundane matters of everyday operations. Miguel Rodríguez-Orejuela, leader of one of the largest Cali wheel networks, reportedly managed every aspect of his vast smuggling operations, including selecting the best hiding spot for cocaine inside

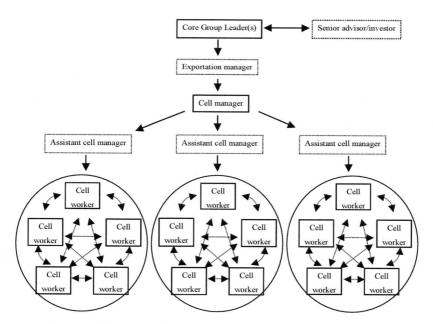

Single-headed arrows denote vertical social relations: decisions flow downward, accountability flows upward. Double-headed arrows indicate horizontal accountability and lateral information flows. However, dotted arrows suggest that cell workers may or may not communicate with all their working group colleagues, depending on their coordination needs. Roles in dotted boxes do not exist in all trafficking networks

Fig. 3   Management levels within Colombian wheel network

boxes of frozen vegetables. Rodríguez-Orejuela also had a habit of send-ing supervisors to the United States to conduct "integrity checks" of his cell managers and monitor their performance. While micromanage-ment may guard against sloppy execution and inferior performance, it requires constant communication between the leader and his charges, reducing one vulnerability by creating another. Although Rodríguez-Orejuela achieved tremendous success over the years, his administra-tive style came back to haunt him when U.S. law enforcers recorded incriminating telephone conversations he had with different subordi-nates and used transcripts of these phone calls as material evidence in several successful prosecutions.

To protect themselves against such depredations, traffickers often delegate much of their day-to-day authority to trusted confidants and senior-level supervisors such as exportation managers. In these net-works the leader may keep abreast of major developments but step in only when problems develop. "I made all the decisions in the U.S.," recalls Arturo, "from whom to sell to, to how to get to that person, to what house to be rented as a stash house, to how the money was to be brought back to Colombia . . . to what price I agreed to on the receiving end." According to Arturo, every week or ten days he would travel to Colombia, where he would meet with his mentor, one of four leaders in the network, to discuss problems and set policy for the enterprise.[16] While Arturo was evidently proud of his decision-making authority, the structure of the operation was assuredly designed to protect his mentor and other network leaders back in Colombia.

The Rules of Drug Trafficking

Rules permeate Colombian trafficking enterprises. "Oh yeah, we had a lot of rules," observes Arturo, providing an obvious example: "We would never say anything on the phone."[17] "When you go to work for an organization," explains Freddy, "there are a series of rules. You have to know the rules and apply them. These rules are simple . . . do your work and don't leave traces. . . . The most important rule is to avoid exposing your network of contacts, so that if someone falls [to law en-forcement], it doesn't compromise everyone."[18]

In addition to maintaining operational security, trafficking groups use rules to distribute resources, perform tasks, communicate information, and make decisions. Rules and procedures structure relations among participants and reflect network leaders' values and beliefs about how their operations should be organized. Traffickers employ rules when processing, transporting, and distributing drugs; collecting, laundering, and repatriating drug proceeds; assigning responsibility for failed transactions; recruiting new members; and performing a host of related activities. The rules of drug trafficking emerge over time and through experience. Trafficking enterprises incorporate "lessons" from experience into practices and procedures that guide subsequent behavior, in the process developing larger, more diverse repertoires of action.[19]

Because they operate in hostile environments, trafficking enterprises often refrain from codifying their rules in written documents. Instead, rules are embodied in informal, intersubjective understandings among participants about the "way things are done around here." "We never said, 'Be careful,' or, 'If you go this far, you going to be dead,' or something like that," explains a former drug pilot for Carlos Lehder, a prominent Colombian smuggler during the 1980s with links to the Medellín "cartel." "You don't have to say it. It was implicit. We knew that because of who the people were that we were working with, we had to keep a low profile."[20] These implicit understandings are communicated through conversations, stories, body language, and social gatherings that allow veterans to share norms and experience with less knowledgeable colleagues.

Some trafficking enterprises convene meetings in which network leaders or their associates interview prospective employees and lay out the rules of behavior. Recruits may be asked to provide contact information for their immediate family members as a hedge against cooperating with the police. For similar reasons, some enterprises require potential employees to fill out an application that details previous work experience and supplies personal information to their employer. During a criminal trial of several alleged members of the Cali "cartel" in Miami, Guillermo Pallomari, a former accountant for the Rodríguez-Orejuela network and the U.S. government's star witness in the case, explained that his former boss regularly held meetings with incoming employees to clarify the conditions of their employment. "What rules did Miguel Rodriguez establish for each of these people who were joining the Cali Cartel?" the prosecuting attorney asked Pallomari.

"That they should be people who were trustworthy, who would keep loyal to the Cali Cartel structure and that should they ever be arrested, they should never cooperate with the authorities," Pallomari replied.

"If in fact they were ever arrested," the prosecutor continued, "what rules are you aware of Miguel Rodriguez-Orejuela stating to each of these members who were joining the Cali Cartel?"

"To keep silent."[21]

Pallomari went on to explain that during these meetings participants were warned that providing information to the police would not be tolerated, and that those who did should expect violent reprisals, not only against themselves but towards their family members as well. Pallomari himself apparently suffered the consequences of cooperating with the authorities. After he provided incriminating information to Colombian officials about his former boss, enforcers working for Rodríguez-Orejuela allegedly kidnapped his wife to pressure him to return to the enterprise. Pallomari refused, turning himself in to U.S. DEA agents stationed in Bogotá instead. By his own account, he never saw or heard from his wife again.[22]

Trafficking Routines

Colombian trafficking networks develop numerous practices and procedures to achieve their objectives, many of which are designed to minimize their exposure to law enforcement officials and other adversaries. They recruit family members and childhood friends as co-conspirators. They pool resources from different groups and offer informal insurance to drug shipment investors. They use multiple smuggling routes and shipping methods simultaneously. They design transportation and delivery routines that limit contact between participants. They withhold sensitive information from low-level workers until the last moment, to reduce the risk of robbery and police penetration. They communicate through pay phones, beepers, cell phones, cloned cell phones, phone cards, and e-mail to evade electronic surveillance. And they coerce, intimidate, and, if necessary, harm those who jeopardize enterprise security.

Many trafficking routines are reasonably simple, such as recruiting family members and life-long friends to join a trafficking group. These practices can be executed without much coordination or planning among participants. Other routines are more complicated, involving a series of actions among numerous participants from different groups.

In general, the greater the risks of a particular transaction, the more intricate the procedures for carrying it out.

Distribution cells have developed elaborate practices for delivering large amounts of drugs to independent wholesalers. Allowing for local variation, one popular delivery routine during the 1980s included the following steps. Once a large load of cocaine was received, counted, and stored within a stash house run by a distribution ring (a complicated routine in itself), the distribution manager would telephone core-group leaders or their intermediaries in Colombia to confirm receipt of the cocaine and receive a delivery list for the shipment. Delivery lists contained beeper numbers for different wholesalers, the amount of cocaine to be delivered to each, and specific code words and aliases to be used when arranging transfers. The distribution manager would then call each beeper number on the list and punch in the number of a pay phone where he would wait for wholesalers' return calls. When a wholesaler or his contact called the distributor, they would discuss the details of the exchange using the coded terminology and arrange to meet in a public setting, such as a popular restaurant. If possible, the distribution cell would conduct reconnaissance on this location beforehand to make sure that it contained easy vehicle access and ample pedestrian traffic. After meeting face to face in the parking lot, the distribution manager and the wholesaler would quickly confirm the arrangements of the transaction and retire together to the restaurant. Here the two managers would pass the time while their respective subordinates carried out the transaction. Workers from both groups would exchange motor vehicles—one containing drugs, the other money—drive to separate stash houses, and unload, inspect, and count the contents of the vehicle. Once they confirmed that everything was in order, the subordinates would return to the restaurant and signal their supervisors that the transfer was complete, whereupon the distributor and wholesaler would go their separate ways.

This antiseptic delivery routine was designed to reduce the risks that independent distributors and wholesalers face from law enforcers—and each other. By avoiding any direct handling of the money or merchandise, the routine made it more difficult, but not impossible, for police and prosecutors to demonstrate beyond a reasonable doubt that the two men talking over a cup of coffee in the local diner were in fact conducting an illegal transaction. By meeting in public, surrounded by potential eyewitnesses, the routine also made it more difficult—but again, not impossible—for the distribution manager and wholesaler to steal from each other. Of course, if the wholesaler and distribution manager belonged to the same organization, as "cartelized" depictions of the drug trade suggested, such elaborate precautions would have been unnecessary. But in fact distributors and wholesalers, and for that matter exporters, transportation rings, and money launderers, often belong to different groups. The delivery routine was effective because it allowed independent groups to conduct arms-length transactions at minimal risk to both. In addition, the routine was relatively easy to execute and flexible in the details. When planning their delivery, participants could choose from a wide variety of meeting places, code words, and transportation methods. In this manner the routine adapted to fit the circumstances of the moment and the preferences of collaborators.

Joining the Crew: Participation in Trafficking Networks

Whether they operate in processing labs, in distribution cells, or as independent brokers, participants in trafficking networks make decisions, plan strategy, devise tactics, and communicate with co-conspirators. Because of the illegal nature of their occupation, traffickers do not enter into formal contractual relations with their employers that spell out their rights and responsibilities as professional drug smugglers. Instead, membership claims are informal. Traffickers identify themselves as participants in a specific group, claims that other participants and leaders validate by recognizing that they have a legitimate role to play. Membership claims may be supported by kinship, friendship, or geographic ties, or the specialized knowledge and skills a person brings to the operation. Whatever the justification, the member generally identifies him- or herself as part of a larger collective. "I work for a *mafioso* as a cooker [cocaine processor]," explains "Freckles," an informant interviewed by a Colombian sociologist who conducted extensive research on the Colombian drug trade. "We are a group of four people, all strong acquaintances, generally family members or old friends."[23] "We had like thirty-five to forty members," recalls Homero, a former drug distributor I interviewed who worked in a small transportation and distribution network. "Of course, we all identified ourselves as members. We all had our part. Some supervised the merchandise, others the distribution, others the money."[24] What Homero recognizes, Freckles clearly implies: individuals identify themselves as belonging to a specific group by virtue of the roles they perform on behalf of the enterprise.

Getting Started

In what might be called the gateway theory of drug trafficking—not to be confused with the gateway theory of drug *consumption* popular among prohibitionists—many career criminals become involved in the narcotics trade gradually, through participation in parallel pursuits such as contraband smuggling and money laundering. These activities provide the skills, experience, and connections aspiring traffickers need to expand into the more lucrative drug business. Freddy recalls that he smuggled black market sugar and cloth for more than a decade before joining a large trafficking network. His descent (or ascent—depending on one's point of view) into the cocaine trade occurred through contacts he developed while smuggling contraband and purchasing dollars from established traffickers. "I began to buy dollars," he explains, "and this was one of the things that most connected me to a series of people involved in the drug business. I bought dollars and they, the traffickers, developed a certain confidence in me."[25]

Homero's involvement in drug trafficking also came gradually. In the mid-1980s, drug dealers he knew in Bogotá gave him the opportunity to make money by brokering cocaine deals. After arranging several transactions, Homero became a dealer in his own right, which put him in contact with international traffickers who traveled to Colombia to buy drugs and transport them back to the United States. "I began to meet these people," he recalls, "and they interested me in the business when I realized how much money there was to be made." He soon connected with a Colombian-based network that sent cocaine and heroin to the United States through human couriers. After completing a couple of carries himself, he remained in the United States to receive "mules" and provide them with lodging and other support during their stay.[26] Over time and repeated transactions, Homero proved himself a reliable and trustworthy associate, and his superiors increased his responsibilities to include delivering drugs to independent wholesalers. Working as a distributor allowed Homero to expand his contacts, which he used to develop his own clientele.

As these examples suggest, social networks are critical to the Colombian drug trade. Freddy, Homero, and other former participants I interviewed were recruited into smuggling enterprises through personal connections based on family and friendship ties or professional relationships. Freddy's connection to the Cali wheel network came through a friend of the family, someone who knew of his involvement in contraband smuggling and vouched for his reliability to network leaders. Homero exploited friendship ties among several drug dealers to become a cocaine broker, initiating his long-term participation in the trade. Néstor and Arturo drew on professional contacts in otherwise legitimate export-import businesses to become involved in drug smuggling gradually. In each case social relationships steeped in criminal activity developed over time, as established and prospective traffickers developed mutual trust through multiple interactions and transactions. These social networks are the bedrock of interorganizational trafficking networks. They bring new people into the trade, allowing groups to replace captured participants; they create social identities based on trust and accommodation among established participants; and they facilitate not just the exchange of drugs and money but the knowledge required to trade these commodities.

Turnover and Promotion

Popular mythology suggests that the only way out of the drug trade is through imprisonment or death. While lots of traffickers are eventually apprehended and incarcerated by American and Colombian authorities, and while others are violently eliminated by their competitors, many smugglers exercise more mundane exit options. Some traffickers simply retire from the trade following a period of criminal activity. The reasons for retirement are numerous and vary with the personalities and motivations of the individuals involved. Some traffickers "burn out" from the high levels of stress that accompany this hazardous occupation, where individuals live under constant threat of exposure to the police and illegal competitors. Others recoil from the steady progression in deviant behavior that sustained participation in the trade often brings. Some participants have no qualms about guarding a stash house or collecting and laundering drug proceeds, but balk at the prospect of engaging in physical intimidation or violence. Others eventually tire of the hedonistic lifestyle that inspired their entry into the trade. Drug abuse, family problems, depression, and a heavy conscience prompt some to cease their activities voluntarily. Other traffickers may retire because they have reached their personal enrichment goals or found employment in a more appealing, legally sanctioned line of work. Retirement may be driven by a combination of factors. An unwelcome brush with the law, for example, may compel a participant to reconsider his priorities, making him less tolerant of work-related stresses and more open to gainful employment in "dull" but less dangerous occupations.

The causes of involuntary expulsion from the drug trade are also numerous. Participants may be laid off from trafficking enterprises during difficult times, as when law enforcement crackdowns force some networks to cancel smuggling ventures or downsize their operations. Participants may be fired for engaging in irresponsible behavior that puts the enterprise at risk, such as abusing alcohol or consuming cocaine while working, showing up late for meetings, and repeatedly getting into trouble with friends and family.[27] In some cases errant workers may be subject to more drastic sanctions. If someone is believed to have knowingly cooperated with the police, stolen product or proceeds from the enterprise, or deliberately engaged in reckless behavior that threatens the existence of the network, he may be subject to intimidation, violence, and, in extreme cases, murder.

Finally, every year law enforcers in Colombia and the United States remove thousands of participants through apprehension and arrest. Unfortunately, the impact of these apprehensions on the drug trade is muted by law enforcer's tendency to arrest low-level violators, such as drug couriers and street dealers, and by Colombia's relatively ineffective criminal justice system, as manifested in case overloads, low conviction rates, and porous prisons.[28] Moreover, a number of traffickers incarcerated in Colombia have continued their criminal activities from behind bars. After surrendering to Colombian officials in 1990, Pablo Escobar, the notorious "kingpin" of the Medellín "cartel," ran his criminal operations largely unimpeded during a year of incarceration at the Cathedral, a luxurious correctional facility of his own design. While unable to build their own penitentiaries, other Colombian traffickers, including Miguel and Gilberto Rodríguez-Orejuela, Jorge Luís and Fabio Ochoa, and Ivan Urdinola Grajales, were also accused by government officials of continuing their trafficking activities from behind bars. "They clearly feel they are safer and can operate more comfortably from a prison they control than they could as fugitives," one Colombian police official claimed. "They have a sophisticated communications network they run through a pay phone at the prison and carry on business without interference."[29]

Traffickers who avoid apprehension readily migrate to other nodes or networks when their former colleagues are jailed. "This happens a lot, depending on your role," explains Néstor. "Say one guy gets popped—you go work for another group or another guy."[30] Traffickers who maintain robust social networks connecting them to other enterprises are well positioned to continue their involvement in the trade. In some cases they will even join competitors.

Whatever the cause of turnover, participants must be replaced if the enterprise is to continue. Network leaders enjoy access to an abundant pool of labor, even for the low-level jobs that face the greatest risk, such as drug couriers. "The mules beg these organizations to keep them in mind," explains the head of a counterdrug enforcement unit in the detectives' branch of the Colombian National Police. "We have intercepted many phone lines and you always hear the mules asking, 'Please, keep me in mind for a trip.' And the *capo* or the owner of the route says, 'No, because you just traveled a month ago and they are going to see a lot of entrances in your passport.' So the mule says, 'The thing is, I have problems.' They beg them. For just one trip there are five or six mules that want to travel."[31]

To reduce their exposure to law enforcers, network leaders may recruit people "of confidence," drawing on their own and their participants' family and friendship networks. Other recruits may be sought for the particular skills they bring to the enterprise, such as bilingual fluency or expertise in information systems, international finance, criminal law, and undercover surveillance. Colombian trafficking enterprises also replace participants by promoting from within. Ironically, the stimulus for promotion often comes from successful law enforcement operations. When police and prosecutors remove traffickers from a particular network through indictment, arrest, or incarceration, they provide opportunities for remaining participants to rise. Workers who have caught their manager's eye through proficiency and diligence may benefit from these incidents.

"Initially, I was a mule," explained Homero, "but after I traveled to the U.S. they needed someone they could trust to stay here to deliver mules to others, and that was how I became involved in that aspect of the business."

"So it functioned as a form of promotion?" I asked.

"Yes, of course," he replied. "Because what happens is that you go and return a couple of times, and you are a competent person, so possibly in the U.S. or whatever country, they lose someone. For whatever reason, he goes to prison, or he doesn't want to work anymore, so they need someone of confidence to ensure that the drug distribution gets to the consumers. So I began to receive mules that arrived first in Miami, then I went to New York, to obtain mules. Then I was contracting cars, etcetera."[32]

Promotion is more complicated when enterprise leaders are the ones to be replaced. Who succeeds the "kingpin"? In small, clan-based groups, where decision-making authority is concentrated in a single figure, the leader may be irreplaceable. In these enterprises, removal of the boss may signal the end of the enterprise itself. Yet, given that they transact in negligible quantities of drugs and usually represent redundant nodes in smuggling networks, the termination of small groups does not exert a significant impact on larger trafficking systems. Larger groups, such as core nodes and distribution cells in wheel networks, may survive a limited degree of executive turnover. In these groups incarcerated leaders often turn over the day-to-day management of their operations to trusted subordinates, such as family members or long-time confidants. In some groups the act of turning over operations may be as simple as supplying the new leader with the necessary contacts and vouching for his credibility with suppliers and customers. "Every time they capture a group of narcotics traffickers," explains a Colombian prosecutor, "naturally, they never catch all of them. There are people that sell the information, people that know the contacts outside the country and here inside."[33]

The leader himself may sell this knowledge in exchange for a fee or a cut of the profits, or he may rent his route to trusted associates. "The kingpins cede their routes to their men of confidence," notes another Colombian official. "They tell them, 'Take the route, I rent it to you, I have nothing to do with this.' So they hand over the routes and just receive some dividends for renting them. The ones that become stronger are from the lower levels. Now they are the owners of these routes."[34]

In this manner some trafficking enterprises continue their operations following the removal of their original leaders, demonstrating substantial flexibility and underscoring the challenges facing head-hunting approaches to drug control. Law enforcers may sever "kingpins" from their wheel networks, as they did in disrupting the Medellín and Cali "cartels" during the 1990s, but other leaders appear in their place, eager to draw on surviving nodes to continue their activities.

Understanding the architecture of the Colombian drug trade requires exposing a powerful myth that remains prevalent in the United States. Contrary to what some politicians, law enforcers, journalists, and filmmakers would have us believe, Colombia's illicit commerce has never been dominated by one or more criminal organizations exerting monopoly control over what in practice has always been a fluid and diffuse industry. Even as the DEA pursued its "kingpin strategy" in the 1990s and Hollywood created sensationalistic portrayals of the "drug lord" lifestyle, hundreds of criminal enterprises flourished in Colombia, producing, processing, brokering, transporting, and distributing cocaine, heroin, marijuana, and other psychoactive substances. While independent groups pooled their resources to coordinate drug shipments and suborn public officials, they did not form monolithic associations that established international drug prices. Instead, many of these groups formed flat, loosely coupled interorganizational networks that coordinated their activities when opportunities arose. Embedded within these intergroup networks were social or interpersonal networks among participants that facilitated commerce by creating social relations based on shared identities, trust, and accommodation. To help manage the necessary tension between concealment and coordination, traffickers developed flexible operating procedures to conduct sensitive transactions and reduce their exposure to law enforcers and other adversaries. These routines doubled as repositories of organizational experience, allowing traffickers to build and refine their criminal expertise over time, often in ways that made it more difficult for law enforcers to apprehend them. While personnel turnover was common in many enterprises, its disruptive impact was ameliorated by internal promotion procedures, contact sharing among established traffickers, and an abundant supply of labor.

Drug trafficking in Colombia, then and now, occurs in fluid social systems where intergroup networks, buttressed by interpersonal ones, expand and contract according to market opportunities and law enforcement pressure. Trafficking networks—be they wheels, chains, or variations on a theme—are fundamentally dynamic. They change over time owing to internal developments and external stresses. Even the largest trafficking groups, the transnational wheel networks with many years of smuggling experience and strong ties to corrupt officials, are often compelled to "react to the action of the government," in Néstor's words. How these illicit networks adapt their operations in response to information and experience is a critical feature of Colombian trafficking systems and the subject of the next chapter.

During the 1981 Christmas drug-smuggling season, U.S. law enforcers intercepted a suspicious airplane flying over Florida carrying more than nine hundred pounds of cocaine.[1] A smuggling ring led by Max Mermelstein, one of several that provided transportation and distribution services for the Ochoa wheel network, had flown the cocaine from Colombia to the Florida straits, where the pilots engaged in a pursuit chase with DEA helicopters, U.S. Customs airplanes, and air force F-16 jets. As the smugglers maneuvered their way through the not-so-friendly Florida skies, they jettisoned their illegal cargo over the Gulf of Mexico before being forced to land at Tampa International Airport. The Tampa incident represented a major setback for Mermelstein's group. While the smugglers were drug free on landing, the authorities confiscated the plane and arrested one of the pilots, forcing other group members into hiding. Mermelstein's ring lost an estimated US$12 million dollars' worth of cocaine that day, some of it found floating in the Gulf by local fishermen.

In the frantic days following the bust, Mermelstein and his colleagues held several meetings in which they sought to make sense of the events that led to disaster. As they reflected on their misfortune, the smugglers discussed several ideas for improving their operations, including one that Mermelstein hoped would provide a solution to their problem. "We knew now that coke floated, and we did a lot of sitting around bullshitting and brainstorming. Mickey told me about all the pot he had brought in from Jamaica in the old days and how a lot of times they'd drop the pot in the water to be picked up by boats below."[2]

Intrigued by Mickey's experience, Mermelstein considered the possibility of using airdrops for cocaine. After receiving the go-ahead from their Colombian suppliers, Mermelstein and his colleagues began gathering the information necessary to transform idea into innovation. This included studying local maritime conditions, including the tides, currents, and water depths of potential airdrop locations in the Caribbean. Once they had gathered sufficient information, Mermelstein's ring conducted a series of practice runs in the Bahamas, using flour instead of cocaine as they tinkered with the routine. The practice drops revealed that the most difficult part of the operation lay in wrapping the cocaine so that it would not rupture upon hitting the water and would float for several minutes, allowing the boaters enough time to retrieve the packages. Mermelstein's group experimented with different wrapping methods, losing several bales of flour before developing a method that worked well enough to try on the real thing.

Having settled on a wrapping method, Mermelstein sent precise instructions to the exportation group in Colombia, along with a sample package as a model. More costly experimentation, including the loss of more than one hundred kilograms of cocaine, and a hands-on demonstration in Colombia were required before workers in the exportation group learned how to wrap the packages properly. But once this information was effectively communicated to the exporters, the airdrop lived up to its initial promise, allowing Mermelstein and his colleagues to eliminate the danger of unloading stationary drug planes. As the smugglers gained experience with their new routine, they improvised further by replacing the plastic bags with more resistant fiberglass boxes, improving the effectiveness of the airdrop.

Following his arrest by law enforcers in 1985, Mermelstein's associates took over the smuggling ring, continuing the airdrop as part of their transportation practices. Other groups began using the airdrop as well. By the early 1990s numerous trafficking enterprises, including those affiliated with rival groups, were air-dropping cocaine in the waters off the Bahamas, Puerto Rico, and other Caribbean islands. Indeed, Freddy, one of the former traffickers I interviewed, claimed that his Cali-affiliated transportation cell air-dropped cocaine during the 1990s.[3] Some smuggling rings made additional improvements to the practice, using radio transmitters and global positioning system devices to make it easier to locate the floating drug packages. Today the airdrop remains standard practice for trafficking groups that smuggle illegal drugs along Caribbean routes.[4]

The airdrop story is significant not so much for what it says about the criminal exploits of a particular smuggling ring but for illustrating how drug traffickers learn, the subject of this chapter. In the course of conducting a risky but routine operation, Mermelstein's ring experienced a grave surprise when law enforcers interrupted their drug shipment. Confronted with the possible termination of their lucrative enterprise and their identity as professional smugglers, Mermelstein and his colleagues engaged in what organization theorists call sensemaking.⁵ They held meetings, talked, and shared stories about the Tampa bust and other relevant events in ways that allowed them to make sense of their experience. By retrospectively "bullshitting and brainstorming," they negotiated plausible, if not necessarily accurate, interpretations of the causes of the disaster—for example, their new airplane had flown too high and too fast, triggering the U.S. military's air inspection protocol. Communicating and negotiating among themselves, the members of Mermelstein's crew and their intermediaries in the larger trafficking network created a collective interpretation based on their identities as drug traffickers operating in a hostile law enforcement system.

This interpretation proved functional in that it allowed Mermelstein and his colleagues to develop alternative practices for everyday activities. Mermelstein's crew went beyond mere sensemaking to change their practices based on their new understanding of reality. They enacted their shared understanding by creating a new set of routines they hoped would allow them to overcome the unsettling interruption to their activities. In doing so, they moved from sensemaking to organizational learning. Eager to return to business and reaffirm their identities as competent criminals, the smugglers turned misfortune to their advantage by drawing on the Tampa bust to improve their operations. This innovation centered around a disarmingly simple yet crucial understanding. Mermelstein's realization that "coke floated," combined with Mickey's memory of marijuana airdrops, led to the collective insight that it might be feasible to run airdrops for cocaine. After identifying their prospective solution, Mermelstein and his colleagues scanned their environment for relevant cues, collected information about the airdrop, and used this information to build knowledge-in-practice through improvisation. If practice did not make perfect, it did yield experiential knowledge and a new routine, allowing the traffickers to air-drop cocaine in the Caribbean and reducing their vulnerability to American law enforcers. Using knowledge-based artifacts, including the sample wrapped package and a practical demonstration in Colombia, Mermelstein's ring communicated the technical and experiential knowledge embedded in their routine to other nodes in the interorganizational network. By gathering, interpreting, and enacting knowledge and experience, Mermelstein and his crew created a new transportation practice that allowed them to smuggle illicit drugs, at least in the short run, and confirm their identities as resourceful smugglers engaged in an ongoing battle of wits against law enforcers. In sum, Mermelstein and his colleagues made sense of the Tampa bust and learned from it, improving the reliability, if not necessarily the efficiency, of their activities.

Drug Trafficking as Mētis and Techne

As the airdrop story suggests, many of the skills involved in drug trafficking require the ability to adapt quickly to unpredictable events and capricious environments. Mermelstein's crew adapted to the unexpected Tampa bust by developing a new set of practices based on their knowledge of local smuggling conditions and their ability to improvise a new routine under real-world conditions. To be successful, drug smugglers require, in a word, mētis.

The concept, James C. Scott reminds us, comes from the ancient Greek poets and philosophers. Mētis refers to a broad range of practical skills that sailors, athletes, doctors, statesmen, and others use to respond to "a constantly changing natural and human environment," including prudence, perceptiveness, ingenuity, elusiveness, and deceit.[6] This crafty intelligence "bears on fluid situations which are constantly changing and which at every moment combine contrary features and forces that are opposed to each other," observe Marcel Detienne and Jean-Pierre Vernant, a pair of Greek classicists and two of the foremost authorities on the subject.[7] While criminal behavior is not the subject of Homer's *Odyssey*, or of Scott's penetrating critique of state development planning, the ability to adapt to unexpected events as they unfold and "outfox" one's adversaries, defining qualities of mētis, are essential to drug trafficking.

Whether transporting drug shipments, off-loading cargo, distributing loads, corrupting officials, or laundering profits, traffickers confront a variety of situations that demand craftiness and prescience. Illegal drugs must be processed, shipped, and delivered clandestinely, allowing traffickers to elude law enforcers who aim to disrupt their transactions and criminals who hope to rob them. Transporting drugs to consumer markets overseas, to take one example, involves assorted human courier, mechanized vessel, and containerized cargo schemes, all of which require foresight and deceit. Foresight allows smugglers to select transportation schemes that are unlikely to raise suspicion among law enforcers, who exploit established smuggling "profiles" to identify suspected shipments. Physical deception allows traffickers to fool law enforcers into thinking that the drug-laden tourist, fishing yacht, or frozen vegetable shipment under their admittedly brief inspection is not in fact hiding psychoactive substances.

Suborning government authorities, another basic ingredient in drug trafficking, also requires prudence and cunning. Moving large amounts of illegal drugs from South America through the Caribbean, Central America, and Mexico into the United States often requires interacting with multiple authorities who demand compensation for their complicity. Indeed, corruption is a form of adaptation: criminals and cops establish contact, share information, and develop practices that facilitate selective nonenforcement of the law or active collaboration in illegal activity. To begin the process, traffickers require leads for potential law enforcement partners. Once they identify officials who may be amenable to bribery, they approach them, exercising due diligence until they are certain the official is truly crooked and not merely feigning interest in order to trap the smugglers. To guard against that risk, some traffickers ensnare these officials in compromising situations, developing information they can use to blackmail them, should the need arise. Arturo, the U.S. distribution manager for a Colombian trafficking network, provides an example:

> I found out that this guy is interested in protecting us and that we should land drugs there. Then I found out that the guy was a cop, okay? Now, imagine everything that was going through my head. Was this a setup or was it for real? So I did a lot of things to make sure that the guy was for real, like throw two or three parties for him and invite prostitutes. And I took pictures of him with the prostitutes and stuff like that. I had a whole stack of pictures I could use to ruin his life. I had pictures showing him snorting cocaine and so on. I went through a lot of stuff with the guy before that first airplane landed.[8]

As Arturo's remarks suggest, veteran smugglers seek to reduce their exposure to unnecessary risk by preparing their operations with care and building trust among potential co-conspirators. Even the most meticulous planning, however, will fail to eliminate all risks, necessitating a talent for quick thinking and improvisation. Drug traffickers face numerous sources of uncertainty in their operations, including the weather, mechanical problems, communication practices, law enforcement activities, and group associates, all of which may endanger the operation. "The unexpected will happen," explains one former smuggler, describing the critical—and vulnerable—act of landing and unloading drug planes, "and when it does it often comes down to a group member making a spur-of-the-moment judgment call to save the day."[9]

Saving the day requires perceptiveness and adaptability, other essential elements of mētis. Accomplished smugglers, often confronted with such situations, combine these two qualities to survive hostile trafficking systems. Again, Arturo provides a relevant example. "One time I was supposed to make a delivery to this guy, once the cocaine arrived in the States. Usually, they have forty-eight hours to pick the delivery up, but I could not get a hold of this guy for four days. When I finally reached him and I told him that I have something to deliver, using the code that we already established, he asked me a stupid question. At that point I knew the police were involved. So I said, 'Look, you know, this is all a mistake. It was a joke.' Somehow the police were able to locate where I was, but I got out before they arrived."[10] Relying on his instincts and experience to recognize that something was amiss, Arturo immediately changed his behavior, terminating the transaction and moving to a new location. On that day at least, Arturo's common sense and quick thinking allowed him to avoid arrest and continue his illegal activities.

Professional traffickers learn their mētis by doing, observing more experienced colleagues carry out tasks, talking with them about their work, and then performing these activities on their own, adjusting their behavior to the unique—and potentially perilous—circumstances of each transaction. Mermelstein claims that he acquired much of his knowledge about drug smuggling through informal "on-the-job training exercises" in which he observed his supervisor, Rafael Cardona, engage in variety of criminal activities that he was expected to refine and improve.[11] Freddy underwent a similar apprenticeship when he began his involvement in cocaine smuggling, traveling to Miami to learn, as he put it, "the conditions of business," including cell management.[12] Another member of the Rodríguez-Orejuela network was allegedly sent to Venezuela to learn how to hide cocaine inside concrete posts and cornerstones, while a third traveled to Guatemala to learn about shipping containers for hiding cocaine, and a fourth went to

Miami and Los Angeles to show less experienced colleagues how to remove cocaine packages from hollowed-out shipments of lumber.[13]

Consistent with Scott's analysis, these examples suggest that drug-trafficking mētis develops through practical experience gained in local contexts, rather than scientific training. Unlike techne, which consists of abstract technical information expressed in universal propositions, mētis "resists simplification into deductive principles" taught through formal instruction. Practitioners develop mētis through performance rather than "book learning." In the process, they develop an intuitive "feel or knack" for the activity that comes only from direct experience.[14] Drug traffickers acquire mētis by immersion, through informal apprenticeships, practical demonstrations, or simple trial and error. When asked how he learned to process coca leaves into coca paste, one former processor replied, from "watching" his neighbors.[15] Another processor elaborated, "At first I just watched and asked questions about the quantities [of precursor chemicals] that you had to use, but afterward I memorized the formulas and little by little I became knowledgeable in the matter. I myself taught the practice to another colonist, also for cash, and now today almost all are . . . specialists."[16]

Trafficker Training Programs

While apprenticeships are common among Colombian traffickers, some groups seek to distill smuggling techne that can be codified in operations manuals and taught through training programs. Several Cali-based wheel networks reportedly trained their operatives in security and countersurveillance, including evasive driving techniques and communications practices, to avoid detection by police.[17] In 1989 a former member of a paramilitary group with close links to Medellín traffickers testified before the U.S. Senate that he received training from Israeli and British mercenaries. He claimed that his group, Muerte a Secuestradores (Death to Kidnappers), maintained two separate training camps in Colombia, where courses were taught on light weapons, munitions, and assassinations. Members of his paramilitary death squad learned the *parrillero,* an assassination technique in which the killer rides on the back of a motorcycle armed with a semiautomatic firearm while his partner careens through congested urban streets searching for their victim. A video was even made at one camp, he explained, "so that other patrolmen who were not able to attend the

courses given by these instructors would have an opportunity to watch the film and learn something."[18]

As these examples suggest, trafficking enterprises seek to combine experiential mētis with technical knowledge that can be applied across a range of activities. While many groups tend to privilege the former, both mētis and techne are important for developing trafficking expertise. To be sure, many skills essential for drug smuggling, including prudence and adaptability, are not readily taught by abstraction. Developing a feel for quick thinking and foresight requires immersion in the activity itself. But other trafficking-related activities, such as processing coca paste into cocaine hydrochloride or discharging a weapon, are based on general knowledge that can, at least in part, be boiled down to logical, step-by-step action sequences that are codified in formal artifacts and taught through training programs.

Drug-trafficking techne complements mētis. Smugglers who receive training or read operations manuals and other literature can enhance their abstract knowledge by applying it in the field. At the heart of such learning is the smuggler's ability to tailor his general knowledge to the specific needs of the moment. In doing so, he or she intuitively develops rules of thumb for dealing with a variety of contingencies, any one of which may be generalizable across different situations. In this manner trafficking mētis and techne interrelate and partially create one another. Traffickers extend their general knowledge through practical experience, which in turn enriches their general understanding of drug smuggling and related pursuits.

Knowledge-Based Artifacts

Participants in drug-trafficking enterprises share, record, and create knowledge through organizational memories. These knowledge-based artifacts include files, manuals, notebooks, correspondence, and computers that document and store techne, as well as stories, myths, and conversations that transmit experiential mētis.[19] Traffickers draw on the knowledge contained in these artifacts when engaging in organizational sensemaking or acting on behalf of the enterprise. Record keeping also allows leaders to keep track of inputs and outputs, supervise group members' behavior, and, theoretically at least, deter theft.

Numerous trafficking groups disseminate information through writ-

ten guides that describe rules and procedures for different activities. In the 1980s one transnational enterprise based in Medellín produced a pamphlet outlining various practices for managing stash houses, including suggestions for keeping the lawn trim, going to the movies every Thursday night, and other tips on "how to live like Ozzie and Harriet," according to one DEA intelligence analyst who read the document.[20] In the 1990s U.S. law enforcers seized manuals produced by the Cali wheel network that described procedures for transporting illicit cash and communicating with participants in different cities. And in 1997 Colombian authorities discovered two booklets in the prison cell of a Rodríguez-Orejuela associate. The first manual, brazenly entitled, "To Successfully Carry Out an Illegal Flight, Analyze the Following Aspects," included radio frequencies monitored by air traffic controllers, a list of radar installations in different Latin American countries, and suggestions for avoiding detection by drug enforcers. The second booklet, "How to Give Testimony and Receive Judicial Benefits," provided instructions on favorable crimes to confess and other tips for reducing prison sentences.[21]

Some wheel networks maintain records on nearly every aspect of their operations. Before his arrest in 1995, Miguel Rodríguez-Orejuela ordered his cell managers to keep diligent records of their criminal activities, which were faxed to the core group in Cali on a regular basis. He also hired accountants to maintain records of income and expenses related to drug trafficking, payments and gifts to government officials and politicians, contributions from other traffickers for the network's numerous political projects, the number of foreign law enforcement personnel believed to be entering Colombia, and telephone and motor vehicle records for enterprise employees and enemies. Handwritten records were stored in accounting ledgers, often using aliases and coded notations. Electronic records were maintained on laptop computers, with backup copies stored on diskettes. When Colombian law enforcers forced Rodríguez-Orejuela into hiding, he developed an elaborate system for filing important documents in numbered briefcases stored in secret locations throughout Cali.

Other records were stored on an IBM AS/400 midrange server that accountant-turned-government informant Guillermo Pallomari purchased for the enterprise.[22] Thomas Cash, the former head of the DEA's Miami field division, explains how computer analysts working for the

Rodríguez-Orejuela enterprise used this computer to monitor the telephone calling patterns of important employees.

> They were able to get the phone numbers that their drug couriers and the people that worked for them in critical positions dialed from Colombia to the U.S. embassy in Bogotá or to the United States, and they entered these telephone numbers into a database. Then they created another database, which was the telephone numbers of U.S. government agencies, such as the attorney general's offices and the prosecutors' offices. These numbers can be found in the Yellow Pages. This basic use of computer science was used to identify any numbers called by these people on their cell phones or whatever to a law enforcement agency in the United States. The idea was to determine whether—and in fact a couple of times I think they did find that—some of their cohorts were calling the FBI, DEA, Customs, the Coast Guard, or whomever they were calling.[23]

Of course, not all trafficking enterprises maintain such sophisticated artificial memories, nor need they. Groups that transact in smaller quantities of drugs require fewer documents to track their activities. In these enterprises the leader may scribble a few records into handwritten notebooks, while the bulk of operational mētis resides in the group's daily practices and the collective mind of group members. In hostile trafficking systems, record keeping represents an important source of vulnerability that police and prosecutors exploit to undermine their adversaries (I explore this point in greater detail in Chapter 4).

Collecting Information Through Social Networks

Before they can store information, organizations have to gather it. Trafficking groups have developed a variety of methods to gather information about their activities, new smuggling innovations, and the latest law enforcement efforts. "That's part of the beauty of drug smuggling," says one former trafficker, "the game constantly changes. Quick adaptation ensures continued success . . . but how can one know when the game is changing? The answer is to read and listen. Watch CNN, read *Time* and *Newsweek,* the *Miami Herald,* and *High Times.* Combine these with the local newspaper where you plan your area of operation, and you're going to be well informed about current happenings."[24]

Perhaps. But Colombian traffickers go well beyond the news media to exploit additional sources of information, including fellow traffickers, consultants, corrupt officials, and government reports. To access such knowledge, traffickers often rely on their associates' family, friendship, and professional ties, which channel tips about smuggling innovations and local law enforcement activities. Through their members' social networks, smuggling groups maintain access to a diversity of information sources and search routines.[25] When knowledge about new practices or government enforcement efforts cannot be supplied in-house, traffickers leverage their participants' social networks to find outside consultants or professionals with the desired expertise. In this manner smuggling enterprises with sufficient resources—and connections—expand their knowledge base by obtaining information and expertise that would otherwise remain beyond their reach.

Knowledge is a critical resource for drug traffickers—and those who have it can sell it to those who want it. Some trafficking groups use their members' social networks to access outside consultants who, in the words of one observer, "beat a path to their door with new ideas, technologies, techniques, and investment opportunities."[26] Several of the more exotic smuggling methods that have been uncovered by law enforcers over the years, including molding cocaine into plastic suitcases and constructing semisubmersible vessels that glide along the surface of the Caribbean Sea, have come from independent consultants who sold their ideas to established enterprises. Some groups hire professionals with specialized knowledge in particular areas. Colombian traffickers have reportedly hired chemists to teach them how to process opium latex into heroin, lawyers to show them how to manipulate legal statutes and criminal proceedings, and former soldiers and cops to instruct them in building intelligence networks and assassinating enemies.[27] When I asked Arturo how he developed the idea for hiding cocaine shipments inside diesel engines, which he maintained was an effective ruse against police "sniffer" dogs, he recalled that the innovation came from a law enforcement officer working on behalf of the enterprise.[28]

Through such specialists, trafficking groups obtain not just techne, which can be documented and stored for future use, but mētis, which largely resides in the heads and hands of experienced practitioners. Experts hired for this purpose share their hard-earned knowledge with less experienced colleagues through dialogue and demonstration. Acolytes then perform the activity themselves, developing their own expertise through practice. The smuggling group appropriates the experiential know-how to suit its needs, adding to its collective knowledge base, even if the original expert leaves the enterprise.

As suggested in the airdrop story that begins this chapter, the impetus for information gathering in trafficking enterprises is often, but not always, an interruption or setback that compels the group to direct its attention toward resolving the impasse.[29] When law enforcers succeed in interdicting a drug shipment or arresting an important trafficker, the affected enterprise will collect and analyze information about the event, in some cases sending participants on fact-finding missions to research local press clippings and criminal court proceedings. In the wake of the Tampa bust, Rafael Cardona sent Mermelstein to Tampa to learn more about the incident from local media accounts. Cardona then delivered these press reports to network leaders in Medellín, who reviewed them to determine which, if any, participants were at fault for the bust and to change transportation practices to avoid similar mistakes in the future.[30] Other trafficking enterprises exploit the criminal justice system to obtain sensitive information about law enforcement activities.

For a number of years the Rodríguez-Orejuela enterprise manipulated the discovery process to access criminal complaints, indictments, wiretap affidavits, intelligence reports, and other sensitive documents that described in detail how law enforcers investigated the Cali network.[31] American lawyers hired by the group obtained the documents by right of discovery and faxed them to Colombia, where they were analyzed in meetings between network leaders, their lawyers, and other high-ranking participants. The purpose of these sensemaking sessions was to determine how law enforcers penetrated the network's operations, identify confidential informants, and learn about the latest tactics in criminal investigations. On occasion, core group leaders ordered their cell managers to study these materials in order to learn from the mistakes of their predecessors.[32] Thomas Cash, the former head of the DEA's Miami field division, explains:

> The Cali people would get discovery from different lawyers representing different members of their organization who had been arrested, and they would enter that information in data

form into their computers as well. The purpose was to determine whether there was a similar technique as to how they were arrested. What was the weak point? What was the piece of evidence? Was it a wiretap or was it an undercover buy? Was it a transport operation where the government was posing as a pilot or posing as a ship operator or pleasure boat operator? They took in the discovery that was turned over by various government agencies, in accordance with the law, and these reports, be they DEA reports, which they were most of the time, or an FBI report, or a Customs report, were then sent back to Cali for analysis, as to lessons learned, like what they did wrong, and what they could do better.[33]

In Colombia some trafficking groups developed sophisticated intelligence networks with the help of a variety of collaborators, including law enforcers, military officials, legislators, public prosecutors, telephone workers, reporters, hotel clerks, and lawyers, among others. Through their informants, trafficking groups collected valuable information regarding drug enforcement programs, ongoing criminal investigations, and impending antidrug legislation. During the 1990s the Rodríguez-Orejuela enterprise established an intelligence operation in Cali using local taxicab drivers. The traffickers allegedly provided *taxistas* with mechanical assistance and interest-free loans for purchasing automobiles in exchange for regular intelligence reports. These roving surveillance posts were reportedly equipped with two-way radios, beepers, and cellular telephones, allowing the cab drivers to quickly report any suspicious activity to their contacts in the trafficking network. In the United States, numerous transportation rings established electronic listening posts in coastal areas to monitor the radio frequencies of Customs drug interdiction flights and local police units. Some smugglers apparently also obtained lists of radio frequencies used by the DEA, the FBI, and other enforcement agencies from radio shops and public documents. And during the 1980s numerous traffickers cased the Homestead Air Force Base and Boca Chica Naval Air Station in south Florida in order to monitor drug interdiction flights.[34]

Sharing Information Through Communities of Practice

As befits the mētis-type skills of drug smuggling, information among practitioners often spreads informally. Typically, members from a trafficking group meet in casual settings such as restaurants, bars, and dance clubs to discuss business problems, impending activities, and local smuggling conditions. "Sure, we sit down at a restaurant," Néstor recalls from his smuggling days. "I tell them what to do, nothing like a corporate meeting. Sometimes we meet halfway from one location to another. These are very informal meetings, with no set of written instructions."[35] Birthday parties, baptisms, weddings, and other social gatherings provide additional opportunities for swapping stories and exchanging professional gossip. Members of Freddy's circle often shared humorous anecdotes containing useful information about smuggling conditions at such events. In this manner veterans socialize their newer colleagues to the norms and practices of their enterprise and of drug trafficking more generally, creating "communities of practice."

The concept of communities of practice was developed by organization scholars to understand how apprentices in a variety of settings, including Mayan midwives, Liberian tailors, and American butchers, develop a "mastery of knowledge and skill" in a particular trade by moving "toward full participation in the sociocultural practices" of the community. Veterans and novices form these social communities by interacting on a regular basis, creating and re-creating experiential knowledge expressed in shared practices, routines, and narratives.[36] Drug-trafficking communities of practice contain a common language and knowledge base that participants draw on and create in developing their own mētis. Having applied this knowledge in their own activities, traffickers then share the fruit of their experience within the community through storytelling and practical demonstrations. In creating and re-creating experiential knowledge, participants become deeply embedded in the community's cultural norms and practices, solidifying their identity as professional smugglers and creating additional opportunities to learn useful skills.

Drug-trafficking communities of practice are not limited by "organizational" boundaries. Diffusion of trafficking mētis occurs among different groups and individuals who connect through social networks. Traffickers from different cells and even separate organizations share their experiential know-how at parties and in other informal settings. "You know the smugglers; you may not even work with each other but you've got each other's back," explains Néstor. "In restaurants, you might meet up with some guys and you find out about the environment, how the situation is going. This is all useful information."[37] Based on their common identities as professional smugglers, their links through overlapping social networks, and their participation in broader communities of smuggling practice, associates share stories about their activities and law enforcement practices. Members of one group may share stories with members from another about an incident that demonstrates their ability to elude police, without necessarily providing all the details of their operations to these potential competitors. Arturo describes how his group adopted the idea of a "suicide" car (for crashing into police cars conducting surveillance on drug-carrying vehicles) from another trafficking enterprise: "the suicide car, we learned that . . . from Pablo [Escobar]'s organization. We would share information. We would not share information as to exactly how we did things, but we would share information like, for example, the cars you use."[38] Significantly, Arturo's group was independent from and in some respects a competitor to Escobar's enterprise. Yet the two operations connected through social networks, shared knowledge within a common community of practice, and occasionally even pooled their resources in joint smuggling ventures.

Colombian authorities believe that in some areas, such as Medellín, the social diffusion of criminal expertise extends beyond drug trafficking to other forms of organized delinquency, including armed robbery, kidnapping, and murder for hire. A senior advisor on crime and counterterrorism to President Andrés Pastrana argues that Colombian police have identified sophisticated bands of bank robbers and car thieves whose members were previously implicated in drug trafficking.[39] In this manner drug trafficking may have spawned broader communities of practice in Colombia, involving participants from other criminal pursuits that create and share experiential knowledge through regular interactions.

While shared national or subnational identities provide a cultural bond that facilitates trust and information sharing among wary criminals, drug-trafficking communities of practice are not restricted to participants from the same country. When it suits their interests, participants in Colombian enterprises readily interact and exchange information with associates from other countries. This may occur in meetings between leaders of different groups who plan joint transactions or through habitual interactions among lower-ranking operatives who carry out these commercial exchanges. To penetrate new markets, exploit existing competencies, and elude law enforcers, Colombian trafficking groups have created transnational communities of practice with organized criminals from Mexico, Brazil, the Dominican Republic, Guatemala, Russia, Israel, and other countries. These informal arrangements allow participants to tap into their partners' knowledge of local smuggling conditions, spreading trafficking mētis among groups located in different countries. When seeking to expand into European drug markets, for example, some Colombian enterprises have collaborated with established criminal syndicates in Spain, Italy, and the Netherlands. In exchange for access to plentiful supplies of high-grade cocaine, host country syndicates share their knowledge of domestic drug markets, wholesale and retail distribution contacts, and local law enforcement efforts with their Colombian counterparts.

Cross-Generational Learning

The diffusion of trafficking mētis is not only interorganizational but cross-generational. Contraband smuggling is an old business in Colombia, and smugglers tend to learn from the experiences—and mistakes—of those who came before them. Over the years smuggling mētis has proved highly fungible: many of the skills involved in running black market emeralds and whiskey transfer reasonably well to smuggling illegal drugs, and some of the practices used to transport and distribute bulk quantities of Colombia's first transnational drug of choice, marijuana, apply equally well to cocaine and heroin.

During the 1960s and 1970s, a number of contraband smugglers drew on the experiential knowledge they developed when transporting "legitimate" goods, such as cigarettes, whiskey, and emeralds, to diversify into the illegal drug trade. Emerald traders such as Gonzalo Rodríguez Gacha drew on their practical expertise managing close-knit, clan-based enterprises, coordinating maritime contraband shipments, selling commodities on international black markets, laundering foreign exchange, and providing security to their operations to expand into marijuana and cocaine. In the early 1970s, prior to forming his own cocaine "cartel," Pablo Escobar learned the smuggling business while working as an enforcer for a whiskey and cigarette contrabandist, a man he later referred to as his "maestro."[40]

Several practices pioneered by marijuana smugglers later became popular among cocaine enterprises, such as air-dropping specially wrapped packages of cannabis in the Caribbean, and using large seafaring freighters—known in the trade as "mother ships"—to transport huge quantities of marijuana to prearranged locations off the U.S. coastline, where fast motor boats and private yachts would pick up smaller qualities for the final run into the United States. More recently Colombian cocaine traffickers discovered that, with minor modifications, many of their transportation routes, distribution contacts, and marketing techniques could be used to smuggle heroin. Homero describes how his transportation and distribution ring expanded into the heroin trade. "We began because the clients in New York asked us about heroin, which is when we realized that we could make money with heroin, too. They tried an ounce or two of heroin. They liked it so much that they began to ask for more. For us it was similar to transporting cocaine. At first the police weren't looking for heroin, because they didn't know. Heroin doesn't smell, so the dogs couldn't find it, and it doesn't have a strong taste like cocaine. Heroin was actually easier to transport."[41]

In this manner Homero's network, along with other trafficking enterprises, drew on their knowledge and experience to develop into polydrug organizations. Over time, the diffusion of trafficking mētis among different groups fosters the creation of additional communities of practice in which growing numbers of participants develop the experiential knowledge necessary to establish themselves in the illicit drug trade. Fortunately for law enforcers, these communities of practice remain relatively small, representing a minute proportion of the U.S. and Colombian populations.

Trafficking Adaptations

For many organizations, the ultimate purpose in gathering information is to act on it by applying their knowledge and experience to everyday practices. Over the years, Colombian trafficking groups have exploited mētis and techne to change their routines at every stage of the production, transportation, and distribution of illegal drugs. Initially traffickers select simple, cost-effective smuggling methods, such as shipping cocaine and marijuana directly from Colombia to south Florida on simple fishing vessels. When confronted by law enforcement efforts to impede their commerce, however, they quickly shift to more elaborate practices, including circuitous smuggling routes that wind their way through numerous countries, and intricate financial schemes that launder drug proceeds through various international wire transfers and shell corporations. These adaptations frequently reduce the efficiency of their operations, a cost many smugglers are willing to accept, as long as they maintain their security and provide what they consider to be satisfactory profits. Contrary to the findings of organization theorists and industrial economists who study legally sanctioned firms, trafficking networks often learn to improve their performance by becoming *less* efficient over time, not more.[42] For clandestine enterprises that operate within hostile law enforcement systems, other values, including safety and reliability, commonly trump the desire to produce more for less.

The following adaptations in drug transportation, distribution, and money-laundering practices represent some of the most common and consequential changes in trafficking methods in recent decades. Without secure routes to transport illegal drugs, safe practices for distributing them to independent wholesalers, and dependable money-laundering techniques to keep the proceeds flowing, the illegal drug industry cannot function. For this reason U.S. and Colombian law enforcers prioritize the disruption of these critical bottlenecks, while traffickers privilege their steady execution.

To this point the theoretical focus of this chapter has been on exploring the processes of organizational learning and sensemaking as experienced by Colombian traffickers. In the following sections I survey the "outputs" that result from these processes: changes in practices and procedures made by traffickers in response to knowledge and experience. In analyzing learning as both process and output, we must be careful, as Karl Weick and Frances Westley warn, of "concealing rather than revealing the dynamics of the process and the exact nature of the [result]."[43] In particular we should avoid "explaining" learning by equating it to an output—in this case, by arguing that smuggling ring *a* changed rule *y* and therefore learned. Such explanations are tautological and misleading. While change is necessary for learning, it is not sufficient. Change in and of itself does not signify learning. There are many sources of change in organizations, including leadership turnover, coalition or group dynamics, and political pressure.[44] When an organization changes a practice, this does not necessarily mean it has learned, in a cognitive or even a behavioral sense. Moreover, we cannot explain the theoretical and empirical richness of learning by reducing it to an output. In this chapter I aim to address these concerns by providing a finely grained analysis of the learning processes experienced by trafficking enterprises and illustrating how their adaptations occur in response to knowledge and experience.

Transportation Routes and Methods

Smugglers often respond to law enforcement pressure by changing existing transportation routes and developing new ones. Indeed, the expectation, based on experience, that all routes, no matter how creative or ingenious, will eventually "heat up" or otherwise run into problems prompts some traffickers to continually refine existing transportation programs, even when current arrangements are performing well. "We could never assume that because we had done it right once, bingo, we could do it again," recalls Max Mermelstein. "We never did it exactly the same way twice."[45] "The routes always change," explains Homero, "in order to avoid awakening suspicions."[46] "Someone might smuggle for ten years," says Néstor, "but they're always changing the rules. . . . Weather, surveillance, places, etcetera, all make you change. When a place is heated up, you move. If you don't move after three years then you're dead meat. What happens is that within three years you will get some kind of heat. You have to change your operation and location. You might be working out of some harbor and everything is good there, but some heat comes up, so you have to check out the situation and make sure it's safe again."[47]

Since the late 1970s drug-smuggling routes have changed repeatedly in response to government interdiction efforts. When law enforcers discover large quantities of drugs passing along a particular sea-, air-, or land-based corridor, they concentrate their interdiction and surveillance assets in the offending area. Intensified enforcement leads to an immediate and palpable increase in arrests and drug seizures as authorities disrupt established routes. But these interruptions often prove ephemeral, as smuggling groups quickly move their transportation routes to areas where government pressure is less intense.[48]

When federal authorities created a regional enforcement network to crack down on cocaine smuggling in south Florida in the early 1980s, traffickers shifted their routes to Alabama, Texas, and other Gulf Coast states that lacked extensive counterdrug radar coverage. When confronted with a regional enforcement network in the southwest border area shared by Mexico and the United States, smugglers responded by further diversifying their transportation routes. Some enterprises developed air- and land-based trafficking routes through Argentina, Brazil, and other Southern Cone countries. Others shifted their maritime routes to the Pacific Ocean, disembarking from Colombia's western coast and traveling up the eastern Pacific to Central America, Mexico, California, and Vancouver before transferring their cocaine to land-based vehicles. Meanwhile, south Florida and the Caribbean basin remained important smuggling zones, as numerous transportation rings discovered weaknesses in local interdiction efforts and moved their routes around the Caribbean, corrupting many officials along the way. Today the Caribbean and the eastern Pacific Ocean continue to provide enterprising smugglers with more than enough options to diversify their routes, forcing law enforcers to expand the geographic range of their interdiction activities, and making it harder for authorities to respond to reports of suspected drug shipments.[49]

Traffickers also switch among a variety of air-, sea-, and land-based smuggling vessels in response to law enforcement pressure. "When we started going after the small planes, the Colombian traffickers moved to the big jets," explains a senior analyst with the Office of National Drug Control Policy. "When we had figured that they had moved to the big jets, then they started moving more by maritime. When we started paying more attention to the maritime stuff, then we began to see a lot more go-fast boats. When we started chasing the go-fast boats, then every once in a while we'd see the semisubmersibles."[50]

Pressure to avoid government interdiction efforts has led some traffickers to experiment with elaborate transportation methods. In the early 1990s U.S. authorities discovered that smugglers were using "low-profile vessels" to transport cocaine in the Caribbean. These motor boats measure approximately forty feet in length and can transport one metric ton of cocaine. They are often painted dark gray to blend in with the sea and ride a foot or two above water, making radar detection extremely difficult. Around the same time, DEA officials reported that some Colombian traffickers were experimenting with "semisubmersible" vessels to ship cocaine between Colombia and Puerto Rico. These small craft rest so low in the water that only a portion of the hull remains visible. Like the low-profile vessels, semisubmersibles are constructed of wood and fiberglass, making them virtually undetect-able by most radar systems.[51] In September 2000 Colombian authori-ties discovered a partially built submarine for transporting drugs in the Caribbean. On completion, the submarine would have been 110 feet long and capable of transporting ten metric tons of cocaine while navi-gating completely underwater. The director of the DEA in Colombia remarked to local reporters that he had never seen anything like it in his thirty-two years of practicing law enforcement.[52] While submarines have not been widely adopted by transportation rings, in part because the persistent success of more traditional smuggling methods has made them unnecessary, this incident suggests that some well-heeled groups have the capital and knowledge to experiment with the most elaborate transportation methods.[53]

Traffickers also switch among different types of containerized cargo in response to law enforcement pressure. International commercial cargo from South and Central America provides smugglers with doz-ens of options for hiding drugs alongside legal commodities. Traffick-ers use these exports, including fruits, vegetables, coffee, seafood, soda pop, textiles, clothing, lumber, cut flowers, fence posts, ceramic tiles, toilet paper, cattle, exotic birds, and industrial equipment, to smuggle large quantities of illegal drugs to U.S. and European drug markets. Smugglers also transport cocaine and heroin within maritime cargo ships and bulk cargo containers commonly used in international com-merce. Some groups hide drugs behind false walls built within bulk containers and within the walls and support beams of the containers themselves.

When law enforcers discover a particular scheme, traffickers switch to other containerized cargo routes already in operation or develop new ones, sometimes by purchasing legitimate companies that export these commodities. During the 1990s the Rodríguez-Orejuela network switched among different conveyance methods in response to drug en-forcement efforts. "You constantly saw a changing of technique and tactic," explains Thomas Cash, the former special agent in charge of the DEA's Miami field division, who directed numerous investigations against the transnational wheel network:

> In 1988 they were hollowing out cedar boards with a router, putting cocaine in Styrofoam containers and slipping them into the routed boards. They cut one inch off the two-by-ten

and then they glued it back on. You can imagine the amount of work in that. After that was discovered, the concrete fence post scheme came up. They bought the factory that made these concrete fence posts in Venezuela, and about the twenty-seventh time the ship arrived in the U.S. with fence posts it contained cocaine. Then they had a machine that packaged the cocaine just like frozen broccoli, that wrapped it and had it labeled—and it was frozen too. It was perfect. They bought a factory that did that. Of course, there were real products mixed in. It wasn't all cocaine. It's just like you get in the frozen foods section in the grocery store; the same-size box. Then they smuggled the cocaine in coffee. It looked like vacuum packed containers of coffee. But once we hit a couple of loads of that the coffee stopped. Then they brought it in Lucite blocks. They'd take these big Lucite blocks and put seven kilos of co-caine in and put the Lucite blocks in cans of roofing tar. They bought different facilities to do different things. It was all very well thought out.[54]

When law enforcers disrupted cargo routes used by his transporta-tion rings, Miguel Rodríguez-Orejuela convened meetings with his col-leagues, during which they analyzed lessons from each setback, often using information their American lawyers obtained through the discov-ery process. Guillermo Pallomari, a former accountant for the traffick-ing network, was privy to numerous meetings between 1990 and 1994. In his courtroom testimony in Miami, Pallomari recalled that Miguel Rodríguez-Orejuela mentioned the fall of the lumber route during sev-eral meetings, "in order not to make the same mistakes that led to the falling apart of that route in the United States."[55]

Drug Distribution

Traffickers who receive illicit drugs in the United States and distribute them to wholesalers confront hostile law enforcement systems. Throughout the United States, dozens of enforcement networks made up of hundreds of federal, state, and local police agencies strive to iden-tify and infiltrate these distribution cells, intercept their deliveries, raid their stash houses, apprehend their members, and confiscate their drugs and cash. To reduce their exposure to government authorities bent on dismantling them, distribution cells modify their communications, transportation, and warehousing practices in a variety of ways. To protect sensitive communications from electronic surveillance technologies, including telephone wiretaps and pen registers (which record numbers dialed on the targeted phone, but not actual conversations), distributors regularly change their telephone and fax numbers, switch among different pay phones, purchase prepaid phone cards and cloned cell phones, place calls through third-party switching stations, exploit off-the-shelf encryption technology, and discard cell phones and pagers after a limited period of use. To prevent intelligence analysts from deciphering their written and oral communications, distribution groups change the code words and cryptic notations they use to communicate and record transactions. To counter police surveillance of cars used for delivering drugs and money, distribution groups acquire new (and used) motor vehicles on a regular basis, rent cars instead of buying them, drive ordinary-looking sedans that avoid unwanted attention, repaint automobiles following a drug delivery, and modify delivery cars with secret hiding compartments, special shock absorbers, and customized engines. To protect drugs from seizure, distributors periodically change warehouses and stash houses, create front companies, and construct reinforced steel vaults in stash houses and members' residences to store money, drugs, weapons, and sensitive documents.[56]

Adaptations in distribution practices are frequently driven by law enforcement pressure, and changes within cells often correspond to leaders' perceptions of the threat of police penetration. When danger to the cell is believed to be minor, changes may be relatively modest. If an individual member of the cell is the target of police surveillance, he may simply be removed from the group, with no additional changes made to the operation. However, if a cell manager believes that law enforcers have identified his group's operational "signature," he may order participants to change their telephone numbers, discard old pagers, develop fresh code words, replace motor vehicles, relocate stash houses, and create new front companies. In a well-organized group, these changes can be made within several days or weeks, after which the cell may resume operations with many of its original practices, procedures, and participants in place.

When the damage of police penetration is more severe, adaptations may be more substantial. In addition to replacing participants and changing operational signatures, core-group leaders may decree new practices and procedures for the targeted cell. The arrest of a cell manager is a particular cause for concern, given the manager's knowledge of distribution operations and access to different stash houses. Following the arrest of an important cell manager in Miami, Miguel Rodríguez-Orejuela ordered his replacement to study court documents obtained through the discovery process to learn how U.S. drug enforcers penetrated the cell's communications system. After learning that police investigators gathered intelligence by wiretapping members' cell phones, which were previously thought to be immune from government eavesdropping technologies, Rodríguez-Orejuela came up with new communication rules. Distributors were instructed to avoid using cell phones when discussing business, to use randomly selected pay phones when calling the core group in Colombia, and to pay for these calls with coins or prepaid debit cards.[57]

When police penetration of a distribution cell appears to be systemic, leaders may terminate the group and transfer remaining participants to other nodes in the network or temporarily remove them from duty. Some trafficking enterprises move their distributors to new regions or create new groups in smaller urban areas where local law enforcers have fewer counterdrug resources. In recent years several wheel networks have adapted to intensified law enforcement in major U.S. drug markets, such as New York and Miami, by moving their distribution cells to smaller cities and rural areas, including Charlotte, North Carolina, and Des Moines, Iowa.

In the expectation that their operations will eventually be discovered by the police, some distribution cells change their practices before law enforcers identify them. In these operations members change their communications and transportation equipment and stash house locations every few months. Leaders rotate cell workers and managers among different nodes on an annual, or even semiannual, basis. Some groups draw on their experience to develop new routines for delivering drugs, collecting money from wholesalers, and repatriating profits back to Colombia. By regularly changing their practices, these groups adapt their operations without experiencing the interruption or surprise that often kick-starts the learning process. In effect, they have learned how to learn, institutionalizing adaptation into their standard operating procedures.[58] These groups often remain beyond the reach of police authorities because they change their practices before law enforcers can discover their operational signatures, allowing them to survive hostile trafficking systems for extended periods.

Money Laundering

In the late 1970s and early 1980s, money laundering was a relatively straightforward affair. Traffickers could simply deposit bundles of cash earned from illicit drug sales in banks. For a fee, many financial institutions would reissue the proceeds in another form, such as money orders and cashier's checks, or wire the deposited funds to a bank outside the United States. Some banks offered convenient amenities for cash-burdened criminals, including after-hours operations, night deposit boxes, and electronic counting machines. Federal regulations requiring banking institutions to report any currency transaction greater than US$10,000 to the Internal Revenue Service were routinely ignored.

After federal authorities forced the Bank of Boston to pay substantial fines for not filing the mandatory Currency Transaction Reports to the IRS in the mid-1980s, American banks began to comply with this requirement, making it harder for traffickers to launder their illicit funds. Faced with the prospect of having to file Currency Transaction Reports for large cash deposits, many traffickers began "structuring" their currency transactions by making multiple deposits of less than $10,000 in different banks to avoid IRS reporting requirements. Smuggling enterprises with million-dollar money-laundering needs employed large numbers of people to make deposits in different banks, always slightly less than $10,000, a practice known as "smurfing"—named after the ubiquitous little blue characters that place the deposits. Traffickers and their smurfs easily modified their deposit amounts and methods to keep pace with changing regulations in the banking industry. "[T]hey kept changing the rules," explains one former money launderer, "and you kept changing with the rule-changing."[59]

When government regulators lowered daily and monthly reporting requirements for cash deposits to discourage smurfing, some traffickers switched to nonbanking institutions to exchange their currency, such as money-exchange houses and convenience stores. To thwart law enforcement profiles identifying prototypical smurfs, traffickers turned to depositors who failed to fit the sketch. One money-laundering outfit, called the "Grandma Mafia," relied on middle-aged women to exchange drug proceeds for cashier's checks at numerous California banks.[60] In Colombia mysterious intermediaries recruited foreign tourists to circumvent national currency regulations by paying them to exchange black market dollars, provided by the intermediary, for Colombian pesos.[61] Cocaine traffickers also shipped their proceeds directly to Colombia by hiding large amounts of cash inside legal imports, including refrigerators, televisions, and other consumer durables, and using human couriers to smuggle smaller quantities of money hidden in their clothing, bags, or body cavities. Some transportation rings shipped bulk quantities of cash, along with weapons and other goods, to Colombia on the southern leg of their drug runs, when their aircraft would otherwise be empty.

When American and Colombian authorities made additional changes to their respective banking industries to keep pace with the latest currency-smuggling innovations, some traffickers turned to professional money launderers who understood the laws—and loopholes—of international finance. Knowledgeable in multilayered wire transfers, overseas shell corporations, the black market peso exchange, and other financial schemes, these professionals offered traffickers new ways to keep their proceeds beyond the reach of officials. Money launderers were also proficient at falsifying records—for example, manipulating the value of import invoices to hide drug monies—investing in service industries that generated large amounts of cash to bury illicit earnings, including sporting events and construction, finding banks that were willing to disregard government reporting requirements for currency transactions, and exploiting gaps in international financial regulations, such as purchasing million-dollar life insurance policies that could later be cashed out. Money launderers also exploited new developments in electronic commerce, including smart cards, Internet banking, and online casinos, to launder currency through complex webs of international finance.[62]

The demand for increasingly sophisticated money laundering provides opportunities for well-educated financial advisors to enter the drug trade, which in turn increases the practical skills and acquired intelligence of the trafficking enterprises that employ them. Some smuggling groups learn by putting these wizards to work for them, tapping into their financial acumen and experience to increase the range of money-laundering practices available to their operation. In recent years the talents of professional financial advisors have become increasingly prominent in many smuggling enterprises, as core-group leaders seek to exploit their advisors' social networks and specialized knowledge. Three of the former traffickers I interviewed—Arturo, Freddy, and Néstor—claim they became involved in the drug trade through people they met while engaging in money laundering. A DEA official with extensive experience investigating Colombian trafficking groups describes how some enterprises "breed off the intellect" of their money launderers, asking them to share information about specific practices and exploiting their social networks to recruit other professionals to join the operation:

> In the old days, in the late 1970s and early 1980s, money laundering was pick up the money, put it up in a box, and ship it to Colombia. That was money laundering. Now you have more cerebral people in the equation. You have the money launderer. And what happens is that the money launderer has a degree in international financing and banking. Maybe he worked for a private consortium, finance company, or something else, or the drug organization lured him away with very good money. They also breed off his intellect, since he is a smart guy. They may ask things of him, like, "How did you do this, how did you do that?" The money launderer is oftentimes tasked to go out and get new people for the drug side of the organization. Why is that? Because of perception and profile—how the money launderer looks. He's got a suit, he's educated, drives a nice car, as opposed to the guy who shows up in a sports car with the gold chain, carrying three cell phones. What we have seen over the last ten years in these organizations is a metamorphosis, as the money launderer gains higher positions of respect.[63]

The cross-pollination of money-laundering and trafficking mētis and social networks notwithstanding, many Colombian smugglers continue to rely on traditional methods for repatriating their drug profits, including body carries, appliance stuffing, and airplane smuggling. In 2003, for example, Colombian authorities reported an increase in body smuggling of U.S. dollars and other foreign currencies into Colombia.[64] The resilience of these money-moving basics reflects the desire of some traffickers to avoid the expensive fees charged by professional launderers, which, depending on the nature of the transaction, can run as high as 20 percent of the value of the money being cleaned. While traffickers who avoid the services of professional money launderers probably save money, they do so at the cost of denying themselves access to the specialized mētis and professional networks of financial advisors. Yet the return to simpler methods is also a response to the increasingly stringent efforts to limit money laundering on the part of government authorities. As American and Colombian law enforcers increase their scrutiny of financial transactions in both banking and nonbanking investment industries, traffickers return to the tried-and-true methods of money smuggling, suggesting that sometimes the most effective adaptation is also the simplest.

Drug trafficking involves the collection, storage, and dissemination of knowledge among like-minded delinquents. While the knowledge required to hide cocaine inside maritime shipments or to change cell phones and stash houses pales in comparison with manufacturing weapons-grade plutonium or engaging in counterdrug law enforcement, no one is born knowing how to produce, transport, and distribute illegal drugs. Traffickers learn their vocation by doing it, often with the assistance of more knowledgeable colleagues who distill mētis and techne through apprenticeships, demonstrations, and, less frequently, informal training programs. In performing their activities, traffickers draw on knowledge-based artifacts that document and conserve experience, including ledgers or computer files for tracking operational expenses and pamphlets providing tips for specific activities. Over time and through practice, smugglers develop contextualized knowledge that is not codified in formal artifacts but is generated within and across enterprises through language, stories, and social practices. Knowledge diffusion occurs through social networks connecting individuals from different groups and larger communities of practice that transcend interorganizational networks.

Traffickers apply mētis by changing practices and procedures, often—but not always—in response to feedback. Many of these adaptations are driven by the need to maintain security in hostile trafficking systems and achieve satisfactory profits, rather than to maximize efficiency. Today, smuggling routes and methods are generally more elaborate, more circuitous, and less cost-effective than in the past. Many traffickers have been willing to accept increased transportation costs and reduced profits to keep their commodities flowing to American and European drug markets. Ironically, increased law enforcement pressure has been a boon to some smugglers. By compelling resolute traffickers to develop new transportation routes, shipping methods, distribution practices, and money-laundering schemes, law enforcers have encouraged their adversaries to diversify their repertoires and tap the knowledge and experience of professional outsiders, including lawyers and financial advisors. And by forcing smugglers to search the region for fresh transshipment points, front companies, import-export arrangements, and financial havens, law enforcers have encouraged their adversaries to create transnational communities of practice with criminals from other countries, including but not limited to Brazil, the Dominican Republic, Guatemala, Italy, Mexico, the Netherlands, and Russia. With more transportation options to choose from and greater mētis to exploit, contemporary trafficking networks are well positioned to respond to counterdrug crackdowns. The law enforcement networks that lead these efforts also change their practices and procedures in response to experience. How drug enforcement agencies learn is the subject of the next chapter.

It was an offer few of the computer distributors could refuse: three days of fun and sun on the beaches of Miami with all expenses paid, including travel, five-star hotel accommodations, and tickets to Comdex, a leading computer trade fair, where they would sample the latest trinkets and gadgets in information technology. There was only one catch. The invitation was part of an elaborate undercover sting by American law enforcers to lure Colombian merchants to south Florida, where they faced criminal indictments for money laundering and drug trafficking. The sting was part of a larger three-year investigation known as "Operation Cashback," targeting computer distributors and black market peso brokers believed to be exploiting a brisk trade in personal computers to launder drug profits. Undercover agents from the DEA and IRS set up fake export and import companies in Miami and Bogotá to infiltrate the money-laundering network and develop evidence for prosecution. Agents used the front companies to export personal computers from Miami, sometimes stuffed with cash, and computer parts to Bogotá-based wholesalers. These "controlled" transactions allowed law enforcers to gain the trust of their putative business partners and eventually trick them into making the trip to Miami, where they were arrested and prosecuted in American courts. By the conclusion of Cashback, police and prosecutors had convicted fifty Colombian and American money launderers and taken back close to $4 million in illicit cash.[1] Essential to the operation's success was law enforcers' ability to outfox their adversaries through of a combination of ingenuity, cunning, and deceit. Mētis, as we shall see in this chapter, is indispensable not only for drug traffickers and money launderers who operate outside the law but for law enforcers who work within it.

Before the 1980s, undercover investigations of the size and shrewdness of Operation Cashback were virtually unknown. In the 1970s, while Colombian traffickers expanded into the marijuana and cocaine trades, agents from the newly formed Drug Enforcement Administration were arresting low-level street dealers and confiscating small amounts of drugs. While popular among politicians eager to show their constituents they were getting tough on crime, the transactional approach to drug control was ill suited to a "super" law enforcement agency created to dismantle the largest transnational smuggling networks. For much of its first decade of existence, the DEA came under intense scrutiny for its inability to target higher-level traffickers through complex conspiracy investigations.

In response to these external pressures, as well as to changes in the international drug trade, during the 1980s and 1990s the DEA developed numerous innovations in its undercover operations, including controlled deliveries and reverse stings. The agency also placed greater emphasis on intelligence collection and analysis, while increasing its use of electronic surveillance technologies such as telephone wiretaps and pen registers. During the same period, Washington and Bogotá created binational enforcement networks composed of elite drug enforcement units in Colombia that shared intelligence with their American partners and carried out joint investigations and interdiction operations. In part thanks to these reforms, by the late 1990s the DEA and the Colombian National Police had become more competent in identifying, infiltrating, and disrupting trafficking networks than they had been in the early 1970s. In making these improvements, neither agency has proved to be immune from the corruption scandals, bureaucratic rivalries, and civil rights violations that have periodically undermined counterdrug law enforcement in both countries. They have, however, shown themselves to be adaptive institutions, capable of responding to feedback from other government organizations and changes in the international drug trade.

Drug Enforcement as Techne and Mētis

As illustrated in the previous chapter, drug traffickers require technical and experiential knowledge to perform their activities. But if drug smuggling involves knowledge about how to produce, export, conceal, and distribute illegal drugs, the information needs of contemporary law enforcement are substantially greater and more complex. Counterdrug law enforcement is a specialized form of police activity that requires knowledge of drug pharmacology, criminal investigation, penal law, civil rights, and telecommunications technologies, among other things. To be effective, law enforcers must learn how to identify different illegal drugs, initiate investigations against suspected smugglers, gather intelligence from a variety of human and electronic sources, plan and carry out undercover operations, provide persuasive testimony in criminal trials, and conduct a host of related activities, all without violating an assortment of laws and bureaucratic regulations that define acceptable standards of professional behavior.

To learn the practices and procedures of their trade, U.S. and Colombian law enforcers undergo a variety of probationary and in-service training programs. The DEA identifies training as the "cornerstone" of its efforts and requires all trainees to complete a sixteen-week course of instruction at the agency's training facility prior to being sworn in as special agents. During basic training, probationary agents receive instruction in case initiation, conspiracy investigation, criminal law, drug identification, computer information systems, intelligence analysis, interrogation techniques, undercover operations, surveillance, report writing, operational planning, courtroom testimony, emergency driving, firearms, and law enforcement ethics. In the field, agents supplement their formal training with in-service seminars covering more advanced aspects of conspiracy investigations, electronic surveillance, informant handling, asset forfeiture, and clandestine drug laboratories.

In addition to training its own agents, the DEA offers a range of instructional programs to law enforcers from Colombia and other countries. In Colombia, DEA training teams provide seminars on conspiracy law, asset forfeiture and money-laundering investigations, extradition and mutual legal assistance treaties, clandestine laboratory investigations, precursor chemical diversion investigations, airport operations, intelligence collection and analysis, and forensic chemistry. The content of these international training programs, according to one DEA publication, changes regularly "in response to experiences, changes in law enforcement emphasis, current international narcotics trafficking situations, new technologies, and specific requests" from Colombia and other host country governments.[2] The DEA also brings talented agents and administrators from the Colombian National Police to the United States for advanced training. The Sensitive Investigative Unit training program provides members of elite drug enforcement units with five weeks of specialized instruction in criminal investigations at the Justice Training Center in Quantico, Virginia. Following their return to Colombia, select participants receive additional instruction in management and institutional training.[3]

The stated purpose of these international programs is to improve host country law enforcement capabilities and build working relationships, based on "cop-to-cop" social networks, between the United States and its allies in the drug war. Just as important, however, are the creation of informal communities of practice among American and foreign law enforcers. Training programs and international gatherings, such as the annual International Drug Enforcement Conference, increase interactions among law enforcers from different countries, providing opportunities for the United States to socialize its partners to the cultural norms and practices of American-style drug enforcement while solidifying their identities as competent professionals engaged in meaningful pursuits. When trainees return to their respective countries they are expected to exemplify the professional norms imparted during training and build on their knowledge by investigating major trafficking enterprises. Colombian law enforcers who perform well and capture the attention and trust of their American colleagues may be selected for additional training opportunities and select job assignments, including participation in one of the elite Colombian counterdrug enforcement units that Washington has supported over the years (more on this below).

Much of the information contained in DEA and CNP training programs and seminars resembles techne, the sort of abstract technical knowledge that can be decomposed into "small, explicit" steps of instruction, as found in algebraic formulas or cooking recipes. Practitioners can acquire techne—unlike mētis—prior to engaging in the activity itself, allowing it to be taught as a formal discipline or vocation with theoretical or practical applications.[4] Counterdrug techne has a strong practical orientation: recruits and agents learn deductive principles of law enforcement as they prepare to apprehend narcotics violators and develop material evidence for prosecution. This knowledge is codified in textbooks and manuals that instruct agents in how to manage informants, conduct electronic surveillance, complete undercover operations, perform searches and seizures, handle physical evidence, testify in criminal proceedings, and perform other tasks essential to their craft.[5]

As important as techne is to contemporary law enforcement, many of the skills involved in criminal investigations are best acquired through practical, on-the-job experience. Like drug trafficking, counterdrug law enforcement is a mētis-based activity that requires improvisation and responsiveness if it is to be successful.[6] Effective agents often supplement their formal training with practical know-how and intuition that comes from performing their activities repeatedly in local environments. Like the narcos they seek to apprehend, law enforcement "narcs" cultivate mētis in carrying out investigations and adapting their activities in response to unanticipated circumstances.

Undercover Operations as a Source of Mētis

Undercover investigations, which involve deceptive practices to gather evidence of criminal behavior, offer an illuminating example. When working undercover, police agents and confidential informants assume misleading identities and try to trick traffickers into trusting them and exposing their illicit operations. Undercover operatives use their knowledge of criminal subcultures, including appropriate dress, jargon, and mannerisms, to portray themselves as willful participants in illegal transactions. The need for close contact with mistrustful armed perpetrators frequently places agents and informants in risky situations. Wily smugglers test their fealty to the criminal lifestyle and try to deceive them into exposing their true identities. Gaining the trust of suspicious criminals and infiltrating their illicit conspiracies without blowing one's cover requires a number of talents not readily imparted through formal training programs, including a cool disposition, persuasive acting, and a knack for quick thinking and improvisation.[7]

While law enforcers learn abstract rules and procedures for planning and conducting undercover operations during training, it is not until they are actually in the field, working investigations of their own, that they apply their technical knowledge to specific cases. With the accumulation of experience, agents deepen their formal training by developing personal intuition and rules of thumb for interacting with suspects and criminal informants. Effective agents intuitively adapt their general knowledge to each case, an important if understated skill given that every investigation brings them into contact with unique individuals with their own idiosyncrasies. Because even the most meticulous planning will not account for all contingencies that may arise in undercover encounters, agents must be able to respond to unforeseen situations with poise and precision. The practical challenges of undercover work require that agents balance their formal training with an acquired feel for the particularities of individual investigations, a responsiveness to changing circumstances, and localized knowledge.

In this manner, mētis complements, but does not replace, counter-drug enforcement techne. Following training, agents enter the field with abundant abstract knowledge. But their professional education has only just begun. New agents enter existing communities of practice through informal apprenticeships with more experienced colleagues who possess knowledge of local criminal and law enforcement settings.[8] Veterans socialize newcomers to the norms, practices, and organizational cultures of their units, expressing themselves through personal narratives or "war stories." These narratives contain useful information about counterdrug practice circulated among community participants. In their daily activities, new agents enact the knowledge gleaned from training and apprenticeships in responding to and interacting with their environment. They begin to see that general rule x regarding informant handling is not always applicable to undercover situation y and may need to be modified, depending on the context of the investigation. As they improvise their practices to meet the demands of each case, they also modify their understanding of law enforcement, using experiential "know-how" to inform abstract "know-what." In this manner, counterdrug mētis and techne are mutually constitutive. Law enforcers create and transform both types of knowledge through interaction and performance in everyday settings. They act by knowing and know by acting, generating knowledge that allows them to practice and understand their craft, becoming full members in their respective communities of practice.

Criminal Investigation as Sensemaking

Criminal investigations are exercises in organizational sensemaking through which government authorities construct plausible interpretations of their clandestine adversaries and their own efforts to destroy them.[9] Police, prosecutors, and policymakers "structure the unknown"[10] by piecing together strands of seemingly obscure information, including names, telephone numbers, accounting notations, surveillance photos, and conversations, to create coherent narratives of illegal behavior. These social understandings serve a variety of purposes. Police officials and administrators construct their interpretations with an eye toward identifying and apprehending suspected traffickers, disrupting their criminal activities, seizing their products and profits, and securing additional government resources to continue their efforts. Prosecutors construct plausible narratives of criminal activity that satisfy the evidentiary standards of trial law procedure, withstand the legal machinations of clever defense attorneys, convince jurors to convict defendants, and secure additional resources to continue their efforts. Policymakers create memorable narratives of organized criminality that capture the public interest, build support for bureaucratic and legislative agendas, and communicate messages laced with political symbolism that the United States is fighting, and ultimately winning, a war against drugs. Police, prosecutors, and policymakers negotiate their shared understandings through meetings, hearings, reports, conversations, and other practices that facilitate regular interaction and communication. They enact their interpretations by carrying out criminal investigations and prosecutions against suspected smugglers, and by creating counterdrug programs, and policies.

During criminal investigations, police and prosecutors convene meetings and conferences to share information and form collective understandings of their adversaries. Steeped in their identity as professional law enforcers and as private citizens with families, officials create social interpretations that highlight the perceived dangers drug trafficking poses in the United States, and the importance of defeating the criminals who conduct it.[11] Within this interpretive frame, officials discuss problems with ongoing investigations, coordinate their operations with agents from different offices, and negotiate shared understandings of targeted groups. Their interpretations tend to be tactical and operational in nature, focusing on the illicit enterprise's "command-and-control" structure, operating methods, and links to additional perpetrators. One Los Angeles–based DEA agent recalls holding numerous interoffice meetings in a multijurisdictional investigation, during which agents sought to make sense of the trafficking group's communications code and to brainstorm investigational strategy:

> Periodically, as the case got going, we would have a meeting. We'd sit down, myself and my supervisor, and then Miami would come, their supervisor and their agent, and New York and New Jersey and wherever we were "spinning off" to. . . . A lot of what was going on at the meetings was each of us telling the others what was happening on our wiretapped phones . . . like when we sat with Miami and we said, "We have this code

that comes out of Colombia. It's partially this." We'd sit together and just brainstorm.[12]

In sensemaking with their Miami counterparts, the Los Angeles
agents deciphered one of the codes the traffickers allegedly used to discuss transactions, deepening their knowledge of the conspiracy and fur-
thering the investigation. Another purpose of the meetings was to
coordinate operations and negotiate compromises to conflicts between
different field offices. One particularly sensitive issue involved determining a "take-down" date for arresting the perpetrators that was acceptable to all the investigating offices. After several drug seizures in
Los Angeles, the case agent and his colleagues became concerned that
their primary target, a suspected cell manager for one of the Cali wheel
networks, would flee to Colombia before they had a chance to arrest
him. Agents from other jurisdictions, however, were still hoping to spin
off their own investigations from intelligence provided by wiretaps
from the Los Angeles office. Some of these agents wanted more time
to develop sufficient evidence against their local targets. The Los
Angeles case agent explains:

> We started talking about when should we end this? That be-
> comes the most testy time because we may have been listening
> to the wiretap for two months, but St. Louis may have only
> been listening for a week, and they're not ready to end. That's
> an issue that comes up. In this case everyone was pretty good
> about it. I don't think we had any one really mad at us for the
> date we ended up taking down. We did have a meeting to de-
> cide when the target date was, based on things that were hap-
> pening in the investigation.[13]

At the conclusion of major cases, U.S. and Colombian law enforcers
convene additional meetings and conduct informal after-action reviews
to identify weaknesses in the investigation and attempt to learn from
their mistakes. Officials also use these sessions to brainstorm innovations in their investigative techniques, including undercover operations, based on their perceptions of the drug trade. "Once we terminate
a case," notes the head of an investigative unit with Colombia's Department of Administrative Security (DAS), "we have a meeting in which
we all contribute information and we say, 'Now we are going to work

in this form,' because we saw this type of criminal activity."[14] The purpose of these sensemaking sessions, according to another DAS agent, "is to improve the investigative form, so that we can better our investigations, to try to see how the traffickers are working with respect to topic *x*—and how we can counteract it."[15] When authorities modify existing practices or develop new ones as a result of their sensemaking, the link between shared realities and organizational routines is revealed: collectively negotiated understandings lead to changes in investigational practices that agents hope will improve their ability to dismantle drug traffickers, validating their identities as professional law enforcers engaged in a Manichean struggle against malevolent adversaries.

As plausible as these interpretations may be, they are not necessarily accurate. Given the clandestine orientation of smuggling networks and the consensual nature of their transactions, criminal investigators confront an exceedingly opaque and secretive environment. How does an investigator know what he thinks he knows about his adversaries? Investigations of drug trafficking and money-laundering violations often commence with tips provided by human informants who participate in these activities. "The most valuable informants," observes Ethan Nadelmann, author of an influential study on counterdrug law enforcement, "tend to be those who are directly involved in illicit drug dealing."[16] One common tactic is to apprehend "targets of opportunity," low-level violators who face the greatest exposure to law enforcement, and pressure them to "flip" against their supervisors. Informants who agree to cooperate can provide the kind of timely, detailed tactical intelligence that investigators use to identify other nodes in the network and "spin off" additional investigations.

But just because criminal informants are in a position to provide law enforcers with accurate and reliable information doesn't mean they will. Drug traffickers, to put it charitably, are not always the most accurate sources of information, particularly when they face strong incentives to be less than candid about their criminal activities. Whether they are seeking financial compensation for their assistance, "working off a beef" with the narcs who busted them, or hoping to punish their enemies and erstwhile colleagues, informants may minimize the extent of their own illegal behavior and embellish the alleged criminality of others. Well-trained, experienced investigators who are aware of this tendency may still accept these slanted presentations, in part because they view them as plausible, but also because, owing to the nature of their work, they depend on their informants for raw intelligence and access to other criminals, both of which are essential to job performance and career advancement. This can lead to wasted resources as law enforcers pursue false leads or, worse, build cases based on false evidence and subsequently arrest, indict, and prosecute innocent people. In the most egregious cases, case agents and their informants cross the line from investigating crime to instigating it, tricking or coercing unwitting suspects into perpetrating illegal acts they otherwise would not have committed.[17]

Misinterpreting the Colombian Drug Trade

Even when knowledgeable informants provide accurate accounts of their smuggling operations, these narratives may get warped by government officials whose own view of the drug industry is shaped by their institutional interests. As described in Chapter 1, U.S. policymakers and police administrators, with the complicity of the news media, have long created mythical interpretations of the Colombian cocaine trade centered on the dramatic but ultimately false notion of drug "cartels" that allegedly control Andean cocaine production and set international prices. Beginning in the mid-1980s officials claimed that the Medellín "cartel," led by Pablo Escobar and the Ochoa brothers, was responsible for no less than 80 percent of the cocaine entering American drug markets. Escobar was said to have concentrated the production and transportation of Colombia's large cocaine industry in his own hands through cunning, violence, and intimidation. No sooner was Escobar captured and his Medellín "cartel" disrupted by law enforcers and special operations forces than American officials created a new interpretation of the Colombian drug trade, arguing that the Cali "cartel," led by Gilberto and Miguel Rodríguez-Orejuela, was now the source of 70 percent of the cocaine flooding the United States and 90 percent of the cocaine entering Europe.[18] Several years later, when the Colombian National Police, in cooperation with the DEA and the CIA, apprehended the Rodríguez-Orejuela brothers and other leaders of the Cali "cartel," officials again changed their story, claiming that the industry was now dominated by the North (Cauca) Valley and Atlantic coast "cartels" that had allegedly taken over the trade from the fallen Cali empire.

These hyperbolic interpretations conflicted with more sober accounts of the Colombian drug trade provided by the people actually involved in it. Like other traffickers-turned-government informants, Max Mermelstein emphasized the sprawling, segmented nature of the Medellín "cartel" in his testimony at several criminal trials and a hearing before a U.S. House banking subcommittee. Mermelstein insisted that his transportation ring was only one of four to six operations based in Miami at the time, and that the cocaine shipments he smuggled were "owned" by different investors "who had their own distribution networks in place in the United States."[19] Former traffickers I interviewed, several of whom had worked for one or more of the alleged "cartels," made similar observations. Arturo pointed out that the Colombian end of his network was composed of four independent groups or "families," each of which had its own organization and source of supply. The families pooled their resources to share the costs—and risks—of exporting their precious cargo to the United States, but they maintained separate organizations.[20] Homero stressed that although his distribution ring sometimes received cocaine from large-scale importers affiliated with the Medellín or Cali "cartels," his group steadfastly maintained its independence from these organizations, in part by relying on other cocaine suppliers and maintaining its own clientele of retailers.[21] Néstor emphasized that exportation, international transportation, and wholesale distribution in the United States were all handled by "small, independent groups" brought together by brokers like him for the purpose of completing transactions. "There was no central operational structure with some big map or cartel," he insisted toward the end of our interview. "It was simply lots of small, independent groups: small clans, friends, relatives, family."[22]

While cartel-centered interpretations of the Colombian drug trade may not have been particularly accurate, they were useful. Sensemaking allowed U.S. and Colombian officials to create memorable narratives that focused public attention on the drug war and marshaled substantial resources for counterdrug efforts. U.S. officials also used the cartel myth to keep political pressure on their Colombian colleagues, who they feared would be less likely to apprehend major traffickers who maintained a more discreet, less violent profile than Escobar and his associates. Policymakers and administrators promoted this interpretation by creating law enforcement programs, such as the DEA's "kingpin strategy," designed to dismantle the "cartels" and capture their leaders. As law enforcers caught, killed, or compelled high-level traffickers to surrender, which they often did between 1989 and 1996, when the entire original leadership of the Medellín and Cali "cartels" was removed from the trade, government officials crowed that they were winning the war on drugs and that the days of the "cartels" were over.

These officials were right about one thing: the days of the "cartels" were over—because they had never really begun. Removing Pablo Escobar, Jorge Luis Ochoa, Gilberto Rodríguez-Orejuela, and other "kingpins" did not have much impact on the overall trade because the industry was not dominated by one or two organizations. Instead, the Colombian drug trade was composed of hundreds of independent enterprises connected through wheel and chain networks. The "post-cartel" drug industry in Colombia became even more diffuse and decentralized, as smaller networks, often led by experienced traffickers who had worked for one of the "cartels," moved into the vacuum created by the disruption of the Medellín and Cali enterprises. Left-wing guerrilla organizations, such as the Revolutionary Armed Forces of Colombia, and right-wing paramilitary groups also increased their involvement in the trade, in some cases becoming directly involved in cocaine processing and transportation in Colombia. As government officials became aware of this trend, they adjusted their interpretations accordingly, speaking nonsensically of "microcartels" that they now claimed ran the industry, in conjunction with "narco-guerrillas" and "narco-terrorists." These interpretations formed the basis of Plan Colombia and Plan Patriota, the latest extensions of the U.S. government's long-standing militarized supply-reduction strategy in Colombia, which directly targeted the guerrillas and, to a lesser extent, paramilitaries now held responsible for Colombia's drug trade. As this analysis suggests, the social understandings generated by state authorities are inherently malleable, even if the broader drug-control strategy they serve— reducing cocaine consumption in the United States by targeting its supply in Colombia—is not.

Evolving Drug Enforcement Operations

Many of the basic tools of counterdrug law enforcement, including confidential informants, undercover work, and electronic surveillance, have been around for decades. In the 1930s U.S. Treasury agents were running undercover operations, recruiting informants, and installing listening devices to gather intelligence against suspected drug traffickers in Mexico. During the 1950s and 1960s agents from the Federal Bureau of Narcotics, one of the DEA's predecessor agencies, routinely used criminal informants and undercover operations when conducting investigations, sometimes, as Ethan Nadelmann recounts, by evading legal prohibitions against these tactics in the host country.[23]

In 1970 concerns about the perceived growth of organized crime and narcotics trafficking in the United States led Congress to add several instruments to the drug enforcement tool kit: the Continuing Criminal Enterprise statute, the Racketeer Influenced and Corrupt Organizations statute, and the Bank Secrecy Act. These laws allowed criminal investigators to link high-level traffickers to drug and money-laundering violations in the United States even if they did not participate directly in these crimes themselves or conducted their activities from outside the United States.[24] While the new laws eventually proved instrumental in prosecuting organized crime families in the United States, they were highly complex, encompassing a variety of offenses that traditionally did not violate federal statutes. Years passed before criminal investigators and prosecutors learned how to use these statutes effectively, much as counterterrorism officials today are still learning how to use the increased investigative powers provided by the PATRIOT ACT to their advantage (see Chapter 6).

Within the DEA the shift to complex conspiracy investigations occurred gradually and was driven by the need to placate vociferous congressional critics and respond to changes in international trafficking, including the rise of sophisticated marijuana- and cocaine-smuggling networks from Colombia. Changes in DEA investigative tactics were made possible by improved training programs, sophisticated eavesdropping technologies and intelligence systems, and additional developments in conspiracy law, including the Comprehensive Crime Control Act of 1983 and the Money Laundering Control Act of 1986.

Banshee or Buy-Bust?

Operation Banshee offers a compelling case in point. In the early 1970s the DEA and New York City police conducted a joint undercover investigation targeting a large, loosely coupled network of alleged criminals who transported cocaine and marijuana from Colombia through Panama, Puerto Rico, Toronto, Los Angeles, and Miami to distribution points in Queens and Manhattan. Beginning with a tip provided by a criminal informant, DEA-NYPD task force investigators gradually pieced together the strands of this transnational conspiracy through physical surveillance, telephone wiretaps, and informants who turned state's evidence. After more than eight months of investigation, police agents moved against the smuggling network, arresting dozens of distributors, brokers, and couriers. Drawing on the new conspiracy statutes and evidence from the wiretaps and informants, federal prosecutors convicted numerous traffickers, disrupting what was then described as "the biggest Colombian narcotics organization ever uncovered." Unfortunately, the alleged leaders of the network, including Alberto Bravo and Griselda Blanco, eluded capture and continued to direct their smuggling activities from Colombia.[25]

Instead of following up on Operation Banshee's limited success by prioritizing the capture of Bravo, Blanco, and other high-ranking targets, over the next several years the DEA refrained from pursuing cocaine conspiracy cases. Robert Nieves, a former DEA official and a participant in the original investigation, explains why: "Operation Banshee had taken over a year to put together, involved large numbers of agents, and was costly in terms of man-hours, dollars expended, and investigative time. To many DEA managers, Operation Banshee was just the type of case that we should not be getting involved in. Consequently, cases of this type were discouraged."[26]

At the time, many DEA investigations relied on traditional "buy-bust" techniques, where undercover agents or criminal informants purchased small quantities of illegal drugs from street dealers, who were immediately arrested. Unlike conspiracy investigations, buy-bust cases were resource-light and easy to execute. Law enforcers merely had to identify a drug dealer, covertly approach him, "flash" some money to entice him into making a transaction, and arrest him when he took the bait. Although agents often attempted to flip dealers in the hope of identifying their suppliers, many buy-bust investigations effectively ended with the arrest of one or two low-level violators. But DEA promotion procedures rewarded field agents and their supervisors who used the technique to "put powder on the table" and dealers behind bars. Field office managers and regional administrators also benefited when they added their buy-bust statistics into impressive-sounding performance reports, demonstrating to agency executives and policymakers that

they ran productive divisions. Politicians eager to capitalize on President Nixon's war on crime contributed to the body-count mentality by
praising law enforcement efforts that focused on apprehending local
drug dealers.

But the DEA's primary mission, since it was cobbled together from a
hodgepodge of federal agencies to form a comprehensive drug enforcement bureau, was to apprehend *major* drug traffickers and dismantle
their transnational smuggling networks. With its focus on street dealers, the buy-bust tactic was ill suited to such efforts. During the 1970s
the DEA came under increasingly severe criticism from independent
observers and Congress for targeting too many low-level narcotics violators through buy-bust tactics.[27]

The reprimands reached a peak in 1976 with a series of hard-hitting
congressional hearings into the agency's investigative practices. Convened by the Senate Permanent Subcommittee on Investigations under
the leadership of Henry Jackson, the hearings culminated in a report
that censured the DEA's use of buy-bust tactics, questioned the integrity
of its undercover operations, and characterized the agency's overall performance as abysmal.[28] So oppressive was the atmosphere surrounding
the Jackson hearings and report that some agents openly wondered
whether their organization would survive. Peter Bensinger, the person
chosen to lead the embattled bureaucracy in the midst of the hearings,
reportedly announced at his first staff meeting with senior agents that
"[o]ur only goal is to keep this agency alive."[29] Over the next several
years critics continued to push the DEA to abandon its transactional
approach to drug enforcement and devote greater resources to complex
conspiracy investigations targeting major trafficking networks.

Meanwhile, criminal activity in New York and south Florida suggested that the international drug trade was changing. After several
decades of serving as intermediaries for Chilean, Cuban, and Italian
American trafficking groups, by the mid-1970s a number of Colombian
entrepreneurs had established their own transportation and distribution networks in the United States. The growing presence of Colombian traffickers in Miami and New York, along with an increase in drug-
related violence in these cities, convinced some law enforcement officials of the need to identify and dismantle these enterprises. Law enforcers also recognized that many of these enterprises contained
organizational features, including extensive family and friendship networks, compartmented cells, and clan-based core groups, that protected

leaders from simple buy-bust operations. If the DEA and other law enforcement agencies hoped to target these smuggling enterprises effectively, they would have to make better use of the legal and investigative
tools available to them.

More Electronic Surveillance, Better Intelligence Analysis

In the following decades, the DEA made a sustained effort to target
major trafficking groups in the United States and Colombia by conducting more electronic surveillance, strengthening its intelligence programs, and introducing several innovations to its undercover
operations. In the process, the agency demonstrated its ability to exploit
existing drug enforcement competencies to greater effect. Like many
trafficking enterprises, the DEA learned, at least in the limited sense of
modifying established routines in response to experience—in this case
to negative feedback from powerful external actors (i.e., Congress) and
the agency's own belated realization that its traditional buy-bust practices were ineffective against the sophisticated transnational networks
they now confronted.

Beginning in the early 1980s the DEA made greater use of electronic
surveillance in criminal investigations targeting major traffickers.
While Operation Banshee and other investigations demonstrated the
evidentiary value of electronic surveillance as early as 1974, throughout
the 1970s the agency made sparing use of wiretaps, pen registers, and
trap-and-trace devices. Between 1973 and 1980, for example, the DEA
conducted 195 court-approved electronic surveillance orders, an average
of twenty-four operations per year. The low number of surveillance orders during this period was due to a number of factors, including the
agency's institutional preference for short-term buy-bust cases and a
corresponding shortage of properly trained personnel available to exploit electronic surveillance. In the early 1980s, however, the DEA's
electronic surveillance operations began to increase. In 1981 the DEA
conducted thirty-six surveillance orders across the United States. One
year later this figure had risen to sixty-four, a 77 percent increase. This
expansion continued throughout the decade. In 1985 the DEA conducted 142 court-approved electronic surveillance operations; in 1989,
196 such orders.

But the real growth in electronic surveillance came in the 1990s,
when agency officials became convinced that telephone communica-

tions between traffickers and their associates represented a critical vulnerability that law enforcers could exploit. Between 1990 and 1995 the number of DEA electronic surveillance orders grew from 217 to 330, a 52 percent increase. In 1994 the agency created a new division at headquarters to help field offices develop multijurisdictional conspiracy cases based largely on intelligence provided by wiretaps. In the Special Operations Division's first year (fiscal year 1996), the DEA carried out 546 electronic surveillance orders, an increase of 65 percent over the previous year (see Fig. 4). While external critics have castigated the DEA's reliance on criminal informants to make drug cases and its practice of seizing financial assets from suspected, as opposed to convicted, traffickers, they have largely ignored the explosive growth in DEA wiretaps, pen registers, and trap-and-trace devices during the 1990s, along with the disquieting possibility that such aggressive electronic surveillance infringes on Americans' basic civil liberties.

Complementing the DEA's more aggressive use of electronic surveillance orders, the agency has emphasized the role of intelligence in counterdrug investigations over the past several decades. In the early 1970s the DEA's intelligence programs were headquartered in a small office staffed primarily by administrative personnel and agents with little training in intelligence collection and analysis. Many "intelligence analysts" were clerical workers rewarded for loyal service to the agency;

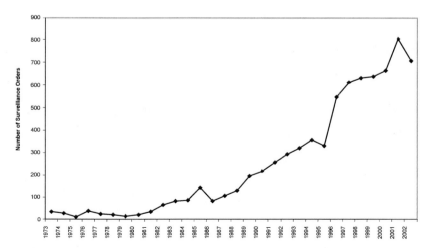

Fig. 4   DEA court-approved electronic surveillance orders (Title III), Fiscal Years 1973–2002. Drug Enforcement Administration, Statistical Services Section.

others were veteran narcotics agents at the tail end of relatively undistinguished careers and mediocre upstarts lacking the kind of mētis-based skills necessary for drug enforcement on the street. To make matters worse, the agency's organizational culture downplayed the significance of intelligence. Intelligence specialists were often seen as little more than glorified secretaries best used for answering telephones and performing menial administrative duties. As the DEA began to pursue conspiracy investigations more aggressively, however, managers came to appreciate the value of link diagrams, association matrices, financial investigations, and other analytical tools that intelligence specialists use to discern patterns in criminal activity and connect nodes in trafficking networks.

Since the early 1970s the DEA's intelligence program has grown from a handful of underinstructed clerks and cops to more than seven hundred professionally trained research specialists in 2003 (see Fig. 5). While the number of DEA agents increased during the same period, the percentage of intelligence analysts tripled, from less than 5 percent of DEA agents in 1977 to 15 percent in 2000. Today, intelligence analysis is considered a legitimate occupation in federal law enforcement, complete with its own specialized training programs and career ladders. DEA intelligence specialists receive intensive analytical training and are stationed in all of the agency's domestic field divisions and more than

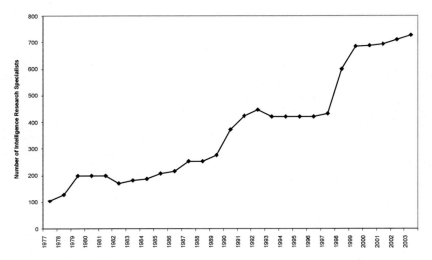

Fig. 5   DEA intelligence research specialist positions, fiscal years 1977–2003. Drug Enforcement Administration, Statistical Services Section.

twenty foreign countries, including Colombia. The intelligence program gained divisional status in 1992, emphasizing its importance to the DEA's overall mission and improving the agency's ability to coordinate counterdrug intelligence internationally.

    In recent decades the DEA and other U.S. agencies have also sought to improve the intelligence capabilities of their Colombian colleagues. In the 1970s and 1980s American officials were often reluctant to share intelligence with Colombian law enforcers for fear that sensitive information would reach suspected traffickers, putting DEA informants in the country at risk and compromising ongoing investigations. In response to these problems, the United States and Colombia created transgovernmental enforcement networks composed of elite law enforcement and intelligence units in Colombia that cooperated closely with American agencies.[30] The United States supported these elite units with extensive training and material assistance, including sophisticated weaponry, surveillance equipment, and transportation and communications technologies. Such capacity building, as noted earlier, was designed not only to beef up Colombia's counterdrug capabilities but to create social networks and communities of practice that fostered trust and enhanced information sharing between law enforcers from both countries. As a result of these changes, Washington and Bogotá manage a number of programs that strengthen counterdrug cooperation and intelligence sharing. These include, but are not limited to, joint criminal investigations that target specific trafficking conspiracies, joint task forces that coordinate maritime and aviation interdiction operations, and joint intelligence centers that combine tactical and operational intelligence from both countries into shared clearinghouses. By improving bilateral communication and coordination, these programs have enhanced law enforcers' ability to identify and disrupt trafficking networks in both countries. In Colombia, elite police and military units use U.S.-supplied intelligence to track down and capture the leaders of different trafficking groups, while in the United States law enforcers use Colombian-supplied intelligence to identify members of distribution cells and intercept drug shipments.

Innovations in Undercover Operations

Beginning in the late 1970s the DEA and other agencies carried out a series of undercover investigations that made innovative use of conspir acy statutes, electronic surveillance, controlled deliveries, and financial analysis. While these investigations experienced problems with inter-agency rivalries and convicting core group leaders, they allowed law enforcers to learn more about their adversaries and develop counter-drug mētis. For example, in 1977 DEA and FBI agents conducted a joint undercover financial investigation called Operation Banco that targeted a large marijuana-smuggling ring. Criminal investigators exposed the ring's extensive money-laundering activities by analyzing Currency Transaction Reports, tips from confidential informants, and intelligence stored in the DEA's Narcotics and Dangerous Drugs Information System (NADDIS) database. Revealingly, Banco failed to prosecute any leaders from the smuggling network, in part because the investigation was unable to infiltrate the ring through criminal informants. But the investigation did yield considerable strategic intelligence about how Colombian and American traffickers were using the banking community to launder illegal profits. Federal agents also exploited tactical intelligence from Banco to spin off additional investigations, including an imaginative FBI operation in which agents set up a clandestine front company to provide drug traffickers with money-laundering services.[31]

The 1980s witnessed numerous innovations in undercover operations, prompting one senior DEA official to characterize these years as a "laboratory for experimentation in international drug law enforcement."[32] Law enforcers modified the traditional buy-bust technique in a variety of ways, allowing them to infiltrate major smuggling networks. In the "reverse undercover" sting, the role of the undercover agent or criminal informant changed from a buyer to a *supplier* of illegal drugs. By masquerading as successful smugglers, agents tricked numerous traffickers into exposing their operations, which were subsequently disrupted by law enforcers. Law enforcement officials considered the reverse undercover sting so effective in apprehending "high-value" targets that they expanded and modified the tactic. Undercover agents posed as transportation specialists and off-loaders, suppliers of precursor chemicals, financial advisors and money launderers, and merchants in everything from airplanes, to weapons, to computer parts.

Through these reverse undercover stings, the DEA, the FBI, Customs, and other federal agencies were able to exploit the fundamentally decentralized nature of the Colombian drug trade. Ironically, this occurred at the same time that bureaucratic administrators and policy-makers were promoting mythical interpretations of the Colombian industry. If the cocaine traffic was as centralized and monolithic as these policymakers claimed, law enforcers would have experienced greater difficulty in penetrating these trafficking conspiracies. In fact, however, undercover agents and their informants were able to infiltrate numerous smuggling networks by forming support nodes that linked with other nodes to carry out a small number of controlled transactions, before arresting the alleged criminals and seizing their assets. Confidential informants often facilitated this process by introducing undercover narcs to established narcos and brokering phony business deals between them. The effectiveness of this practice underscored the importance of brokers in a decentralized industry where independent groups conduct occasional arms-length transactions with other independent groups. Exploiting their modified versions of the traditional buy-bust practice, law enforcers were able to disrupt different exportation groups, transportation rings, distribution cells, and money-laundering outfits, in the process demonstrating that the Colombian drug trade was more diffuse than some government officials wanted to believe.

Experimentation in undercover operations continued throughout the 1990s, as law enforcers developed increasingly sly schemes to outsmart their adversaries. In Operation Green Ice, the DEA established a bogus investment firm and several front companies to launder drug proceeds for several Cali-based trafficking networks. Confidential informants identified prospective targets and introduced these smugglers to undercover agents posing as money launderers. The DEA used intelligence from Green Ice to spin off a second investigation, Green Ice II, where undercover agents established fake money-exchange houses and bank accounts to further penetrate trafficking networks. In Operation Dinero, DEA and IRS agents created numerous front companies, corporate bank accounts, and a fake offshore bank in the Caribbean island of Anguilla to provide loans, cashier's checks, wire transfers, and other money-laundering services to their putative clients. In Operations Zorro I and II, DEA agents used dozens of court-approved electronic surveillance orders, including pen registers, dial-digit searches, and fixed and roving telephone wiretaps, to infiltrate Colombian and Mexican trafficking groups operating in multiple jurisdictions.

In these and other undercover operations, law enforcers combined cunning and deception to penetrate the shrewdest criminal conspiracies, including the Cali wheel networks. "What we learned," explains the

Los Angeles case agent for Operation Zorro, which dismantled two Cali-affiliated distribution cells, "was how to extend an investigation to bring in more players and to learn more about the upper echelons of the conspiracy. In the old days, we would have simply seized a load of cocaine, even if we did a wiretap. We would have heard about drugs coming out of the stash house, we'd have seen it, grabbed the buyers, run back, do that house, and arrest the guy. All the other stash houses and people would have been out of the mix—and we would have been happy with that. But what we learned was that by being a little more patient in our seizures we could bring the major players into the mix."[33]

In moving beyond low-level buy-bust cases to build investigations focusing on broader trafficking networks, the Los Angeles case officer and agents from other criminal investigations captured more of the "major players" the DEA was supposed to pursue. In doing so, they learned to exploit existing technologies and practices to better effect. Under pressure from external critics, and in response to perceived changes in the international drug trade, the DEA targeted high-level traffickers by making greater use of electronic surveillance technologies and improving their intelligence operations. The DEA and other law enforcement agencies also modified their traditional buy-bust practices, developing several undercover innovations that helped them penetrate trafficking networks. Meanwhile, government officials modified their social interpretations of the Colombian drug trade, demonizing one "cartel" after another to focus public attention on the drug war, secure additional funding for law enforcement programs, and maintain pressure on Colombian authorities to target the latest incarnation of Public Enemy #1.

But if the DEA and U.S. policymakers learned, they did so in the limited, tactical sense of becoming more competent at using existing practices, rather than exploring new ways of enforcing drug laws that might have produced better results in the long run, or considering broader changes in organizational goals and strategies.[34] This type of learning, common among law enforcement agencies, concentrates on exploiting established practices and technologies, without exploring potentially superior alternatives or questioning whether existing bureaucratic objectives are appropriate for achieving larger goals, such as reducing millions of Americans' harmful dependence on cocaine and other psychoactive substances. Such exploratory learning is difficult because it requires that policymakers reexamine the basic assumptions underlying the drug prohibition paradigm and reconsider the supply-reduction approach to drug control. The trade-off between exploitation and exploration is a persistent, if unfamiliar, theme in U.S. drug control—one that I return to in the concluding chapter of this study.

Drug trafficking and counterdrug law enforcement resemble an end-
less game of narcs and narcos, in which law enforcers seek to identify,
apprehend, and dismantle smuggling enterprises, while traffickers aim
to elude or co-opt their sovereignty-bound competitors. These spirited
dynamics feature adversarial yet interdependent players. Narcos rely on
narcs, and the drug prohibition regime they enforce, to inflate prices
artificially and hence boost profits for the illicit commodities they trade.
Narcs rely on narcos to serve as targets for law enforcement operations
and to validate their existence to external stakeholders, including Congress, the White House, and the American public. When law enforcers
identify smuggling conspiracies for disruption, traffickers often react
by changing their daily routines. When traffickers succeed in reducing
the "heat" of drug enforcement by doing so, law enforcers must change
their practices to keep up with their adversaries or seek new targets.

   While the preceding chapters showed how drug traffickers and law
enforcers change practices in response to feedback and experience, this
chapter highlights the interactive nature of narco-narc adaptation.
Narcs and narcos learn not in isolation but from each other. Cops and
criminals interact, acquire information about each other from these
interactions, and alter their behavior accordingly. Such learning is
problematic, not automatic. Narcs and narcos find it difficult to learn
because of the secretive nature of their activities and the hostile nature
of their environment. To protect their operations from competitors,
trafficking enterprises and law enforcement agencies organize their
participants into different "compartments" and restrict information
sharing on a need-to-know basis. While such practices may enhance
operational security, they make it harder to learn from feedback and
experience. Trafficking networks are particularly vulnerable to learning
disabilities associated with compartmentation and informal organizational memories. But they also enjoy a number of advantages over their
state competitors—among them stronger incentives to adapt, smaller
coordination costs, flatter organizational structures, and fewer institutional impediments to action. These advantages influence, but do not
determine, outcomes in competitive adaptation. Narcs can and do beat

narcos, even as the larger trafficking system they populate proves relatively impervious to these ephemeral victories.

Understanding Competitive Adaptation

Information is the lifeblood of competitive adaptation. Narcs and narcos seek technical and experiential knowledge that allows them to accomplish organizational objectives while outmaneuvering their opponents. They gather intelligence from a variety of sources, including informants, physical and electronic surveillance, government documents, and news reports. As they acquire techne and mētis, players modify existing practices and create new ones. Traffickers use their adaptations to slacken, or better still sever, connections to law enforcers in hot pursuit, while law enforcers use theirs to strengthen links to identified traffickers, improving their ability to disrupt ongoing conspiracies. These interactions are fundamentally dynamic: tactics and strategies that work well during one period may perform poorly in others. This means that the ability to change practices quickly in response to feedback and unforeseen events is essential for success. Players who fail to think fast and outfox their adversaries do not perform well in hostile trafficking systems.

Narcs and narcos are intentionally adaptive: they tend to select and retain practices and procedures that achieve satisfactory results, while (sometimes) disregarding those that do not. But in making their adaptations, players lack access to complete or perfect information. Decisions are often made in conditions of profound uncertainty. Given the clandestine nature of drug trafficking and criminal investigations, narco-narc interactions are shrouded in mystery, complicating players' efforts to learn about their adversaries. While narcs and narcos may be aware of the broad strategies of their opponents, many particulars remain unknown, which inhibits their ability to respond to ongoing events. In competitive adaptation players seek to make better decisions by reducing uncertainty; yet the knowledge needed to do so is often difficult, if not impossible, to obtain.[1]

Law enforcers, for example, often possess strategic intelligence about general trafficking patterns but lack tactical intelligence—names, addresses, telephone numbers, dates—about specific conspiracies. This is problematic because police agents cannot identify, let alone disrupt, trafficking operations without it. Traffickers may comprehend the standard tools of counterdrug law enforcement, including the use of confidential informants, undercover operations, and electronic surveillance, without realizing that one or more of their associates are actually government informants or, worse, undercover agents. Depending on their ability to corrupt government officials, some smugglers may even have access to sensitive intelligence, such as the license plate numbers of unmarked police vehicles and the identities of certain "confidential" informants. But even the best-informed enterprises, such as the Cali wheel networks, lack complete knowledge of criminal investigations. In tracking down Miguel and Gilberto Rodríguez-Orejuela, U.S. and Colombian law enforcers relied heavily on intelligence supplied by informants within the criminal enterprise. While Miguel Rodríguez-Orejuela reportedly suspected that at least two of his closest associates were government informants, he was unable to figure out who they were until it was too late.[2] For all their sophistication and cunning, the Rodríguez-Orejuela brothers were unable to resolve critical information uncertainties that resulted in their eventual apprehension by government authorities.

Advantages of Information—and Force

In competitive adaptation, to paraphrase Gordon McCormick, drug traffickers initially enjoy an information advantage over law enforcers, while law enforcers enjoy a force advantage over traffickers.[3] Narcos' information advantage stems from the secretive nature of their trade and their need for less information to perform their activities, as compared with law enforcers. When smugglers decide to engage in criminal activity, they generally do so without the knowledge of law enforcers.[4] Hence the initiative belongs to narcos. Law enforcers cannot penetrate enterprises they have not identified, nor can they develop intelligence about unknown criminal acts before they are committed. For this reason they usually respond to criminal violations that have already occurred, often between willing accomplices who share a strong interest in shielding their activities from interlopers. While traffickers often do not know the identities and specific operating tactics of the law enforcers who target them, unlike their adversaries they do not need this information to perform their jobs, even if such intelligence would undoubtedly assist them.

Given their clandestine status and law enforcers' tendency to concentrate their resources on criminal conspiracies they have already identified, traffickers often enjoy undisturbed and profitable dealings when beginning new criminal ventures. Pino Arlacchi makes a similar point in his study of drug trafficking and organized crime in Italy: "When a new channel of illegal dealing is opened, operations are at first undisturbed, and big profits can be made in this initial period."[5] The reason for this, according to Arlacchi, is that drug dealers enjoy a head start over preoccupied law enforcers, an advantage he calls the "time factor." Here I am suggesting something different. Narcos' real advantage in competitive adaptation is informational, not temporal. Traffickers know when, where, and how they are going to carry out a crime—law enforcers do not. This suggests that criminal investigators will not be able to resolve their information problem simply with the passage of time but only by acquiring tactical intelligence about specific targets. As long as narcos remain below the radar screen of narcs, regardless of the amount of time that has passed since their illicit operations began, they will continue to conduct their activities largely free from state penetration.

Many trafficking groups enhance their information advantage by periodically changing their routines irrespective of law enforcement pressure, as described in Chapter 2. When law enforcers identify a "new" smuggling practice or technology, traffickers have often already moved on to different innovations. "When we discovered *la cocaína negra* [cocaine mixed with charcoal and iron fillings]," explains one Colombian official, "which was a smuggling method they had been using for many years, the traffickers had already switched to another method, which they were using to transport cocaine past our authorities without us realizing it."[6]

Law enforcers seek to close the gap between their understanding of smuggling methods and what trafficking groups are actually doing. This requires the timely production and dissemination of tactical intelligence they can use to identify, track, and apprehend violators. "We try to stay one step ahead of the traffickers," explains a DEA official in Bogotá. "If we can intercept their communications, then we can be successful against them. We have to follow what they're doing. The hard part is figuring out what the Colombians are doing."[7]

On occasion law enforcers succeed, as evidenced by the disruption of several major trafficking conspiracies in the 1990s. In Operation

Millennium, a joint investigation between the D EA and the Colombian National Police, agents caught thirty-three members of an elaborate smuggling network that worked with trafficking groups in Colombia and Mexico. Critical to Millennium's success, explains the D EA case agent in Colombia, was law enforcers' ability to generate real-time intelligence on the network's smuggling activities.[8]

However, once the enterprise and other targets were removed from the trafficking system, law enforcers confronted a host of criminal conspiracies about which they knew next to nothing. For government agents, the cycle of competitive adaptation began all over again, this time against different narcos exploiting their own information advantage. Thus the quest for real-time, actionable intelligence remains a perennial challenge for law enforcers. No matter how well narcs play the game, they often remain a step or more behind their illicit adversaries. "We're always behind the traffickers on the learning curve," concedes the D EA case agent for Millennium.[9]

Fortunately for law enforcers, information represents only one side of the information-force asymmetry that characterizes narco-narc interactions. Armed with sophisticated surveillance technologies, professionally trained agents, and other accoutrements of state power, many law enforcement agencies enjoy a significant advantage in capability over their criminal adversaries. Traffickers are able to avoid the bruising implications of this force disparity only as long as law enforcers cannot see what they desire to attack and government officials lack the resolve to attack what their law enforcers see.[10] Periodic corruption scandals in the United States and Colombia notwithstanding, since the mid-1980s law enforcers from both countries have used their force advantage to capture and convict hundreds of traffickers, destroy thousands of drug-processing labs and transportation vessels, seize tons of illegal drugs, and freeze millions of dollars in illicit assets.

One reason why law enforcers are able to exploit their force advantage is that the information advantage enjoyed by some traffickers tends to be fleeting. As narco-narc interactions proceed, traffickers' information advantage tends to decline because of competing tensions between organizational growth and the need to maintain security. In drug smuggling, as in many areas of economic exchange, the ability to achieve satisfactory profits encourages additional transactions and commercial expansion. But for every new transaction undertaken, for every new conspirator, customer, and node added to an existing network, traffickers increase their exposure to risk and uncertainty. This is particularly true in hostile environments where numerous law enforcement agencies aggressively target criminal enterprises. In these systems, illicit success invites a robust response from law enforcers, who focus their superior resources on the largest, best-known smuggling enterprises. Some trafficking groups seek to mitigate the liability of largeness by changing locations, compartmenting information and workers, modifying electronic signatures, and making other tactical adjustments to their daily operations. Other groups purposely limit the size and scope of their operations, discounting potential profits in favor of organizational security. In drug trafficking, small is often beautiful.

Co-Adaptation and Environmental Selection

When law enforcers confront criminals who adapt in such fashion, they too must adjust their approach. As narcos change phone numbers and stash house locations, criminal investigators must update their surveillance affidavits or apply for roving wiretaps to keep their suspects under observation. When narcos alter their drug-smuggling and money-laundering schemes, law enforcers must gather intelligence about these new practices and technologies and devise effective countermeasures. In capitalizing on their force advantage, law enforcers remove some smugglers from the Colombian trafficking system, a victory—of sorts—for the state. Many traffickers, faced with the loss of large investments, the disruption of established trading routes, and the prosecution of leaders and key members, find the environment too hostile to continue their activities. This is especially true of smaller groups with fewer resources to replace personnel, capital, and equipment captured by the state.

But even the most successful counterdrug operations cause only temporary disruptions to the larger trafficking system. Police crackdowns tend to weed out individuals and groups that face the greatest exposure to law enforcement. In Darwinian fashion, these targets either adapt to ecological stresses or find themselves selected out of the system, replaced by other individuals and groups, some of which—but not all—may be better organized and more accomplished. Depending on the extent of state penetration, some networks will survive setbacks by revamping their operations and replacing members with new recruits. When individual nodes are dismantled, network leaders turn to other nodes that provide the same service or function. Redundant nodes make for resilient networks. When leaders are captured and incarcerated, they may arrange to continue their smuggling operations from behind bars. Alternatively, incarcerated "kingpins" may cede day-to-day managerial authority for the network to trusted associates by lending or renting their routes to them, as described in Chapter 1. Surviving networks may emerge from law enforcement crackdowns a little smarter from the wear and tear, extrapolating lessons from mistakes and modifying their operations accordingly. Enterprises that escape detection by law enforcers altogether may still learn from their competitors' experience through the diffusion of mētis among smugglers who share informal communities of practice.

Other groups may benefit from the removal of their competitors without absorbing any lessons from the experience. Rather than being sharper than their predecessors, these enterprises fortuitously enjoy another advantage in competitive adaptation: they are less known to law enforcers. While targeted narcos face significant environmental pressures to adapt or perish, survival in hostile trafficking systems does not necessarily demonstrate optimality in form and function. Some individuals and groups slip through the drug enforcement net as police agencies focus limited resources on targets they have already identified. Hence the selection processes at work in competitive adaptation do not inevitably yield more efficient, or more sophisticated, criminals.[11] Many narcos survive hostile trafficking systems merely because they are unknown to law enforcers.

The Double-Edged Nature of Organizational Memories

The ability to draw on organizational knowledge quickly and accurately is an important attribute in competitive adaptation, and a challenge for narcs and narcos alike. Trafficking networks and law enforcement agencies rely on records, computers, and other knowledge-based artifacts to document and store techne, monitor resource flows, and conserve organizational experience. But when narcs and narcos store information in knowledge-based artifacts, they confront a trade-off between information security and accessibility that has important implications for their ability to exploit this resource. If the information is not available, participants will not be able to use it when needed; if the information is not protected, adversaries will exploit it to their own advantage. With their greater information costs and more elaborate organizational memories, the trade-off between information security and access is a pressing concern for law enforcement agencies such as the DEA.

In general, the larger and more complex an organization's activities, the greater its corresponding need to document at least part of its experience. For this reason, transnational enterprises such as the Cali wheel networks, which coordinate several multiton cocaine shipments a year involving dozens of suppliers, transporters, distributors, and money launderers, tend to maintain larger, more elaborate record keeping systems than do small, independent smuggling groups that perform smaller transactions less frequently. Freddy, the former seafaring smuggler who worked for a large Cali network, explains: "You can't distribute drugs in such quantity, in such a large volume, without records. It's like dealing in cattle. You can't remember where you sold your cattle, nor to whom, without documents. Or say something goes wrong with the merchandise. Documenting who is involved and responsible for the deal will help you fix the problem. It's very similar to how you would manage a company. It's the same thing."[12]

Large smuggling networks such as Freddy's rely on a variety of paper, electronic, and, more recently, online technologies to store information about their transactions, employees, and government counternarcotics efforts. The formal organizational memories of even the most sophisticated trafficking networks pale in comparison, however, with the volume of records stored by federal law enforcement agencies (more on this below). Traffickers also rely heavily on stories and informal conversations to share and store information. But for narcs and narcos alike, the ability to exploit information depends largely on its availability. Frequently and recently used information stored in artifacts that are easy to access will be more readily exploited than old, stale information salted away in locations that are hard to reach.[13] Although recent advances in information technology have reduced the costs of recording and retrieving information, much organizational experience remains undocumented, underscoring the importance of conversations, stories, and other informal artifacts that build and transmit experiential knowledge.

With their relatively low information costs, and the persistent need to protect their operations from outside interference, narcos tend to maintain fewer, less formal organizational memories than narcs do. "The worst thing a trafficker could possibly do is store and document and put in some form of ledgers his activity," explains Thomas Cash, the former head of the DEA's Miami division. "Because when I seize that, it becomes evidence that puts the noose around his neck."[14] Still, as Freddy suggests, the size and complexity of some transactions will necessitate some form of record keeping, creating a significant vulnerability that law enforcers may exploit. When U.S. and Colombian law enforcers cracked down on several leading Colombian networks in the 1990s, they discovered a great many documents, accounting ledgers, and computer files that they used to carry out additional raids, capture more participants, and develop material evidence for prosecution.

Drug traffickers seek to reduce their exposure to law enforcers by limiting their documentation, a kind of informal paperwork reduction act that helps them remain beyond the purview of state authorities. To minimize record keeping, managers and associates memorize operational details, including shipment quantities, wholesale drug prices for different customers, bank account numbers, stash house locations, code words and aliases, and telephone and pager numbers. This reduces one vulnerability while creating another. When sensitive information is stored only in the minds of select individuals, their removal from the enterprise, or their failure to recall the information correctly, hinders the group's ability to access this knowledge and function effectively. Moreover, if such individuals become government informants, as occurred when Cali "cartel" accountant Guillermo Pallomari flipped against his former colleagues, their human memories, fallible as they are, can become invaluable sources of courtroom evidence and counterdrug intelligence.

Drug Enforcement Databases

In comparison with their illicit adversaries, law enforcement bureaucracies such as the DEA and the Colombian National Police maintain massive repositories of knowledge-based artifacts housed in dozens of interagency databases. The DEA's Narcotics and Dangerous Drugs Information System (NADDIS) contains nearly six million records, including names, telephone numbers, social security numbers, motor vehicle licenses, criminal backgrounds, businesses, and vehicle identification numbers for thousands of known and suspected drug traffickers.[15] The

DEA also administers the interagency El Paso Intelligence Center, which integrates tactical intelligence from NADDIS and thirty-two other federal databases to provide participating agencies with access to more than a hundred million computer records on the movement of illegal drugs and aliens in the Western Hemisphere. Criminal investigators in the United States and Colombia draw on the vast wealth of law enforcement intelligence stored in these artifacts to identify trafficking patterns and coordinate with other law enforcement agencies.

The collection and dissemination of millions of sensitive records among hundreds of domestic and foreign law enforcement agencies, while keeping them secure from inquisitive criminals, presents special knowledge-management challenges for government officials. One challenge is to encourage case agents to gather and record all relevant leads during their investigative work without overloading them with cumbersome reporting requirements. "Written reports are vital to the conduct of DEA operations," states the DEA Agents Manual. "They are our formal means of communicating among ourselves, with other agencies, and with the court."[16] During investigations, agents spend considerable time simply documenting their activities and recording information containing evidentiary or intelligence value in standardized reports. This creates an opportunity cost for law enforcers by reducing their availability for other activities, such as meeting with informants and investigating leads. "For every hour on the street," observes the DEA's deputy chief inspector, "an agent may spend up to three hours on reports."[17] Another DEA agent describes the paperwork involved in managing informants, a critical activity in drug enforcement. "Every time you ride or meet with an informant, you have to log it. If anything happens, you've got to do a report. If the guy calls you up, and says, 'Hey, I know where so-and-so is meeting, and they're dealing X-Y. Here's their pager numbers and cell phones,' you have to do a report. So you would end up writing reports. You'd be on your laptop all day."[18]

The DEA has sought to reduce burdensome reporting requirements by exploiting advances in information technology and computerized reporting systems. But the shift from pen and paper to electronic reporting has not reduced the workload but merely altered the method of documentation. Computerized reporting has also intensified the DEA's reliance on a knowledge-management system designed more than twenty years ago, creating additional problems for information processing. The agency's vast intelligence holdings are stored in more than sixty computer silos in different locations. This antiquated system forces agents to pull together information from separate areas manually, impeding their ability to access case-specific intelligence in a timely fashion. In spite of the El Paso Intelligence Center's celebrated around-the-clock information-sharing capability, agents often complain that by the time they actually receive tactical intelligence from El Paso, it is no longer useful for ongoing investigations.[19]

Information security presents another management challenge for law enforcement officials. For obvious reasons, drug traffickers place considerable value on intelligence from active investigations, and they have been known to pay top dollar for this information. Over the years, corrupt U.S. and Colombian officials have sold classified intelligence to traffickers or their intermediaries about impending arrests and prosecutions, providing them with ample warning to elude their captors and jeopardizing the lives of undercover agents. In one case, an eleven-year DEA veteran ran several names through NADDIS and called two fellow agents to learn the details of an ongoing investigation targeting a Los Angeles–based money-laundering ring. The agent passed the information to an intermediary, who sold it for US$150,000 dollars to one of the principal targets in the investigation. The stolen intelligence included the useful tip that two undercover agents posing as drug traffickers were traveling to Miami to meet with the person purchasing the information.[20] In another case, a seven-year DEA veteran was convicted of passing along highly sensitive NADDIS intelligence documenting the identities of several informants to a former DEA colleague-turned-drug trafficker.[21] In Colombia, corrupt officials from Cali's Regional Prosecutor's Office allegedly provided Miguel Rodríguez-Orejuela with confidential documents regarding criminal proceedings targeting Rodríguez-Orejuela and his associates. In his courtroom testimony, Guillermo Pallomari, Rodríguez-Orejuela's former accountant, claimed that his boss asked the head of the Regional Prosecutor's Office to "lose these documents within the prosecutors' office, so that the whole process against them would be delayed," adding that this "was a normal tactic that the Cali Cartel used when it came to prosecutions against them."[22]

While the U.S. and Colombian governments have implemented a variety of administrative and technological reforms to protect sensitive information from leaking to their adversaries, the sheer volume of intelligence generated by law enforcers, the demand for this information among the criminal element, and the propensity of some officials to corruption or ineptitude, suggest that classified records will remain vulnerable to exploitation. As if to underscore this point, in February 2004 a legal technician from the FBI's Freedom of Information Act and Privacy Unit was sentenced to twelve months in prison for sharing information she retrieved from the agency's automated case system files with suspected drug violators.[23] Several months later a DEA laptop computer containing more than four thousand pages of case files, including detailed information on confidential informants, was misplaced, ironically, by an auditor performing a review of the agency's payments to informants for the Department of Justice's Office of Inspector General.[24]

The trade-off between information security and accessibility suggests that as the DEA and other law enforcement agencies institute more stringent classification procedures and advanced technological systems, they reduce the availability of tactical intelligence to front-line agents and investigators. Protecting sensitive intelligence, as the DEA has done, by storing it in separate locations and instituting elaborate classification protocols enhances information security at the expense of easy availability. Knowing that the information they desire may be dated by the time it winds through the necessary security channels, agents and investigators will be less likely to draw on these artifacts, which defeats the purpose of storing knowledge in the first place. In hostile and dynamic trafficking systems, law enforcers depend on their ability to access information with speed and precision, a challenge made more difficult by the push for greater information security.

Compartmentation as an Impediment to Learning

The trade-off between information accessibility and security also manifests itself through compartmentation. To maintain the integrity of their operations, protect associates from unnecessary risk, and prevent competitors from exploiting their proprietary tricks of the trade, narcs and narcos channel communication flows into separate "compartments," where information is distributed on a need-to-know basis. While secrecy is often necessary for trafficking groups and law enforcement agencies, sequestering information in functional or geographic compartments that maintain little contact with other parts of the organization limits their ability to learn from experience.

This problem is particularly acute for clandestine smuggling networks that operate in hostile trafficking systems. Over the years Colombian trafficking enterprises have developed numerous innovations in their transportation, distribution, and money-laundering practices. These adaptations are essential for helping narcos maintain their competitive advantage over government adversaries. But innovations developed in one part of the network are unlikely to spread to other nodes that may benefit, unless the information they contain moves through interconnected links. Such links are provided by transportation coordinators who communicate regularly with different cell managers, brokers who facilitate transactions between different nodes, and other intermediaries. Many trafficking operations rely on these go-betweens or "cut-outs" to communicate valuable information about smuggling practices and law enforcement techniques to different cells. This is often done informally, as described in Chapter 2, through social gatherings that provide opportunities for intermediaries and associates from different nodes and networks to swap stories and share trade secrets.

Still, some trafficking networks are so tightly compartmented that they do not benefit from such connectivity. In these intergroup networks, learning tends to remain localized: individual cells absorb only those lessons they have experienced directly. To the extent that learning occurs, it never becomes truly organizational. Knowledge does not spread through the network, and different cells end up learning the same lessons their colleagues in other nodes have already experienced. Moreover, because participants are told only what they need to know to carry out their immediate activities, they lack information about the overall enterprise, limiting their ability to suggest improvements to existing practices. During our two-hour prison interview, Freddy unwittingly demonstrated this aspect of compartmentation. While he described his own maritime smuggling activities at length, he was unable to explain even the most basic operations of the larger network, let alone offer suggestions for improvement.[25]

Compartmentation not only prevents trafficking networks from sharing knowledge about smuggling innovations, it also prevents them from communicating tips about police activities, which plays into the hands of law enforcers. In highly compartmented operations, participants in one node will not be able to warn their colleagues in other parts of the network about law enforcement crackdowns because there are no intermediaries to pass along the information. The failure to communicate can also become a hindrance in less segmented operations, where tactical intelligence about police activities could be shared but isn't. In one conspiracy investigation targeting a Colombian trafficking network, law enforcers were able to seize drugs from different wholesalers on several occasions without scaring off their primary target, a large-scale cocaine importer, because the wholesalers refused to share their unfortunate, if seemingly relevant, news with the importer, for fear of losing access to his prodigious drug supply. Case agents exploited this principal-agent dilemma by developing links to other nodes in the network, which they targeted for additional investigation, thus expanding the range of their investigation.[26]

Compartmentation in Drug Enforcement Agencies

Narcos are not the only players who compartment information and employees. Law enforcers also segment their operations and limit information sharing on a need-to-know basis. The DEA and other police agencies divide their agents into different work units, organized along functional and regional areas of expertise. While drug enforcers are not formally prohibited from communicating with their colleagues from other units and agencies, most interaction and information sharing takes place within units, where agents develop strong interpersonal bonds and cohesive organizational subcultures. This can impede information sharing when law enforcers, whose professional identities are largely defined by their agency and unit, believe that they will harm the interests of their organization. In addition, agents follow numerous classification procedures, restricting their access to information they are not authorized to see and limiting their ability to learn from the knowledge-based artifacts maintained by their bureaus. Law enforcers exacerbate these formal constraints by engaging in informal practices that further limit information sharing. For example, agents often maintain tactical intelligence from specific investigations in off-line case files rather than enter this information into computerized databases that other agents and agencies can access and exploit.

One purpose of compartmentation is to protect ongoing investigations from public exposure, which can disrupt weeks or months of labor-intensive police work and endanger the lives of confidential informants and undercover agents. Another, less salutary, objective is to protect proprietary intelligence-gathering methods and keep embarrassing secrets from competing agencies. A third is to safeguard productive intelligence sources, particularly human informants developed with great care by their handlers, from competing law enforcers. Professional rivalries within and across police agencies have been a persistent, if unfortunate, feature of U.S. drug enforcement. Agents and agencies have been known to withhold information they perceive to be potentially damaging to institutional and individual interests.

These formal and informal information-sharing constraints are often detrimental to counterdrug law enforcement. By limiting communication within and across agencies, compartmentation and classification procedures hinder law enforcers' ability to learn from their colleagues. Knowledge embodied in an effective undercover technique, for example, may fail to reach other agencies, limiting the utility of the practice despite its potentially widespread applicability. As in trafficking networks, adaptation may remain localized, with different units and agencies learning only what they have experienced themselves. In extreme cases, learning may fail to become organizational, as different units relearn the same lessons already experienced in other parts of the agency.

Compartmentation also impedes ongoing criminal investigations when it prevents law enforcers from learning about the activities of their colleagues in other jurisdictions. This can have negative implications when different agencies pursue targets in the same trafficking network through their own investigations, an all too frequent occurrence in the war on drugs. When agents in one region arrest suspects without informing their colleagues in other locations, the latter may lose important targets as word spreads in the trafficking network that people are being apprehended (assuming, of course, that the trafficking network itself is not highly compartmented). Lack of communication between agencies from different jurisdictions also limits law enforcers' ability to determine the full scope of trafficking conspiracies that, by definition, are multijurisdictional. Finally, compartmentation prevents lessons learned in specific cases from spreading to other police agencies that would benefit, undermining the value of such "lesson drawing" for future investigations.

To their credit, policymakers and law enforcers have created institutional mechanisms to alleviate these shortcomings. These include

forming regional enforcement networks to enhance information sharing between agencies, and creating computerized "deconfliction" systems to let agents from different jurisdictions know when they are
pursuing the same target. While these task forces and databases have
improved communication and coordination between participating
agencies, they have not overcome traditional bureaucratic rivalries
among federal, state, and local agencies, nor have they eliminated institutional and individual incentives to hoarding information. Ultimately,
the effectiveness of information-sharing networks is contingent on the
ability and willingness of agents to use them, which remains problematic. Like narcos, if to a lesser degree, communication within and
between law enforcement agencies continues to suffer from compartmentation.

The Survival Imperative

Outside of warfare and counterterrorism, it is difficult to imagine a
more hostile social system than the one shared by narcs and narcos.
The purpose of law enforcement agencies such as the DEA and the
Colombian National Police is to identify, disrupt, and destroy trafficking conspiracies. Special units and interagency networks in the United
States and Colombia target alleged smugglers through physical and
electronic surveillance, satellite imagery, undercover operations, and direct action raids. Law enforcers monitor traffickers' phone calls, flip
their associates, search their properties, burn their processing labs,
seize their drug shipments, freeze their assets, capture their participants, and, in extreme cases, hunt them down and kill them. The force
advantage enjoyed by well-equipped, highly trained narcs provides narcos with a clear and pressing incentive to adapt: their survival as criminal enterprises often depends on it.

For drug enforcement agencies, the stakes of competitive adaptation
are not so high. To survive, agencies must secure sufficient funding to
carry out their programs. This depends more on responding to shifting
winds in domestic politics and maintaining fruitful relations with policymakers who control the purse strings than on responding to the latest
trends in drug trafficking. When congressional oversight of the DEA
became rancorous during the mid-1970s, the DEA responded with a
vigorous campaign to improve relations with key members of Con-

gress. The agency invited influential lawmakers on international fact-finding junkets and allowed them to reap the symbolic benefits of drug war politics by alerting them when successful criminal investigations were near completion in their home districts.[27] In the early 1990s, when news leaked that the Clinton administration, eager to reduce bureaucratic redundancy among federal law enforcement agencies, was considering merging the DEA with the FBI, DEA executives rallied the troops, encouraging agents and their families to contact their congressional representatives and implore them to oppose the merger.[28]

While dexterity in bureaucratic politics helped the DEA weather these and other threats to its autonomy, these stratagems are far removed from the agency's stated purpose of dismantling major drug-trafficking organizations. Indeed, as a public bureaucracy serving numerous stakeholders with the diverse interests of the White House, Congress, domestic and foreign police agencies, the American public, and its own members, the DEA performs functions that, however laudable, have little to do with its primary enforcement mission. These include delivering drug-prevention educational programs in schools and communities and, more recently, homeland security. In the wake of the terrorist attacks of September 11, 2001, hundreds of DEA agents were shifted from counterdrug enforcement to counterterrorism investigations, the Sky Marshals program, even active military duty. While these activities ensure that the DEA remains viable among a broad cross section of stakeholders, they do not improve the agency's ability to identify large trafficking conspiracies.

Still, drug enforcement remains the heart of the DEA's mission, and the agency must demonstrate at least some degree of proficiency in dismantling trafficking conspiracies if it is to justify its existence and continued funding. Press conferences following major investigations and congressional oversight and appropriations hearings, during which agency executives trumpet their latest achievements and outline future initiatives, are critical in this regard. But as important as these exercises are for the politics of the war on drugs, they also provide drug traffickers with valuable "open source" intelligence about existing programs. Néstor, the former cocaine and marijuana broker, explains: "They [law enforcers] start talking, publicizing their activities. You find out they had some boat in Miami, so you ask yourself, 'What the hell do they want with this boat?' Then the smugglers know something is going on, so they switch modes. When the government came out in the media saying, 'We've got helicopters, we're doing this and that,' the smugglers would say, 'Okay, let's switch the operations.'"[29]

Because existing measures of counterdrug success are inherently ambiguous, adaptations by trafficking groups can actually benefit law enforcement agencies by underscoring the need for continued funding. As Peter Andreas observes, "Almost any outcome (for example, either a decrease or an increase in arrests and seizures) can be politically interpreted both as a sign of law enforcement progress and as a sign that much more enforcement is needed."[30] When drug seizures increase, law enforcers can claim that they are doing a better job of stopping the flow of drugs, or that drug trafficking is increasing, or both—all of which can be used to justify additional funding. At the same time, when drug seizures are down, officials can argue that this is a sign that their efforts are working because smuggling patterns have shifted in response to their activities. Once again additional funding is necessary—and well deserved.

This does not mean that agencies such as the DEA and the Colombian National Police are immune to failure. Law enforcement agencies that consistently fail to achieve satisfactory performance, however ambiguously policymakers may define this, or that come under fire for repeated corruption scandals, humans rights violations, and other tainted activities, may find their budgets dwindling and their leaders facing pressure to implement reforms and improve measurable results. In 1968 the Federal Bureau of Narcotics, plagued for more than a decade by a series of corruption scandals, was moved from the Treasury Department to the Justice Department, where it was folded into a rival organization to create the Bureau of Narcotics and Dangerous Drugs (BNDD). Five years later federal law enforcement underwent a second major reorganization when the BNDD was combined with the Office of Drug Abuse Law Enforcement, the Office of National Narcotics Intelligence, seven hundred Customs Service agents, and fifty former CIA operatives to form the Drug Enforcement Administration.[31] During the 1990s the DEA and the Colombian National Police were compelled to reform their organizations in response to external political pressure, including calls that their agencies be abolished.

The continued functioning of the DEA and the Colombian National Police is only partly attributable to the reforms they implemented and the bureaucratic battles they won. In both the United States and Colombia, if for very different reasons, narcotics control retains considerable political significance, and it is not likely that either government will abolish their flagship counterdrug agency in the near future. The survival of these bureaucracies is all but assured, as long as both countries continue to follow prohibitionist drug policies—and have drug traffickers to chase.

The symbiotic relationship between drug trafficking and counterdrug law enforcement further clouds the incentive structure for police agencies. As traffickers depend on prohibitionist policies to boost the value of their illicit commodities, so law enforcers depend on traffickers to channel their efforts. If law enforcers somehow managed to eliminate drug production and trafficking in their respective countries, they would also destroy their raison d'etre. Without narcos to dismantle, narcs would have no formal reason to exist.

Transnational police agencies such as the DEA, which operates in more than fifty countries, may find this prospect fanciful, given the ubiquity of drug supplies throughout the world and the tendency of smuggling networks to shift their operations to areas where police pressure is less intense. But drug enforcement agencies that operate within the national territory of a single state may view this scenario as more plausible—and as threatening to their institutional interests. Should the Colombian police and military eventually succeed in pushing the drug trade out of Colombia, as they currently aim to do, they are likely to lose substantial funding, training, and other material assistance as policymakers direct limited government resources elsewhere. Indeed, when coca leaf production in Bolivia and Peru declined during the latter half of the 1990s, in part owing to aggressive eradication programs by the Banzer and Fujimori administrations, U.S. officials responded by reducing counterdrug assistance to those countries and dramatically increasing it to Colombia, where coca leaf production was believed to be growing rapidly.

Colombian law enforcers understand this dilemma, along with its budgetary implications for their agencies. "If the Colombian police are too successful and wipe out all the narcos," explains a high-level official in the intelligence branch of the Colombian National Police, "they will end up hurting themselves, because their budget will get cut."[32] As this official suggests, law enforcers in Colombia confront competing pressures to demonstrate proficiency against individual targets, such as the Medellín and Cali "cartels," without destroying the overarching trade that, in effect, keeps them working. However unlikely the complete elimination of the Colombian drug trade may be, what matters here is the *perception* among law enforcers that it could be, if they and the policymakers who fund them were to devote sufficient resources to wiping out the trade. To the extent that such attitudes are widely shared, they foster complacency and cynicism among law enforcers, undermining their commitment to winning the war on drugs.

The Flatness Advantage

Players who process information and make decisions faster than their opponents enjoy a formidable advantage in competitive adaptation. To counter their adversaries' latest maneuvers with effective adaptations of their own, traffickers and law enforcers must gather, interpret, and apply information quickly and reliably. Research by organization theorists suggests that numerous factors influence decision cycles in organizations, including size, the number of management layers, and the degree of administrative centralization.[33] Other things being equal, organizations with fewer (but sufficient) participants, flatter authority structures, and decentralized decision rules tend to make decisions more rapidly than those that combine tall administrative hierarchies with centralized decision protocols.

U.S. and Colombian law enforcers work in large bureaucracies oppressed by many layers of management and cumbersome decision protocols. The DEA has more than nine thousand employees organized in different divisions and field offices. The agency's chief executive is the administrator, who oversees six administrative divisions, twenty domestic field divisions, and eighty foreign offices located in fifty-eight countries. Administrative divisions cover numerous functions, including operations, intelligence, operational support, financial management, human resources, and internal inspections. Each division is run by an assistant administrator who oversees, in descending order in the bureaucratic food chain, different offices, sections, and units within his or her domain.

The Operations Division is the DEA's primary enforcement body. It contains separate offices of Domestic Operations, International Operations, Special Operations, Aviation Operations, Operations Management, and Diversion Control, each of which is run by managers overseeing different sections and units covering different functions or geographic regions. The head of the International Operations office su-pervises different sections covering South America, Central America and Mexico, the Caribbean, Europe and the Middle East, and Southeast Asia, along with several administrative units. Each geographic section contains numerous country offices, all of which are led by a country attaché or special agent-in-charge. The head of the DEA's Colombian country office directs two assistant special agents-in-charge who man-age three enforcement groups and one intelligence unit. Each group contains a supervisor that manages the agents in his or her area. From top to bottom, eight management levels separate the DEA's chief execu-tive in Washington from its street-level narcotics agents in Colombia (see Fig. 6).

The Colombian National Police is similarly big and bureaucratic. It has more than ninety thousand uniformed officers, around two thou-sand of whom work in DANTI, the specialized counterdrug enforce-ment division. Organizationally, the CNP contains eleven divisions, including DANTI (short for Dirección Anti-Narcóticos), Intelligence, Operations, Judicial Police, Special Services, Anti-Kidnapping and Ex-tortion, and several administrative support departments. The head of the CNP is the general director, who, in a Colombian twist of historical institutionalism, reports to the minister of defense rather than the min-ister of justice. Each division contains its own director, who manages different areas of operation. The head of DANTI supervises offices in Interdiction, Eradication, Aviation, General Coordination, and Preven-tion. Each office is likewise broken down into separate groups, all of which have their own management structure. The Office of Anti-Nar-cotics Interdiction, to take one example, contains four groups, each with its own managers and assistant managers: Judicial Police, Heroin Control, Intelligence, and the Central Airmobile Company.

Compared to these bureaucratic behemoths, Colombian trafficking enterprises are small and organizationally flat. Many trafficking opera-tions can be conceived as intergroup wheel or chain networks, with different nodes that perform specific tasks, such as international trans-portation and wholesale distribution. Cells often contain fewer than a dozen members, and even "large" wheel networks generally have fewer than a hundred people working directly in drug trafficking. Each cell is led by a manager who supervises several workers; some larger cells also contain one or more assistant managers. Cell managers may report to an exportation manager, an intermediary, or in some cases directly to

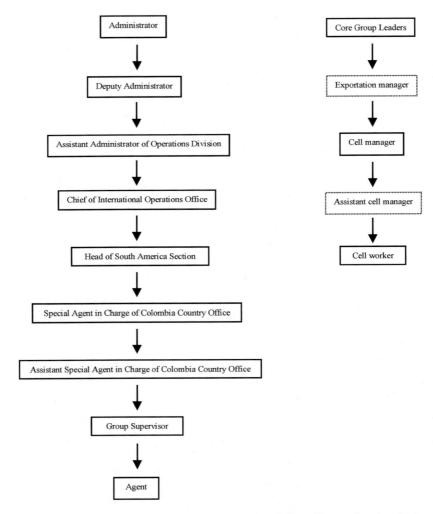

Arrows signify vertical managerial relations; roles in dotted boxes do not exist in all trafficking networks.

Fig. 6　**Management levels in** DEA and Colombian wheel network.

network leaders. Some bosses prefer to concentrate decision-making authority in their hands, which has the potential to slow down decision cycles, particularly when the boss insists on having the final say in most operational decisions. However, even the biggest networks contain only three or four management layers, ameliorating—but not eliminating— this centralization effect. Yet many wheel networks are not led by micromanagers. In these enterprises cell managers enjoy significant decision-making authority. As revealed in Chapter 1, law enforcement crackdowns against the Medellín and Cali networks in the 1990s led to the formation of smaller, more loosely coupled chain networks composed of independent groups that coordinate their transactions on an ad hoc basis. Many of these enterprises contain only a single manager—the boss—assisted by a handful of subordinates.

With their smaller size and flatter structures, smuggling enterprises tend to process information and make decisions faster than law enforcement agencies. In trafficking networks, information flows through fewer channels, reducing the number of administrative bottlenecks that can slow decision making. Flat decision-making hierarchies also limit opportunities for distorting information because there are fewer managers who, whether because of human fallibility or self-interest, manipulate, misplace, or withhold information from superiors and subordinates, or leak it to external competitors. Whether they contain three or four levels of management, Colombian trafficking networks enjoy a flatness advantage over their state adversaries. Leaders' decisions are communicated quickly to cell managers, and through them to cell workers, allowing the network to change its behavior rapidly, an essential attribute for organizations in hostile trafficking systems. A DEA official with considerable experience investigating Colombian smuggling networks emphasizes how quickly these groups share information and make decisions:

> With the decision process in the company [trafficking group], they can make a decision instantaneously and it will be translated in a day by everyone in the chain of command. It gets transmitted immediately. The kingpin can jump into the middle of it immediately and say, "Look, guys, for the sake of business, for our own sake, this is what we will be doing." We have seen them do that. For example, we used to hit them a lot on Amtrak, the train. In New York they would take the drug money, put it in suitcases with wheels, and they would have different old people transporting their suitcases. And no one [in law enforcement] would look at them. We actually popped some of these guys three or four times. It took them like a day to make this adjustment. Because down in Colombia they got the call from an attorney, say, in a particular state where we

made one of the arrests and we have a narcotics trafficker
jabbed in the middle because he just lost three or four million
dollars in a day. So the kingpin says, "Look, do not put your ass
on a train. If anyone is on the train with my papers [money], he
will be killed." End of story. They cannot jump on the train.
You cannot do that in traditional systems.[34]

Comparable decisions in law enforcement agencies often take days
or weeks to make their way through the bureaucratic chain of command before obtaining approval from all the requisite officials. "There
are too many levels of management," complains one Colombian official, "and this slows decisions because they have to pass through too
many steps."[35] During criminal investigations, agents must run basic
operational decisions by their supervisor, including whether to use electronic surveillance, carry out a controlled delivery, or allow a confidential informant to work undercover. In some cases the supervisor may
then consult with his boss, who checks with his boss, and so on. Each
step of the way, decisions may be delayed or impeded by mistakes,
personal conflicts, bureaucratic politics, or more urgent concerns.

The involvement of other federal, state, and local law enforcement
agencies, essential in multijurisdictional investigations targeting major
trafficking networks, further complicates the decision-making process.
To conduct a wiretap, for example, investigating agents must clear the
request with DEA brass, both in the field and at headquarters. From
there, the request goes to Main Justice, the Department of Justice's
headquarters in Washington, D.C., and the regional U.S. Attorney's Office. At each stop, the request drifts through multiple offices, such as
the Office of Enforcement Operations at Main Justice, where it must
be approved by authorized officials before returning to the regional assistant U.S. attorney, who finally presents it before a district court
judge.

Approval for wiretaps can take months to obtain, during which time
traffickers continue their illegal activities, changing phone numbers
and stash houses identified in the original affidavit. When smugglers
change their phone numbers, law enforcers—assuming they are even
privy to the new information—must update their affidavits, which
again requires the consent of their superiors and a magistrate's formal
sanction. In this manner, traffickers can slow criminal investigations
to a crawl merely by changing their operational signatures on a regular

basis, forcing law enforcers to revisit cumbersome electronic surveillance protocols again and again.[36]

Government authorities have created a number of reforms to alleviate this situation. These include creating special review boards to quicken decision making on various technical matters and forming interagency enforcement networks, such as the Organized Crime Drug Enforcement Task Forces and the High Intensity Drug Trafficking Areas, to combine police and prosecutorial resources in "high-value" investigations, while flattening administrative hierarchies. In an effort to speed up decision making in the field, a number of elite drug enforcement units in the United States and Colombia provide their members with considerable discretion when conducting tactical operations.

These efforts enjoy limited success. In certain issue areas and investigations, reforms have accelerated decision cycles and improved coordination between participating agencies. Yet the creation of interagency networks has not eliminated law enforcers' basic need to coordinate their activities across numerous organizational boundaries, a requirement that narcos do not confront, at least not to the same degree. Effective counterdrug operations require close coordination between different agencies from multiple jurisdictions, each with its own decision rules, organizational culture, and investigational priorities. The preceding chapter highlights the challenges involved in coordinating conspiracy investigations across different jurisdictions. While task force members may work closely with colleagues from other bureaus to coordinate operations, resolve disputes, and track their illicit adversaries, they are not immune to the bureaucratic rivalries that have traditionally hampered counterdrug law enforcement in the United States and Colombia. Moreover, in seeking approval for their surveillance affidavits and search warrants, task force members must follow the same bureaucratic decision chains as other police agencies. In sum, law enforcers must overcome significant transaction costs to exploit their force advantage in competitive adaptation. Their smaller, flatter adversaries, by contrast, require much less coordination to carry out their relatively simple transactions.

The Red Tape Trap

While traffickers operate outside the law, law enforcers work within it, which exposes them to legal and bureaucratic constraints their criminal competitors avoid. "We have laws and rules that we have to abide by," emphasizes one DEA manager. "We're regulated by rules and policies set from above. Our agents have a lot of discretion, but we have to follow rules, too."[37] Indeed, law enforcers carry out their daily activities within complex institutional frameworks that must obey constitutional law, criminal statutes, and bureaucratic regulations.

Before they can search alleged drug violators without their consent or seize their property, law enforcers must have "probable cause" that the suspect has committed a crime. Otherwise they must obtain a valid search warrant from a magistrate or judge demonstrating probable cause of a criminal act and specifying, as the Fourth Amendment stipulates, "the place to be searched, and the persons or things to be seized."[38] Likewise, before they can raid suspected drug labs, law enforcers usually need a search warrant demonstrating probable cause of a criminal violation. Agents establish probable cause by gathering intelligence from a variety of sources, including physical and electronic surveillance and tips from informants—all of which must be corroborated by independent sources, according to agency procedures. To use pen registers and trap-and-trace devices to record telephone numbers used by unknowing suspects, agents must demonstrate to an independent magistrate that the sought-after information is relevant to an ongoing investigation. If agents want to conduct nonconsensual phone wiretaps, they must meet the more stringent evidentiary standard of "probable cause plus" and demonstrate that the targeted phone, pager, fax machine, or computer is being used for illegal activity.[39]

Bureaucratic rules and procedures regulate other areas of counterdrug law enforcement as well. To purchase equipment for criminal investigations, DEA agents must prove their need for the technology to supervisors, submit the necessary request forms, and wait for approval. To penalize agents who fail to do a satisfactory job, managers must show sufficient cause for disciplinary action, while granting agents the right to appeal minor penalties through grievance procedures and major penalties through the Merit Systems Protection Board.[40] To prosecute alleged traffickers, police and prosecutors must share all relevant information from their criminal investigations with defense attorneys, under the rules of the discovery process. For all of these activities, and many more—handling evidence, managing informants, interrogating suspects, working undercover, extraditing suspects—law enforcers follow numerous rules and procedures that impose strict limits on what they can and cannot do.

Drug traffickers lack equivalent constraints. When narcos require information about law enforcers, they hire outside consultants or assign participants to collect it. When they need equipment for their activities, they research the technology they want and they buy it. When they wish to interrogate suspicious associates or search their belongings, they direct their henchmen to the task. When associates perform poorly or threaten the integrity of the enterprise, they remove them from the operation, by force if necessary.

To be sure, trafficking enterprises are not disorganized anarchies, lacking all manner of rules, roles, and operating procedures. The architecture of drug trafficking, described in Chapter 1, includes many time-tested routines that guide participant behavior in numerous activities, including processing, transporting, and distributing drugs. Associates understand that they may face the ultimate sanction if they fail to follow behavioral norms or otherwise endanger their enterprise. Yet in trafficking groups rules are fewer in number and generally less restrictive than those regulating their law enforcement counterparts. Many of the rules of drug trafficking are commonsensical, widely shared understandings of behavior that have developed with experience. The informal structure of smuggling networks allows a degree of institutional permissibility and flexibility their government adversaries do not enjoy. Whereas traffickers are often free to adapt existing rules to meet their daily demands, provided their creativity does not place the enterprise in jeopardy, law enforcers work within more established and bureaucratized settings, where they "face a variety of formal and informal sanctions if they are too unorthodox."[41]

Before lamenting this arrangement, we should remember that constitutional safeguards, criminal laws, and bureaucratic procedures regulating contemporary law enforcement arose over several centuries of evolution in Western jurisprudence and democratic institutions. Their purpose is both noble and necessary: to protect citizens' political rights and civil liberties and hold authorities accountable to the rule of law. These rights and protections are indispensable features of contemporary liberal democratic states—and I am not, tacitly or otherwise, endorsing their abolition. But as important as these legal and bureaucratic constraints are to healthy, functioning democracies, a focus on competitive adaptation illustrates how the regulatory regimes governing narcs confer indirect benefits on narcos. "There are norms and parameters the police have to obey, which isn't necessarily bad," explains a Colombian official, "but when the competitor doesn't have to obey them, he has the advantage."[42]

Indeed, the red tape trap confers several advantages on traffickers. First, by slowing down police agencies, it prevents law enforcers from responding as quickly as their illicit adversaries to changes in hostile trafficking systems. As discussed above, agents working active investigations spend much of their time waiting to have their search warrants, wiretap affidavits, and other requests approved by higher-level authorities, within and outside the agency. Meanwhile, traffickers proceed with their transactions and change their practices largely unencumbered by such constraints. Second, by obligating undercover agents to follow certain rules, such as forbidding them to partake in what amounts to obligatory social behavior in many deviant settings and forcing them to seize all drugs contained in controlled deliveries before they reach consumer markets, the trap limits their ability to establish credibility with criminals and use cunning, deception, and other mētis-based skills against them. In Chapter 2, Arturo recalled how he confirmed that a police official was on the take by photographing him with prostitutes and snorting cocaine, activities from which legally bound narcs would presumably have abstained. Other former traffickers and undercover agents emphasize that laws and bureaucratic regulations often prevent the kind of "deep penetration" required to effectively dismantle transnational wheel networks, which rely on intermediaries and compartmentation to shield core-group leaders from street-level drug enforcement.[43] Third, by increasing the transparency of criminal investigations, the red tape trap provides traffickers with plentiful opportunities to gather information about their adversaries, such as using their lawyers to gain access to law enforcement intelligence through the discovery process. "It is more difficult for us to learn from them than for them to learn from us," explains a senior DEA official. "Because everything we do is above board, everything we do is done legally. We do it and it is exposed. It is discovered in court, and that is the law. They have rights and essentially that is the way the game is played. Thank God. That is what democracy is all about, the rule of law, due process and everything. And it is satisfying to know that we comply with the rules and we adhere to their rights, and we still win on occasion."[44]

In fact, the capture, extradition, and conviction of numerous Colombian "kingpins," including Carlos Lehder, Fabio Ochoa, and Bernal Madrigal, has been enormously satisfying to American officials. Unfortunately, it is also true that frustration with the rule of law, combined with an ambitious, amoral resolve to get their man, regardless of the costs, leads some authorities to break rules and regulations. The hunt for Pablo Escobar, led by an elite Colombian task force and supported by DEA agents, CIA operatives, and Special Forces soldiers, was particularly troubling. Escobar had humiliated the Colombian government by escaping from a lavish correctional facility he built with his own money following a year of "imprisonment." Desperate to catch Escobar, Colombian security forces allegedly committed a rash of human rights violations in Medellín, the trafficker's hometown and base of support, including killing a number of his associates. They also established unsavory links with rival trafficking groups from Cali and los Pepes, a paramilitary death squad dedicated to the single-minded pursuit of exterminating the kingpin (the group's name was a Spanish acronym meaning people persecuted by Pablo Escobar). "Frustrated by the legal and logistical restrictions on their operations against Escobar," reports Alma Guillermoprieto, Colombian police and army volunteers "were eager to join an effective organization like the Pepes, who operate in small patrols, with sure targets and with trial-and-paperwork free executions to show for their efforts."[45] A number of them apparently did, exploiting their connections with U.S. and Colombian law enforcers to share intelligence and conduct paramilitary raids against Escobar's family members and closest associates. The hunt for Escobar exposes a tragic irony in competitive adaptation: exasperated by what they see as unnecessary legalistic and procedural niceties, some overzealous authorities place themselves above the law, ignoring the due process rights of the citizens they are supposed to protect.

Narcs and narcos learn not in isolation but through interaction. Competitive adaptation provides one way of thinking about these interactions, illustrating how interdependent, imperfectly informed players gather information about their adversaries and change their practices in response to what they learn. Given the hostile and dynamic nature of Colombian trafficking systems, players who respond quickly to unforeseen circumstances tend to perform well in competitive adaptation. But such mētis-based adaptations are easier studied than done. For one thing, narco-narc interactions are embedded in secrecy, making it difficult for players to learn about their competitors. The clandestine nature of drug trafficking is especially problematic for law enforcers because, unlike narcos, they need precise intelligence about their adversaries—names, dates, phone numbers—in order to perform their activities effectively. But if narcos benefit from an information advantage over narcs, narcs enjoys a compelling force advantage over narcos. Hyperbolic media accounts notwithstanding, even the most sophisticated trafficking enterprises, such as the Cali wheel networks, cannot match the material and logistical capabilities of the DEA and the Colombian National Police. The primary challenge for law enforcers in competitive adaptation is to translate their force advantage into an information advantage by intercepting traffickers' most sensitive communications and gathering real-time intelligence on impending transactions. Even when law enforcers succeed in doing so, effectively removing one player from the Colombian trafficking system, they confront numerous narcos about whom they know very little, which forces them to begin the competitive adaptation struggle anew, this time against less familiar foes.

Narcos confront their own challenges to learning. These include compartmented operations that limit information sharing across trafficking networks, the tendency to store sensitive details in error-prone human memories, and the covert nature of criminal investigations, which creates information uncertainty for smuggling groups that have been targeted for disruption. Some trafficking networks are so tightly compartmented, or manage their collective knowledge so poorly, that they lack the connectivity needed for network learning. In these enterprises, learning, if it occurs at all, tends to remain localized, with different cells processing only those lessons they have learned directly. Poor learners face significant vulnerabilities from experienced law enforcers who exploit traffickers' lack of information sharing to their advantage. However, such highly compartmented networks are few and far between due to the informal spread of smuggling mētis among like-minded practitioners from different groups and networks, and the role intermediaries play in maintaining connectivity between different nodes and networks.

Law enforcers confront even greater obstacles to the sort of rapid organizational learning that is essential in competitive adaptation. These include tall and centralized authority structures that slow decision cycles and organizational action, interagency coordination problems that further complicate, and decelerate, decision making, comprehensive legal and bureaucratic constraints to action, and ambiguous incentive structures that undermine some agents' willingness to share information—and others' commitment to winning the war on drugs. In view of these limitations, it is not surprising that many agile trafficking networks process information, make decisions, and change practices faster than their bureaucratic rivals. Yet these factors do not determine outcomes in competitive adaptation. There are times when law enforcers exploit their force advantage to overwhelm their adversaries, as exemplified in several law enforcement crackdowns in Colombia during the 1990s. But the combination of factors often tilts the playing field in favor of narcos, many of whom extend their information advantage over law enforcers simply by changing their activities and operational signatures on a regular basis. With the promise of prodigious profits and pressing incentives to "adapt or die" driving them, these criminal networks are poised to survive even the most hostile trafficking systems. In the next two chapters I extend the competitive adaptation framework by examining how terrorist networks and state counterterrorist agencies learn, and fail to, in response to information and experience.

Terrorism is a violent form of political action that requires knowledge of demolitions, weaponry, and clandestine operations, among other things. "No one is born with the knowledge of how to build bombs, use a pistol, conduct surveillance, or hijack airplanes," explains Larry Johnson, former deputy director of the State Department's Office of Counterterrorism. "These are skills that must be taught and practiced."[1] Like other skilled practitioners, including the law enforcers and intelligence agents who confront them, extremists learn their tradecraft through training programs, apprenticeships, and practice (in this case, combat). In recent years Al Qaeda and other terrorist networks have developed instructional materials, many of which are now available on the Internet, to teach their brand of guerilla warfare and terrorism to aspiring fanatics. Training courses and other instructional programs serve the dual purpose of spreading terrorist techne among thousands of militants, while allowing leaders to observe and recruit the most promising trainees for membership. Yet terrorists also rely on local knowledge and cunning intelligence they gain from experience, particularly when planning and executing their attacks. They develop mētis by participating in extremist communities of practice and carrying out acts of political violence against noncombatants, adapting their know-how to opportunities and constraints in each operation.

Learning lies at the heart of terrorists' ability to spread their knowledge among like-minded militants and to adapt their tactics in response to government efforts to destroy them. Indeed, the ability to learn from training and experience helps account for the resilience of Al Qaeda and other extremist networks since the war on terror began in the fall of 2001. Today, despite the elimination and capture of hundreds of "high-value" terrorists, state officials from Washington to Jakarta confront a decentralized Islamist movement that includes surviving elements of Al Qaeda and self-organizing, homegrown militants who continue to adapt their activities throughout the world in response to counterterrorism operations. Drawing on the concepts and analytical framework developed in previous chapters this chapter illustrates how terrorists acquire their skills through training and experience and adapt their practices in response to counterterrorism.

Training in Terrorism

Traditionally, terrorists have learned their tradecraft through military-style training programs, often with the support of obliging state sponsors. During the Cold War, the United States and the Soviet Union, either directly or indirectly through proxies, provided military training to belligerents later identified as terrorists and government security agencies subsequently implicated in state terror. Recipients of Soviet largesse included al Fatah and the Popular Front for the Liberation of Palestine, both of which established training camps modeled after Soviet facilities. Palestinian militants in turn provided training in guerrilla warfare and urban terrorism to revolutionaries from Western Europe, South Asia, and Latin America. During the 1970s, Palestinian instruction served as an important catalyst in fomenting international terrorism, foreshadowing the role that Al Qaeda's training camps in Afghanistan would play two decades later. Beneficiaries of Palestinian training made contact with comrades from different groups and countries, shared information and tips on terrorist tradecraft, studied a common paramilitary curriculum, and, on occasion, cooperated in joint operations on behalf of the Palestinian cause, including the 1972 Lod Airport attack in Israel that killed twenty-six people.[2]

During the war against Soviet occupation forces in Afghanistan in the 1980s, the CIA provided funding and weapons to the Pakistani Inter-Services Intelligence Directorate, which distributed these resources among various resistance groups fighting in Afghanistan. Afghan resistance fighters in turn trained foreign Islamic militants who helped them overthrow the Soviets. Tragically, some of these foreign *mujaheddin* subsequently expanded their holy war to include the United States and other Western countries. Also during the Cold War, Washington provided substantial military aid and training to state security agencies in Chile, Colombia, El Salvador, and Guatemala, several of which were later directly or indirectly implicated in carrying out acts of political repression against their own citizens. For decades the United States provided matériel and instruction to the Colombian army, elements of which covertly trained and supported right-wing paramilitary forces as part of its counterinsurgency strategy.[3] On September 10, 2001, under pressure from human rights groups, Washington formally classified one of these paramilitary organizations, the United Self-Defense Groups of Colombia, as a terrorist organization.

The United States and the Soviet Union have not been the only direct or indirect state sponsors of paramilitary instruction for political extremists. Terrorist training facilities have been discovered in Afghanistan, Algeria, Iran, Iraq, Ireland, Lebanon, Libya, Pakistan, and the Sudan, among other countries. For years, Libya, under the protection of Muammar Qaddafi, provided training in guerrilla warfare and terrorist tactics to a variety of militant groups, including the Provisional Irish Republican Army (IRA), the Popular Front for the Liberation of Palestine, the Basque Fatherland and Liberty, the Secret Army for the Liberation of Armenia, and the Japanese Red Army. In Syrian-controlled areas of Lebanon's Bekaa Valley, Iranian Revolutionary Guard fighters, many of whom received training from the Palestine Liberation Organization, provided Hizballah activists with instruction in automatic weapons, explosives, rocket launchers, clandestine infiltration, and combat at close quarters. Hizballah members also received training directly from the Palestinians. Hizballah later established its own training camps in Lebanon, where instructors provided training in munitions, intelligence, and bombing attacks to the Palestine Islamic Jihad, Hamas, the Popular Front for the Liberation of Palestine-General Council, and Al Qaeda.[4] As these examples suggest, terrorists often rely on training camps to teach their associates tradecraft. The transfer of terrorist techne through formal instruction creates significant vulnerabilities that counterterrorists can exploit by locating and destroying training camps (I will have more to say about this weakness in the conclusion).

Al Qaeda Training

During the 1990s Al Qaeda supplied training to thousands of supporters at camps located in Afghanistan, Bosnia, Chechnya, Indonesia, the Philippines, Somalia, the Sudan, and Yemen. In Afghanistan alone, dozens of camps provided basic and advanced training in guerrilla warfare and terrorism to anywhere between ten thousand and twenty thousand foreign fighters, according to U.S. intelligence officials. Most participants in the camps received only basic training, which included instruction in Islamic law and history, guerrilla warfare, small arms (handguns and rifles), and explosives.[5]

Recruits who performed exceptionally well in Al Qaeda's basic training, and others with highly prized linguistic or paramilitary talents, or citizenship in countries where the network hoped to develop "sleeper" cells, were invited to continue their extremist education, sometimes by Osama bin Laden himself. Advanced training took place at smaller camps in Afghanistan and included courses in heavy weapons, explosives, kidnapping, assassination, surveillance and countersurveillance, and cell management. Following basic training, one promising student, Mohamed Rashed al-Owhali, received an audience with Osama bin Laden, who encouraged him to continue his military instruction. The aspiring terrorist apparently did so, receiving advanced training in information security, intelligence, hijackings, and related activities. When al-Owhali later agreed to participate in the U.S. embassy bombing attack in Nairobi, Kenya, in 1998, a crime for which he was later convicted in a Manhattan courthouse, he underwent, as one FBI agent recalls, "very specialized training" in cell management.[6] Other associates, following their selection for what was then being called the "planes operation" inside Al Qaeda, received some training in Afghanistan for carrying out skyjackings, disarming air marshals, and handling knives and munitions. Several hijackers from the 9/11 plot also traveled to Karachi, Pakistan, where they received personalized instruction in basic English, the Internet, sensitive communications, and living in the United States from Khalid Shaikh Mohammed, the alleged "mastermind" of the attack, who lived in North Carolina for several years.[7]

The experience of Mohamed Rashed al-Owhali, and testimony from various Al Qaeda supporters turned government informants, including L'Houssaine Kherchtou, Ahmed Ressam, Ali Mohammed, and Jamal al-Fadl, suggest that these training programs were designed not only to spread the network's terrorist techne to thousands of supporters but to evaluate, recruit, and vet the most promising trainees for membership in Al Qaeda.[8] A select few were invited to pledge their loyalty to bin Laden and receive more advanced instruction. Former FBI special agent John Cloonan, who debriefed several Al Qaeda militants-turned-informants, explains: "It was only a very small group of people that ever transitioned from the basic training camp into the more specialized camps, where they ended up getting more intense training. These people would have been completely vetted. . . . What they wanted to do is to have people, either the leader of the camp or good teachers, try to find the students that were more intense, more religious, and less selfish than others and willing to work harder, longer, and nurture them, develop their specialties, and eventually move them into higher positions of responsibility, and give them specialized training."[9]

The number of militants who entered Al Qaeda's "professional development" program was relatively small, probably hundreds rather than the thousands who received basic training in guerrilla warfare. Following basic instruction, some recruits were sent to fight in *jihads* then raging in Bosnia, Chechnya, and Kashmir. Other acolytes returned to their respective countries, sometimes with instructions to form sleeper cells and await further orders from Al Qaeda leaders. While not as well schooled in terrorist techne as their colleagues selected for advanced training, militants who received only basic training became better prepared to carry out lethal attacks, becoming a force multiplier for Islamic extremism.[10]

In addition to spreading technical knowledge about guerrilla warfare and terrorism, Al Qaeda's training camps fostered the development of informal communities of practice and social networks among the Islamists. Whether or not they became card-carrying members of Osama bin Laden's network, trainees learned norms and practices associated with the Islamist cause, as interpreted by their instructors and other experienced mujaheddin. Regular, sustained interactions among veterans and novices allowed the former to share their mētis through conversations and war stories. Through this socialization process, novices solidified their identity as Salafi jihadists and their commitment to political violence, moving toward deeper participation in the Islamist community of practice. Trainees also formed new friendship ties and deepened preexisting ones among fellow Islamists with whom they trained. These social networks, developed through participation in broader communities of practice, fostered trust and reciprocity among participants and created additional opportunities for knowledge sharing and collaboration. In this sense, terrorist training camps became incubators of extremist social networks and communities of practice, which later spread to other countries. Following training, militants either returned to their countries of origin or traveled to active theaters of combat, and they took their norms, practices, and friendship ties with them, expanding their social networks and communities of practice as they interacted with new sympathizers and supporters of the Islamist cause.

Terrorist Knowledge

Terrorist techne is codified in handbooks, novels, videos, CD-ROMs, and other knowledge-based artifacts—all of which, in an age of exploding information technology, are widely shared among extremists.[11] Militiamen, white supremacists, environmental activists, Marxist revolutionaries, and Islamic radicals have all "published" manuals with the aim of spreading their destructive knowledge among larger audiences. The *Militia of Montana Field Manual* provides instruction on urban guerrilla warfare and includes plans for sabotaging the U.S. economy, eliminating "traitorous" government officials, and assassinating prominent public personalities. *Ecodefense: A Field Guide to Monkey Wrenching* contains detailed information on how to spike trees, destroy logging roads, immobilize vehicles and heavy equipment, build smoke bombs, disable computers, and conduct other acts of economic sabotage. The *Anarchist's Cookbook* provides step-by-step instructions on how to make various household poisons and incendiary devices, while the *Terrorist Handbook,* published by Gunzenbomz Pyro-Technologies, teaches readers how to manufacture different explosives and acquire ammunition for a variety of weapons.[12]

While these and other "direct-action" manuals are available to amateur militants through mail-order publishers and the Internet, many of their recipes are, to put it mildly, imprecise. A munitions expert in the U.S. military, who has read portions of the *Anarchist's Cookbook* and other terrorist manuals, points out that the "bomb-making recipes are missing several steps" and that it would be hazardous for would-be terrorists to construct munitions based solely on information found in these recipes. "It only takes the right conditions, which the books do not address, to cause an accident."[13] Another military expert explains that considerable training is necessary to put together "anything more complicated than the most fundamental explosive weapon." To learn how to use mercury tilt fuses, remotely controlled detonators, and electromagnetic firing devices, already knowledgeable students "must be taught by experts."[14]

In order to prevent their members from blowing themselves up, many militant groups produce their own handbooks and operations manuals. Members learn the principles and recipes of terrorism, as practiced and preached by their respective organizations, through these artifacts. IRA recruits absorb an entire curriculum of training materials, including the infamous *Green Book, the Handbook for Volunteers of the Irish Republican Army,* and other instructional manuals. The *Green Book* covers "the duties and responsibilities of volunteers," along with "the history of the movement, the rules of military engagement, and anti-interrogation techniques," explains one former Provo.[15] Other manuals discuss bomb making, weapons handling, and intelligence collection. These handbooks are often written by senior volunteers and draw heavily on their experiences confronting British troops. Even Provos who have been captured and incarcerated by the British provide valuable information that is codified in instructional materials. In one example, reminiscent of the manuals found in the jail cell of a Colombian trafficker, the IRA "debriefed Volunteers who had gone through the process of detection and trial and produced a 9,000 word document whose title could have been 'How Not to Incriminate Yourself.'"[16]

Al Qaeda has produced several training and operations manuals for its members, including the *Encyclopedia of Afghan Jihad* and the *Declaration of Jihad Against the Country's Tyrants.* Network supporters compiled the encyclopedia to document the experience of Islamic resistance fighters in Afghanistan's war against the Soviet Union and share this knowledge with their fellow mujaheddin in Bosnia, Chechnya, and Kashmir. The multivolume document includes material on guerrilla warfare, intelligence, weapons, explosives, topography, training, and other areas. The encyclopedia also contains diagrams copied from the U.S. Army's field manual series, allegedly acquired by Ali Mohammed, a former Al Qaeda member turned U.S. government informant. According to one of Mohammed's government handlers, former FBI agent John Cloonan, the Islamic militant obtained copies of the manuals while serving as a supply sergeant at Fort Bragg, home of the U.S. Army's Special Operations Command. He later translated the documents into Arabic and sent them to Osama bin Laden and other Islamists in Afghanistan.[17]

The *Declaration of Jihad* contains eighteen "lessons" for successful terrorist operations, including sections on "Counterfeit Currency and Forged Documents," "Member Safety," "Prisons and Detention Centers," "Training," and two separate chapters on "Espionage." Both manuals outline religious and ideological justifications for various acts of violence and describe rules and routines in detail. For example, the declaration's fifth lesson, "Means of Communication and Transportation," reminds readers that communication in clandestine operations is always a "double-edged sword," and describes numerous security precautions, including the use of code words in telephone conversations and secret signals in face-to-face meetings.[18] The manuals are updated to accommodate, record, and disseminate the network's growing body of terrorist experience. Al Qaeda supporters have enhanced the encyclopedia by adding supplementary volumes to the document, including one on chemical and biological warfare that is available on CD-ROM.[19]

In recent years, despite an increasingly hostile counterterrorism environment, individuals and groups linked to Al Qaeda have continued to circulate a variety of instructional materials. Since 9/11 numerous operation manuals aimed at Islamists have appeared in electronic form, among them the *Al-Aqsa Jihad Encyclopedia,* which contains detailed instructions for preparing a variety of explosives, and the *Encyclopedia of Preparation,* which includes URLs linking readers to specific content about guerrilla warfare, weaponry, and training. Moreover, through the Internet Al Qaeda supporters have published several trade journals, including the *Sawt al-Jihad* (the Voice of Jihad), which provides religious and ideological rationales for waging holy war, and *Mu'askar al-Battar* (al Battar Training Camp), a virtual training guide that provides instruction in covert operations, surveillance, secure communications, weapons handling, kidnappings, and many other practices for waging guerrilla warfare.[20]

Two installments of another Al Qaeda–affiliated periodical, *In the Shadow of the Lances,* discuss lessons learned in Operation Enduring Freedom, including deploying fighters in small, mobile units led by experienced mujaheddin to minimize losses from U.S. precision-guided bombs, and using human couriers to communicate, rather than advanced communications systems that can be intercepted by American forces. In keeping with Al Qaeda tradecraft, a senior operative wrote the installments as an after-action review of sorts to be shared with fellow insurgents then preparing to fight American forces in Iraq.[21] In January 2004 Al Qaeda supporters reportedly issued a new online publication, *The Base of the Vanguard,* aimed at fresh recruits and supporters who operate below the radar of state intelligence agencies and who may not wish to risk undergoing formal training. The document includes articles on physical training, security procedures for operations cells, and the use of small arms, along with testimony from a reputed suicide bomber.[22] And in April 2006, the "Media Committee" of Al Qaeda in Afghanistan published its sixth issue of *The Vanguards of the Kharasan* (Kharasan is the historical name for the present-day territory of Afghanistan). The ninety-page document includes an analysis of the U.S.-led war on terror in Afghanistan and Iraq, a report on mujaheddin operations in Afghanistan between October 2005 and January 2006, and a discussion of common mistakes made by Islamic fighters.[23] As these examples suggest, Al Qaeda–affiliated groups use these trade journals not just to propagandize their interpretation of Islam and share technical information with their far-flung supporters, but to analyze lessons learned from previous encounters against enemy troops in order to improve existing operations.

Over the years Al Qaeda supporters have also recorded a series of videos offering instruction on assassinations, bomb making, chemical weapons, paramilitary raids, destruction of bridges and communication lines, even motorcycle drive-by shootings similar to the *parrilleros* perfected by Colombian killers in the 1980s. Like its training manuals, the videos document Al Qaeda's extensive experience in guerrilla warfare, while serving as recruiting tools for extremists. While a primary purpose of these artifacts is to encourage would-be militants to join the cause, they also contain lessons on the religious and ideological justifications for waging jihad and operational techniques for carrying out specific attacks.[24] One set of Al Qaeda videos obtained by CNN contained "step-by-step instructions on how to use a surface-to-air missile" and lessons on "complex hostage-taking techniques and assassination operations."[25] Along with Al Qaeda's other knowledge-based artifacts, the videos are copied and shared among militants through human couriers, postal services, and, increasingly since 9/11, the Internet. The dissemination of these artifacts ensures that the knowledge they contain continues to spread throughout the broader Islamic extremist movement, even as the United States and its allies destroy Al Qaeda's training camps in Afghanistan and elsewhere.

Terrorist Mētis

Not all the skills of terrorism can be boiled down to abstract, formally codified principles and rules of thumb. Militants complement their training in terrorist techne with intuition and local knowledge gained from practical experience. To take an example from the previous section, in order to use bomb-making recipes successfully, would-be bombers must adapt abstract technical knowledge regarding explosives and triggering devices to their specific needs and constraints, which may include limited resources for acquiring the necessary ingredients and bomb-making conditions that are less than ideal. To build bombs, militants require practical knowledge of local bomb-making conditions—that is, mētis. Like drug traffickers, terrorists learn mētis by doing: building bombs and detonators, discharging rifles and handguns, engaging in actual armed combat, infiltrating "enemy" lands, casing potential targets, writing intelligence reports, maintaining cover in hostile environments, communicating by code words and secret signals, establishing safe houses, and performing a host of other clandestine activities. "Most trade craft," emphasizes J. Bowyer Bell, a leading authority on terrorism and guerrilla warfare, "must be learned in action."[26]

In the field, surrounded by potential enemies, terrorists use deception and cunning to mask their intentions from people with whom they interact, even close friends and family members. After several 9/11 hijackers traveled to Afghanistan, where they accepted their martyrdom mission and pledged loyalty to Osama bin Laden, they returned to Germany to begin preparing for the operation. "Once back in Hamburg," explains the 9/11 Commission Report, Mohammed Atta, Ziad Samir Jarrah, and Marwan al Shehhi "distanced themselves from conspicuous extremists like Zammar, whom they knew attracted unwanted attention from the authorities." "They also changed their appearance and behavior. Atta wore Western clothing, shaved his beard, and no longer attended extremist mosques. Jarrah also no longer wore a full beard and, according to Senguen [his wife], acted much more the way he had when she first met him. And when Shehhi . . . held a belated wedding celebration . . . a friend of his was surprised to see that he had shaved off his beard and was acting like his old self again."[27]

Unlike law enforcers who go undercover for short periods of time to arrange drug deals, professional terrorists must convincingly play their roles for weeks, even months at a stretch, sometimes while living in foreign countries. Such deep undercover assignments require talents not readily imparted in training programs, including mental alertness, prudence, and emotional stamina. Clandestine militants must be able to interact repeatedly with a variety of individuals—neighbors, fellow workers, mosque acquaintances, family members—as they gather intelligence and otherwise prepare for terrorist operations, all without raising suspicion regarding their true intentions and activities. This is not easy. Undercover operatives frequently experience "burn syndrome," the pervasive fear that other people know what they're doing, which leads them to make awkward movements, often without realizing that their actions make them appear more, not less, suspicious. "[L]earning to fight 'burn syndrome,' observes a former U.S. counterterrorism agent, "is one of the key elements of tradecraft, and it is impossible to master simply by reading about it."[28]

While the *Declaration of Jihad Against the Country's Tyrants* distills Al Qaeda's extensive knowledge of undercover operations in the form of simplified recipes and rules of thumb, the manual also emphasizes the need for caution and perceptiveness when conducting countersurveillance, interrogating enemy personnel, and performing other activities. The declaration describes several actions militants can take to detect government surveillance during an operation, such as "[w]alking down a dead-end street and observing who is walking behind you," but warns that these "exercises are not well defined, but are dependent on the time, place, and the ability to be creative"—in other words, on mētis. Recognizing that their enemies will try to deceive them, the manual counsels that a militant who questions enemy personnel should be careful, "extremely patient," be "able to act, pretend, and mask himself," "have knowledge and expertise about people's behavior and morals," and "possess a sixth sense based on practice and experience."[29] Significantly, Al Qaeda seeks recruits who already possess many of these skills. Among the "necessary qualifications and characteristics" for membership outlined in the declaration's second lesson are patience, prudence, unflappability, intelligence and insight, the ability to keep secrets and conceal information, the ability to observe and analyze, and the ability to act, change positions, and conceal oneself.[30]

Terrorists develop mētis through informal apprenticeships, on-the-job training, communities of practice, and combat. In some cases trainees undergo lengthy apprenticeships with knowledgeable practitioners, which allows them to gain greater experience under controlled settings. Following preliminary instruction in weapons handling and undercover operations, a member of the Abu Nidal organization was assigned to senior operatives who socialized him to the organization's rules and routines and provided him with a series of increasingly challenging assignments, such as obtaining false passports and photographing American and Israeli embassies in Europe.[31] Another recruit underwent a similar apprenticeship with the Provisional Irish Republican Army. During a two-year period the terrorist-in-training participated in a series of increasingly lethal operations, starting with simple reconnaissance before advancing to bombings and assassinations under the tutelage of more experienced IRA members. "I look back on that time as my apprenticeship," he recalls in his memoirs. "I learned how to be an effective member: how to gather intelligence, how to set up operations, how to avoid mistakes."[32] In some groups the apprentice graduates from his training through an act of political violence, such as assassinating a local politician, police informer, or, when one is available, soldier. "Through this 'passing-out ceremony,'" observes Alistair Horne of the Algerian National Liberation Front, "the apprentice became both proven in reliability and bound, Faust-like, to the rebel cause by his act of outlawry."[33]

Through their apprenticeships militants also become acculturated to the norms and practices of extremist communities of practice. Veterans share their practical knowledge with novices through demonstrations and narratives. As novices acquire the expertise to conduct violent attacks, they also develop the necessary mindset. Through intensive interaction with more experienced, more radicalized comrades, they develop social interpretations of their enemies and themselves that normalize the most extreme perceptions and behavior. Following a period of intensive indoctrination and sensemaking, novices begin to perform their own activities, at first under the watchful tutelage of senior colleagues and then, after the completion of successful actions, with greater independence. With the accumulation of experience, novices gradually develop their own mētis-based skills, moving beyond their apprenticeships to become legitimate practitioners in their own right. When these practitioners pass along their knowledge to newer recruits through their own war stories and exhibitions, they add to organic communities of practice, deepening their identities as militants engaged in a cosmic war where acts of unspeakable violence are viewed not only as justified but as necessary.[34]

When preparing for large-scale attacks, Al Qaeda militants hone mission-specific skills and rehearse different aspects of the operation, in much the same way that Western Special Operations Forces train for specific missions. In the weeks leading up to the 9/11 attacks, several of the "muscle" hijackers worked out at local gyms, and at least one militant brushed up on his kickboxing and knife-fighting skills by tak-ing martial arts classes. Meanwhile, the prospective hijacker-pilots en-rolled in flight-training courses, flew practice flights on small rented planes, did test runs on commercial flights to gather intelligence on cockpit access and airport security, and purchased commercially avail-able flight-deck simulation videos and software. Careful preparation in-creased the hijackers' ability to perform their assigned tasks, with tragic results for the United States.

Of course, not all extremists benefit from lengthy apprenticeships and meticulous preparation. Many militants receive only rudimentary instruction in weaponry and guerrilla warfare, and some not even that, before undergoing their "real education": combat against enemy forces. During the 1980s, Arab mujaheddin, including many of the original leaders of what would later become Al Qaeda, learned fighting skills and developed personal contacts with other Islamic insurgents while battling Soviet troops in Afghanistan. Later on, conflicts in Bosnia, Chechnya, Kashmir, and Iraq provided additional opportunities for Is-lamists, including those who went through the Al Qaeda camps and, subsequently, those who did not, to supplement whatever training they might have had with actual combat experience.

Like the socialization that occurs in Islamist training camps, not to mention some radical mosques and *madrassas,* immersion in combat fosters the development of communities of practice and social net-works among participants. Battling with their fellow mujaheddin for a righteous cause in which they devoutly believe, fighters form enduring friendships with Islamists from different countries and regions, creat-ing a transnational brotherhood that transcends borders.[35] Through conversations and war stories they share norms and practices about their tradecraft, swapping tips for defeating their adversaries and valid-ating their identities as Salafi warriors. The friendships, skills, and ex-perience they acquire fighting enemy combatants, which may include the ability to improvise explosive devices and kidnap and assassinate people, often transfer well to urban terrorist operations in other coun-tries. Recognizing this, many counterterrorism officials today are deeply concerned with what they call "bleed out," whereby seasoned foreign fighters from Iraq and other jihadi theaters return to their home countries to continue the struggle against "apostate" regimes and Westerners (I revisit this theme in the conclusion).[36]

Transnational Networks

Numerous terrorist groups are embedded within interorganizational networks that contain multiple nodes spread across different countries.[37] Hizballah, part terrorist organization, part political party, and part social welfare agency, includes several administrative groups that issue directives to various military, political, financial, ideological, and social committees based in Lebanon and Iran. The movement also maintains an extensive international presence, with operatives and cells located in Africa, the Middle East, Europe, and North and South America. Overseas cells perform support functions for the larger network, including recruiting new members, disseminating propaganda, acquiring weapons and equipment, transporting operatives, conducting surveillance for possible attacks, and raising money through Islamic charities, contraband smuggling, and money laundering. Hizballah cells have also been implicated in terrorist attacks, including the bombing of the Israeli embassy in Buenos Aires, Argentina, in 1992, and the blasting of a Jewish cultural center in the same city two years later.[38] Magnus Ranstorp, a prominent authority on Hizballah, argues that its dispersed transnational structure is held together by "a coalition of Lebanese Shi'ite clerics, each of whom has their own networks of followers and ties to Iran's clerical establishment," rather than a centralized directorate.[39] In this respect Hizballah resembles a bureaucratic network hybrid that coordinates and to varying degrees controls different groups of Shi'ite extremists.

Other terrorist networks are reportedly even flatter and more decentralized than Hizballah, containing fluid linkages among separate nodes.[40] The Palestinian resistance movement Hamas, whose military wing has carried out dozens of self-styled "sacred explosions" in Israel and the occupied territories since 1993, is made up of a decentralized network of mosques, schools, orphanages, health clinics, and paramilitary cells. While Hamas contains administrative bodies, including an advisory council and politburo, that provide strategic guidance, moral backing, and funding for major operations, local groups and clandestine cells enjoy substantial autonomy in carrying out their day-to-day affairs, even at the expense of contradicting the movement's "official" policy.[41] Abu Sayyaf, a Filipino extremist group with ties to a national secessionist movement as well as to Al Qaeda, operates as a decentralized network of loosely coupled groups that conduct bombings, kidnappings, assassinations, and other acts of political violence in pursuit of a common goal: establishing an independent Islamic state in the southern Philippines. Even "traditional" terrorist organizations known for their bureaucratic disposition, including the Palestine Liberation Organization (PLO) and the now defunct Red Army Faction, more closely resemble interorganizational networks containing loosely affiliated groups of supporters that share common objectives rather than monolithic bodies with formally defined lines of administrative accountability.[42]

Paradoxically, the decentralized nature of these network forms of organization, where relations between nodes are characterized by horizontal accountability and a shared commitment to a common cause, does not preclude the existence of vertical decision-making hierarchies within nodes that carry out the network's most dangerous activities. Indeed, decision making in many paramilitary cells that conduct terrorist attacks tends to be fairly hierarchical: leaders issue orders and underlings carry them out. While cell workers may enjoy limited autonomy in conducting their daily activities, even standard operational decisions must be cleared by their supervisors. This structure is designed to safeguard the integrity of ongoing operations and prevent low-level workers from exposing the terrorist network to unnecessary risks. Cell leaders and workers alike understand their basic roles in the enterprise and the corresponding limits to their discretion. One member of a Palestinian extremist group describes the top-down nature of decision making in his organization, where supervisors made the basic decisions: "the rank and file were ready to follow through fire and water. I was subordinate to just one person, my relations to him were good, as long as I agreed to all that was asked of me. It was an organization with a very clear hierarchy, and it was clear to me that I was at the bottom [of] the ladder and that I had to do whatever I was told."[43]

Al Qaeda as a Wheel Network

With flat decision-making hierarchies and loosely coupled support nodes spread across dozens of countries, Al Qaeda is the archetype of networked, transnational terrorism. Prior to the U.S. invasion of Afghanistan, Osama bin Laden's movement was organized primarily as a transnational wheel network, similar to the drug "cartels" that dominated cocaine production in Colombia in the 1980s and 1990s. The "general emir," bin Laden, provided inspiration, strategic guidance, and oversight to his followers, in close consultation with several lieutenants and a senior advisory body known as the *shura majlis* (consultative council). Experienced shura members directed Al Qaeda's training programs, military operations, and external affairs. Outside this core group stood several "committees" specializing in different functions.[44]

The military committee proposed terrorist operations, recruited participants, and, with the assistance of a subcommittee, managed Al Qaeda's numerous training camps. The security committee was responsible for intelligence collection, counterintelligence, and the physical protection of network leaders. The business and finance committee ran a number of profit-making enterprises in Sudan, including construction, transportation, and agricultural firms, and managed Al Qaeda's finances through investment companies, financial institutions, and humanitarian relief agencies. The foreign purchases committee acquired weapons, munitions, and technical equipment for Al Qaeda. The *Sharia* committee prepared the religious pronouncements, ostensibly grounded in Islamic law, through which Al Qaeda justified its terrorist attacks. The media committee disseminated information about Al Qaeda and the larger Sunni extremist movement through an Arabic-language daily newspaper and a weekly report. The committees maintained linkages with the core group and dozens of peripheral nodes, including training camps, warehouses, communications facilities, commercial businesses, and operations cells (see Fig. 7).

Decision-making authority in Al Qaeda was hierarchical yet diffuse. Within the core group and peripheral nodes, decisions and accountability stemmed from vertical social relations. At the top stood Osama bin Laden and his fellow shura members, who determined general policy and may have helped plan major operations, such as the East African embassy bombings and the 9/11 attacks. Bin Laden and other shura members also issued general directives and detailed instructions to different functional committees, which in turn supplied funding, logistical support and guidance to peripheral nodes. Members of the core group communicated with other network nodes using cell phones, satellite phones, e-mail, fax machines, websites, and paper and electronic documents delivered by human couriers.

Peripheral nodes were often loosely coupled to the core and exercised considerable discretion in carrying out their day-to-day activities, including planning and conducting attacks. Mohammed Atta essen-

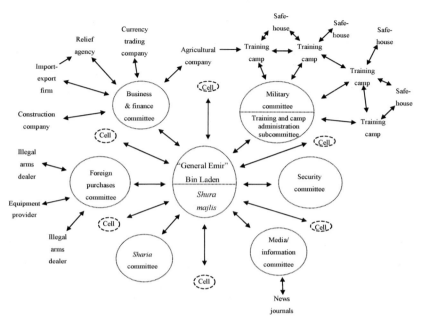

Fig. 7   Al Qaeda's wheel network

tially determined the final dates and targets of the 9/11 attack, with input from bin Laden, Khalid Shaikh Mohammed, and Ramzi bin al-Shibh, based on what he felt was feasible given local conditions in the United States. Indeed, the 9/11 Commission points out that there was some disagreement among Al Qaeda leaders and attack planners on this issue, with bin Laden pushing for earlier attacks to coincide with political events, such as Israeli prime minister Ariel Sharon's planned visit to the White House in the summer of 2001, and Khalid Shaikh Mohammed and Atta insisting that the attacks not proceed until all the hijacker teams were ready. Mohammed Atta and Khalid Shaikh Mohammed apparently carried the day and the attack did not take place until after the first week of September, when Atta knew that the U.S. Congress would be back in session following its summer recess.[45]

Peripheral nodes also contain their own decision-making hierarchies with leaders who supervise other members of the group. Peripheral nodes communicate with the core group through human couriers, oblique telephone conversations, and encrypted e-mail messages. If problems arise, such as personality clashes between group members, the core group may intervene to resolve the problem. For the 9/11 attacks, Al Qaeda maintained a relatively flat organizational structure that ensured a degree of vertical accountability within individual nodes and administrative oversight of the overall operation. Mohammed Atta reportedly supervised and coordinated other members of the conspiracy in the United States, apparently with the assistance of Nawaf al-Hazmi, his second in command. When disagreement arose between Atta and Ziad Samir Jarrah, another pilot in the operation, Khalid Shaikh Mohammed interceded, urging Ramzi bin al-Shibh, who communicated directly with Atta and Jarrah, to maintain peace between the two hijacker-pilots. While tension persisted between Atta and Jarrah, they were evidently able to smooth over their differences enough to keep the conspiracy from unraveling.[46]

Compartmentation in Terrorist Networks

Terrorist networks frequently organize their activities by dividing adherents into separate working groups, or cells, that perform different tasks. Over the years, many terrorist groups, including the PLO, the Abu Nidal Organization, the Popular Front for the Liberation of Palestine, the IRA, Hizballah, Hamas, and Al Qaeda, compartmented their operations. As with Colombian trafficking enterprises, compartmentation helps protect these clandestine actors from infiltration by state security agencies and limits the damage of penetration when it does occur.

"Cell or cluster methods should be adopted by the Organization," explains Al Qaeda's *Declaration of Jihad Against the Country's Tyrants*. "It should be composed of many cells whose members do not know one another, so that if a cell member is caught the other cells would not be affected, and work would proceed normally."[47] Former Al Qaeda members-turned-informants have identified a number of different cells for major operations, including reconnaissance, surveillance, logistics, and attack. Each cell contains several militants who use code names to hide their true identities from their colleagues. Cell members are told only what they need to know to perform their tasks. While many terrorist cells contain flat authority structures, task relations among members are structured through informal decision-making hierarchies that assign greater responsibility to more experienced, higher-skilled, and better-trained members. Al Qaeda commanders enjoy considerable autonomy in conducting their day-to-day operations. Cells that operate on enemy soil direct their members to blend into their surrounding communities, avoid attracting unnecessary attention to the group, and protect their communications with the utmost secrecy. Al Qaeda members in Western countries are instructed to shave their beards, avoid contact with neighbors, consolidate daily prayers into few sessions, and use general terminology and code words when communicating sensitive information by telephone.

In practice, the degree to which terrorist networks actually compartment their operations is limited. Hizballah paramilitary units typically contain "fighting clerics," religious figures trained in guerrilla warfare who communicate with their colleagues in different regions and up the Hizballah chain of command.[48] Through the fighting clerics, different cells in the Hizballah network can share information and experience across nodes and regions, ameliorating problems with learning found in some terrorist networks, where lessons learned tend to be localized, limited to the nodes that experienced them directly. Indeed, many groups, including Al Qaeda, recognize that the ability to carry out complex operations requires communication between cells located in different areas. When asked how Al Qaeda cells communicate with the rest of the terrorist network, former FBI agent Cloonan explains:

> You have a go-between. Typically, the emir [leader] of the cell crosses functional lines between the different cells. There is a common factor between cells: Generally the emir knows everything there is to know about the operation involved. . . . People in the logistics cell would not necessarily know who was involved in the surveillance cell. And people in surveillance would not necessarily know who is involved in the attack cell. But there would be the emir, who is in charge of the overall operation who is likely to know all the players and trust them. This person would communicate back to the leadership through an intermediary or in some cases they would just go back to bin Laden directly.[49]

Like the cutouts found in many trafficking networks, cell leaders in terrorist networks communicate valuable information between nodes, which allows them to draw on the experience of their colleagues in other parts of the network. Even the more flexible procedures Cloonan describes may be violated if this will enhance communication between nodes. In the 9/11 attacks, militants from different hijacking teams apparently traveled together and met in Las Vegas and Florida in preparation for their synchronized attacks on New York and Washington, D.C.[50] When planning and carrying out complex attacks, terrorists often weigh the benefits of cross-group communication in facilitating their operations against the risks of police infiltration. Like trafficking enterprises, different nodes in terrorist networks are linked through their participants' social networks—long-standing friendship and family ties that diminish the risks of state penetration—and allow planners greater flexibility in carrying out their attacks.

While some observers have pointed to cross-cell communication in the 9/11 hijackings as evidence of Al Qaeda's "sloppy tradecraft," such an assessment misses an important point: militants are likely to view compartmentation as a useful guide in planning their operations rather than a sacrosanct principle that is never violated. Terrorist guides such as the *Declaration of Jihad Against the Country's Tyrants* are just that—guides. In the field, extremists enjoy flexibility in improvising their practices and procedures as necessary to meet the demands and contingencies of the moment, provided they do not violate the physical security of the operation. As in Colombian trafficking networks, operating rules and procedures in terrorist groups are set in sand, not stone. This procedural malleability is critical to helping terrorist and trafficking networks maintain their suppleness in hostile enforcement systems.

Collecting Intelligence

Terrorists routinely gather information about their activities and government counterterrorism efforts in order to learn from past events and identify vulnerabilities in their adversaries' operations. Sources of inspiration and imitation include media accounts that describe successful attacks, publications detailing counterterrorism measures, and judicial proceedings against fellow extremists. Many extremist groups conduct surveillance prior to planning and conducting terrorist attacks and adjust their tactics accordingly. "There has been a lot of learning by the terrorists," explains a former high-ranking official in the CIA's Counterterrorist Center: "All these guys engage in extensive casing of potential targets and reconnaissance of security around targets. They look at possible targets to see the security measures protecting them and try to identify vulnerabilities. Does the security look vulnerable? . . . Terrorists engage in careful reconnaissance of targets and then change their targeting decisions and policies in response."[51]

For example, activists from the Animal Liberation Front (ALF) and the Earth Liberation Front reportedly read trade publications and video-tape potential targets in preparing for property damage attacks against logging companies, ski resorts, animal breeders, and other perceived culprits of animal abuse and environmental degradation.[52] ALF activists have infiltrated businesses they plan to attack by developing ties with workers or becoming employees themselves in order to gather informa-tion about the offending firms' security routines. They then use this intelligence, developed through social networks, to carry out economic sabotage and animal "liberation" raids against targeted firms.[53] In an interview with *Bite Back Magazine,* John Curtin, a veteran animal rights activist who has been incarcerated for participating in numerous ALF actions, describes the surveillance involved in liberation raids:

> We took in definitely weeks, if not months, of surveillance for the raid. It involves a lot of sitting out in the dead of night in the wind, rain, sitting in the side of a hedge just watching, waiting. That is a large part of all the raids I've ever known of—the surveillance beforehand. You really want to know the run of the place, you want to know what time the staff come in, what time do the rotators change, what time does the day staff change, when does the security make their rounds—and you want to know all of this like the back of your hand. That involves just sitting there, and getting wet and getting cold. . . . Its [sic] like . . . I imagine robbing a bank, which would take a lot of work, and because you're dealing with animals there could even be more problems. So for the few hours it takes to do the raid . . . it takes many, many weeks of 24/7 concentra-tion on it in order for it to go well. There may be times when you could do something spur of the moment, but you don't want to rush into that intentionally. I would always want to know my enemy before I went there.[54]

Political extremists have also developed numerous practices to moni-tor law enforcement and military activities, frequently with an eye toward improving existing operations and preventing costly errors. "Terrorists often analyze the 'lessons' to be drawn from mistakes made by former comrades who have been either killed or apprehended," writes Bruce Hoffman, former head of the RAND Corporation's terrorism research unit. "Press accounts, judicial indictments, courtroom testimony, and trial transcripts are meticulously culled for information on security force tactics and methods and then absorbed by surviving group members."[55] During the 1980s members of the Red Army Faction, a small German terrorist group, studied professional law enforcement journals and court testimony from police officials to learn antiterrorist techniques and develop appropriate countermeasures, such as applying a special ointment to their fingers that prevented them from leaving incriminating prints for criminal investigators.[56]

When IRA militants land in British or Irish prisons, "they are immediately approached by other incarcerated cadre and debriefed on their capture," explains another source. "This information is smuggled out of the institution and provided to the command structure for analysis by leaders and promulgation to members at large."[57] Debriefings of incarcerated Provos and suspected informants are the primary means by which the IRA gathers information about British law enforcement practices, according to another RAND researcher: "The internal [IRA] security unit that performed this function applied interrogation techniques learned from, among other sources, their own interrogations by security services . . . debriefings occurred whenever anyone was arrested, an operation was penetrated, or events during an action did not go as planned."[58] Like Colombian trafficking networks, the IRA also learned to exploit the British criminal justice system to gather intelligence about counterterrorism efforts. After initially refusing to defend themselves for fear of legitimizing the Crown's judicial system, IRA defendants began to plead not guilty to compel British law enforcers to divulge their counterterrorism methods in open court.[59]

Hizballah has long gathered tactical intelligence about the Israeli Defense Forces, even in the most rudimentary fashion. According to a major in an IDF intelligence unit stationed along Israel's fortified border with Lebanon, when the Israelis used to conduct regular border patrols along the security perimeter, Hizballah fighters would collect information about their adversaries by sneaking up to the border fence and shaking it, creating a ruckus. The Hizballah fighters would then study the Israeli response, counting the number of IDF soldiers who came to investigate the disturbance, the types of vehicles they drove, where the commander of the forces positioned himself, what he wore, and so on. Hizballah then used this information in its attacks on Israeli border guards.[60]

Al Qaeda similarly emphasizes intelligence collection. Network associates gather information from personal contacts, public officials, newspapers, news broadcasts and movies, courtroom testimony, and other open sources, taking advantage of the press freedoms and transparent government reporting enjoyed in many Western democracies. According to an unclassified CIA memorandum, Al Qaeda operatives search the media for information about U.S. counterterrorism activities and alter "their practices in response to what they have learned in the press about our capabilities,"[61] including restricting their use of cell phones.

Al Qaeda and its predecessors have also been known to send associates on undercover assignments overseas to gather intelligence for guerrilla warfare and conduct reconnaissance of potential targets for attacks. In the 1980s Ali Mohammed was allegedly tasked by Ayman al-Zawahiri, then leader of the Egyptian Islamic Jihad, part of which later merged with Al Qaeda, to travel to the United States and infiltrate the security services there. According to former FBI agent Cloonan, after failing to join the FBI as a translator, Mohammed enlisted in the army, where he was eventually able to obtain unclassified maps and training manuals while serving as a supply sergeant at Fort Bragg in North Carolina:

> Mohammed ends up joining the army and goes to Fort Bragg, where he comes to the attention of the faculty of John F. Kennedy Special Warfare School. They see him as a pretty good adjunct instructor and they used him to help teach military officers who were going overseas to the Gulf countries and other Islamic countries on how they should operate and so on. At the same time, he had access to the map shack and he would go there and take maps. They were readily available, they were not classified maps, as I understand, but they were maps that he took and downsized at a local copy store and sent them over to Afghanistan. This was when the Soviet-Afghan war was still going on. Plus, he was able to take a lot of training manuals out of the army, translate them, and give them to Osama bin Laden. He did so routinely.[62]

Eventually, bin Laden came to view the United States as a legitimate target for terrorist operations and he redirected his network's information-gathering activities accordingly. Before bombing the U.S. embassy in Nairobi, Kenya, in 1998, Al Qaeda scouts allegedly entered the embassy by posing as informants carrying the ominous warning that unidentified terrorists were preparing to bomb the building. "The men then watched the embassy over the following days taking notes on the security measures put in place to ward off the threat," two *Newsweek* journalists reported.[63] Then they packaged their intelligence in operational plans containing handwritten notes, photographs, and maps, which they sent to Al Qaeda leaders for review. In Afghanistan, Osama bin Laden and other shura majlis members met to discuss the intelligence, analyze vulnerabilities in the embassy's security precautions, and design an attack plan based on their analysis. The ensuing operation, along with a simultaneous bombing at the U.S. embassy in Dar es Salaam, Tanzania, killed more than three hundred people and injured five thousand others.[64]

Shortly before the 9/11 attacks, another Al Qaeda operative allegedly flew from Amsterdam to Tel Aviv, then traveled throughout Israel on a scouting mission for the terrorist network. According to a report on the mission, apparently written by an Al Qaeda member, the scout collected intelligence on security procedures used by El Al, the Israeli national airline, and cased potential targets in Jerusalem, Haifa, Bethlehem, and Tel Aviv, including skyscrapers, public transportation systems, and the Wailing Wall. The report, obtained by the *Wall Street Journal*, contained information that could aid future reconnaissance missions, including a list of questions El Al security officers asked the scout and advice that operatives with Pakistani visas "wash" their passports before traveling so as to remove their incriminating credentials. The report also recommended that Al Qaeda conduct a follow-up mission in order to gather additional intelligence on El Al's security procedures, and suggested that the operative carry "an article that would imitate a container to be carried during an actual operation."[65]

Terrorist Sensemaking and Adaptations

For operation-minded militants, the ultimate purpose of gathering intelligence is to act on it. Al Qaeda and other terrorist networks use reconnaissance collected by their agents to plan and execute operations that achieve group objectives. They hold meetings and engage in sensemaking to analyze their intelligence and identify vulnerabilities they can exploit against potential targets. John Cloonan, who debriefed several Al Qaeda members-turned-informants during his tenure as an FBI counterterrorism agent, provides an example of such sensemaking, which eventually culminated in the U.S. embassy bombing in Nairobi in 1998. Recalling his numerous interviews with Ali Mohammed, Cloonan describes how Osama bin Laden and other leaders, drawing on their identities as Islamists, analyzed the feasibility and utility of attacking the U.S. embassy using the intelligence gathered by Mohammed and other field operatives:

> When bin Laden decided to attack the U.S. Embassy in Nairobi, Ali Mohammed conducted a surveillance of the building. Using a first-generation laptop computer with average software, he produced an intelligence report with attachments containing pictures and diagrams. The report was presented to bin Laden in his office in Khartoum. It was in an office around a conference table, just the way you would make a presentation to your class or something like that. The report was laid out, and bin Laden, Mohammed Atef, Ayman al-Zawahiri, Ali Mohammed, and others discussed every aspect of the report. Ali Mohammed had to make a presentation based on his report. They discussed it in detail, whether it was feasible, whether it was Islamically correct, whether it was going to accomplish the goals and objectives they wanted to. There was an issue of killing fellow Muslims, and what time of day to do it. They discussed what would be the best method of attack. Then, according to Ali, bin Laden looked at one of the pictures or diagrams and concluded that the U.S. embassy was extremely vulnerable. The embassy was not set back from the road and there was nothing really in the way of a physical structure to prevent a bombing of the building; security guards were walking around, they were unarmed, I think they had night sticks. And so bin Laden and the others decided, first of all in 1993, that they were going to put a bomb in a car or truck in the parking space that they could access. . . . Later, that particular surveillance was updated, before the attacks in '98. . . . The

[Nairobi] plan was not haphazard; it was not done on the spur of the moment. It was well planned, well thought out, an attack with a high probability of success against a weak target.[66]

Of course, not all terrorist operations are as carefully planned as Al Qaeda's 1998 and 2001 "spectaculars." Many terrorist attacks carried out since 9/11, when the counterterrorism environment became extremely hostile for Islamic militants, appear to involve ad hoc planning by less experienced mujaheddin, sometimes with the assistance of veteran fighters.[67] Yet even these operations require basic preparations, including reconnaissance of the target, and a process, however imperfect, by which militants make sense of their environment to determine the prospects for executing attacks.

In addition to planning attacks, terrorists use intelligence to modify their operations to prevent state security officials from destroying them. Success for political extremists who operate in hostile environments depends on their capacity to outmaneuver law enforcement and military bureaucracies. To this end they routinely alter their activities to prevent state authorities from identifying patterns and practices they can use to infiltrate their operations. "You change your tactics to keep them guessing," explains an experienced IRA militant. "If you stick to one tactic, you can become predictable and be tracked down."[68]

These tactical adaptations are often fairly simple, yet maddeningly effective—sometimes with devastating results. Following a suicide bombing of the American embassy in Beirut by Shia extremists that killed sixty-three people in April 1983, media sources reported that intelligence officials had intercepted radio communications between the alleged planners of the attack in Syria and their counterparts in Iran. "Shortly thereafter," observed Katherine Graham, then head of the Washington Post Company, "the traffic ceased. This undermined efforts to capture the terrorist leaders and eliminated a source of information about future attacks." Five months later, Shia extremists carried out another, far more devastating bombing of the Marine barracks in Beirut, this time killing 241 American servicemen.[69]

As noted above, government officials believe that Al Qaeda operatives also learn about U.S. counterterrorism efforts through media reports. After published accounts that U.S. intelligence agencies were monitoring his satellite telephone calls, Osama bin Laden apparently switched phones and reduced his use of the technology, making it harder for American authorities to track him. "Once that information was out," complained deputy secretary of defense Paul Wolfowitz, referring to the unauthorized leaks by government officials to newspaper reporters that allegedly tipped bin Laden off, "we never again heard from his satellite phone."[70] More recently, numerous Islamists reportedly stopped using Swisscom cell phones, which they erroneously believed protected their anonymity, to communicate sensitive messages, switching to e-mail, Internet phone calls, and human couriers. Investigators maintain that the alleged extremists changed their communications because they learned their cell phones were vulnerable to government interception. Indeed, "[c]ell phones have played a major role in the constant jousting between terrorists and intelligence agencies," report Don Van Natta and Desmond Butler of the *New York Times.* "Each success by investigators seems to drive terrorists either to more advanced—or to more primitive—communications."[71]

Terrorists also adapt their activities in response to difficulties that arise when planning and executing operations. The 9/11 attacks provide a glaring example. Belying its catastrophic outcome, the 9/11 operation was beset by problems during the preparation stages, forcing Khalid Shaikh Mohammed and Mohammed Atta to alter their plans repeatedly. The original plot, as conceived by Khalid Shaikh Mohammed, drawing on his experience from the failed Oplan Bojinka incident, was decidedly more ambitious, calling for ten planes to attack various targets on the East and West Coasts of the United States.[72] This operation was downsized several times, apparently owing to Osama bin Laden's objections that it would be too difficult to coordinate and to the inability of several aspiring hijackers to obtain U.S. visas. Operational problems that threatened to derail the mission included the failure of two hijackers to obtain sufficient pilot training; several participants who unexpectedly backed out of the mission or were removed by Al Qaeda leaders; and interpersonal conflicts between Atta and Ziad Samir Jarrah. Khalid Shaikh Mohammed, Ramzi bin al-Shibh, and Mohammed Atta changed their plans in response to each challenge by reassigning participants to tasks for which they were better suited, recruiting and training more skilled hijackers, and persuading operatives to overcome personal animosities for the greater good of the mission.[73] The terrorists' ability to fix their mistakes and adapt to a changing environment, defining qualities of mētis, ensured that the 9/11 operation, imperfect as it was, was ultimately carried out with devastating results.

Terrorists' adaptations are frequently driven by the need to safeguard organizational integrity in hostile environments and to keep pace with developments in counterterrorism tactics and technologies. Over the past several decades airlines have instituted a number of security procedures designed to protect domestic and international flights against bombings and hijackings. While these precautions have undoubtedly enhanced aviation security, enterprising extremists have responded to each innovation by circumventing new technologies and procedures. After terrorists carried out a number of airline hijackings in the late 1960s, the United States and other countries responded by installing metal detectors and X-ray machines in airports to screen passengers and deter potential attacks. While this policy decreased the number of skyjackings worldwide, it led to an increase in terrorist assassinations and hostage takings, as militants switched to other forms of political violence.[74]

Nor did improvements in airport security prevent all skyjackings. In 1985 Hizballah members circumvented screening devices during their hijacking of TWA Flight 847 by having airline workers hide weapons in the airplane lavatory, which prompted airlines to conduct background checks on ground crews. A year later, as Gregory Raymond recounts, explosives were found in a woman's luggage in London, apparently hidden there by her erstwhile boyfriend. Airlines responded by requiring workers to ask passengers if they packed their own baggage. Terrorists countered by checking their own bomb-laden baggage and then not boarding the flights. Again, the airlines responded, this time by matching checked luggage with boarded passengers, under the now tragically discredited assumption that terrorists would avoid suicide skyjackings.[75]

Driven by what Bruce Hoffman describes as a fundamental "organizational imperative" to continue their attacks, terrorist groups adapt in response to all manner of counterterrorism tactics. Hoffman describes the case of the Provisional Irish Republican Army, where bomb makers, under considerable pressure from British authorities and hoping to reduce the risk of accidental explosions to IRA militants, repeatedly modified their explosive devices and detonation systems. When British Ministry of Defense engineers responded to the Provos' bombing innovations by developing successful countermeasures, IRA technicians returned to their basement labs, where they improved their triggering devices. Each successive innovation allowed the IRA to overcome the government's countermeasures, enhancing their ability to conduct violent attacks within an intensely hostile environment.[76]

Recently another RAND scholar, Brian Jackson, has built on Hoffman's work by describing how the Provos repeatedly changed their detonation devices in response to counterterrorism pressure:

> One of the earliest detonation mechanisms adopted by the
> PIRA [IRA] was the use of long command wires, usually buried
> to avoid detection. . . . The buried wire could also be detected,
> potentially compromising an operation. This drove PIRA to ex-
> plore remote detonation, beginning with remote-controlled or
> radio systems. . . . PIRA's first transmitters were based on a
> commercial unit designed for model airplanes or boats. To
> counter this new tactic, security forces began transmitting jam-
> ming signals on the transmitter frequencies, preventing deto-
> nation or prematurely detonating PIRA bombs. . . . PIRA
> answered this innovation by adopting more sophisticated elec-
> tronic switches. . . . The back-and-forth innovation/counter-
> measure developments led to a "chase" across the radio
> spectrum. Once the security forces jammed a frequency, PIRA
> had to seek out a new area of the spectrum to reconstitute its
> capabilities. . . . PIRA tested new technologies to ensure that
> their signals could penetrate the security forces' protective
> countermeasures. . . . For these innovation efforts, PIRA drew
> on expertise within the commercial sector . . . and on experts
> from abroad and within the military.[77]

The IRA and the British army are not the only terrorists and counterterrorists to engage in competitive adaptation. Hizballah has also shown its ability to change bombing practices and technologies in response to counterterrorism operations by the Israeli Defense Forces. Over the years, Hizballah's paramilitary wing has created numerous innovations in its bombs and triggering devices, building an increasingly diverse operational repertoire in what one technical intelligence sergeant with the IDF's combat engineers unit describes as an "evolutionary process."[78] In their long-standing confrontation with Israeli security forces, which escalated into open warfare in the summer of 2006, Hizballah guerrillas have repeatedly increased the power and accuracy of their explosives. They began with simple improvised explosive devices before shifting to homemade shaped charges, then to direct fragmentation charges, and finally to military standard shaped charges. Hizballah operatives have also modified their initiation devices, progressing from electric wire triggers to simple wireless triggers to cell phone triggers and finally to infrared detectors based on household alarm technologies. Hizballah has also adapted its bombing practices by hiding explosives inside artificial false rocks, hollowed-out books, paint buckets, beer cans, egg crates, and other camouflaged artifacts, and creating laboratories for making explosives from fertilizers and liquid chemicals.

Hizballah's technological improvements are propelled by its own internal innovations and the need to respond to IDF countermeasures. The pressure to learn, in other words, comes from both within and outside the organization. Advances in Hizballah's explosives, for example, are generally made internally, as technicians seek to build more accurate, concentrated, and powerful charges that can be fired over greater distances. But many of Hizballah's triggering innovations develop in direct response to IDF successes in blocking or impeding existing triggers, compelling its bomb makers to innovate further. The use of commercially available infrared detectors, for example, is designed to bypass electronic jammers used by the IDF to block radio-wave detonators, including cell phone and garage door triggers. While the use of infrared detectors, which are based on light waves, does not yet appear to be widespread among Hizballah units, the IDF fears that this is just a matter of time, as knowledge of this innovation spreads within the militant network and to Palestinian resistance fighters in the occupied territories. Israeli concerns are exacerbated by the IDF's apparent lack of effective countermeasures to neutralize infrared triggers. "We have not been able to counter this type of triggering device," observes the IDF technical intelligence sergeant.[79]

Of course, no discussion of terrorist adaptations would be complete without reference to the Iraqi insurgency. The U.S. invasion of Iraq in 2003 had the (presumably) unintended effect of creating a country-wide training camp in guerrilla warfare and terrorism, essentially replacing the role played by Afghanistan during the 1990s. Like previous insurgencies in Algeria, Malaysia, Vietnam, and elsewhere, domestic and foreign guerrillas fighting in Iraq quickly learned to adapt their tactics and technologies in response to their opponent's successes and their own failures.[80] As early as mid-July 2003, two and a half months after President Bush triumphantly declared the end of major combat operations in Iraq, General John Abizaid, the commander of the U.S. Central Command, observed that the Iraqi insurgency "is adapting to our tactics, techniques, and procedures, and we've got to adapt to their tactics, techniques, and procedures."[81] The general's recognition of a competitive, adaptive dynamic between coalition forces and Iraqi insurgents did not prevent the latter from continuing to study their adversaries and change their practices in response to U.S. countermeasures. Throughout 2004 and 2005 reports emerged in the press about insurgents' ability to repeatedly improve their improvised explosive devices (IEDS) by developing more sophisticated triggers in response to U.S. countermeasures and, apparently borrowing a page from Hizballah, making greater use of shaped charges to punctuate the armor of reinforced Humvees and Bradley fighting vehicles.[82]

In fact, as documented by Anthony Cordesman and others, the insurgents have adapted their combat operations in a variety of ways over the past several years, including but not limited to their use of IEDS. As they gained combat experience battling coalition forces, insurgents learned to make better use of mortars, rocket-propelled grenades, and other light weapons; to prepare more complex and deadly ambushes; and to "swarm" U.S. and Iraqi forces by attacking them from multiple directions simultaneously. To gather intelligence about coalition operations, insurgents learned to monitor the media and the Internet on a regular basis, to infiltrate Iraqi security forces with their own informants, and, like the IRA, to question released prisoners and detainees about their capture and interrogation at the hands of U.S. forces. To protect their communications from electronic eavesdropping by American military and intelligence agencies, insurgents learned to use Internet-based communications more securely and to rely more on human couriers and cell phone text messaging. To increase their operational capacity, insurgent groups learned to cooperate with each other to share intelligence, trade weapons, and conduct joint training exercises. And to protect their operations from penetration by security forces, insurgents learned to organize participants into separate compartments that divide operational and support functions, to minimize command-and-control communications from leaders, and to exercise greater caution when selecting new recruits for membership.[83] As these adaptations suggest, the war in Iraq has provided insurgents with a rich learning environment in which to experiment with different tactics, technologies, and organizational structures, while developing invaluable mētis-based skills that will serve them well in the years to come.

Terrorism, like drug trafficking and counterdrug law enforcement, is a specialized pursuit, demanding knowledge of demolitions, light weapons, covert operations, and a host of related activities. Terrorists learn their violent tradecraft through informal apprenticeships and formal training programs that convey the abstract ideals of their political ideologies and the concrete techniques of asymmetric warfare, while strengthening their identities as committed militants. Many terrorist networks, including Al Qaeda, Hizballah, and the IRA, devote considerable resources to instructing their members, as reflected in the quantity and variety of their training materials. To be sure, most terrorism training, generally carried out under conditions of secrecy and limited resources, does not match the sophistication of military training provided by contemporary states. But terrorist networks such as Al Qaeda are similar to their government adversaries in several respects: they provide basic military training to recruits; they select promising candidates for advanced and specialized instruction; and they provide members with specific tasks and responsibilities based on their level of training and expertise. Many professional terrorists are better trained than the Colombian traffickers examined in the preceding chapters.

Yet, like traffickers, terrorists supplement their formal training with the shrewd intuition and intelligence that comes from practical experience. Over time, extremists develop the sort of experiential mētis that is difficult to codify in knowledge-based artifacts. For this reason the capture of senior militants matters, and governments can—at least temporarily—degrade the capabilities of terrorist networks by apprehending their most experienced members. Like Pablo Escobar, however, Osama bin Laden, Ayman al-Zawahiri, and even Al Qaeda itself are not irreplaceable. What remains of Al Qaeda today is more of an ideology than an organization, with local Salafi jihadists in different countries pursuing their own operations under the purported inspiration—but not necessarily the supervision—of Al Qaeda leaders. Meanwhile, terrorist techne and mētis continue to spread among increasingly diffuse, electronically mediated Islamist communities of practice, suggesting that Al Qaeda's knowledge will continue to persevere even as the original network metastasizes into new organizational forms.

Like narcs and narcos, terrorist networks and counterterrorism agencies engage in repeated interactions through which law enforcers attempt to identify, apprehend, and dismantle terrorist networks, while terrorists aim to elude, co-opt, and assault their state adversaries. These contests pit flat, decentralized extremist networks that operate outside the law against tall, multilayered government bureaucracies that exist within it. Terrorists and counterterrorists gather information about each other and use it to modify existing practices and technologies and develop new ones. While counterterrorism agencies enjoy greater resources than law enforcement bureaus, the speed and precision of decision cycles and information flows still matter in competitive adaptation, influencing—but not determining—outcomes in these struggles.

The Counterterrorism Force Advantage

In the campaign against terrorism, the United States and its allies enjoy an enormous advantage in capability over their illicit rivals. Since the 9/11 attacks, Washington has devoted substantial human, technological, and financial resources to tracking down and eliminating Al Qaeda and other terrorist networks. Following the coordinated attacks on the World Trade Center and the Pentagon, Congress approved US$15.5 billion in emergency supplemental funding for homeland security, while the federal counterterrorism budget increased by 68 percent, from US$28.9 billion in 2002 to US$48.6 billion in 2003. To place these figures in comparative counterdrug perspective, in 2003 the federal government allocated less than half that amount, approximately US$19.2 billion, for all drug-control programs.[1] Significantly, these homeland security budget figures do not include additional funding for unconventional warfare and direct action, essential—and increasingly expensive—components in the Bush administration's counterterrorism strategy.[2]

Federal counterterrorism resources are embodied in a broad range of domestic and foreign programs designed to detect, deter, and ultimately defeat terrorist networks. These activities are administered by dozens of agencies spread across numerous departments.[3] While the FBI, located within the Department of Justice, has traditionally been a domestic law enforcement agency, in the 1980s it expanded its role in both international terrorism investigations and international drug enforcement.[4] The bureau's counterterrorism role has grown dramatically since 9/11, and today it administers many programs to investigate, prosecute, and dismantle terrorist organizations in the United States and abroad, including the National Joint Terrorism Task Force, the Counterterrorism Watch program, the Foreign Terrorist Tracking Task Force, the Office of Law Enforcement Coordination, the National Intel Share Project, and the elite hostage rescue teams.[5]

The Defense Department commands a variety of direct action and intelligence capabilities to disrupt terrorists abroad, including elite Special Operations Forces, regional joint military commands, and several intelligence agencies. Preeminent among the DoD's intelligence agencies is the National Security Agency, the largest intelligence organization in the United States and the leading provider of electronic surveillance. The CIA also runs numerous programs that gather, analyze, and disseminate counterterrorism intelligence using human and technological sources, including interagency "fusion" centers and units focusing on specific terrorist threats, and covert paramilitary forces that seek to capture and in some cases kill suspected terrorists. The National Counter-Terrorism Center integrates and analyzes terrorism threat reporting from throughout the intelligence community and oversees interagency groups that monitor federal counterterrorism efforts while keeping tabs on extremist groups that seek to attack American interests. Other agencies from the Departments of Homeland Security, State, and Treasury contribute to America's counterterrorism and homeland security mission by patrolling the nation's borders, intercepting ships transporting alleged extremists, identifying and freezing finances from terrorist organizations and their support networks, sharing intelligence among government agencies, facilitating international cooperation, providing rewards for information leading to the arrest of suspected militants, and arranging for the extradition and extraordinary rendition of terrorism suspects to the United States and allied countries.[6]

No extremist network, however global its reach and well financed its activities, can match the technological wizardry and military might embodied in these programs—a point dramatically underscored by Operation Enduring Freedom in Afghanistan and similar counterterrorism activities elsewhere. These joint actions featured coordination between the U.S. Special Operations Command, the CIA, the FBI, and their host country counterparts. In Afghanistan, CIA paramilitary operatives and Special Operations soldiers organized ethnic Uzbeks, Tajik Afghans, and Pashtun tribesmen into a coordinated opposition force, and provided targeting intelligence that allowed U.S. Navy, Marine, and Air Force pilots to launch more than ten thousand precision-guided bombs against Al Qaeda and Taliban fortifications. They also hunted Osama bin Laden, Ayman al-Zawahiri, and other "high-value" targets through reconnaissance operations and direct action raids.[7] In Pakistan, Special Operations Forces and FBI agents worked closely with Pakistani police and intelligence officials to identify and apprehend Al Qaeda fighters fleeing Afghanistan into Pakistan's cities and semiautonomous western tribal areas.

Sensemaking in Counterterrorism

Many counterterrorism missions resemble the sort of organizational sensemaking that law enforcers engage in when targeting drug traffickers. Like criminal investigators from the DEA and the Colombian National Police, Special Operations soldiers, CIA operatives, and FBI agents piece together bits of seemingly discrete intelligence to identify terrorist groups, disrupt their operations, and apprehend their members. In the process they generate shared understandings of their adversaries and themselves, based on their interpretation of previous experience, including terrorist attacks and counterterrorism efforts. Intelligence analysts, law enforcement agents, and policymakers create these understandings through meetings, informal conversations, and other social settings where officials communicate information and negotiate plausible interpretations of reality. These interpretations are plausible, as opposed to necessarily accurate, because rationally bounded sensemakers confront time constraints, information overload, and perceptual biases in seeking to understand clandestine opponents who are constantly changing their methods and movements. Collective interpretations inform counterterrorism strategies and tactics, as government officials create new practices and procedures and amend existing ones based on their understanding of how both terrorists and counterterrorists operate. For example, in response to information sharing and policy coordination problems, the federal government has created a variety of interagency programs over the years (I discuss these programs, which have produced mixed results in the war on terror, in greater detail below).

Tactical intelligence is critical to counterterrorism sensemaking. Government agents combine a variety of information sources to learn more about their adversaries' methods and operations. In the hunt for Osama bin Laden, Ayman al-Zawahiri, and other Al Qaeda leaders, intelligence analysts sift through mountains of high-tech "signals" intelligence provided by satellite surveillance systems, unmanned aerial reconnaissance drones, and data-mining software, and share promising leads with CIA operatives and Special Forces soldiers on the ground, who coordinate their activities with Afghan and Pakistani commandos. Northern Alliance and Pakistani officials, in turn, share low-tech human intelligence from undercover operatives and confidential informants with their American colleagues. As they gather and disseminate tactical intelligence, analysts and operatives re-create and renegotiate their interpretations of Al Qaeda, focusing on the network's command-and-control structure and the identities of remaining militants. When these retrospective interpretations appear sufficiently plausible to decision makers, American and host country commandos enact their understandings by conducting strategic reconnaissance and direct action raids that, according to one report, more closely resemble "high-stakes police work than traditional military combat: secret stake-outs followed by lightning raids on suspected terrorist compounds."[8] On occasion, security forces capture Al Qaeda and Taliban fighters, along with documents, computers, cell phones, phone directories, and other knowledge-based artifacts. FBI and military document exploitation teams extract information from these artifacts, which they use to update their interpretations of Al Qaeda and continue their pursuit of Osama bin Laden and other terrorist leaders.

The enactment of these social understandings in counterterrorism operations has produced noteworthy results. According to senior Bush administration officials, many of Al Qaeda's leaders have been captured or killed since 9/11 and more than three thousand militants have been placed in custody. Government authorities also claim to have seized or frozen more than US$200 million in terrorism-related assets and disrupted dozens of potential attacks by Al Qaeda and its affiliated groups in, among other places, Bosnia-Herzegovina, France, Italy, Jordan, Macedonia, Singapore, Turkey, and Yemen.[9] Widely reported kills include Mohammed Atef, the alleged military leader of Al Qaeda, Ali Qaed Sinan al-Harethi, the suspected operations chief killed by a Predator drone strike in Yemen, and, more recently, Abu Musab al-Zarqawi, the notorious leader of an independent Islamist group in Iraq who in 2004 formally pledged his loyalty to Osama bin Laden.

More important, from the perspective of organizational sensemaking, numerous militants, including Khalid Shaikh Mohammed, Tawfiq Attash Khallad, Ali Abd al-Rahman, Abu Zubaydah, Ibn al-Shaykh al-Libi, Ramzi bin al-Shibh, and Riduan Isamuddin (Hambali) have been apprehended and turned over to American authorities. Several prize catches, under immense pressure from prolonged "stress and duress" interrogations administered by the CIA at undisclosed locations in Afghanistan, Thailand, and unnamed eastern European countries, reportedly provided the kind of detailed intelligence, including names, addresses, and phone numbers, that investigators used to identify other nodes in the network and prevent additional attacks. For example, government officials claim that the CIA's admittedly harsh treatment of Abu Zubaydah coerced him into detailing Khalid Shaikh Mohammed's central role in the 9/11 attacks and providing information about José Padilla, a low-level Al Qaeda associate subsequently arrested by the FBI in Chicago for allegedly plotting to conduct a radiological "dirty bomb" attack. Other "enhanced interrogation techniques," some of which are prohibited under international law, reportedly compelled Khalid Shaikh Mohammed and Ramzi bin al-Shibh into providing government investigators with details about the 9/11 operation.[10]

Other terrorists-turned-informants have willingly contributed to counterterrorism sensemaking by identifying Al Qaeda safe houses in Afghanistan, deciphering code words used to communicate details of impending attacks, and providing inside knowledge of sleeper cells and core-group leaders. Following the 9/11 attacks, over which there was considerable disagreement in Al Qaeda's shura majlis, and Operation Enduring Freedom, which flushed many Al Qaeda leaders from their state-sponsored sanctuary in Afghanistan, the CIA was reportedly able to recruit several highly placed informants in what remained of the original network's leadership core, including at least one informant who apparently provided detailed intelligence that led to the arrest of

several figures.[11] Like highly placed informants in Colombian drug-trafficking networks, terrorist turncoats are influenced by a variety of considerations, including a desire to distance themselves from decisions
and operations with which they strongly disagree, to escape the stresses
and strains that come with this perilous vocation, to receive lenient
treatment from government captors, to obtain so-called "snitch" visas
to immigrate to the United States or other Western countries, and to
collect good old-fashioned greenbacks for their cooperation.[12]

Whatever their motivations, informants can deepen investigators'
understanding of terrorist groups by providing an insider's perspective
that is often lacking in counterterrorism analysis. Depending on the
timeliness of the intelligence and the objectives of policymakers, this
knowledge can be used to hunt down and kill suspected extremists or
prosecute them for terrorism-related crimes. Former FBI agent John
Cloonan, who handled several Al Qaeda militants-turned-informants
during his career as a criminal investigator, describes how one informant's firsthand knowledge helped the Department of Justice prosecute several Al Qaeda associates in the east African embassy bombing
trial held in Manhattan in 2001:

> Jamal al-Fadl provided our first window into Al Qaeda in a very
> significant way. . . . We debriefed him for the better part of two
> years and we got an incredible amount of information from
> him, which led to further indictments and to other people
> being identified. He was your classic cooperating witness, pro-
> viding the government, in this case the FBI, with an insight
> into Al Qaeda that had not existed. . . . This information was
> not a verbatim transcript of an interrogation, it was not a posi-
> tion paper from the CIA. This stuff was coming from a real,
> live, walking, talking member of Al Qaeda. . . . [In the trial] he
> was able to provide the jury an insight into Al Qaeda, explain-
> ing what the group was, explaining its structure, and providing
> real-life testimony and firsthand accounts of what bin Laden
> was up to. He was able to explain the *fatwas* that were first
> issued in 1996, declaring war on the United States, and he was
> able to provide evidence against the defendants who had been
> charged.[13]

Drawing on their real-life experiences as "walking, talking" terrorists,
Jamal al-Fadl and other informants can offer important insights for

counterterrorism sensemaking, allowing analysts and policymakers to renegotiate their interpretations of their clandestine adversaries and exploit these social understandings to justify existing policies—or call for new ones.

In his own way, Jamal al-Fadl can be considered the Max Mermelstein of Al Qaeda: a prominent former member of an illicit enterprise turned star informant who provided American investigators with detailed intelligence about the structure and operations of his network. In both cases, government officials drew on their informers' testimony to gauge the danger to American citizens posed by Islamic terrorism and Colombian drug trafficking, respectively, and to validate plausible interpretations of these clandestine operations. While Mermelstein emphasized the decentralized nature of the drug trade during his testimony before a House banking subcommittee, his insights from this hearing and several criminal trials were often manipulated by prosecutors and law enforcers to create a misleading interpretation of the Colombian drug trade as highly centralized, with so-called cartels exerting monopoly power over the entire industry.[14]

If Jamal al-Fadl has not yet provided formal testimony before the U.S. Congress, this has not prevented observers from using his and other informants' testimony to present similarly plausible, yet misleading, interpretations of a monolithic Al Qaeda somehow directing the operations of all Salafi jihadists throughout the world.[15] Such interpretations persist not only because they are plausible but because they serve the interests of a variety of actors who seek to emphasize the threat posed by their illicit adversaries. In the case of counterterrorism sensemaking, these actors include politicians eager to advance their agendas and focus public attention on the continuing danger of terrorism, as well as their own efforts to protect Americans; bureaucratic administrators hoping to increase government funding for their sundry counterterrorism programs; and a horde of independent analysts, media commentators, and lobbyists who profit handsomely from the burgeoning counterterrorism and homeland security industry.

Yet, like "cooperating" drug traffickers, terrorist informers have strong incentives to deceive their captors, particularly about their own involvement in violent and illegal activities. Al Qaeda members are reportedly trained to provide misleading information to interrogators, or to provide large amounts of intelligence that appears plausible, based on their role and location in the terrorist operation, but that is actually false or dated and takes investigators a long time to substantiate.[16] In the aftermath of 9/11, concerns about Al Qaeda's counterintelligence practices, along with a desire to extract information from suspected terrorists to prevent further attacks, led some policymakers and intelligence officials to advocate the use of aggressive interrogation techniques, under the assumption that roughing up and manipulating detainees psychologically would compel them to provide accurate information to investigators more quickly than noncoercive methods would. Law enforcers and intelligence agents have long warned, however, that torture often produces false information, particularly from victims who are willing to say just about anything they believe their tormenters want to hear in order to spare themselves further humiliation and brutality.[17] In fact, according to James Risen of the *New York Times,* Khalid Shaikh Mohammed, who was treated to "harsh interrogation techniques" about a hundred times during one two-week period, later repudiated some of his coerced testimony, placing the intelligence community and the 9/11 Commission, which relied heavily on his interrogations in its report, in the challenging position of trying to separate Mohammed's tortured truths from lies.[18] Abu Zubaydah's coerced confession regarding José Padilla has likewise been called into question, particularly since the Bush administration decided to prosecute the Muslim convert on the relatively minor charge of providing material support to terrorists, a far cry from the government's original accusation that he planned to carry out a dirty bomb attack in the United States.[19]

Finally, Ibn al-Shaykh al-Libi, the first high-ranking Al Qaeda figure to fall into American custody after 9/11, admitted that he fabricated a story, in order to escape harsh treatment from his Egyptian interrogators, that Iraqi officials had provided Al Qaeda operatives with training in explosives and chemical weapons. The CIA had secretly surrendered al-Libi to Egypt, a country with a well-deserved reputation for its aggressive handling of terrorism suspects, where he apparently concocted the story. Al-Libi later changed his account when Egypt turned him over to the United States and American investigators confronted him with evidence from their own informants questioning the veracity of his claim. But this was after al-Libi's original story had proved so valuable to White House officials as they sought to create a plausible narrative justifying the U.S. invasion of Iraq in 2003. Without mentioning al-Libi by name, President Bush used his original allegation in a campaign speech in Cincinnati in October 2002, in which he suggested that a strong operational relationship existed between Al Qaeda and Saddam Hussein's regime in Iraq. Several months later, Secretary of State Colin Powell drew on al-Libi's subsequently discredited story to argue the case for preemptive war against Iraq in a major speech before the UN Security Council.[20]

As these examples indicate, a basic problem with torture-tainted intelligence, indeed any intelligence derived from unreliable extremists, is that it often leads to grave distortions in counterterrorism sensemaking and policymaking. Rather than quickly producing accurate intelligence that can be used to create more effective policy, torture can have the opposite effect: with little regard for reliability, victims share information they believe their tormenters want or expect to hear in order to get them, quite literally, off their backs. Such biased yet plausible accounts can waste resources—and worse—as investigators chase down false leads, bureaucratic chiefs allocate funding based on poorly understood threats, and politicians promote shortsighted policies based on fabricated intelligence.

Competitive Adaptation and the Counterterrorism Bureaucracy

For all the technological sophistication and intelligence capabilities that the United States and other countries have marshaled in the campaign against terrorism, terrorist networks enjoy a number of advantages over their government adversaries, including flatter authority structures, quicker decision cycles, and fewer legal and bureaucratic constraints. These organizational features have enabled remnants of Al Qaeda to survive the post-9/11 counterterrorism crackdown, even as the former wheel network evolves into a diffuse social movement that unites its supporters under a shared ideology and local extremist networks that take their inspiration, but not their marching orders, from Osama bin Laden (I return to this theme in the conclusion).

Several of the most dangerous terrorist enterprises in recent memory, including Hamas, Hizballah, and Al Qaeda, are embodied within larger interorganizational networks containing relatively few layers of administrative accountability. Even in relatively centralized wheel networks, such as Al Qaeda before Operation Enduring Freedom, only one or two intermediaries separate the core node from the operations cells responsible for planning or executing terrorist attacks. Peripheral nodes enjoy considerable discretion in conducting their daily activities, including the freedom to improvise their practices and procedures in response to unexpected developments. While rank-and-file cell members may be told only what they need to know to carry out their tasks, linkages exist between peripheral and core nodes, whether in the form of Hizballah's fighting clerics or Al Qaeda's cell emirs. These network structures facilitate rapid information flows and decision cycles, processes that are enhanced by the relatively small size of extremist groups and their standing as illegal organizations subject to few bureaucratic and legal constraints to action. Of course, linkages between nodes also create operational vulnerabilities in extremist networks that counterterrorists can exploit if they capture the people who serve as intermediaries and persuade them, by force or by fortune, to turn state's evidence.

The U.S. counterterrorism apparatus, in contrast, is immense, stretching across a handful of departments, including Defense, Homeland Security, Justice, State, Treasury, and dozens of military, intelligence, and law enforcement agencies. Many of these agencies are large and cumbersome, employing thousands of people organized in numerous divisions characterized by multiple management layers and Byzantine decision-making protocols. Post-9/11 administrative reforms by the U.S. government, which include the creation of the Department of Homeland Security in 2003 and the creation of the National Counter-Terrorism Center and the National Intelligence Director in 2004, have made this bureaucratic apparatus even larger and more convoluted.

Department of Homeland Security

Formed in direct response to Washington's inability to prevent the 9/11 attacks, the Department of Homeland Security (DHS) is a bureaucratic behemoth that consolidates 180,000 employees from twenty-two separate agencies, each containing distinct organizational histories, missions and authorities, under the roof of a single department with an expansive mandate: to protect the United States from terrorist attacks. While the Bush administration's reorganization is designed to streamline the institutional structure of the new department, top-down decision-making hierarchies and abundant management layers permeate DHS, as is inevitable in any large bureaucracy with such a sweeping mission. In addition, a "cumbersome retooling process" is under way as numerous agencies involved in the homeland security shuffle, including the Customs Service, the Coast Guard, the Federal Emergency Management Agency, and the Immigration and Naturalization Service (INS), reconfigure their missions, operations, and organizational cultures to fight the war on terrorism—without surrendering their original missions.[21] One important aspect of this retooling lies in retraining thousands of government employees with the skills needed for homeland security, such as instructing immigration agents in customs law and inspection procedures and teaching police officers about biological weapons poisoning.[22]

"In many ways," observes public administration scholar Donald Kettl, the DHS's creation "was the most complicated restructuring of the federal government ever proposed,"[23] an assessment shared by the officials who handled the reorganization. "Managing the start-up of the Department of Homeland Security is surely one of the greatest managerial challenges any Cabinet official has ever had to face," testified Richard Falkenrath, former White House deputy homeland security advisor, before the Senate Committee on Homeland Security and Governmental Affairs: "The scale and complexity of the task can hardly be underestimated; the time frame for action was tight and unforgiving; the daily operational and policy demands were relentless; the interagency environment could be treacherous; the external constituencies, perpetually discontented. With circumstances such as these, no Cabinet officer will ever succeed at all tasks, all the time."[24]

A year after this vast reorganization began, a report from the DHS inspector general acknowledged that despite "major strides in protecting U.S. borders . . . the challenges are immense, and it will take years to address them fully."[25] Unfortunately, government bureaucrats and policymakers may not have years to prepare for the next terrorist attack on the United States. The DHS's numerous achievements notwithstanding—and they include the creation of counterterrorism preparedness doctrines, the consolidation of multiple human resource systems, and increased protections for the U.S. air transportation system—basic challenges remain. These include strengthening security for land- and sea-based transit systems, improving information sharing between the DHS and other federal, state, and local agencies, and reducing critical vulnerabilities at thousands of hazardous chemical production and transportation facilities throughout the United States, many of which are owned by private firms that have few incentives to increase costly security protections at their facilities.[26]

Some of these challenges have been exacerbated by turf battles among different DHS agencies, technological barriers to information sharing, and substantial personnel turnover among high-level officials. For example, the Transportation Security Agency's effort to project its authority over all matters relating to transportation security led to bureaucratic fights between the agency and other DHS bodies, including the department's infrastructure protection division and the Bureau of Immigration and Customs Enforcement. These debilitating battles, which one former official characterized as "a civil war within the U.S. government," created lengthy delays in protecting trains that carry hazardous chemicals and deciding which government databases would be used to monitor foreigners and cargo entering the United States.[27] Meanwhile, different DHS agencies continue to rely on separate information technologies to collect and store data, making intelligence sharing within the department—let alone between DHS and external agencies—most cumbersome.[28] And while some organization theorists suggest that a limited amount of leadership turnover may help established organizations "unlearn" detrimental practices,[29] the appointment of two secretaries, three deputy secretaries, and numerous undersecretaries and assistant secretaries in a little more than two years appears excessive for a newly created bureaucracy that is trying to accumulate mission-critical expertise in a novel area of government responsibility. In fact, according to the *New York Times,* more than ninety domestic security officials from the Department of Homeland Security, the White House Office of Homeland Security, and other executive agencies have left their positions since 2002, many of them to seek lucrative employment in the fledging homeland security industry. An optimist might suggest that because so many high-ranking former officials continue to work in the field of homeland security, this might help lessen the DHS's problems with lost knowledge and experience due to executive turnover. A less sanguine assessment would emphasize that many of these former officials now represent private firms that seek to sell security-related products to DHS and other government agencies, raising serious questions about the impartiality of the expertise they choose to share with their erstwhile colleagues.[30]

Developing Homeland Security Mētis from Training Simulations

Further hampering the Department of Homeland Security's ability to learn is its relative lack of experience in dealing with catastrophic terrorist attacks, what organization theorists refer to as the small-sample problem. Organizations learn from experience, adjusting their practices in response to feedback about the actions they took, or failed to take, when confronted with similar problems in the past.[31] Organizations often find it difficult to learn when history offers only a limited amount of experience on which to draw. This problem is "particularly acute," observe Barbara Levitt and James March, when organizations seek to learn from "low-probability, high-consequence events," such as natural disasters and terrorist attacks. The political, legal, and institutional ramifications of catastrophic events make it difficult to disentangle meaningful inferences about their cause "from conflict over formal responsibility, accountability, and liability."[32] Organizations seek to build on their lack of knowledge by experiencing limited histories more richly. One way they do this is by focusing their attention on critical, world-changing events from which they construct hypothetical histories that re-create the experience in new ways, allowing them to draw lessons from the expanded sample.[33]

The coordinated terrorist attacks on 9/11 certainly qualify as a critical incident for the United States, changing the way Americans view the world and leading to numerous government reforms. While policymakers have drawn a variety of lessons from the experience, learning from the attacks also became highly politicized as Democratic and Republican lawmakers, White House officials, and intelligence agencies squabbled over who was ultimately responsible for the tragedy and what institutional reforms, if any, should be implemented. The desire to avoid appearing weak in such a politically charged climate encouraged politicians and policymakers to exaggerate the magnitude of the threat they faced, creating strong incentives for security bureaucracies to do the same (I explore this theme further in the conclusion).

Fortunately, the United States has not experienced a major terrorist assault on American soil since 9/11, and it suffered only a handful before. This means that the Department of Homeland Security has a limited historical sample from which to learn. To their credit, DHS and other agencies are trying to expand their experience by creating hypothetical histories based on simulations of terrorist incidents. For example, the DHS's Office for Domestic Preparedness has developed an elaborate exercise program, including the Top Officials Exercise Series (TOPOFF), to help government officials and private-sector administrators learn by responding to simulated terrorist attacks. These training simulations test a variety of counterterrorism preparedness capabilities, including cross-agency coordination and command, hazardous materials management, and emergency medical response.[34] TOPOFF exercises allow government agencies and private-sector firms to develop mētis by practicing their response capabilities in a simulated environment. As hospitals, fire departments, police stations, hazardous materials units, and businesses cope with hundreds of role-playing actors performing their assigned tasks, officials can evaluate how their agencies respond to the simulated emergency and workers gain valuable first-responder experience.[35]

The simulations also provide opportunities for organizational sensemaking. DHS exercises include an after-action review process, which allows agencies to reflect on the experience, identify problems, and share their interpretations with DHS. Federal officials then encourage the agencies to enact their interpretations by making recommendations for improvement, which the agencies are expected to follow. "The exercise process is not over when the field exercise component ends," explains one program manager. "The jurisdictions have about sixty days to get an after-action report and improvement plan to us, and then we review it and send it back to them with our recommendations. And we actually follow up with them, to make sure the improvement plan is being implemented, and that the recommendations in the improvement plan are being followed."[36]

While DHS and other counterterrorism agencies have expanded their experience with these simulations, it is not clear that they are learning suitable lessons for homeland security. By design, hypothetical histories are embedded with fake contrivances, which can lead participants to make invalid inferences. For a variety of reasons, including the prohibitive costs involved in simulating actual disasters, the training demands of participating agencies, and the need to protect participants and avoid creating a public panic, DHS exercises are largely artificial. Although exercise managers strive to maintain a delicate balance between "maximizing reality" and "minimizing safety risks," the latter often necessarily trumps the former. Scenarios are scripted, sometimes in detailed playbooks numbering in the hundreds of pages; participants know the broad outlines of each role-play in advance, including the location of the "attack" and emergency response sites; and role players are instructed to inform unwitting participants, including police officers and emergency workers, that they are performing in a simulation, lest the officials respond a little too realistically to the event.

It is difficult to know how first responders would respond to the intensified stresses and strains that accompany an actual assault. One potential danger is that, having learned their tradecraft primarily through formal training and simulations, emergency workers will possess an abundance of general technical knowledge (techne) without knowing how best to apply this information to the demands of specific emergencies, the hallmark of mētis. But, to paraphrase James Scott, each terrorist attack is unique, and "half the battle is knowing . . . when to throw the book away and improvise."[37] Compounding this problem, local officials and emergency workers who have experienced only simulated terrorist attacks may possess an inflated sense of competence, which may cause them to overestimate their ability to respond to a real event.

Another concern is that law enforcers and other first responders will make invalid inferences about terrorist behavior based on these hypothetical histories, leading them to misinterpret cues from perpetrators before and during an attack. To simulate terrorist attacks for the TO-POFF exercises, DHS has developed an elaborate database called the Universal Adversary (UA), which models a range of extremist threats facing the United States, including Islamic terrorists, domestic radicals (antiwar, environmentalist, right-wing militia groups), states that sponsor terrorism, even alienated loners and disgruntled workers.[38] While DHS is to be commended for the database's expansive coverage, such a broadly conceived adversary is not well suited to capturing the behavioral signatures of specific groups, which can provide law enforcers in local jurisdictions with critical clues in tracking down suspected militants. If law enforcement agents or intelligence analysts are searching for suspected terrorists based on their knowledge of the UA's stylized model, they may miss important clues pertaining to adversaries they are more likely to face, whether those clues stem from local Islamic extremists, abortion clinic bombers, or environmental saboteurs.

To avoid this problem, Jacob Shapiro and Rudolph Darken suggest that government officials need to run more exercises based on different types of terrorists. They also suggest that the DHS should develop additional simulations to test intelligence analysts' ability to separate the wheat of meaningful intelligence from the chaff of environmental noise. Unfortunately, resource constraints currently prevent the DHS from doing so.[39] When the department runs a new simulation, what changes are the parameters of the attack scenario rather the parameters of the attacker. The upshot is that DHS simulations are premised on a highly generalized—and static—understanding of the adversary. Yet, as illustrated in the previous chapter, the nature of the terrorist threat facing the United States, where extremists routinely gather intelligence about their adversaries and change their practices in response to counterterrorism pressure, is anything but stagnant. How well the UA prepares counterterrorists to deal with such malleable real-world rivals remains an open question.

Ironically, we may not be able to determine whether TOPOFF and other exercise drills have actually reduced America's vulnerability to terrorist attacks until there is another catastrophic attack. This exposes a tragic paradox in homeland security learning. While experience is ultimately the best teacher for emergency response and counterterrorism agencies, the costs and consequences of catastrophic failures are higher than the "value of the lessons learned from them," explain two scholars.[40] The Department of Homeland Security, not to mention the American people, are better off learning from exercise scenarios and "near failures" than real failures, even when the value of such lessons remains uncertain.

Bureaucratic Complexity and Culture

Similar to the drug enforcement agencies examined in Chapter 4, the sheer size and organizational complexity of counterterrorism bureaucracies hinders their ability to learn in complex adaptive systems. Like other bureaucratic players in the war on terror, the Department of Homeland Security contains numerous divisions, agencies, and offices with centralized decision making, multiple management levels, and ungainly operating procedures, through which information, the lifeblood of organizational learning, must flow. Designed to ensure government accountability and transparency in liberal democratic states, these institutional structures also impede robust information sharing, while ensuring that government decision cycles remain slower than terrorist ones. "Right now, there are 18 food chains, 20 levels of paperwork and 22 hoops we have to jump through before we can take action," complains one Bush administration official. "Our enemy moves faster than that."[41]

Different agencies also have their own organizational mandates, cultures, interests, and procedures, complicating the intelligence sharing and interagency coordination necessary for effective counterterrorism. Consider the missions of two lead agencies in the war on terror, the FBI and the CIA. The FBI is a law enforcement agency whose traditional counterterrorism mandate has been to develop material evidence for prosecuting alleged terrorists for crimes committed against the United States *after* they occur. In contrast, the CIA is an intelligence agency whose chief counterterrorism mission has been to gather and analyze intelligence for stopping terrorist attacks against American interests *before* they occur. Both tasks are critical to effective counterterrorism, but each requires different training, skills, and attitudes and distinct rules of engagement.

Diverse ways of thinking and doing counterterrorism can—and do— lead to conflict among intelligence analysts and law enforcers as they seek to coordinate their activities. FBI agents, trained to avoid committing civil rights abuses and to follow statutory and judicial guidelines for collecting and processing material evidence (so that it will be admissible in court), often take a different view of intelligence collection and informant handling than do their CIA colleagues, who are trained and socialized in the morally ambiguous world of foreign intelligence gathering, where information and informers are treated with different standards. Different views on permissible behavior, reflected in diverse institutional mandates and bureaucratic cultures, sometimes create tensions when agents from the two organizations work together in joint operations. Although FBI agents were originally assigned to assist their CIA counterparts in the questioning of high-ranking Al Qaeda detainees, they were eventually pulled out of these interrogations, apparently because the sessions proved too realistic in "simulating" torture for the bureau's taste. As reported by James Risen, at least one FBI agent who observed Abu Zubaydah in custody was convinced that he was being tortured.[42]

Another sensitive issue that arises in joint FBI-CIA operations involves whether to devote limited resources to building a prosecutable case against a specific target or whether to eliminate the target altogether. In the late 1990s an interagency unit dedicated to combating Al Qaeda housed at the CIA's Counterterrorist Center grappled with this issue as it developed human intelligence sources from bin Laden's network. Former FBI agent John Cloonan, who worked with bureau investigators assigned to the unit, code-named the Alec Station, describes the conflict that arose as one confidential informant, Jamal al-Fadl, shared his knowledge of Al Qaeda with intelligence officials:

> Tension filled at this point because now you have a guy [al-Fadl] that is an excellent source of intelligence, but also an excellent source and potential witness for prosecution. How much information is he going to divulge and in what format, and how can you maintain him as a witness for the prosecution without jeopardizing that? That is a very difficult issue for the agency and the bureau to deal with, particularly when the stakes are as high as what we are discussing here. I think the CIA agent that headed the Alec Station would have preferred to exploit a lot of information from al-Fadl more proactively through more robust operations targeting Al Qaeda. But we saw him as a valuable tool in the prosecution of bin Laden, and eventually our aspect of this case became more important to the [Clinton] administration, because they said if we are going to the bring these guys to justice, this is how we are going to do it.[43]

With clear guidance from senior White House officials, who emphasized bringing terrorists to justice through arrest and prosecution, the FBI and CIA were able to work through their differences in handling Jamal al-Fadl and in conducting other counterterrorism investigations. This is welcome news in the wake of the 9/11 *Commission Report* and other investigations which suggest that the FBI-CIA relationship is profoundly dysfunctional. It is also true, however, that the Alec Station and other counterterrorism units struggled to share vital intelligence with their interagency partners in the face of institutional procedures that compartment information on a need-to-know basis, legal and bureaucratic constraints on disseminating intelligence between intelligence collectors and criminal investigators, intelligence agencies' tendency to hoard information to protect their bureaucratic interests, and simple misunderstandings between agencies regarding their respective information-sharing responsibilities.[44]

These cultural, legal, and bureaucratic constraints to information sharing are not academic. The inability of the FBI, CIA, Customs Service, INS, State Department, and military intelligence agencies to share actionable intelligence in a timely manner has been repeatedly cited as one of the major intelligence failures that precipitated the tragic events of 9/11. Over a period of eighteen months, from January 2000 to August 2001, the CIA failed to provide the names of two Al Qaeda militants it was tracking—Khalid al-Mihdhar and Nawaf al-Hamzi—to a watch list used by State Department officials and INS and Customs agents to prevent suspected terrorists from entering the United States. By the time agency officials added al-Mihdhar and al-Hamzi to the list it was too late: both militants were already in the United States preparing for their roles in flying American Airlines Flight 77 into the Pentagon. When FBI headquarters belatedly realized that al-Mihdhar and al-Hamzi were in the country, it authorized an intelligence investigation to find al-Mihdhar but refused to allow criminal investigators from its New York office to participate in the search for fear of violating agency and Foreign Intelligence Surveillance Act procedures regarding the separation of criminal and intelligence investigations.[45] These incidents, along with dozens of other "missed signals" and "lost opportunities" detailed in separate investigations of the 9/11 attacks by the congressional joint intelligence inquiry, the 9/11 Commission, and the Justice Department's own inspector general, illustrate the many obstacles facing officials within and across bureaucracies in sharing information, marshaling resources, and coordinating activities quickly enough to keep track of their terrorist adversaries.[46]

The national crisis of 9/11 provided a powerful stimulus for analysts and agents from the CIA, FBI, State Department, and other federal agencies to overcome distinct operating styles, bureaucratic cultures, and traditional rivalries for the greater good of homeland security. Moreover, legislation proposed by the Bush administration and passed by Congress in the weeks and months following the attacks, particularly the controversial USA PATRIOT ACT, removed legal and procedural constraints to information sharing between law enforcement and intelligence agencies—not without alarming civil libertarians and legal scholars, who fear that the PATRIOT ACT undermines Americans' civil rights. The act unambiguously breaches the procedural "wall" separating foreign intelligence gathering from criminal law enforcement, and changes an important rule of federal criminal procedure that prohibited intelligence analysts involved in international investigations from accessing domestic grand jury testimony.

While the PATRIOT ACT reportedly makes it easier for intelligence analysts and law enforcement agents to share information relating to foreign terrorism, more than two years after it was signed into law confusion remained among law enforcers about what the complex statute actually permits. Moreover, the judicial review process for terrorism-related electronic surveillance, as authorized under the Foreign Intelligence Surveillance Act (FISA), remains cumbersome, requiring multiple levels of administrative review, even if the overwhelming majority of wiretap applications are eventually approved. The increased number of surveillance requests since 9/11, which more than doubled between 2001 and 2003, has aggravated the problem, creating bottlenecks in the FISA approval process that have the potential to slow eavesdropping orders in counterterrorism investigations.[47] Bush administration officials have expressed concern that existing rules and regulations would prevent intelligence agencies from obtaining swift approval for the large number of electronic communications they wish to monitor, even though FISA procedures allow for a seventy-two-hour grace period during which investigators can install a wiretap before obtaining court approval. These concerns reportedly led President Bush to sign a controversial executive order allowing the National Security Agency (NSA), which has traditionally focused on overseas intelligence collection, to scrutinize the telephone calls and e-mail messages of around five hundred people *inside* the United States without obtaining FISA warrants.[48]

In spite of the president's secret authorization of what amounts to warrantless electronic spying in the United States, and other possibly illegal efforts by the Bush administration to expand the government's surveillance authorities in the war on terror, the post-9/11 administrative landscape continues to feature tall management hierarchies, cumbersome bureaucratic procedures, and internal (i.e., inspectors general, general counsel) and external (interagency review committees, presidential regulatory boards, congressional committees, private watchdog groups, investigative journalists) oversight mechanisms. As in the war on drugs, these programs, when they are functioning properly, are indispensable in protecting Americans' civil and political liberties and holding officials responsible for abuses of government authority.

Nor are officials impervious to the vicissitudes of the larger political environment surrounding the war on terror, where events in one area can have important implications for counterterrorism operations elsewhere. In the wake of the Abu Ghraib prison scandal in Iraq, after numerous detainees were subject to vile mistreatment by American soldiers and military intelligence personnel, the CIA's interrogation program, which is separate from the military detention facilities in Iraq and Guantánamo Bay, Cuba, came under increasing scrutiny. In June 2004, under growing pressure from human rights groups, legal scholars, and even some military officials who questioned the effectiveness and legality, let alone the morality, of coerced confessions, the CIA suspended the use of its "enhanced interrogation techniques" pending further review by Justice Department and White House lawyers.[49] Also in 2004, concerns raised by the chief judge of the FISA court and other government officials about the NSA's domestic spying compelled the Bush administration to scale back the surveillance program, at least temporarily, and authorize external oversight and other administrative checks for the program. But the surveillance program later came back on line, and even the public outcry and political fallout that emerged in the aftermath of the spying "scandal" has not stopped the Bush administration from continuing the contentious program, which it views as essential for tracking suspected Al Qaeda militants.[50]

As these incidents suggest, existing institutional mechanisms are not foolproof, but they do provide some measure of government transparency and accountability. For this reason policymakers would be rightfully loath to allow their dissolution to underwrite an overzealous war on terrorism, a danger that even counterterrorism practitioners wish to avoid. "Western democracies have many rules and regulations," observes a former deputy director of the CIA's Counterterrorist Center. "This is a good thing because it helps prevent against a counterterrorism policy that sacrifices our core values. Tactical counterterrorist operations may be impeded by rules and regulations, such as rules that keep the FBI from barging into Islamic mosques without probable cause. If we don't abide by laws, we are undermining U.S. counterterrorism. If people think that the FBI and CIA are rogue government agencies, this will hurt our efforts."[51]

Unfortunately, as illegal nonstate actors who operate outside the rule of law, terrorists lack comparable restraints, giving them an advantage in competitive adaptation. "Terrorists have very little in the way of rules and regulations they need to follow," the former CIA official adds. "Midlevel figures may feel constrained by higher-ups, particularly leaders that micromanage them. Some extremists may feel inhibited due to this and feel they need to run their decisions by their leaders, but there are few formal rules for them to follow."[52] When extremists require their own intelligence, about both counterterrorism efforts and new ideas for conducting attacks, they can scour the Internet and other information sources without wondering whether they are violating anyone's right to privacy. When they wish to pass knowledge from one network node to another, they communicate through coded terminology, electronic encryption, and human couriers without considering whether their communications violate legal statutes or security clearances. And when terrorists wish to assault their adversaries, they plan and carry out attacks to the best of their capabilities, without worrying whether they are violating international or domestic law. Extremists follow rules that define appropriate standards of behavior, but these routines are informal, flexible, and generally free from legal review and external oversight. Such is the operational nature of terrorism, which contrasts sharply with the institutional environment that constrains—and slows down—its sovereign competitors.

Counterterrorism Networks

Many officials are keenly aware of the impediments to information sharing and coordination among counterterrorism agencies, which they hope to eliminate by enhancing communications flows within and across these bureaucracies. Since the 1980s Washington has created a number of institutional mechanisms to strengthen information flows and increase interagency coordination, including National Security Council (NSC) policy coordination committees, interagency personnel exchange programs, and interagency task forces. These programs, many of which are modeled on transgovernmental enforcement networks in the war on drugs, seek to combine the expertise of different law enforcement, military, and intelligence organizations, while removing cultural and procedural barriers to cooperation. The interagency coordination trend has accelerated since 9/11, as more policymakers come to accept, however uncritically, the notion that it "takes networks to fight networks" (I explore this proposition further in the conclusion).[53]

Interagency coordination is led by the NSC, which runs several counterterrorism committees and working groups, including the

Counterterrorism Security Group, the Terrorist Financing Working Group, and the Hostage Crisis Working Group. These interagency bodies, composed of high-level officials from key agencies and departments, coordinate counterterrorism policy and make recommendations to the president. At the operational level, interagency networks seek to improve communication and coordinate policy among different law enforcement, intelligence, and military agencies. The FBI administers numerous task forces, including the National Joint Terrorism Task Force, the Foreign Terrorist Tracking Task Force, and eighty-eight local Joint Terrorism Task Forces—all of which aim to improve information sharing and enhance coordination among participating agencies. The Department of Defense oversees several regional military commands, including Joint Task Force Horn of Africa, Joint Task Force 150, and Joint Task Force 180, as well as special operations task forces in Afghanistan, Pakistan, the Philippines, and Yemen. These interagency networks share information, coordinate decisions, and conduct joint counterterrorism operations among different American, and in some cases foreign, military service branches.[54] Finally, a number of intelligence and law enforcement bureaus, including the FBI, CIA, Customs Service, INS, Defense Intelligence Agency, and NSA, take part in personnel exchange programs by lending their agents to work in different fusion centers specializing in counterterrorism.

Interagency networks have produced mixed results in the campaign against terrorism. During the 1980s, a small, informal NSC working group featuring representatives from the CIA, FBI, State Department, office of the secretary of defense, and the Joint Chiefs of Staff overcame numerous obstacles to interagency cooperation within the large, organizationally fragmented counterterrorism bureaucracy. The working group's small size, stable membership, and frequent meetings allowed representatives from different agencies to build trust and share information more openly than they were accustomed to doing in larger institutional settings. Group meetings, which were often informal, provided a regular forum in which members could listen to their colleagues, air their own views, and create shared understandings on policy-related issues. Group interpretations were enacted by coordinating interagency responses to specific terrorist incidents, such the hijacking of an Italian cruise ship, the *Achille Lauro,* by the Palestine Liberation Front in 1985. The working group's ability to coordinate the Reagan administration's counterterrorism policy, in effect serving as the core node for a larger interagency wheel network, was bolstered by the support it received from cabinet-level officials, reflecting the president's heightened concern over international terrorism in the wake of several attacks in the mid-1980s. "This increased the effectiveness of the group by increasing its ability to cut through the obstacles presented by the interagency bureaucracy," explains David Tucker, former director of policy planning in the Defense Department's Special Operations and Low Intensity Conflict office, who interviewed working group participants.[55]

Following several domestic and international terrorist incidents in the early 1990s, the Clinton administration strengthened the NSC's Counterterrorism Security Group (CSG), giving greater priority to counterterrorism operations and policy coordination. The working group was led by a seasoned NSC official, Richard Clarke, in a new, awkwardly titled position he helped create: the national coordinator for security, infrastructure protection and counter-terrorism. Under Clarke's direction, the CSG met frequently—sometimes daily during crisis situations—to facilitate interagency sensemaking and strengthen presidential oversight. Like the earlier NSC working group, the CSG provided an important forum for senior officials to negotiate shared understandings of the terrorist threat. The CSG also served as a core node for the larger counterterrorism network, allowing policymakers to enact their interpretations through interagency coordination.[56]

At the level of policy implementation, cross-agency personnel assignments have reportedly improved communication and coordination among traditional bureaucratic rivals. Several intelligence officials I interviewed credit these interagency assignments with improving information sharing between the FBI and the CIA. "Detailees" form social networks and communities of practice with their colleagues from different agencies, building trust and fostering honest communication. Participants also share knowledge-in-practice as they pool their professional mētis in specific investigations. Participants in the Joint Terrorism Task Forces (JTTF), for example, have facilitated numerous investigations by permitting the FBI to tap into their organizational expertise. "[T]he most highly lauded member of the JTTF is often the INS," reports the staff director of the congressional joint intelligence inquiry. "INS membership in the JTTF repeatedly has allowed the FBI personnel in the New York, Boston, and Phoenix field offices to use violations of the immigration laws to disrupt and obtain information from individuals the FBI suspects of being terrorists or having terrorist connections. The INS-FBI collaboration has been instrumental in getting relevant information from these individuals."[57]

Even the U.S. military, the largest and most administratively complex counterterrorism bureaucracy of them all, has sought to benefit from interagency networks by coordinating its operations through Special Operations task forces and shortening decision cycles. During Operation Enduring Freedom, air force pilots and planners participating in a Special Operations task force adapted their targeting selection process to the challenges of the Afghan landscape and essentially abandoned the air force's standard three-day bomb-planning cycle in favor of a streamlined selection and strike process executed in twelve hours or less. On the ground, air force liaison officers assigned to interagency "A-teams" shared knowledge-in-practice with their special forces colleagues, teaching them how to call in close air support and "to talk in a language that pilots understood: smooth, calm, peppered with Air Force slang," writes Dana Priest of the *Washington Post*.[58] Once they received authorization for specific actions, A-teams were capable of responding even more quickly to actionable intelligence. In one raid a team of forty U.S. and Danish forces captured an important Taliban figure after receiving intelligence from a Predator surveillance drone that their target was on the run. "We planned, designed, and executed that operation with one hour's notice," recalled the task force commander. "Once we heard that he was moving, my guys went off and put together a plan in 30 minutes. And 30 minutes later, it was all over."[59]

Problems with Interagency Counterterrorism Networks

These accomplishments notwithstanding, interagency working groups, task forces, and personnel exchanges have not eliminated problems with information sharing and coordination within and across counterterrorism bureaucracies. The NSC working group credited with improving interagency cooperation during the 1980s did not always resolve conflicts or streamline policy coordination among participating agencies. Moreover, political fallout from the Iran-Contra arms-for-hostages scandal in 1986 resulted in the dismissal of the group's NSC representative, Oliver North, and brought increased scrutiny from Justice Department lawyers and the NSC counsel, who began to attend the weekly meetings. As the meetings grew in size, leaks to the press occurred, reducing trust among participants, along with their willingness to share sensitive information.[60]

Despite broad agreement over the threat to American interests posed by Al Qaeda and other terrorists, the Counterterrorism Security Group led by Richard Clarke became bogged down in a series of disagreements over counterterrorism strategy and operations in the late 1990s, fueled in part by contending institutional interests and personal mistrust among participants from the NSC and the CIA. "There was a natural tension between Richard Clarke's counterterrorism shop at the White House and the CIA's Counterterrorist Center," writes Steve Coll in *Ghost Wars,* his Pulitzer-Prize-winning account of U.S. counterterrorism efforts in Afghanistan before 9/11. "The CIA, in particular, had been conditioned by history to recoil from gung-ho 'allies' at the National Security Council. Too often in the past, as in the case of Oliver North, CIA managers felt the agency had been goaded into risky or illegal operations by politically motivated White House cowboys, only to be left twisting after the operations went bad. White House officials came and went in the rhythm of electoral seasons; the CIA had permanent institutional interests to protect."[61] The agency's decision in the summer of 2004 to suspend the coercive interrogation techniques used to extract intelligence from Al Qaeda detainees, techniques that were originally approved by the White House, reflected its fears of being accused of illegal activities. Some intelligence officials have expressed concern that the decision to suspend the interrogation program, and confusion over the legal limits of coercive techniques, are impeding efforts to obtain intelligence from Al Qaeda figures in American custody.[62]

While personal mistrust and the desire to protect one's institutional interests may prevent some participants at interagency meetings from being completely forthcoming with their colleagues, officials also fail to share information simply because they make mistakes. High-level counterterrorism officials work in a demanding environment that forces them to manage numerous events, policies, and bureaucratic interests simultaneously. Faced with significant constraints on their time and attention, and swamped with daily streams of problems, choices, and solutions, policymakers apply frames of reference and other cognitive shortcuts that select some issues at the expense of others. Cognitive schema reflect policymakers' personal and professional experiences and bias their interpretations, leading them to miss—or misinterpret—some problems and solutions. One former CIA executive, who sat in on numerous CSG meetings at the White House, describes how rationally bounded officials relied on individual and institutional biases to interpret information and make decisions about counterterrorism policy. In the process she provides a sympathetic critique of rational choice theory, which suggests that people make decisions by comparing a range of possible choices based on the expectation that some choices will satisfy their preferences more than others.[63] Instead, decision-making processes in these interagency meetings often resemble "garbage cans," the suggestive metaphor coined by James March and his colleagues. In the garbage-can model of decision making, problematic preferences, fluid participation, and complex problems compel policymakers to match solutions to problems not because they are necessarily optimal or correct but because they happen to be available at the time and appear satisfactory.[64]

> The real problem is that there is a huge amount of information that policymakers have to select and wade through, and often they don't have the time to do this. Ideally, you'd like to see the policymaker go through an elaborate balance of alternatives where they are considering the pros and cons of different options. Under this scenario they're carefully considering all the relevant factors that should inform the ultimate policy decision. But in reality they pick certain pieces of information, often with the help of their assistants, because they don't have the time to do an adequate balance of alternatives. Institutional biases become relevant here as the mission of the person's agency or department will largely determine what information they look at. They will also incorporate their own selection bias, which is very human and based on their own frame of reference and interests. . . . There's a tremendous amount of information out there and decision makers cannot perfectly balance the different alternatives. It's not possible. . . . I cringe when I hear some of the criticisms made of intelligence in the media and even the 9/11 Commission. They're identifying some real shortcomings, but they neglect the fact that in the heat of the battle there is no way people can absorb everything they need to every time.[65]

Several rungs down the bureaucratic ladder, members of the CIA's Counterterrorist Center, the FBI's Joint Terrorism Task Forces, and other interagency bodies have experienced their own problems with information sharing. As noted earlier, in the months leading up to the 9/11 attacks the CIA failed to share relevant intelligence regarding two Al Qaeda operatives, Khalid al-Mihdhar and Nawaf al-Hamzi, with the FBI despite the fact that five agents from the bureau were detailed to the Alec Station, the CIA's counterterrorism unit focusing on Al Qaeda. When one of these agents, who read classified CIA reporting on Al Qaeda, requested that the agency pass along information to the FBI that al-Mihdhar possessed a valid multiple-entry U.S. visa, his request was denied, then apparently forgotten.[66] Another FBI agent assigned to the Alec Station emphasized that there was a significant amount of animosity from agency employees towards the bureau's agents. He described his own arrival to the unit as akin to "walk[ing] into a buzz saw."[67]

Cross-agency employees have also experienced problems in the JTTFS managed by the FBI. Many non-FBI participants in the JTTFS essentially serve as liaisons to their home institutions rather than as full working partners in the task forces, which limits their access to both FBI information systems and their own agency's databases. For something as simple as running name traces on suspected terrorists, task force members need approval from FBI headquarters, which means navigating their way through unwieldy bureaucratic protocols. While JTTF members possess top-secret security clearance, they often have poor access to information systems, which curtails their ability to draw on these databases. To access Intelink and other intelligence databases, for example, members of the New York JTTF must leave their office building, cross the street, and enter a second building containing a secure documents room that is reportedly so small it cannot accommodate more than one agent at a time. These limitations on classified information technologies hamper FBI agents as well as the non-FBI members of the JTTFS. In the bureau's New York and San Diego field offices, even full-fledged FBI agents lack sufficient access to secure telephone lines that can be used to discuss classified material and desktop computers that store the sort of highly classified intelligence the CIA routinely deals in.[68]

The numerous classification procedures that compartment information on a need-to-know basis are another impediment to information sharing. When participants on interagency boards and task forces obtain classified intelligence that could prove useful to their home institutions, "originator control" (ORCON) and other classification procedures prevent them from sharing this information without the host agency's approval. The FBI agent assigned to the Alec Station who sought to share intelligence on al-Mihdar with the bureau was blocked from doing so by the CIA's ORCON procedures. "Agencies fight over who owns the information, who controls it, who investigates, and who disseminates," explains a Department of Justice trial attorney with thirty years of experience in prosecuting terrorism cases: "If the CIA owns the information and I am sitting on an interagency board, as I do, I'll have access to that information but I can't do anything with it. I can't discuss it with any colleagues, I can't disclose it to the court until I get permission from the CIA to do so. This is time consuming. Then, if I receive permission to share the information, other issues arise. I may be allowed to share the information, but not necessarily the source of the intelligence, whether it was from an electronic intercept or whether it is based on a single-source human informant."[69]

Initially designed to protect intelligence collection methods and sources from sophisticated counterintelligence threats, such as Cold War spies from behind the Iron Curtain, ORCON procedures have been abused by some agencies to, as one former CIA analyst puts it, "hide embarrassing secrets or information that might cause them damage."[70] Intelligence agencies also manipulate ORCON to protect proprietary methods of collecting intelligence and preserve their bureaucratic power.[71] Even when ORCON and other knowledge compartmentation procedures are used correctly, they may prevent more knowledgeable, lower-level analysts from seeing intelligence that could allow them to construct meaningful interpretations of terrorist methods and behavior, an essential component of counterterrorism sensemaking. The former CIA intelligence executive explains:

> Sometimes an issue is so sensitive, rights of readership are given only to senior people, which means that the lower-level person who has more expertise in this subject area can't see the information. But oftentimes it is only if you see lots of pieces of information from different sources that you can make the connection. With this system of security clearance and need to know, we end up relying on fewer people to make con-

nections. This is not bureaucratic caprice but is intrinsic to the problem. It's a pickle, because you don't want to put your human informants at risk. No amount of bureaucratic reorganization can resolve this. . . . In my work, I concluded that compartmentation was one of the biggest risks we faced because pieces of relevant information were not being shared with those that should have seen it. These people needed this information to make more comprehensive assessments.[72]

While some agencies have been working to reduce the use of ORCON on terrorism-related reporting since 9/11, many current and former officials acknowledge that it continues to impede the production of relevant and timely intelligence analysis.[73] "Originator control procedures are still a problem," one high-level CIA official explains. "This has not been solved. Information flows get blocked due to ORCON. It slows down the flow of information and restricts the dissemination of knowledge. Sometimes analysts will take the information out of circulation rather than have to deal with these cumbersome procedures."[74] When this happens, ORCON distorts sensemaking by forcing analysts to build interpretations, which may eventually inform counterterrorism operations and policy, without the benefit of knowledge that could improve the reliability and validity of their analyses. In a well-intentioned effort to prevent past and present adversaries from learning about them, intelligence agencies have created an anachronistic institutional environment that makes it harder for their own analysts to learn about the terrorists.

Such telling ironies are not restricted to civilian agencies. Special Operations task forces that have been pursuing Osama bin Laden and other high-value targets in Afghanistan, Pakistan, and elsewhere also suffer from information-sharing problems and slow decision cycles. Many of these difficulties are an inevitable outgrowth of the way these military organizations are designed, with compartmented planning, tall management hierarchies, and "risk-averse" decision makers who, to their credit, seek to minimize the loss of civilian casualties in counterterrorist attacks.

In Afghanistan military planning was highly compartmented, as is often the case in war, when information is jealously guarded to protect operational security—and military interests.[75] Task Force Mountain, the military body responsible for planning Operation Anaconda, did not include the air force until late in the planning stages, even though the air force was expected to provide crucial bombing support in the battle. The reason, according to former U.S. Army War College professor Stephen Biddle, who conducted a seminal review of the conflict based on dozens of classified interviews with key decision makers in Afghanistan, was that military planners feared that a more inclusive process would allow enemy Afghan fighters to learn of their plans, jeopardizing operational security. "They [Task Force Mountain] wanted to keep the number of people that knew about this operation to the absolute minimum that they believed was necessary. Their experience was telling them that if too many people know about something, then sooner or later the indigenous Afghans will find out, and as soon as the indigenous Afghans find out, one way or another it will flow around the country and get into bad places. So after having been burned a couple of times, Task Force Mountain was trying to hold the number of people involved with planning to a small number, so small, in fact, that it handicapped the efficiency of the plan."[76]

Thus, like civilian intelligence agencies, the military creates its own self-perpetuating irony: to keep their adversaries from learning their battle plans, decision makers create an institutional structure that stifles information sharing and retards sensemaking, in this case making it harder for interagency task forces to conduct joint operations. The tension between concealment and coordination with which drug traffickers and terrorists are well acquainted was not the only impediment to interagency coordination in Afghanistan. As Biddle recalls, a variety of classification practices kept Special Operations Forces, which culturally and procedurally tend to be very secretive, from sharing intelligence with the regular military forces with whom they were coordinating. Other classification procedures, in turn, kept American troops from sharing information with military units from allied countries participating in the transgovernmental network.[77]

Counterterrorism operations in Afghanistan were also hampered by an inherent tension between military doctrine, which states that the quality of intelligence determines the size of direct action raids, and the tactical imperative to maintain stealth and surprise against fast-moving adversaries. "The more uncertain the intelligence," observes Steve Coll, "the larger the required force."[78] When military planners confront unreliable intelligence—a persistent problem when dealing with shadowy, adaptable militants who frequently change their location and methods—they must marshal enough resources to counter resistance if they are to minimize the potential loss of American soldiers. If counterterrorism war planning tends to be compartmented, the operations themselves frequently end up being large and unwieldy, requiring plenty of logistical lead time—not always the best approach for executing clandestine search-and-destroy missions.

While the details of many Afghanistan operations remain classified, several missions have been criticized in the press for slow planning cycles and noisy execution. One direct action raid in Afghanistan targeting Mullah Mohammed Omar, the Taliban leader, featured cumbersome planning by decision makers in the U.S. Army's multitiered central command. The plan called for using overwhelming firepower to blast a set of buildings where military intelligence indicated that Mullah Omar might be hiding, then insert a small team of Delta Force commandos into the compound to capture Omar, along with any documents and other artifacts they might find. The attack drew on a wealth of military assets, including a company of two hundred army rangers, a reinforced squadron of one hundred Delta Force soldiers, at least one AC-130 gunship, Chinook helicopters, and several assault vehicles. After the Delta Force team stormed the complex, they came under heavy attack from Taliban forces that, tipped off by the earsplitting arrival of the bulky American force, were able to organize substantial resistance. "As they came out of the house, the shit hit the fan," one officer recalled, as reported by investigative journalist Seymour Hersh. "It was like an ambush. The Taliban were firing light arms and either R.P.G.s—rocket-propelled grenades—or mortars." In the ensuing firefight, twelve Delta commandos were injured and one Chinook helicopter was damaged. Fortunately, no American soldiers were killed. Unfortunately, the mission failed to achieve its objectives: neither Omar nor any significant intelligence was captured, and Delta Force was unable to insert a small team of undercover operators into the area as originally planned.[79]

Other operations targeting Osama bin Laden and his followers have been hindered by bureaucratic hierarchies that slowed decision cycles, as well as corresponding lags between the moment "actionable" intelligence is developed on the ground and the moment military assets are actually deployed. In 1998 and 1999 U.S. policymakers received numerous reports regarding Osama bin Laden's whereabouts in Afghanistan, prompting the NSC's Counterterrorism Security Group to convene emergency meetings of its cabinet-level officials, the so-called principals, to consider the president's options. In his memoirs, former counterterrorism czar Richard Clarke describes the delays that accompanied the presidential authorization process. "By the time the information reached the CSG, it was already getting old. By the time the Principals met and recommended action to the President, another hour or two would have passed. After presidential approval, it would take at least two hours for the missiles to hit the target. Bin Laden had to stay put throughout that time, perhaps six hours or more."[80] The unobliging fanatic rarely did.

Still, on at least three occasions in 1999 policymakers considered the intelligence on bin Laden fresh enough to authorize Cruise missile attacks. But the strikes were eventually called off because of the unacceptably high risk of harming innocent civilians and because the intelligence was "single threaded," meaning that it came from a single, uncorroborated source.[81] The CIA's subsequent review of these incidents indicated that policymakers' caution was well founded. In only one instance was bin Laden reportedly at the target site, where he was staying in a house next to a hospital. Defense Secretary William Cohen estimated that a Cruise missile strike against the house would have killed "hundreds" of civilians without necessarily eliminating bin Laden, who rarely spent more than one night in the same location.[82] By constantly staying on the move, bin Laden effectively neutralized the Cruise missile option, which during the late 1990s emerged as the Clinton administration's de facto military tactic against Al Qaeda.

These incidents and near misses, which are not limited to U.S. counterterrorism operations before 9/11, understandably increase policymakers' reluctance to make life-and-death decisions regarding potentially innocent human beings. They also have the unintended effect of further slowing government decision cycles and stymieing counterterrorism operations on the ground. In November 2002, more than a year after the war on terror began in earnest, two Predator missile strike missions in Yemen were cancelled by senior American commanders when they learned that the passengers in the targeted vehicles were nomads, not Al Qaeda terrorists. Conflict among military commanders over the nearly disastrous missions, and the five passengers, including an American citizen, who perished in the Predator strike against Al Qaeda operative Sinan al-Harethi, made it increasingly difficult "for

Special Forces teams on alert to take immediate advantage of time-sensitive intelligence," reports Hersh.[83]

Back in Afghanistan, the two-week bombing campaign against Al Qaeda and Taliban fighters in Tora Bora near the conclusion of Operation Enduring Freedom encountered similar problems. Despite several "sightings" of bin Laden, CIA paramilitaries and Special Operations Forces were unable to capture the terrorist kingpin. At one point, a team of Green Berets received precise-targeting intelligence that reportedly placed bin Laden within striking distance. But when the team leader requested approval for a snatch operation from higher-ups in the task force command structure, his request was reportedly deemed too risky and the team was ordered to stand down.[84] As the bombing campaign in Tora Bora dragged on, bin Laden and hundreds of Al Qaeda and Taliban fighters eventually fled the porous mountain region to nearby Pakistan, in some cases with the apparent complicity of Afghan fighters tasked by central command to search the cave complexes in the area. To guide their way through the snow-covered peaks, bin Laden hired members of local Pashtun tribes with intimate knowledge of the dangerous mountain passes separating Afghanistan from Pakistan.[85]

When it became clear that bin Laden had eluded capture once again, the Pentagon came under heavy fire for allowing less reliable Afghan counterparts to conduct the cave searches. But critics often ignored the logistical delays that inevitably accompany the planning and execution of large-scale military operations. "With the U.S. military being such a stylized bureaucratic beast," explains Larry Johnson, a counterterrorism consultant for the Defense Department, "it becomes a fairly significant logistics effort just to move a small group of people, and when you get into large units it becomes an even bigger show—it's like moving the circus."[86] Indeed, Pentagon officials defended their decision to use Afghan proxies to search the Tora Bora caves by pointing out that it would have taken the U.S. Marines in southern Afghanistan as long as three weeks to prepare for the operation, more than enough time for bin Laden and his cronies to slip between the jagged mountain crags to freedom.[87] Simply put, Al Qaeda militants, drawing on the indigenous mētis of their Pashtun guides, moved more quickly than the top-down, resource-heavy, protocol-laden military apparatus could, even with all the intelligence in the world.

This situation has not changed much since 9/11. Military decision making in the war on terror continues to be compartmented and centralized. Decisions and information pass through the appropriate chains of command, navigating the procedural currents established by military doctrine and rules of engagement. In September 2004, Larry Johnson, the Defense Department consultant and former high-level counterterrorism official, described a military planning exercise in which he had participated a couple of weeks earlier. The exercise was designed to test the ability of military units in a specific theater to put together a snatch operation in response to an intelligence "sighting" of a simulated Al Qaeda operative in a foreign city where Special Operations Forces have an established presence. But the process was slowed, for hours at a stretch, as officials followed formal planning protocols, as called for in counterterrorism military doctrine:

> Now, Hollywood and the average American would say, "Great, this is how you come down to the area, this element will get with the CIA guys and local folks to go out and grab the guy and bring him back to the U.S." But here is where the bureaucracy took over. The information was called time-sensitive intelligence, which unleashed a process called time-sensitive planning in the military community. The military units that were responsible for tracking Al Qaeda started to plan the operation and then briefed their general: "Okay, this is where this country is, this is the plan, this is how we are going to get there." The first briefing took place twelve hours after officials received the initial sighting report. Then a subsequent planning process kicked in, which took another twenty-four hours. The process is called time-sensitive planning, specifically geared for the global war on terrorism. It's very bureaucratized and very centralized, because ultimately you do not want anyone to go out and use military force without an authorization and permission. The earliest you would get action out of this process would be forty-eight hours, maybe seventy-two. At this point the concern is, Did the target check out of the motel, how long was he there, has he moved to another place? It is understandable, but when you have these different military, intelligence, and law enforcement agencies involved, they are responsible to their bureaucratic leadership. It is a centralized process within their own organizations, much less so when refereed at the National Security Council.[88]

Following the 9/11 attacks, the United States undertook the largest counterterrorism offensive in history, directing massive military, law enforcement, and intelligence resources in a coordinated effort to root out the transnational terrorists held responsible. In the war on terror, some government organizations have reportedly improved policy coordination and communication by participating in interagency working groups, joint military commands, and personnel exchange programs. But counterterrorism networks have not resolved long-standing problems with information sharing and sensemaking, both of which continue to be hampered by classification procedures that prevent intelligence analysts from seeing information that would allow them to understand their adversaries better; by terrorism prevention and preparedness exercises that encourage officials to draw inappropriate lessons from artificial experience; and by coercive interrogation techniques that push detainees to provide false information to their inquisitors.

Flawed as the data may be, policymakers and politicians rely on them to create plausible interpretations of the terrorist threat facing the United States. Government officials put these interpretations into practice through authoritative acts, privileging what military planners euphemistically call the "interdiction" of terrorist leaders, on the assumption that removing the bin Ladens, Zawahiris, and Zarqawis of the world will eliminate the problem, or at least reduce it to manageable proportions. Yet, as the preceding chapters show, the head-hunting approach to narcotics control has not settled the drug problem, and a head-hunting approach to counterterrorism is unlikely to win the war on terror. Instead, leadership interdiction tends to produce more diffuse trafficking and terrorist systems, as extremists and criminals adapt to military and law enforcement pressures by replacing incapacitated leaders and decentralizing their operations. What allows them to do so are the rapid decision cycles, flat management structures, and lack of bureaucratic and legal constraints that give terrorists and drug traffickers a leg up in competitive adaptation. If a focus on competitive adaptation highlights the institutional impediments facing counterterrorists and law enforcers, a focus on sensemaking suggests that policymakers and politicians help create the world they perceive, and seek to change, by enacting social understandings that often aggravate the problem rather than solve it. In the final chapter of this study I explore how policymakers—and publics—can move beyond these unintended consequences in the wars on drugs and terror.

In the summer of 1997, the DEA's special agent-in-charge (SAC) of Colombia told me that his goal was to drive the drug trade out of Colombia into neighboring countries, where he believed trafficking networks were less sophisticated and would be easier for law enforcers to identify and dismantle.[1] Ten years and several SACs later, this goal remains elusive. Contrary to the agent's prediction, the drug industry remains firmly entrenched in Colombia, as smuggling networks decentralize their operations, flatten their organizational hierarchies, align themselves with local paramilitaries and guerrillas, and make the countless other adaptations necessary to survive hostile law enforcement systems. Since 9/11, what remains of Al Qaeda and other extremist networks have also revealed their protean nature, responding to an increasingly relentless counterterrorism environment by dispersing their activities, recruiting new members, cooperating with independent militants, and exploiting the Internet to wage "virtual" jihad on the West.

As the evolutionary trajectory of Colombian traffickers and Islamic militants suggests, states confront daunting adversaries when they wage war on drugs and terrorism. Drug-trafficking and terrorist networks come in a variety of shapes, sizes, and shades of organizational sophistication, from transnational wheel networks that use core groups to steer their far-flung operations, to decentralized chain networks that rely on ad hoc coordination among largely independent nodes, to numerous cross-mutations that mix and match features of these "ideal types." Despite their variety, many criminals and combatants share basic features that complicate government efforts to destroy them.

Drug-trafficking and terrorist networks both contain relatively flat authority structures that facilitate rapid decision cycles and quick information flows. They compartment participants and information into separate, semiautonomous cells, often based on family, friendship, and geographic ties. They build redundancy into their operations by giving important functions to multiple groups, and they rely on brokers and other intermediaries to span "structural holes" between loosely connected nodes and networks. They place a premium on intelligence gathering and analysis, drawing on various information sources to learn about their adversaries and develop their own innovations. They routinely modify practices and procedures in response to information and experience, often in simple but effective ways that allow them to remain beyond the grasp of government authorities. And they both stand outside the rule of law, disregarding many legal and bureaucratic constraints that inevitably slow their sovereign competitors.

In spite of their tall management hierarchies, cumbersome decision procedures, and interagency coordination challenges, government law enforcement and counterterrorism bureaucracies also gather, record, and interpret information. But these agencies face significantly higher information costs than their illicit adversaries. The knowledge required to dismantle trafficking and terrorist enterprises is greater and more complex than the relatively simple information needed to smuggle illegal drugs or engage in political violence against noncombatants. Compounding this information asymmetry, traffickers and terrorists actors enjoy an important advantage over their government opponents: they know when, where, and how they will carry out their activities; law enforcers do not.

To support their information needs, drug enforcers and counterterrorists have created sophisticated systems to manage knowledge. These vast artificial memories store organizational knowledge and experience for participants, while protecting it from their adversaries. In managing the trade-off between concealment and coordination, many government bureaucracies err on the side of caution, ironically making it harder for their analysts and agents to access information they need when they need it. But, like their illicit adversaries, law enforcers also adjust their practices and procedures in response to experience. Reacting to external critics and changes in the international drug trade, the DEA and the Colombian National Police have made greater use of electronic surveillance and have developed numerous innovations in their undercover operations over the past several decades, improving their ability to penetrate drug-trafficking networks. In response to the 9/11 attacks and the more permissive institutional environment that followed, counterterrorists have pushed the limits of their enforcement tools, relying on warrantless surveillance orders, secret renditions, coercive interrogations, and indefinite detainment of suspected terrorists to combat Islamic extremism.

Law enforcers and counterterrorists also engage in organizational sensemaking, stitching together bits of tactical intelligence to create coherent and plausible narratives of their illicit adversaries. In the process, they weave memorable narratives that celebrate their identities as public servants engaged in mortal combat with malicious antagonists. Their intersubjective understandings, reinforced by agency administrators, help governments focus public attention on the threat du jour, be it controlled substances or terrorism, while marshaling sufficient resources for the "wars" needed to combat them. But sensemaking also tends to generate simplistic understandings of illicit adversaries, whether in the form of centralized drug "cartels" that control worldwide cocaine production or a monolithic "Al Qaeda" that oversees all terrorist attacks against Western interests. Policymakers enact these interpretations through authoritative acts, creating enforcement policies that seek to remove trafficking and terrorist "kingpins" in the mistaken assumption that this will either resolve the problem or at least make it more amenable to state control.

These dynamics unfold within complex adaptive systems featuring dozens of terrorist and trafficking networks and hundreds of law enforcement, military, and intelligence agencies. Competitive adaptation features an asymmetry of information and force between mutually dependent players. Traffickers and terrorists try to maintain their information advantage over the state, allowing them to remain hidden and continue their activities unimpeded, while law enforcers seek to capitalize on their force advantage by generating real-time, actionable intelligence against their adversaries.

Players who do well in such dynamic and hostile environments often exhibit abundant mētis. Traffickers and terrorists survive complex adaptive systems, even when their victims do not, by tapping into intuitive skills and cunning intelligence that allow them to remain more supple, crafty, and polymorphic than their state adversaries. Illicit actors often learn by doing, developing rules of thumb and practices for meeting different challenges that arise in their daily activities. They share improvisational knowledge with their colleagues through conversation and stories, enhancing their identity as smugglers and militants while preserving practices and experience not codified in knowledge-based artifacts.

While mētis is important to survival in hostile law enforcement and counterterrorism systems, the selection processes in competitive adaptation do not inevitably produce stronger, more astute adversaries. Competitive adaptation tends to weed the most exposed players out of

drug-trafficking and terrorist systems, while placing poor learners—
those who fail to swiftly change their activities and operational signatures in response to law enforcement pressure—at considerable risk.
But endurance in such environments does not guarantee superiority in
organizational form and function. In the wars on drugs and terrorism,
states face formidable opponents, not illicit "supermen" who perform
flawlessly. In fact, drug-trafficking and terrorist groups have significant
vulnerabilities that law enforcers can and do exploit. One of the more
sobering insights to emerge from the *9/11 Commission Report* is how
the planes' operation, one of the most sophisticated terrorist attacks
ever attempted, suffered from poor planning, inconsistent coordination, and clumsy execution among resolute yet often inept conspirators.[2] Colombian traffickers, widely regarded as among the best in the
business by law enforcers, have made their own share of mistakes over
the years, including ordering participants to transport large drug shipments they knew were under police surveillance and repeatedly failing
to prevent their own participants from robbing them. Freddy, one of
the former traffickers I interviewed for this book, described a number
of problems that arose in his work, including territorial conflicts between competing groups, poorly paid employees who undermined the
security of the enterprise, and fights between traffickers over women
and other sources of envy. "In this business," he concluded, "I have
seen the biggest stupidities in my entire life."[3] What makes Freddy's
lament notable is that he worked for one of the Cali wheel networks, a
transnational smuggling enterprise that at its peak was considered one
of the most sophisticated criminal organizations in the world.

Nor are the drug traffickers who succeeded Freddy and his colleagues, or the terrorists who succeeded Al Qaeda, necessarily more
sophisticated than their predecessors, although some are clearly capable of learning from the experiences and mistakes of those who came
before them. Many traffickers and terrorists manage to survive hostile
environments not because they are inevitably "smarter" than their predecessors, or because the network forms of organization they embody
are inherently superior to bureaucracies, even if they do tend to enjoy
quicker decision cycles and information flows than their law-bound
competitors. Illicit actors often survive simply because they are less well
known to law enforcers and counterterrorists who apply limited resources to groups and networks they have already identified for disruption.

Traffickers' and terrorists' primary advantage in competitive adaptation is informational: when they lose their covert edge because law enforcers have identified and located them, they face great difficulty overcoming the force advantage of states. Yet, because drug-trafficking and terrorist systems are populated by dozens if not hundreds of illicit actors, by the time law enforcers succeed in translating their force advantage into an information one, other clandestine groups have already replaced their predecessors. When this happens, the cycle of competitive adaptation begins anew, this time pitting law enforcers against different criminals and illicit combatants about whom they know very little. No matter how well law enforcers play the game, they often remain a step or more behind their adversaries.

In the remainder of this chapter, I review and expand on several findings from my research, while exploring its implications for existing law enforcement and counterterrorism policies.

Exploiting Mētis and Techne

The need for knowledge, and the need to communicate sensitive information among fellow conspirators, creates important vulnerabilities in drug-trafficking and terrorist networks. Yet law enforcers' ability to exploit this vulnerability depends in part on the type of knowledge, mētis or techne, being exploited.

Because of the manner in which it is stored and communicated, mētis is more difficult for law enforcers to manipulate. The shrewd, experiential knowledge that is mētis is recorded mostly in the minds of those who have learned it, either through their own trial and error or the experiences of others. Because terrorist and trafficking mētis is not generally codified in documents and computer disks, there are few mētis-based artifacts governments can seize, analyze, and exploit to learn more about their adversaries. Instead, drug enforcers and counterterrorists must rely on the fallible recollections of captured offenders, who have an obvious interest in shielding their hard-earned knowledge from those determined to use it against them. While experienced police officials and intelligence agents employ a variety of mētis-based interrogation techniques—some legal, others regrettably extralegal—to compel detainees to talk, aggressive questioning of recalcitrant combatants often produces unreliable intelligence. When such distorted information becomes the justification for an aggressive drug enforcement or counterterrorism campaign, the results can be disappointing, or worse—as in the case of coerced intelligence from an Al Qaeda source that became one of the evidential nuggets used by the Bush administration to rationalize its invasion of Iraq in 2003.

Even when informants provide reasonably accurate accounts of their activities, the type of intelligence law enforcers generally seek is tactical in orientation: names, phone numbers, addresses, and dates they can use to identify other illicit adversaries and prevent impending crimes. Such a focus is understandable when authorities seek to disrupt terrorist attacks or develop material evidence for prosecution. But a single-minded focus on tactical intelligence becomes a liability when it prevents agents from learning the intuitions and rules of thumb their adversaries use to change their practices and elude government enforcement efforts.

Of course, these conditions do not always apply. There are times when inquisitive law enforcers capture traffickers and terrorists who possess substantial mētis they are willing to reveal in exchange for lenient treatment, financial compensation, or other inducements. Criminals and combatants turned government informants, such as Max Mermelstein, Guillermo Pallomari, and Jamal al-Fadl, can provide valuable insights into their respective operations. Law enforcers exploit this knowledge to negotiate plausible interpretations of their adversaries, build links to additional offenders, and develop intelligence for direct action raids and prosecution.

Yet even under such favorable circumstances, knowledge provided by informants may be of limited value to government officials because of the inherent limitations of mētis itself. Mētis is fundamentally local and contextualized knowledge. It centers on the experiences of individuals performing specific activities within circumscribed contexts. Drug-trafficking and terrorist mētis is oriented toward facilitating illegal, clandestine activities in different countries during limited time periods. The knowledge governments gain from penetrating one illicit network is not necessarily fungible, which limits its applicability to other law enforcement and counterterrorist operations. The knowledge that Miguel Rodríguez-Orejuela, leader of one of the largest Colombian cocaine networks, was a devoted follower of the Virgin Mary, a man who always lit a candle to his celestial icon before retiring for the night, may have helped law enforcers track the elusive kingpin in Cali, Colombia's third-largest city.⁴ But presumably this knowledge has not been particularly helpful to intelligence agents seeking to locate other drug kingpins in Colombia, let alone Osama bin Laden, Ayman al-Zawahiri, and other high-value Salafi jihadists reportedly hiding out in the remote Pashtun tribal areas of western Pakistan.

A second limitation of mētis for law enforcement has to do with the fluid nature of illicit networks. As documented in this study, drug traffickers and terrorists often change their practices and procedures in response to feedback. Such adaptability limits the time period for which their mētis remains "actionable" for law enforcers. By the time government officials develop the sort of finely grained, contextualized knowledge geared toward specific adversaries, traffickers and terrorists have often adapted and moved on. For the same reason, while the capture of experienced terrorists and traffickers can undoubtedly help government officials diminish the capabilities of specific networks, these effects are generally short-lived, lasting only as long as it takes these agile enterprises to replace captured members and modify their practices.

Fortunately for states and the civilians they are authorized to protect, techne is more vulnerable to exploitation. To the extent that criminals and combatants rely on knowledge-based artifacts to document technical information and use training camps to disseminate this knowledge to supporters, they create potent vulnerabilities law enforcers can exploit by seizing these records and destroying their camps. Formal training and record keeping is a double-edged sword for traffickers and terrorists alike. In using manuals and information technology to record sensitive information, they create paper and electronic trails that security forces can use to track them down, learn their modus operandi, and disrupt their activities.

Training camps that double as repositories of organizational knowledge are particularly appealing targets for government authorities. These facilities often contain a treasure trove of information law enforcers use to learn more about their opponents and upset their operations. For this reason, drug enforcement operations in Colombia and counterterrorism operations in Afghanistan often include document exploitation teams that analyze records and artifacts seized during raids. The goal is to identify other network nodes for disruption and spin off additional raids and investigations. Law enforcers in Colombia have damaged numerous trafficking networks by capturing incriminating documents and other knowledge-based documents during raids on

drug-processing labs and paramilitary training camps. And U.S. officials argue that they have weakened Al Qaeda and disrupted its ability
to plan and carry out terrorist attacks by destroying dozens of training
facilities in Afghanistan and Pakistan. In this manner the codification
and storage of techne came back to haunt Al Qaeda, just as it did the
leaders of several trafficking networks in Colombia in the 1990s.

Like drug traffickers, terrorists attempt to diminish their vulnerability to formal documentation by minimizing their record keeping and
disguising their communications through code words, aliases, and electronic encryption. Such tactics, however, have their own liabilities. Dependence on fallible human memories increases the risk that sensitive
information will be lost when participants fail to recall important details—or are captured and killed by state authorities. The simple aliases
and code words commonly used by traffickers and terrorists can be
cracked by law enforcers, particularly when they apprehend participants
and get them to decode their communications. While encryption technology presents considerable challenges to government code breakers,
criminals and combatants do not always enjoy access to the software
and hardware necessary to digitally encode and decipher their communications. Relying on cryptic language to communicate operational details can also lead to misunderstandings and confusion in illicit
enterprises, even in the absence of state penetration.

There are limits, however, to the amount of disruption governments
can expect to cause by seizing knowledge-based artifacts and destroying
training camps. Even elaborate training facilities responsible for instructing hundreds, if not thousands, of aspiring militants often contain little physical infrastructure susceptible to permanent damage by
Cruise missiles and other high-tech weaponry. One reason why senior
Clinton administration officials were reluctant to launch additional
missile strikes against Al Qaeda training camps in Afghanistan during
the 1990s was that there were few buildings the expensive missiles
could actually destroy. Like the ubiquitous "kitchen" drug labs in Colombia, the Al Qaeda camps were highly mobile, allowing trainers,
weapons, and instructional materials to move on short notice to different locations in Afghanistan and elsewhere.

To be sure, Operation Enduring Freedom and the hostile counterterrorism environment that followed have made it increasingly difficult
for extremists to establish training camps and have degraded the quality of their formal instruction. But the training programs of even the

most sophisticated terrorist networks, such as Al Qaeda and the Provisional Irish Republican Army, have always been rather basic, with militants taught rudimentary paramilitary skills they hope to develop further through combat. The substandard quality of terrorism training, at least as compared with the military training of state actors, did not prevent the Provos, Al Qaeda, and other extremists from causing substantial physical and psychological harm, nor is the mediocre training today's illicit combatants allegedly receive likely to prevent the same.

For one thing, Salafi jihadists have adapted to the post-9/11 counterterrorism environment by establishing training camps in new locations, including Pakistan, the Philippines, and various parts of Africa.[5] In other countries, including the United States, they have avoided creating formal camps but still train their followers in small, closely knit groups that get together on weekends and vacations. These informal sessions are led by local extremists who draw on their own military experience to train their fellow militants. Members of one alleged extremist group gathered for secret training sessions in the Virginia countryside, playing paintball to simulate guerrilla warfare and receiving instruction in combat tactics from a former U.S. Marine Corps clerk, who subsequently pled guilty to criminal charges for his participation in the conspiracy.[6] The perpetrators of the Casablanca bombings in May 2003 underwent weekend training in nearby caves by local mujaheddin who previously trained in Afghanistan. As Marc Sageman points out, the quality of training received by the Moroccan bombers was inferior, and the operation itself was plagued by numerous difficulties. Yet these setbacks did not stop the attackers from carrying out several coordinated bombings that killed forty-one people and injured more than a hundred others. A critical breakthrough in the group's attack preparations reportedly came when its members discovered a lighter, more reliable munitions recipe on the Internet.[7]

The Casablanca bombing underscores the importance of another terrorist training mechanism, one that has become increasingly prominent in the post-9/11 security environment: the Internet. The diffusion of terrorist techne among religious and secular militants through videos, CD-ROMs, training manuals, and other knowledge-based artifacts, many of them available on extremist websites, "means you don't need Afghanistan anymore to teach people how to make bombs and chemical agents," notes Magnus Ranstorp, former director of the Centre for the Study of Terrorism and Political Violence at the University of St.

Andrews.[8] Since the war on terror began, authorities have discovered instructional materials produced by Al Qaeda in Pakistan, Indonesia, Iraq, and other countries. After forcing Ansar al-Islam, an anti-Saddam extremist group, from its traditional base of operations in northern Iraq in March 2003, American and Kurdish security forces found digital and paper copies of Al Qaeda manuals, posters, and lesson plans, which one Special Forces officer called "the Al Qaeda mobile curriculum."[9] Much like the DEA's international training teams, described in Chapter 3, Al Qaeda apparently sent instructors and experienced fighters to the area to train militants in demolitions, poisons, and combat tactics, and to assist Ansar al-Islam with its growing administrative needs.

Meanwhile, Internet-savvy supporters of the Salafi extremist movement have created virtual training camps through online publications, asynchronous message boards, and real-time chat rooms, "building a massive and dynamic online library of training materials—some supported by experts who answer questions on message boards or in chat rooms—covering such varied subjects as how to mix ricin poison, how to make a bomb from commercial chemicals, how to pose as a fisherman and sneak through Syria into Iraq, how to shoot at a U.S. soldier, and how to navigate by the stars while running through a night-shrouded desert."[10] One discussion board, apparently popular among users from the Levant and the Maghreb, recently posted a detailed description of a five-day training course in guerrilla warfare. The anonymous author of the posting emphasizes that the course is designed for beginners who operate in hostile counterterrorism environments, where "time is against the brothers, and in which there is the necessity to train by any means available." The course, which according to the blogger has been modified to accommodate shorter training periods, allegedly provides instruction in Islamic law, map reading, intelligence gathering, assassination techniques, and weapons handling, including live-fire exercises.[11]

In addition to recruiting and training supporters, Islamic militants use these websites and discussion boards to build trust among dispersed fellow travelers, spread propaganda and raise funds for their violent activities, research government vulnerabilities and other potential targets, and, increasingly, plan and coordinate terrorist operations. Demonstrating the same mētis in their cyber operations that they have shown in their physical ones, Salafi extremists have adapted to efforts

by government agents and freelance hackers to shut down these websites by moving them to different Internet service providers, many of
them located in the United States. They have also shifted to message
boards and chat rooms hosted by online discussion services and used
encryption and password protection technology, "virtual dead drops,"
and other tricks to elude their electronic pursuers. Numerous observers
have pointed out that the fluid, dispersed nature of the Internet prevents government authorities from significantly impeding the Islamist
movement's online activities.[12] Indeed, some intelligence agencies have
apparently accommodated themselves to the sites, recognizing the vulnerabilities they create for online extremists. Just as the Salafi jihadists
use the Internet to gather intelligence about counterterrorism efforts,
their state adversaries, often with the assistance of nongovernment con-
tractors that specialize in clandestine Internet surveillance, scour Islamist websites and electronic discussion boards to develop intelligence
they can use to monitor extremists' activities and disrupt planned attacks.

While the loss of Al Qaeda's state sanctuary and training camps in
Afghanistan may reduce the skills of Islamic militants in the immediate future, the network's substantial body of terrorist knowledge will
continue to spread within the broader Salafi extremist movement, even
as government authorities press on in the campaign against terrorism.
Weekend training sessions and online discussion boards provide experienced mujaheddin with opportunities to share their knowledge-in-
practice with new recruits and socialize them to the norms and practices of Salafi extremism. Sustained interpersonal contact among militants, whether mediated through the Internet or in face-to-face
meetings, allows them to build social relations based on trust and reciprocity, while deepening their identities as Islamic holy warriors engaged in a cosmic struggle against the "crusaders and infidels."
Whether terrorists learn their tradecraft through formal instruction or
direct participation, online or in battle, the diffusion of knowledge
among ever widening Islamist communities of practice presents contemporary states with pressing, unresolved security challenges.

The Fallacy of Counter-Netwar

What, then, is to be done? One answer, proposed by a growing number
of pundits and practitioners since 9/11, is that it "takes networks to fight

networks." The basic idea, derived from military doctrine on network-centric warfare, is that governments should mimic the institutional features of terrorists, drug traffickers, insurgents, and other practitioners of "netwar" by developing flatter, decentralized decision-making hierarchies and more robust coordination mechanisms. Creating interagency networks that transcend bureaucratic borders within and across governments will, according to champions of counter-netwar, allow authorities to better match the rapid decision cycles and institutional flexibility of their adversaries.[13] While not explicitly grounded in counter-netwar assumptions, many of the strategic decisions made by the Bush administration in the heady days after 9/11, including the expansion of the CIA's extraordinary rendition and "targeted killing" programs, the use of coercive interrogation techniques against suspected Al Qaeda militants, the authorization of warrantless electronic spying in the United States, and the indefinite detainment of "unprivileged" enemy combatants in Guantánamo Bay and elsewhere, were similarly motivated by senior officials' desire to maintain the government's flexibility of response in bringing terrorists to justice as swiftly and decisively as possible.[14]

On the face of it, much of the discussion in the preceding chapters could be read as implicitly supporting the counter-netwar proposition. After all, in describing the challenges of interagency coordination in the wars on drugs and terrorism, I argue that government agencies continue to be hampered by tall and centralized management hierarchies, cumbersome bureaucratic procedures, and numerous legal constraints. Some intrepid readers might infer from my analysis that if state bureaucracies could become as flat, nimble, and diffuse as trafficking and terrorist networks, while maintaining their force advantage, they could effectively destroy their illicit adversaries.

But, as I have also emphasized in this study, governments have been using interagency enforcement networks in campaigns against drugs and terrorism for years. Anticipating proponents of counter-netwar, during the 1980s U.S. and Colombian law enforcers and policymakers created transgovernmental enforcement networks to strengthen information flows, shorten decision cycles, and increase interagency coordination. Underwritten by the generous provision of U.S. training and material assistance, these networks intensified cooperation and generated trust among law enforcement and criminal justice officials from both countries. Around the same time, American policymakers created interagency counterterrorism task forces, modeled on similar efforts in the war on drugs, to combine and coordinate the resources of different military, intelligence, and law enforcement agencies, while removing institutional barriers to cooperation. While these drug enforcement and counterterrorism networks improved information sharing and coordination among participating agencies, they did not eliminate problems with intelligence sharing within and between governments, nor did they succeed in eliminating, or even substantially reducing, the Colombian drug trade and transnational terrorism.

The ultimate failure of drug enforcement and counterterrorism networks illustrates two major shortcomings with the counter-netwar perspective. First, proponents of counter-netwar often discount the inherent, sovereignty-bound nature of state enforcement networks, along with its profound implications for the way these transgovernmental bodies function. Second, and perhaps more surprising given their emphasis on the flexibility of network forms of organization, many advocates of counter-netwar do not sufficiently consider the supple nature of their illicit opponents and its implications for government efforts to destroy them.

Unlike drug-trafficking and terrorist networks, government enforcement networks are, thankfully, bound by the rule of law. To take one example, when law enforcers from the United States coordinate their activities with their Colombian counterparts through interagency networks, they must follow the same constitutional safeguards, criminal statutes, and bureaucratic regulations that restrict their home agencies. In fact, transgovernmental enforcement networks often increase participating agencies' coordination costs, along with their legal and regulatory constraints. When DEA agents carry out joint investigations and intelligence operations in Colombia, they must coordinate their activities with a range of Colombian law enforcement and criminal justice agencies. Because they are operating on Colombian soil, they must also respect the sovereignty and national laws of their host country, while continuing to observe agency regulations, many of which are based on U.S. law. DEA agents working in Colombia and other foreign countries function less as traditional "narcs" with arrest powers and more as government liaisons, diplomats, trainers, and disseminators of intelligence. Yet their diminished operational capability does not immunize overseas DEA agents from contemporary governance standards regarding democratic accountability and transparency. To help ensure that

American agents remain accountable for their actions wherever they operate, and to protect civilians from human rights abuses, enforcement networks in Colombia and elsewhere contain oversight mechanisms and administrative centralization not found in trafficking networks.

In sum, enforcement networks face significant limitations in the degree to which they can decentralize their decision making and quicken information flows because they are beholden to the same standards of accountability and transparency that govern all U.S. government bureaucracies. Even the flattest, most fluid enforcement networks still operate within the bounds of law and bureaucratic responsibility; trafficking networks do not. For this reason, enforcement networks will remain taller, more centralized, and less agile than their illicit adversaries, and this is not likely to change, no matter what proponents of counter-netwar may wish. The notion that it takes networks to fight networks makes an arresting sound bite, but in the real world of law enforcement and counterterrorism the concept is misleading—and potentially dangerous.[15]

But let us indulge the fantasies of counter-netwar enthusiasts for a moment and assume that governments *could* design an interagency network structure that effectively mimics the quick decision cycles, rapid information processing, and institutional plasticity of their rivals. This would still not eliminate drug trafficking and terrorism. While more supple bureaucracies and stronger international cooperation would presumably allow states to conduct enforcement operations with greater speed and effectiveness than before, it would not transform the basic learning capabilities of their opponents. Even if more traffickers and terrorists are killed and captured, and more illicit networks are dismantled, new and surviving criminals and militants will continue to adapt, whether they are confronted by enforcement networks or hierarchies. Traffickers and terrorists will gather information about their government rivals, change their activities in response to experience, and circulate mētis through diffuse communities of practice. Of course, some groups will fail to learn and these will be selected out of the system, resulting in a victory of sorts for states. But whether driven by the pursuit of profit or the hope for political change, enough criminals and combatants will remain to supply drug trafficking and terrorism into the near—and distant—future.

System Effects

When U.S. and Colombian law enforcers succeeded in disrupting the major cocaine networks in Medellín and Cali in the 1990s, some prominent officials declared victory, announcing that drug trafficking was, in the words of the Colombian prosecutor general, "disappearing from Colombia."[16] While many law enforcers offered more realistic assessments of the post-cartel trade, few observers recognized the implications of purging the largest enterprises from the system. Certainly no one—publicly, at least—predicted that cocaine and opium production would flourish as the country's illicit drug industry decentralized.

Yet this is precisely what happened. By focusing their considerable resources on the most prominent narcos, U.S. and Colombian law enforcers created a window of opportunity for smaller, lower-profile trafficking enterprises to emerge from the shadows of the "cartels." They also provided surviving traffickers with a powerful incentive to shift to other products and markets, including heroin and Europe, respectively, and to allow smuggling groups from other countries, particularly Mexico, to face the risks of exporting cocaine directly into the United States. Post-cartel enterprises, including transnational networks based in the North Cauca Valley and Atlantic coast regions of Colombia, proved more than capable of picking up where their predecessors left off, in some cases forming cooperative arrangements with guerrilla fronts and paramilitary groups in Colombia and trafficking enterprises in Mexico and numerous Caribbean countries.

Recent increases in drug seizures, crop eradication, and trafficker extraditions to the United States have not reversed these trends. Today, according to figures released by the United Nations, the government of Colombia seizes more cocaine than any other country in the world, including the United States.[17] This is a remarkable accomplishment for a relatively small, "underdeveloped" country that is all too often seen as a "narco-state" in the United States. But for all of Plan Colombia's successes, hundreds of groups—nobody knows exactly how many—continue to specialize in some facet of drug production and transportation. Smugglers with considerable experience frequently direct these enterprises. A number of post-cartel operations, both offshoots and new enterprises, were founded by mid-level managers of the Cali and Medellín wheel networks. Several prominent smugglers "retired" from the day-to-day business but continued to invest in shipments and share their expertise on request, suggesting that the knowledge and experience of the most prominent networks has not been lost. Numerous groups downsized their operations, flattened decision-making hierarchies, and lowered their profiles, becoming stealthier and less ostentatious, and consequently harder to eliminate. Meanwhile, drug farmers quickly replanted destroyed crops and moved their plantings into new areas, expanding the geographic scope of Colombia's drug industry and making aerial eradication more difficult. Such are the adaptations of post-cartel entrepreneurs that, in the words of the director of the Colombian National Police, "have carefully studied and learned from the mistakes of the groups that went before them."[18]

In effect, supply-reduction programs have produced a more complex trafficking system in Colombia, as hundreds of small-scale enterprises have emerged to replace a handful of large, vertically integrated smuggling organizations. Complementary system effects include the resurgence of the country's cocaine trade, the growth of a nascent heroin industry, the strengthening of armed insurgents and paramilitaries that maintain links to the drug trade, and the corresponding intensification of Colombia's long-standing civil conflict.

Another consequence of the war on drugs has been the creation of counterdrug agencies and interagency enforcement networks in Colombia and the United States whose organizational prosperity depends in no small measure on maintaining the constancy of the threat posed by drug trafficking. Having interviewed scores of narcotics agents in the DEA, the Colombian National Police, and other agencies, I am convinced that many of these individuals are committed to dismantling criminal conspiracies and reducing the supply of illegal drugs to the United States, which they view as genuinely harmful to users. But it is also true that law enforcers work within larger organizations that have their own bureaucratic interests. To preserve their institutional identity and protect their budgets, counterdrug agencies in Colombia and the United States exploit the threat of drug trafficking, emphasizing the danger illicit drugs pose to the general public and highlighting their own efforts to dismantle smuggling networks in press releases and congressional hearings that celebrate their latest achievements in the war on drugs. Meanwhile, millions of cocaine consumers continue to enjoy ample access to their drug of choice, as price and purity levels remain relatively stable throughout the United States, belying official pronouncements that the United States is on the verge of "tipping the balance" in Colombia.[19] And, while it is difficult to determine who bears a greater moral responsibility for perpetuating the Colombian drug trade, American consumers who fuel the industry or Washington policymakers who stubbornly craft the prohibitionist policies that artificially inflate drug prices, the sobering fact remains that Colombian trafficking networks continue to be major suppliers of cocaine and heroin to the United States and other countries.

Nor are Colombian smugglers likely to relinquish this role, even if the Uribe administration, with its American-supported Plan Patriota, eventually pushes the guerrillas and paramilitaries out of the drug business, extraditing the "narco-terrorists" who lead them to the United States. In this admittedly unlikely but not impossible scenario, the Colombian drug system will continue to evolve as captured traffickers turn over their operations to trusted associates, and new and revitalized networks establish alternative sources of supply and create new smuggling routes based on a near-limitless supply of containerized cargo schemes, transportation vessels, and human drug couriers.

The war on terror also appears to be producing a more complex system. While the United States and its allies effectively disabled Osama bin Laden's original network, government authorities have not eliminated the threat posed by the broader phenomenon of Salafi extremism or even the remaining vestiges of Al Qaeda. Following Operation Enduring Freedom in Afghanistan, bin Laden's network adapted by decentralizing its operations, forging ties with local militants in different countries, and broadcasting its Salafi-jihadist message through the Internet and other communication technologies. Today, what passes for Al Qaeda is no longer a transnational wheel network centered around Osama bin Laden and his shura majlis but rather a brand name with strong appeal among Islamic militants throughout the world, and a series of self-organizing, self-adjusting chain networks in Afghanistan, Morocco, Iraq, Indonesia, Pakistan, and other countries that seek to carry out violent attacks under its increasingly diffuse banner. Simultaneously, a larger Salafi extremist movement sympathetic to bin Laden's ideology and goals has flowered, buoyed in part by the American invasion of Iraq in 2003. Just as Colombian trafficking groups adapted to the law enforcement crackdowns of the 1990s by decentralizing their authority structures and dispersing their activities, so too has "Al Qaeda" responded to an increasingly hostile counterterrorism environment by becoming more elusive and amorphous than before.

While both the regional chain networks and the larger extremist movement look to Osama bin Laden and Ayman al-Zawahiri for inspiration, they operate largely on their own in planning and executing terrorist attacks. Attacks are frequently directed against so-called soft targets such as restaurants, housing compounds, hotels, and mass transit systems, where government security measures are less stringent— and civilian casualties are likely to be high. Operations are often organized on an ad hoc basis, with "homegrown" amateurs, connected through friendship networks and an unwavering commitment to jihad, coordinating their activities over a period of several weeks in preparation for a single, often suicidal, attack. While participants in these self-organizing networks do not appear to be as well trained and well financed as the extremists who carried out the 9/11 operation, they are still capable of carrying out devastating attacks, including the coordinated bombings in Casablanca, Morocco, that killed forty-one people and injured 101 in 2003, the train bombings in Madrid that killed 191 people and injured 1,800 in 2004, and the train and bus bombings in London that killed fifty-six people and injured more than 700 others in 2005. If militants from the Salafi extremist movement continue to organize and carry out at least one spectacular, media-attention-grabbing attack per year, matching Al Qaeda's operational "output" prior to 9/11, they will probably sustain the movement's seductive appeal for thousands of sympathizers and supporters throughout the world. In fact, according to *Stratfor Weekly,* there were *more* fatalities in terrorist attacks credited to "Al Qaeda" the movement (more than 800) in the fifty-two months following 9/11 than there were in the fifty-two months preceding it (fewer than 400).[20]

Numerous post–Al Qaeda chain networks appear to be led or advised by former mid-level Al Qaeda associates with considerable experience waging jihad. These battle-hardened veterans reportedly assumed greater responsibility when higher-ranking figures were captured or killed by state authorities. Many of the new leaders possess the terrorist mētis and techne to continue their activities without direct oversight from Osama bin Laden and Ayman al-Zawahiri, whose leadership roles have diminished since Operation Enduring Freedom. Several of these militants have apparently remained in Afghanistan or traveled to Pakistan, Iraq, and other countries to share their knowledge and expertise with local cells and otherwise assist them in preparing for terrorist attacks. Some advisers then leave the area before the attack is carried out, moving on to their next assignment in support of the global jihad.[21] Afghanistan, which has seen a revival in Taliban and Al Qaeda–affiliated attacks in recent months, remains an important battleground for the Salafi jihadists, who have taken advantage of the diversion of U.S. counterterrorism resources to Iraq to reorganize and retrain themselves.[22] In this manner, the diffusion of Al Qaeda's knowledge continues, even as the original network metastasizes into new organizational forms.

Meanwhile, following the U.S. invasion in 2003, Iraq has replaced Afghanistan as a magnet and training ground for Islamic extremism. While estimates of the number of foreign fighters in Iraq vary widely, from several hundred to several thousand, officials and counterterrorism analysts agree that the war is providing militants from the Middle East, North Africa, and Europe "direct, on-the-job training in a real-life insurgency, with hands-on experience in bombing, sniping and all the skills of urban warfare."[23] As described in Chapter 5, domestic and foreign guerrillas in Iraq have adapted their attack methods, communications practices, and organizational structures in response to U.S. military pressure, evolving into a more deadly insurgency in the process.

Counterterrorism officials now worry about the potential for "bleed out" from the Iraqi conflict, where foreign fighters return to their home countries armed with the lethal mētis necessary to carry out terrorist attacks. During his 2005 annual global intelligence threat briefing before the Senate Select Committee on Intelligence, CIA director Porter Goss warned Congress that Islamic militants were exploiting the conflict in Iraq to recruit new supporters, adding that "jihadists who survive will leave Iraq experienced in and focused on acts of urban terrorism. They represent a potential pool of contacts to build transnational terrorist cells, groups, and networks in Saudi Arabia, Jordan and other countries."[24] A classified CIA intelligence assessment prepared in May 2005 argues that the urban nature of the Iraqi insurgency is teaching combatants how to conduct car bombings, kidnappings, assassinations, and other guerrilla tactics that transfer well to terrorist operations, according to officials who have read the report.[25] Even if coalition forces eventually win their savage war of preemption, which appears increasingly unlikely as I bring this study to closure, the conflict may yield a deadly legacy, as more experienced, better-trained, better-connected insurgents return to their countries of origin primed to continue their attacks.

Coda: Transcending Competency Traps

To the extent that policymakers help create the reality they seek to avoid by enacting social understandings that give lesser-known, adaptive adversaries the incentive and the opportunity to emerge from the shadow of targeted enterprises, it is imperative that we begin exploring ways to create alternative scenarios. Understanding the unintended consequences of drug enforcement and counterterrorism implies that we have an opportunity, and an obligation, to learn from them. After all, if the officials who enact these strategies and programs reflect on what they are doing, they may decide to change what they do in the future. The history of U.S. drug-control policy in the twentieth century, characterized by a series of prohibition-style drug wars, counsels caution in this regard. But with the growth of search and surveillance powers in the United States since 9/11, within a national political climate characterized by expanding executive authority and waning legislative oversight, we would be wise to consider how our experience with the first long war might better inform our response to the second.

Above all, the war on drugs demonstrates that clandestine trafficking systems are not likely to be defeated by law enforcement stratagems that focus on reducing the capabilities of criminal networks. Colombian traffickers have adapted in all manners of operation and organization to counternarcotics efforts, increasing their illegal commerce even in the most hostile environments. But in spite of generating consistently poor outcomes, along with some impressive sounding policy outputs, supply-reduction programs continue to receive the lion's share of federal drug-control spending, approximately three-quarters of national antidrug budgets.[26]

Since the mid-1980s U.S. drug control has become mired in what organization theorists call "competency traps."[27] As counterdrug officials develop greater experience with law enforcement strategies and supply-control programs, they become more proficient in using them, promoting their additional use and validating their identities as professional drug warriors. To the extent that U.S. and Colombian drug enforcers have learned over the past twenty-five years, they have done so in the limited tactical sense of exploiting existing intelligence tools and analysis in their investigative work and developing numerous innovations in their undercover operations.

Acquiring competence in a particular policy or set of practices becomes a trap when satisfaction with current efforts prevents practitioners from experimenting with other, potentially superior routines. Policymakers' exploitation of existing drug-control strategies has prevented them from sufficiently exploring the merits of alternative approaches. The persistent skewing of federal drug war dollars in favor of militarized law enforcement, at the expense of drug treatment, prevention, and research reflects this tendency. Yet exploratory learning, which requires trading established certainties for uncertain possibilities, is difficult, particularly when policymakers and practitioners create social interpretations that identify drug trafficking as a national security threat and highlight the corresponding need for a militarized strategy to deal with the drug "cartels" that allegedly dominate this commerce.

Indeed, many officials, steeped in their professional identities and the rhetoric and practice of supply reduction, are likely to read my critique with caution, believing that perceived failures in the war on drugs are not due to a mistaken policy paradigm but because policy instruments in Colombia and the United States have not been pursued with enough force and determination. Such policymakers and practitioners are more likely to call for tactical refinements in existing programs than to question the underlying assumptions and values driving the prohibitionist paradigm.

For these officials, a satisfactory approach will be to continue with the sort of tactical learning that has characterized American drug enforcement in recent decades. Law enforcers and policymakers will continue to exploit existing competencies: developing refinements in undercover operations, expanding the use of electronic surveillance technologies, increasing the range and firepower of eradication programs, all without seriously questioning whether these programs are capable of eliminating, or even substantially diminishing, an international trade in psychoactive substances that enjoy persistently robust demand in consumer markets. If my analysis is correct, the United States will probably require much greater experience with failed supply-control strategies before its policymakers—and public—embrace policy paths less traveled. Meanwhile, Colombian traffickers will be content to exploit their own competencies to substantial pecuniary effect, taking advantage of the persistently high profit margins supply-reduction helps create.

If the United States hopes to achieve enduring success in the campaign against terrorism, policymakers must avoid, if it is not too late already, the sort of competency traps that have driven out exploratory learning in drug-control policy. This will require trading established certainties in existing counterterrorism policies with uncertain but potentially rewarding possibilities in alternative programs. In particular, the government should move beyond a militarized counterterrorism strategy that concentrates on reducing the capabilities of terrorist networks and devote greater political, cultural, and economic resources to addressing the root conditions of terrorism. To do so, policymakers and practitioners will need to balance existing competencies in counterterrorism and homeland security with innovations in public diplomacy, institution building, and multilateral development assistance.

In considering such exploratory learning, policymakers must candidly confront the numerous ways in which American foreign policy stirs popular resentment in the Middle East and elsewhere. Islamic extremists depend on the United States and other Western states to sustain support for their violent attacks by enacting policies that are widely detested in the Muslim world. Of course, there is probably no policy change Washington could undertake, short of reverting to a counterproductive isolationist posture, that would eliminate the desire of Osama bin Laden and other incorrigibles to attack America. But it may be feasible for the United States, working closely with the international community, to limit the spread of Salafi extremism and other violent movements by addressing the deeply felt historical and political grievances these militants seek to exploit. If this is to occur, counterterrorism policies must speak to the broader populations that provide recruits and other support for terrorists—and give them compelling reasons not to join.

A final critical lesson to be drawn from the war on drugs is that policymakers should be wary of creating organizational structures and incentives that reward threat mongering. As detailed in Chapter 6, Washington has implemented a number of sweeping administrative reforms since 9/11, including the overhaul and creation of law enforcement, intelligence, and military agencies that share a broad institutional mandate to protect American interests from terrorist attacks. When the U.S. government undertook similar measures in the war on drugs, creating and reforming specialized counternarcotics agencies, it created an institutional setting that provided politicians and bureaucrats with strong incentives to play up the same threats they sought to combat. This tendency was exacerbated by a body-count mentality among officials that defined "success" in terms of outputs—the number of traffickers captured, drugs confiscated, assets frozen, "kingpins" extradited to the United States—while largely ignoring the inputs that sustained the Colombian trafficking system—the number of leaders replaced, networks reorganized, smuggling routes resurrected, drug fields replanted. In seeking to protect Americans from harmful psychoactive drugs and reduce the social and economic costs of drug abuse and addiction, politicians and policymakers encouraged law enforcers to maintain the constancy of the threat, which was essential in focusing public attention on the drug problem and securing the resources necessary to continue their supply-reduction efforts. Along the way, they repeatedly altered their interpretations of the Colombian drug trade, creating one "cartel" after another to channel their efforts—and to celebrate their accomplishments when they succeeded in "dismantling" each one. The upshot is that Colombia's war on drugs, while superseded by other threats to U.S. national security, never really ends, as one generation of "kingpins" is replaced by an indefinite procession of others. An elite counterdrug task force within the Colombian National Police currently identifies more than three hundred "kingpins" for capture, more than enough to keep law enforcers in both countries busy in the years ahead.[28]

A clear and present danger in the war on terrorism is that politicians and policymakers, in their level-headed desire to protect Americans from attacks by violent extremists, are creating counterterrorism bureaucracies with a vested interest in magnifying the threat posed by Islamic extremism. Various agencies, including the Department of Homeland Security, the National Counter-Terrorism Center, the Joint Special Operations Command, and the CIA and the FBI, depend on the perceived dangers terrorism poses to the American people to maintain their institutional identities and secure government funding. At the same time, politicians are willing to exploit the threat of terrorism to advance their political agendas and build support among their constituents, particularly during election years.

To the extent that politicians and counterterrorism agencies stake their political and institutional legitimacy on the danger of "Islamist" terrorism, they create powerful incentives to maintain the severity of this threat over time, not by failing to crush our adversaries but by destroying those they can, trumpeting their accomplishments in the war on terror, and highlighting the perils posed by the "next generation" of extremists. Satisfaction with such a paradigm, reinforced by a body-count approach to success that largely disregards the "intake" of Islamic extremism, may lead to counterterrorism competency traps, where security forces become better at exploiting their existing capabilities, producing impressive-sounding policy outputs, and receiving additional funding to intensify their activities, all without exploring alternative strategies that address the root conditions of political extremism. In a policy environment where politicians, military planners, and intelligence officials increasingly speak of the war on terror lasting not months or years but decades, this is an unsettling prospect.

To avoid such competency traps, politicians should shun the temptation to manipulate the public's fears of terrorism for their own benefit, and policymakers should strive to create counterterrorism agencies whose legitimacy depends less on amplifying the threat of extremism and more on creating realistic expectations of our government's ability to stop it. In the end, the American people will have to be persuaded to accept a most politically unpalatable truth: in spite of our best efforts we will continue to be targeted by clandestine, agile adversaries who wish to harm us using conventional and catastrophic weaponry. No matter how energetically the government reorganizes the intelligence community, no matter how jealously it protects its institutional "flexibility" in bringing terrorists to justice, no matter how intrusively it spies on suspected extremists, no matter how aggressively it apprehends and interrogates them, at least some of what the bad guys do will remain, as one leading analyst notes, "for all practical purposes, unknowable. Some terrorist plots will go undiscovered, and some terrorist attacks, including some major ones, will occur."[29]

From this grim conviction follows a second, equally significant, corollary: in seeking to prevent our adversaries from hurting us, and in punishing them when they do, we must avoid sacrificing the political values and institutions that define us as a society.[30] If we overreact to the threat of terrorism by creating public policies and bureaucratic structures that undermine our national identity while weakening our global leadership, we run the risk of causing greater harm to ourselves than our adversaries ever could. Terrorists can and will continue to hurt us, but they cannot destroy our values and institutions; only we can do that. Competency traps are dangerous precisely because they appear effective in the short run, but they often prove self-destructive in the long.[31]

Sidestepping this scenario in wars on drugs and terrorism requires not that we fight networks with networks but that we fight networks with states, liberal democratic states steeped in accountability, transparency, and due process protections for citizens, aliens, and enemy combatants alike. These are the values and institutions that separate us from drug traffickers and terrorists. They must be nurtured and preserved, not ignored, manipulated, and subverted. Otherwise, the trap into which we readily descend to "defeat" our adversaries may prove exceedingly difficult to escape from. As slow, deliberative learners, with multiple checks and balances on executive power, constitutional democracies have the tools to avoid such an outcome. Ultimately, we rely on the openness and vitality of our political system to make sure that we do so.

Preface

1. Captain Joaquin F. Buitrago, director of International Liaison Office, Anti-Narcotics Division, Colombian National Police, Bogotá, interview by author, 18 June 1997 (my translation).

2. Homero (pseudonym), former drug trafficker, interview by author, Federal Correctional Complex, Coleman, Florida, 19 September 2000 (my translation).

3. See, for example, the analysis and policy recommendations in Louise Richardson, *What Terrorists Want: Understanding the Enemy, Containing the Threat* (New York: Random House, 2006); and Robert J. MacCoun and Peter Reuter, *Drug War Heresies: Learning from Other Vices, Times, and Places* (New York: Cambridge University Press, 2001).

4. Michael Ignatieff, *The Lesser Evil: Political Ethics in an Age of Terror* (Princeton: Princeton University Press, 2005), xi.

Introduction

1. For a vivid account of Pablo Escobar's violent death, see Mark Bowden, *Killing Pablo: The Hunt for the World's Greatest Outlaw* (New York: Atlantic Monthly Press, 2001), 246–49. For a description of Abu Zubaydah's apprehension, see James Risen, *State of War: The Secret History of the CIA and the Bush Administration* (New York: Free Press, 2006), 20–21.

2. Paul Kaihla, "Weapons of the Secret War," *Business 2.0* (1 November 2001), http://www.business2.com/b2/web/articles/0,17863,514068,00.html (accessed 8 July 2004).

3. In a speech at OCDETF's twentieth anniversary conference in the summer of 2002, U.S. attorney general John Ashcroft proclaimed, "Twenty years ago, America was under attack—assaulted by an enemy that would not just take lives, but destroy freedom and extinguish hope. Illegal drugs flooded the nation. . . . Almost eleven months ago, America came under attack once again. Just as before, the enemy that attacked on September 11 aimed not merely to kill Americans, but to obliterate our freedom, and to destroy our hope. In response, we have adopted a strategy of cooperation and coordination between law enforcement at the federal, state, and local levels. . . . This strategy of interagency cooperation and coordination is not a new one. It models the example set twenty years ago by the Organized Crime Drug Enforcement Task Force." U.S. Department of Justice, Office of the Attorney General, "Prepared Remarks of Attorney General John Ashcroft," speech given at the Organized Crime and Drug Enforcement Task Force Twentieth Anniversary Conference, Washington, D.C., 30 July 2002, http://www.usdoj.gov/ag/speeches/2002/073002ocdetfremarks.htm (accessed 24 June 2003).

4. Plan Colombia is an ambitious—and controversial—program designed to reduce the cultivation and production of illegal drugs in Colombia by 50 percent over a six-year period (1999–2005). The bulk of American assistance under the plan has gone toward the creation of several military battalions to destroy drug-processing labs and support coca eradication efforts in Putumayo and Caqueta. However, these southern Colombian prov-

inces are also traditional strongholds of the Revolutionary Armed Forces of Colombia (FARC), a fifty-year-old guerrilla insurgency that aims to overthrow the Colombian state whose local commands often tax coca growers and regulate their transactions with the *traqueteros* (trafficking middlemen) who purchase their coca paste. Although the time period for the original Plan Colombia has passed, the United States continues to provide several hundred million dollars a year in antidrug aid to the Colombian military and police through the Andean Counter-Drug Initiative. Plan Patriota is actually a Colombian counterinsurgency offensive targeting FARC forces in southern Colombia. However, U.S. support for Patriota comes from the same funding that helps finance Plan Colombia, terminating the legal fiction that American military assistance in Colombia is exclusively counternarcotic.

5. Of course, accurate and reliable measures of illegal drug production and availability, along with estimates of government drug enforcement outputs, are fraught with methodological problems and should be interpreted with caution. Over the years the U.S. government has consistently underestimated illicit drug production in Colombia, and on several occasions it has revised its drug cultivation and production methodologies to account for these deficiencies. I use these figures to illustrate broad, admittedly uncertain trends rather than to suggest perfect knowledge of clandestine drug markets. See U.S. Department of State, Bureau for International Narcotics and Law Enforcement Affairs, *International Narcotics Control Strategy Report 2006*, vol. 1, *Drug and Chemical Control* (March 2006), http://www.state.gov/p/inl/rls/nrcrpt/2006/vol1/ (accessed 10 July 2006); U.S. Department of Justice, National Drug Intelligence Center, *National Drug Threat Assessment 2006* (Johnstown, Pa., January 2006), http://www.usdoj.gov/ndic/pubs11/18862/18862p.pdf (accessed 11 July 2006); and United Nations, Office of Drugs and Crime, *World Drug Report 2006*, vol. 1, *Analysis,* http://www.unodc.org/pdf/WDR_2006/wdr2006_vol ume1.pdf (accessed 11 July 2006).

6. The 2005 *National Survey on Drug Use and Health* estimates that there are 2.4 million "current" cocaine users in the United States. This number pales in comparison with other drugs consumed illegally in the United States, including marijuana (with an estimated 14.6 million current users, according to the 2005 survey), and the nonmedical use of psychotherapeutic drugs (6.4 million estimated current users). The survey, administered regularly since the mid-1970s, defines a current user as someone who has used the drug during the month prior to the survey interview. With its national multistage sampling strategy and confidential data-collection methods, the survey is considered a reliable barometer for broad trends in drug consumption. However, it probably underestimates the amount of drug use and abuse in the United States because its sample excludes certain institutionalized subpopulations, including prisoners and residents of drug treatment centers, who other surveys suggest have higher prevalence rates. For more on the survey's results and methodology, see Substance Abuse and Mental Health Services Administration, *Results from the 2005 National Survey on Drug Use and Health: National Findings,* NSDUH Series H-30, DHHS Publication No. SMA 06-4194 (Rockville, Md.: Office of Applied Studies, 2005), http://www.oas.samhsa.gov/nsduh/2k5nsduh/2k5results.pdf (accessed 21 September 2006), 13–14, 99–101, 107.

7. As long ago as 1947, in his pathbreaking text on public administration, Herbert Simon discussed how government organizations learn from experience and "intelligently" adjust routines in response to external stimuli. In 1963 two of Simon's colleagues at the Carnegie Institute of Technology, Richard Cyert and James March, developed a theoretical model for conceptualizing organizations as "adaptive institutions" that respond to environmental "shocks" by altering decision rules and engaging in problem-solving activities. Three years later Karl Deutsch applied the concept of cybernetics to communications systems in governments and other public-sector organizations. Like Simon, Deutsch argued that government organizations receive information from the external environment through

feedback loops and modify their behavior accordingly. In the early 1970s Abraham Lowenthal, Ernest May, and other political scientists and diplomatic historians became interested in how policymakers draw on the "lessons of the past" when making decisions. Then, in 1976, Robert Jervis systematically applied theories of social and cognitive psychology to understand how government decision makers reason and learn from previous experience. Since Jervis, a number of political scientists and international relations scholars have sought to understand how policymakers and knowledge-based experts learn, and fail to learn, and the implications this has for domestic and international politics. See Herbert A. Simon, *Administrative Behavior: A Study of Decision-Making Processes in Administrative Organizations* (New York: Macmillan, 1947); Richard M. Cyert and James G. March, *A Behavioral Theory of the Firm* (Englewood Cliffs, N.J.: Prentice-Hall, 1963); Karl W. Deutsch, *The Nerves of Government: Models of Political Communication and Control* (New York: Free Press, 1966); John D. Steinbruner, *The Cybernetic Theory of Decision: New Dimensions of Political Analysis* (Princeton: Princeton University Press, 1974); Abraham Lowenthal, *The Dominican Intervention* (Cambridge: Harvard University Press, 1972); Ernest R. May, *"Lessons" of the Past* (New York: Oxford University Press, 1973); and Robert Jervis, *Perception and Misperception in International Politics* (Princeton: Princeton University Press, 1976). Examples of more recent public-sector learning literature include—but are not limited to—George W. Breslauer and Philip E. Tetlock, eds., *Learning in U.S. and Soviet Foreign Policy* (Boulder, Colo.: Westview Press, 1991); Lloyd S. Etheridge, *Can Governments Learn? American Foreign Policy and Central American Revolutions* (New York: Pergamon Press, 1985); Ernst Haas, *When Knowledge Is Power: Three Models of Change in International Organizations* (Berkeley and Los Angeles: University of California Press, 1990); Peter A. Hall, "Policy Paradigms, Social Learning, and the State," *Comparative Politics* 25 (April 1993): 275–96; Yuen Foong Khong, *Analogies at War: Korea, Munich, Dien Bien Phu, and the Vietnam Decisions of 1965* (Princeton: Princeton University Press, 1992); Jack S. Levy, "Learning and Foreign Policy: Sweeping a Conceptual Minefield," *International Organization* 48, no. 2 (1994): 279–312; Joseph S. Nye, "Nuclear Learning and U.S.-Soviet Security Regimes," *International Organization* 41, no. 3 (1987): 371–402; Dan Reiter, *Crucible of Beliefs: Learning, Alliances, and World Wars* (Ithaca: Cornell University Press, 1996); Scott D. Sagan, *The Limits of Safety: Organizations, Accidents, and Nuclear Weapons* (Princeton: Princeton University Press, 1993); and Janice Gross Stein, "Political Learning by Doing: Gorbachev as Uncommitted Thinker and Motivated Learner," *International Organization* 48, no. 2 (1994): 155–83. There is also a large body of literature on organizational learning among private-sector firms. For discussion and examples of this literature, see Chris Argyris and Donald A. Schön, *Organizational Learning II: Theory, Method, and Practice* (Reading, Mass.: Addison-Wesley, 1996); Michael D. Cohen and Lee S. Sproull, eds., *Organizational Learning* (Thousand Oaks, Calif.: Sage Publications, 1996); Mark Dodgson, "Organizational Learning: A Review of Some Literatures," *Organization Studies* 14, no. 3 (1993): 375–94; C. Marlene Fiol and Marjorie A. Lyles, "Organizational Learning," *Academy of Management Review* 10, no. 4 (1985): 803–13; David A. Garvin, *Learning in Action: A Guide to Putting the Learning Organization to Work* (Boston: Harvard Business School Press, 2000); Bo Hedberg, "How Organizations Learn and Unlearn," in *Handbook of Organizational Design*, vol. 1, *Adapting Organizations to their Environments*, ed. Paul C. Nystrom and William H. Starbuck (New York: Oxford University Press, 1981), 3–27; George P. Huber, "Organizational Learning: The Contributing Processes and the Literatures," *Organization Science* 2, no. 1 (1991): 88–115; Daniel H. Kim, "The Link Between Individual and Organizational Learning," *Sloan Management Review* 35, no. 1 (1993): 37–50; and Peter M. Senge, *The Fifth Discipline: The Art and Practice of the Learning Organization* (New York: Doubleday, 1990).

8. Lynn Eden, *Whole World on Fire: Organizations, Knowledge, and Nuclear Weapons Devastation* (Ithaca: Cornell University Press, 2004), 292. See also Diane Vaughan, "The

Dark Side of Organizations: Mistake, Misconduct, and Disaster," *Annual Review of Sociology* 25 (1999): 271–203; and Diane Vaughan, *The Challenger Launch Decision: Risky Technology, Culture, and Deviance at NASA* (Chicago: University of Chicago Press, 1996).

9. Argyris and Schön, *Organizational Learning II*, 19, 193; Michael Berenbaum, *Witness to the Holocaust* (New York: HarperCollins, 1997); Michael Berenbaum and Abraham J. Peck, eds., *The Holocaust and History: The Known, the Unknown, the Disputed, and the Reexamined* (Bloomington: Indiana University Press, 1998).

10. Jessica Stern, *The Ultimate Terrorists* (Cambridge: Harvard University Press, 1999), 60–65; John Parachini, "Aum Shinrikyo," in Brian A. Jackson et al., *Aptitude for Destruction*, vol. 2, *Case Studies of Organizational Learning in Five Terrorist Groups* (Santa Monica, Calif.: RAND Corporation, 2005), 11–35.

11. Barbara Levitt and James G. March, "Organizational Learning," *Annual Review of Sociology* 14 (1988): 320, 327; Argyris and Schön, *Organizational Learning II*; Michael D. Cohen and Paul Bacdayan, "Organizational Routines Are Stored as Procedural Memory: Evidence from a Laboratory Study," *Organization Science* 5, no. 4 (1994), reprinted in *Cognition Within and Between Organizations*, ed. James R. Meindl, Charles Stubbart, and Joseph F. Porac (Thousand Oaks, Calif.: Sage Publications, 1996), 341–67; Eden, *Whole World on Fire*; Martha S. Feldman, "Organizational Routines as a Source of Continuous Change," *Organization Science* 11, no. 6 (2000): 611–29; Edgar H. Schein, "Organizational Culture," *American Psychologist* 45, no. 2 (1990): 109–19.

12. Levitt and March, "Organizational Learning," 320, 327.

13. James C. Scott, *Seeing Like a State: How Certain Schemes to Improve the Human Condition Have Failed* (New Haven: Yale University Press, 1998), 313–15. This sort of cunning intelligence, which is not captured in conventional distinctions between "tacit" and "explicit" knowledge, is essential to drug trafficking and terrorism. For a fascinating analysis of mētis and techne, see ibid., especially chapter 9; also see Marcel Detienne and Jean-Pierre Vernant, *Cunning Intelligence in Greek Culture and Society*, trans. Janet Lloyd (Sussex, UK: Harvester Press, 1978); and Martha C. Nussbaum, *The Fragility of Goodness: Luck and Ethics in Greek Tragedy and Philosophy* (Cambridge: Cambridge University Press, 1986). For a discussion of tacit and explicit knowledge, see Michael Polanyi, *Knowing and Being: Essays by Michael Polanyi*, ed. Marjorie Grene (Chicago: University of Chicago Press, 1969); Ikujiro Nonaka and Hirotaka Takeuchi, *The Knowledge-Creating Company: How Japanese Companies Create the Dynamics of Innovation* (New York: Oxford University Press, 1995); and Ralph D. Stacey, *Complex Responsive Processes in Organizations: Learning and Knowledge Creation* (New York: Routledge, 2001).

14. Wanda J. Orlikowski, "Knowing in Practice: Enacting a Collective Capability in Distributed Organizing," *Organization Science* 13, no. 3 (2002): 252; Jean Lave and Etienne Wenger, *Situated Learning: Legitimate Peripheral Participation* (New York: Cambridge University Press, 1991); Davide Nicolini, Silvia Gherardi, and Dvora Yanow, eds., *Knowing in Organizations: A Practice-Based Approach* (Armonk, N.Y.: M. E. Sharpe, 2003); John Seely Brown and Paul Duguid, "Organizational Learning and Communities-of-Practice: Toward a Unified View of Working, Learning, and Innovation," *Organization Science* 2, no. 1 (1991): 40–57; Julian E. Orr, *Talking About Machines: An Ethnography of a Modern Job* (Ithaca: Cornell University Press, 1996); and Pierre Bourdieu, *The Logic of Practice*, trans. Richard Nice (Cambridge, UK: Polity Press, 1990).

15. Levitt and March, "Organizational Learning," 320, 327; Scott D. N. Cook and Dvora Yanow, "Culture and Organizational Learning," *Journal of Management Inquiry* 2, no. 4 (1993), reprinted in Cohen and Sproull, *Organizational Learning*, 449, 451; and Karl E. Weick, *Sensemaking in Organizations* (Thousand Oaks, Calif.: Sage Publications, 1995).

16. These transnational criminal enterprises are "Colombian" in the sense that their leaders are based in Colombia. However, network "nodes" are located in numerous countries, and their participants represent a variety of nationalities. In this study I use the

ethnic modifier "Colombian" as shorthand to refer to illicit networks that in fact are often multinational enterprises. I am not implying that these enterprises can be understood according to the nationalities of their participants, nor do I mean to suggest that most Colombians are engaged in drug trafficking and related activities. For discussion of the "ethnicity trap" that has plagued much research on organized crime, see Jay S. Albanese, *Organized Crime in America,* 3d ed. (Cincinnati: Anderson, 1996), 145–46; and Jeffrey Scott McIllwain, "Organized Crime: A Social Network Approach," *Crime, Law, and Social Change* 32, no. 4 (1999): 308.

17. Herbert A. Simon, "A Behavioral Model of Rational Choice," *Quarterly Journal of Economics* 69 (1955): 99–118.

18. Robert Axelrod, "Schema Theory: An Information Processing Model of Perception and Cognition," *American Political Science Review* 67, no. 4 (1973): 1248–66; Reiter, *Crucible of Beliefs.*

19. James G. March and Johan P. Olsen, "The Uncertainty of the Past: Organizational Learning Under Ambiguity," *European Journal of Political Research* 3 (1975): 147–71; Martha S. Feldman, *Order Without Design: Information Production and Policy Making* (Stanford: Stanford University Press, 1989), 5–6; Garvin, *Learning in Action,* 28–29; and Michael T. Hannan and John Freeman, "The Population Ecology of Organizations," *American Journal of Sociology* 82, no. 5 (1977): 931.

20. Different scholars refer to the latter type of learning as "exploration," double-loop" learning, "strategic" or "fundamental" learning, and "third-order" learning. For a discussion of exploitation vs. exploration, see James G. March, "Exploration and Exploitation in Organizational Learning," *Organization Science* 2, no. 1 (1991): 71–87. For more on single-loop vs. double-loop learning, see Argyris and Schön, *Organizational Learning II.* For a discussion of tactical vs. strategic learning, see Philip E. Tetlock, "Learning in U.S. and Soviet Foreign Policy: In Search of an Elusive Concept," in Breslauer and Tetlock, *Learning in U.S. and Soviet Foreign Policy,* 20–61. For more on first-order, second-order, and third-order learning, see Hall, "Policy Paradigms, Social Learning, and the State."

21. The notion of learning ecologies stems from the work of James March and his colleagues, who argue that organizations learn not only from their own experience but from other organizations with which they interact. The classic type of learning ecology is a "collection of competitors," in which rivals are closely linked through the diffusion of experience and the effects of their activities on one another. Despite March's profound influence on organization theory, learning ecologies remain an understudied phenomenon. However, learning ecologies are similar to Paul DiMaggio and Walter Powell's notion of coercive, mimetic, and normative isomorphism, which has been influential in the new institutionalism literature in sociology and political science. According to DiMaggio and Powell, managers from different organizations who populate the same organizational field adapt their structures and practices in response to environmental pressure and uncertainty, leading to greater institutional isomorphism over time. Complexity theory involves the study of actors who share natural or social systems and their relations, which may include combat, trade, communications, and partnership. Complexity seeks to understand how the adaptive agents who populate these systems interact—and the "emergent properties" or adaptive behaviors that result from their interactions. Empirical work in complexity, such as it is, generally takes the form of agent-based computer modeling. As elegant and sophisticated as these simulations have become, they remain computerized thought experiments designed to "aid intuition" rather than provide accurate representations of reality. In contrast, competitive adaptation offers an empirically grounded application for understanding how sets of interdependent, diametrically opposed actors engage in repeated interactions, process information from those interactions, and change their practices in response to what their competitors are doing. For a discussion of learning ecologies, see Levitt and March, "Organizational Learning," 329, 331–32. For a discussion of institutional isomor-

phism, see Paul J. DiMaggio and Walter W. Powell, "The Iron Cage Revisited: Institutional Isomorphism and Collective Rationality in Organizational Fields," *American Sociological Review* 48 (April 1983): 147–60. For more on complexity, see Joshua M. Epstein and Robert Axtell, *Growing Artificial Societies: Social Science from the Bottom Up* (Washington, D.C.: Brookings Institution Press, 1996); Robert Axelrod, *The Complexity of Cooperation: Agent-Based Models of Competition and Cooperation* (Princeton: Princeton University Press, 1997); Robert Axelrod and Michael D. Cohen, *Harnessing Complexity: Organizational Implications for a Scientific Frontier* (New York: Free Press, 1999); John H. Holland, *Hidden Order: How Adaptation Builds Complexity* (Cambridge, Mass.: Perseus Books, 1995); and Robert Jervis, *System Effects: Complexity in Political and Social Life* (Princeton: Princeton University Press, 1997).

22. Walter W. Powell, "Neither Market nor Hierarchy: Network Forms of Organization," in *Research in Organizational Behavior*, vol. 12, ed. Barry M. Staw and L. L. Cummings (Greenwich, Conn.: JAI Press, 1990), 303. See also Margaret E. Keck and Kathryn Sikkink, *Activists Beyond Borders: Advocacy Networks in International Politics* (Ithaca: Cornell University Press, 1998), 8.

23. See Steve Coll, *Ghost Wars: The Secret History of the CIA, Afghanistan and bin Laden, from the Soviet Invasion to September 10, 2001* (New York: Penguin Books, 2004), and Richard A. Clarke, *Against All Enemies: Inside America's War on Terror* (New York: Free Press, 2004).

24. For a gripping account of this period, see Gabriel García Márquez, *News of a Kidnapping*, trans. Edith Grossman (New York: Penguin Books, 1996).

25. Bruce Hoffman, *Inside Terrorism* (New York: Columbia University Press, 1998), 43; Brian M. Jenkins, "International Terrorism: The Other World War," in *The New Global Terrorism: Characteristics, Causes, Control*, ed. Charles W. Kegley Jr. (Upper Saddle River, N.J.: Prentice-Hall, 2003), 18; Stern, *Ultimate Terrorists*, 11–14; and Alex P. Schmid and Albert J. Jongman, *Political Terrorism: A New Guide to Actors, Authors, Concepts, Data Bases, Theories, and Literature*, exp. and updated ed. (New Brunswick, N.J.: Transaction Publishers, 1988), 28.

26. Jonathan P. Caulkins, Mark A. R. Kleiman, and Peter Reuter, "Lessons of the 'War' on Drugs for the 'War' on Terrorism," in *Countering Terrorism: Dimensions of Preparedness*, ed. Arnold M. Howitt and Robyn L. Pangi (Cambridge: MIT Press, 2003), 79–80.

27. John Cloonan, former FBI counterterrorism official, interview by author, 10 December 2004; "Direct Testimony of Jamal Ahmed Al-Fadl," *United States of America v. Usama Bin Laden, et al.*, U.S. District Court, Southern District of New York, 7 February 2001, http://news.findlaw.com/hdocs/docs/binladen/binladen20701tt.pdf (accessed 2 June 2004).

28. For more on Al Qaeda's chilling aspirations, see the published *fatwas* (decrees) and interviews by Osama bin Laden in Barry Rubin and Judith Colp Rubin, eds., *Anti-American Terrorism and the Middle East: A Documentary Reader* (New York: Oxford University Press, 2002).

29. Caulkins, Kleiman, and Reuter, "Lessons of the 'War' on Drugs," 80.

30. Stephen Mastrofski and Gary Potter, "Controlling Organized Crime: A Critique of Law Enforcement Policy," *Criminal Justice Policy Review* 2, no. 3 (1987): 275; Victor E. Kappeler, Mark Blumberg, and Gary W. Potter, *The Mythology of Crime and Criminal Justice* (Prospect Heights, Ill.: Waveland Press, 1993), 83.

31. Alan A. Block, "The Snowman Cometh: Coke in Progressive New York," *Criminology* 17, no. 1 (1979): 94.

32. Kathryn Meyer and Terry Parssinen, *Webs of Smoke: Smugglers, Warlords, Spies, and the History of the International Drug Trade* (Lanham, Md.: Rowman & Littlefield, 1998), 4–5.

33. Friedrich Heckmann, "Illegal Migration: What Can We Know and What Can We Explain? The Case of Germany," *International Migration Review* 38, no. 3 (2004): 1121; Peter

Andreas, *Border Games: Policing the U.S.-Mexico Divide* (Ithaca: Cornell University Press, 2000), 95–97; and Sheldon Zhang and Ko-Lin Chin, "Enter the Dragon: Inside Chinese Human Smuggling Organizations," *Criminology* 40, no. 4 (2002): 737–67.

34. Eva Bertram et al., *Drug War Politics: The Price of Denial* (Berkeley and Los Angeles: University of California Press, 1996); Patrick L. Clawson and Rensselaer W. Lee III, *The Andean Cocaine Industry* (New York: St. Martin's Press, 1996); Ciro Krauthausen and Luis Fernando Sarmiento, *Cocaína y Co.: Un mercado ilegal por dentro* (Bogotá: Tercer Mundo, 1991); David W. Rasmussen and Bruce L. Benson, *The Economic Anatomy of a Drug War: Criminal Justice in the Commons* (Lanham, Md.: Rowman & Littlefield, 1994); and Peter Reuter, Gordon Crawford, and Jonathan Cave, *Sealing the Borders: The Effects of Increased Military Participation in Drug Interdiction* (Santa Monica, Calif.: RAND Corporation, 1988).

35. See Charles A. Russell, Leon J. Banker Jr., and Bowman H. Miller, "Out-Inventing the Terrorist," in *Terrorism: Theory and Practice,* ed. Yonah Alexander, David Carlton, and Paul Wilkinson (Boulder, Colo.: Westview Press, 1979), 3–42; Manus I. Midlarsky, Martha Crenshaw, and Fumihiko Yoshida, "Why Violence Spreads: The Contagion of International Terrorism," *International Studies Quarterly* 24, no. 2 (1980): 262–98; Edward Heyman and Edward Mickolus, "Observations on Why Violence Spreads," *International Studies Quarterly* 24, no. 2 (1980): 299–305; Edward Heyman and Edward Mickolus, "Imitation by Terrorists: Quantitative Approaches to the Study of Diffusion Patterns in Transnational Terrorism," in *Behavioral and Quantitative Perspectives on Terrorism,* ed. Yonah Alexander and John M. Gleason (New York: Pergamon Press, 1981), 175–228; and Amy Sands Redlick, "The Transnational Flow of Information as a Cause of Terrorism," in Alexander et al., *Terrorism: Theory and Practice,* 73–95.

36. U.S. Congress, Senate, Select Committee on Intelligence, testimony of George J. Tenet, "The Worldwide Threat 2004: Challenges in a Changing Global Context," *Current and Projected National Security Threats to the United States: Hearing Before the United States Senate Select Committee on Intelligence,* 108th Cong., 2d sess., 24 February 2004, http://intelligence.senate.gov/0402hrg/040224/tenet.pdf (accessed 26 February 2004), 3.

37. Jessica Stern, *Terror in the Name of God: Why Religious Militants Kill* (New York: Ecco, 2003), 254.

38. See Mia Bloom, *Dying to Kill: The Allure of Suicide Terror* (New York: Columbia University Press, 2005), 120–22; and Robert A. Pape, *Dying to Win: The Strategic Logic of Suicide Terrorism* (New York: Random House, 2005), 73.

39. See Jackson et al., *Aptitude for Destruction;* and James J. F. Forest, ed., *Teaching Terror: Strategic and Tactical Learning in the Terrorist World* (Lanham, Md.: Rowman & Littlefield, 2006).

40. For discussion of sovereignty-bound states and sovereignty-free nonstate actors, see James N. Rosenau, *Turbulence in World Politics: A Theory of Change and Continuity* (Princeton: Princeton University Press, 1990).

41. Andreas, *Border Games,* 24.

42. Charles Tilly, "War Making and State Making as Organized Crime," in *Bringing the State Back In,* ed. Peter B. Evans, Dietrich Rueschemeyer, and Theda Skocpol (New York: Cambridge University Press, 1985), 169–91. See also Peter Andreas and Richard Price, "From War-fighting to Crime-fighting: Transforming the American National Security State," *International Studies Review* 3, no. 3 (2001): 31–52.

43. My focus in this study is on the criminal organizations that exist to smuggle illegal drugs (and on the government law enforcement agencies that exist to stop them), rather than on armed insurgents and counterinsurgents who fund their war-fighting activities, in part, with revenues from the drug trade. This admittedly hazy distinction becomes even more obscure in the case of some paramilitary groups that were allegedly founded by drug traffickers. But while the history of illegal drug trafficking in Colombia overlaps with the history of the country's deep-rooted political violence, the two are not identical. In this

study I provide a theoretical framework for understanding the evolution of drug-trafficking networks in Colombia, not the evolution of Colombia's political violence. For an illuminating analysis of the political economy of Colombia's larger "war system" that focuses on left-wing guerrilla organizations, right-wing paramilitary groups, and the Colombian military, see Nazih Richani, *Systems of Violence: The Political Economy of War and Peace in Colombia* (Albany: State University of New York Press, 2002). For a discussion of the emergence of guerrilla groups, paramilitary organizations, and drug-trafficking enterprises as significant, if distinct, actors in Colombia's political drama, see Marc W. Chernick, "Economic Resources and Internal Armed Conflicts: Lessons from the Colombian Case," in *Rethinking the Economics of War: The Intersection of Need, Creed, and Greed*, ed. Cynthia J. Arnson and I. William Zartman (Washington, D.C. and Baltimore: Woodrow Wilson International Center for Scholars and Johns Hopkins University Press, 2005), 178–205; Ricardo Vargas Meza, *Drogas, máscaras y juegos: Narcotráfico y conflicto armado en Colombia* (Bogotá: Tercer Mundo, 1999); and Francisco E. Thoumi, *Illegal Drugs, Economy, and Society in the Andes* (Washington, D.C.: Woodrow Wilson Center Press, 2003).

44. Marc Sageman, *Understanding Terror Networks* (Philadelphia: University of Pennsylvania Press, 2004), 65.

45. Donald R. Cressey, "Methodological Problems in the Study of Organized Crime as a Social Problem," *Annals of the American Academy of Political and Social Science* 374 (November 1967): 101–12; and Howard Abadinsky, *The Criminal Elite: Professional and Organized Crime* (Westport, Conn.: Greenwood Press, 1983).

46. Of course, many scholars seek to draw out the policy implications of their analysis. For an interesting application of social network analysis to counterdrug intelligence, see U.S. Drug Enforcement Administration, *Intelligence Collection and Analytical Methods* (Washington, D.C.: U.S. Government Printing Office, 1987), especially chapter 4. For examples of network analysis by scholars of organized crime and terrorism, see John Arquilla and David Ronfeldt, eds., *Networks and Netwars: The Future of Terror, Crime, and Militancy* (Washington, D.C.: RAND Corporation, 2001); Peter Klerks, "The Network Paradigm Applied to Criminal Organisations: Theoretical Nitpicking or a Relevant Doctrine for Investigators? Recent Developments in the Netherlands," *Connections* 24, no. 3 (2001): 53–65; Peter A. Lupsha, "Networks Versus Networking," in *Career Criminals*, ed. Gordon P. Waldo (Beverly Hills: Sage Publications, 1983), 59–87; Sageman, *Understanding Terror Networks*; Malcolm K. Sparrow, "The Application of Network Analysis to Criminal Intelligence: An Assessment of the Prospects," *Social Networks* 13 (1991): 251–74; and Phil Williams, "Organizing Transnational Crime: Networks, Markets and Hierarchies," *Transnational Organized Crime* 4, nos. 3–4 (1998): 57–87.

47. This metaphor is inspired by Stephen Jay Gould's *A Wonderful Life: The Burgess Shale and the Nature of History* (New York: W. W. Norton, 1989).

48. H. Russell Bernard, *Research Methods in Anthropology: Qualitative and Quantitative Approaches*, 2d ed. (Walnut Creek, Calif.: Altamira, 1995), 165.

49. In snowball sampling the researcher identifies potential informants, interviews informants who agree to participate in the research, and, at the conclusion of each interview, asks respondents to name other suitable informants. The technique is iterative and cumulative and allows researchers to build a small number of key informants into a large, purposive sample, even when some potential informants refuse to participate. I have found snowball sampling to be an effective method for identifying and interviewing hard-to-reach respondents with expert knowledge in drug trafficking or terrorism, including government officials and their adversaries. For further discussion on this nonprobability sampling method, see Bernard, *Research Methods in Anthropology*, 97–98.

50. Institutional review boards (IRBs) are designed to protect human informants against mistreatment and abuse by researchers. In the United States, research organizations that receive federal funding are required to have formal IRBs vet researchers' plans

for interviewing human subjects. For a discussion of the advantages and disadvantages of the IRB process, including reference to my own challenges in securing IRB clearance for this research, see Martha S. Feldman, Jeannine Bell, and Michele Tracy Berger, *Gaining Access: A Practical and Theoretical Guide for Qualitative Researchers* (Walnut Creek, Calif.: Altamira, 2003), 13–22.

51. Semistructured interviewing uses a written guide containing specific questions to ensure that each topic is covered during the interview, while allowing the researcher discretion to explore relevant leads as they develop. Semistructured interviews are well suited to single-session interviews with managers, bureaucrats, and other professionals who expect the researcher to make efficient use of their time. For more on this method of interviewing, see Bernard, *Research Methods in Anthropology*, 209–10.

52. Others who have interviewed drug smugglers also note the relative candidness of their informants. See Patricia A. Adler, *Wheeling and Dealing: An Ethnography of an Upper-Level Drug Dealing and Smuggling Community*, 2d ed. (New York: Columbia University Press, 1993), 15–20; and Damián Zaitch, "The Ambiguity of Violence, Secrecy, and Trust Among Colombian Drug Entrepreneurs," *Journal of Drug Issues* 35, no. 1 (2005): 215.

53. See Sageman, *Understanding Terror Networks*, 68; Daniel L. Schacter, ed., *Memory Distortion: How Minds, Brains, and Societies Reconstruct the Past* (Cambridge: Harvard University Press, 1995); and Daniel L. Schacter, *The Seven Sins of Memory: How the Mind Forgets and Remembers* (Boston: Houghton Mifflin, 2001).

54. During one interview, a former trafficker, illustrating a certain egocentric bias in his memory recall, claimed that his enterprise was the first to use fax machines in its operations. Needless to say, his claim did not make it into my published account—save as an amusing endnote. Arturo (pseudonym), former drug trafficker, interview by author, Atlanta, Georgia, 29 August 2000.

55. Peter B. Evans, *Embedded Autonomy: States and Industrial Transformation* (Princeton: Princeton University Press, 1995), 18; Richard W. Scott, *Organizations: Rational, Natural, and Open Systems*, 4th ed. (Upper Saddle River, N.J.: Prentice-Hall, 1998).

56. Structured, focused comparison is a method of comparing two or more cases in which the researcher explicitly "structures" the data requirements for his research, which he applies uniformly across the cases, while "focusing" his research only on those aspects of each case that are "relevant to the research objectives and data requirements of the study." Process tracing is a method for empirically "tracing" temporal and (possibly) causal patterns between explanatory and dependent variables and outcomes within and across cases by focusing on the decision processes and behavior of the relevant actors and the influence of various institutional arrangements on their activities. Alexander L. George and Timothy J. McKeown, "Case Studies and Theories of Organizational Decision-Making," in *Advances in Information Processing in Organizations*, vol. 2, ed. Robert F. Coulam and Richard A. Smith (Greenwich, Conn.: JAI Press, 1985), 35, 41. Also see Alexander L. George, "Case Studies and Theory Development: The Method of Structured, Focused Comparisons," in *Diplomacy: New Approaches in History, Theory, and Policy*, ed. Paul Gordon Lauren (New York: Free Press, 1979), 43–68; and Andrew Bennett and Alexander L. George, "Case Studies and Process Tracing in History and Political Science: Similar Strokes for Different Foci," in *Bridges and Boundaries: Historians, Political Scientists, and the Study of International Relations*, ed. Colin Elman and Miriam Fendius Elman (Cambridge: MIT Press, 2001), 137–66.

57. George and McKeown, "Case Studies and Theories of Organizational Decision-Making," 41.

58. Clifford Geertz, "Thick Description: Toward an Interpretive Theory of Culture," in *The Interpretation of Cultures: Selected Essays by Clifford Geertz* (New York: Basic Books, 1973), 5, 29.

59. Gary King, Robert O. Keohane, and Sidney Verba, *Designing Social Inquiry: Scientific Inference in Qualitative Research* (Princeton: Princeton University Press, 1994), 36–41.

60. On learning from failure, or near failure, in organizations, see Jervis, *Perception and Misperception in International Politics;* Levy, "Learning and Foreign Policy"; and James G. March, Lee S. Sproull, and Michal Tamuz, "Learning from Samples of One or Fewer," *Organization Science* 2 (1991): 1–13. The phrase is from Modesto A. Maidique and Billie Jo Zirger, "The New Product Learning Cycle," *Research Policy* 14, no. 6 (1985), cited in David A. Garvin, "Building a Learning Organization," *Harvard Business Review* (July–August 1993): 85.

Chapter 1

1. Néstor (pseudonym), former drug trafficker, interview by author, Federal Correctional Complex, Coleman, Florida, 19 September 2000.

2. See, for example, Krauthausen and Sarmiento, *Cocaína y Co.;* Rensselaer W. Lee, *The White Labyrinth: Cocaine and Political Power* (New Brunswick, N.J.: Transaction Publishers, 1989); R. Thomas Naylor, "Mafias, Myths, and Markets: On the Theory and Practice of Enterprise Crime," *Transnational Organized Crime* 3, no. 3 (1997): 1–45; Francisco E. Thoumi, *Political Economy and Illegal Drugs in Colombia* (Boulder, Colo.: Lynne Rienner, 1995); and Damián Zaitch, *Trafficking Cocaine: Colombian Drug Entrepreneurs in the Netherlands* (The Hague: Kluwer Law International, 2002).

3. Sidney Zabludoff, "Colombian Narcotics Organizations as Business Enterprises," *Transnational Organized Crime* 3, no. 2 (1997): 26.

4. There is an established and sundry body of scholarship on criminal networks. Reflecting divisions in the broader social science literature, scholars of criminal networks employ different approaches and levels of analysis in their research. Many researchers, influenced by anthropological and historical methods, examine organized criminality from the perspective of social network analysis, where the theoretical and empirical focus is on individuals and their relational ties to other criminals. Other scholars, influenced by organizational sociology, focus on the organizational level of analysis, examining how different groups within and across criminal networks make decisions, pool resources, and coordinate clandestine transactions in hostile environments. Unlike social network scholars, organizational network analysts tend to view the organizational or interorganizational network as a unique form of organization, one that is superior in many respects to markets and hierarchies. However, both social and organizational network scholars recognize that criminals operate in distinctive social systems that shape their ability to interact and communicate in profound ways. While my own research, with its focus on intergroup coordination and decision making, leans more toward organizational network analysis, I argue that Colombian trafficking networks are made up of both interpersonal networks, based on participants' family, friendship, and geographic ties, and interorganizational networks, which contain distinct groups of criminals who coordinate their activities, often on an ad hoc basis. Social networks are embedded within and crisscross larger interorganizational networks, shaping, as I describe in this study, how the latter build trust, gather information, and learn. For examples of social network analysis applied to organized crime, see Jean Marie McGloin, "Policy and Intervention Considerations of a Network Analysis of Street Gangs," *Criminology and Public Policy* 4, no. 3 (2005): 607–36; Jeffrey Scott McIllwain, "An Equal Opportunity Employer: Opium Smuggling Networks in and Around San Diego During the Early Twentieth Century," *Transnational Organized Crime* 2, no. 4 (1998): 31–54; Carlo Morselli, "Structuring Mr. Nice: Entrepreneurial Opportunities and Brokerage Positioning in the Cannabis Trade," *Crime, Law, and Social Change* 35, no. 3 (2001): 203–44; and Mangai Natarajan, "Understanding the Structure of a Drug Trafficking Organization: A Conversational Analysis," in *Illegal Drug Markets: From Research to Prevention Policy,* ed. Mangai Natarajan and Mike Hough (Monsey, N.J.: Criminal Justice Press, 2000), 273–98. For examples of organizational network analysis applied to organized

crime, see Enrique Desmond Arias, *Drugs and Democracy in Rio de Janeiro: Trafficking, Social Networks, and Public Security* (Chapel Hill: University of North Carolina Press, 2006); James O. Finckenauer and Elin Waring, *Russian Mafia in America: Immigration, Culture, and Crime* (Boston: Northeastern University Press, 1998); Williams, "Organizing Transnational Crime"; and Zhang and Chin, "Enter the Dragon."

5. During the seventeenth and eighteenth centuries, smuggling was common throughout the Spanish vice royalty of Nueva Granada, the area that encompasses contemporary Colombia. To avoid government duties and satisfy consumer demand, contraband smugglers transported food, liquor, cigarettes, machinery, and weapons across Riohacha, Santa Marta, and Cartagena. They also developed a number of maritime smuggling routes through Caribbean sea lanes that drug traffickers would exploit centuries later. For an illuminating account of contraband smuggling in Nueva Granada during colonialism, see Lance Grahn, *The Political Economy of Smuggling: Regional Informal Economies in Early Bourbon New Granada* (Boulder, Colo.: Westview Press, 1997).

6. Wayne Baker and Robert Faulkner identify this dilemma for price-fixing conspiracies, but it is applicable to a wide range of criminal activities. See Wayne E. Baker and Robert R. Faulkner, "The Social Organization of Conspiracy: Illegal Networks in the Heavy Electrical Equipment Industry," *American Sociological Review* 58 (December 1993): 837–60.

7. For a discussion of the advantages of legally sanctioned networks, see Powell, "Neither Market nor Hierarchy"; and Mark Granovetter, "Economic Action and Social Structure: The Problem of Embeddedness," *American Journal of Sociology* 91, no. 3 (1985): 490. On the advantages of illicit networks, see John Arquilla and David Ronfeldt, "The Advent of Netwar (Revisited)," in Arquilla and Ronfeldt, *Networks and Netwars*, 1–25; Lupsha, "Networks versus Networking," 59–87; and Williams, "Organizing Transnational Crime."

8. Phil Williams, "Transnational Criminal Networks," in Arquilla and Ronfeldt, *Networks and Netwars*, 72.

9. Ibid., 81.

10. Ronald S. Burt, *Structural Holes: The Social Structure of Competition* (Cambridge: Harvard University Press, 1992).

11. Bruce M. Bagley, "Globalisation and Latin American and Caribbean Organised Crime," *Global Crime* 6, no. 1 (2004): 32–53.

12. Arturo, interview.

13. Freddy (pseudonym), former drug trafficker, interview by author, Federal Correctional Complex, Coleman, Florida, 19 September 2000 (my translation).

14. Arturo, interview.

15. Freddy, interview.

16. Arturo, interview.

17. Ibid.

18. Freddy, interview.

19. For a discussion of rules and routines in legally sanctioned organizations, see Cohen and Bacdayan, "Organizational Routines Are Stored as Procedural Memory," 348; Feldman, "Organizational Routines as a Source of Continuous Change," 611; Levitt and March, "Organizational Learning," 320; James G. March and Herbert A. Simon, *Organizations* (New York: John Wiley & Sons, 1958), 145; Barry Posen, *Sources of Military Doctrine: France, Britain, and Germany Between the World Wars* (Ithaca: Cornell University Press, 1984), 44; and Karl E. Weick, *The Social Psychology of Organizing*, 2d ed. (New York: Random House, 1979), 112–15.

20. Fernando Arenas (former drug trafficker), *Frontline: Drug Wars*, http://www.pbs.org/wgbh/pages/frontline/shows/drugs/interviews/arenas.html (accessed 30 January 2004).

21. Guillermo Pallomari, direct testimony, trial transcript, *United States of America v. Michael Abbell, William Moran, Luis Grajales, Eddy Martinez, Ramon Martinez, J. L. Pereira-*

Salas et al., U.S. District Court, Southern District of Florida, Miami Division, Case No. 93 470-CR-WMH, vol. 36 (17 July 1997), 5938.

22. Ibid., vol. 40 (28 July 1997), 6481–93; Gerardo Reyes, *Made in Miami: Vidas de narcos, santos, seductores, caudillos y soplones* (Bogotá: Planeta Colombiana Editorial, 1999), 145–49.

23. Darío Betancourt Echeverry, *Mediadores, rebuscadores, traquetos y narcos: Valle del Cauca, 1890–1997* (Bogotá: Ediciones Antropos, 1998), 159 (my translation). Tragically, Darío Betancourt was later murdered by unknown assailants.

24. Homero, interview.

25. Freddy, interview.

26. Homero, interview. A number of traffickers start off as mules and work their way up the trade. "I arrested Juan Ramon Mattaballesteros at Dulles Airport in 1969 with 50 kilograms of cocaine," explains Thomas Cash, a former DEA official, referring to a notorious Honduran trafficker with extensive ties to Colombian groups. "He had flown from Bogotá to Guatemala City to Dulles Airport. . . . He started off like all of them. They start off as grunts. We would call them mules carrying these suitcases and so forth. That typically is the way they start off. But this is not a rapid progression. You don't buy cocaine on your American Express Card. You have to have cash. And, of course, if you don't pay, then you have to die. So it's a high stakes business that not just everybody enters and it takes a long time to build up your credibility." Thomas Cash, former DEA special agent-in-charge, Miami Division, interview by author, Miami, Florida, 3 August 1999.

27. Freddy, interview; Joseph R. Fuentes, *The Life of a Cell*, Ph.D. diss., City University of New York, Criminal Justice Department, 1998, 164–66.

28. Edgar Alfredo Garzón Saboyá, "Aspectos legales y praxis del narcotráfico y lavado de dinero," in *Drogas ilícitas en Colombia: Su impacto económico, político y social*, Francisco E. Thoumi et al. (Bogotá: Planeta Colombiana Editorial, 1997), 347–408.

29. Douglas Farah, "Colombian Drug Lords Ran Empire Behind Bars," *Washington Post*, 26 December 1996, A37.

30. Néstor, interview.

31. Head of counternarcotics unit, Judicial Police Directorate, Colombian National Police, interview by author, Bogotá, Colombia, 21 July 2000 (my translation).

32. Homero, interview.

33. Colombian government prosecutor, National Prosecutor's Office, interview by author, Bogotá, Colombia, 11 July 2000 (my translation).

34. Official in drug enforcement, Colombian National Police, interview by author, Bogotá, Colombia, 21 July 2000 (my translation).

Chapter 2

1. The following example of organizational adaptation is drawn from the autobiography and congressional testimony of Max Mermelstein. See Max Mermelstein, as told to Robin Moore and Richard Smitten, *The Man Who Made It Snow* (New York: Simon and Schuster, 1990), 115–23, 145–48, 154–55; and U.S. Congress, House Committee on Banking, Finance and Urban Affairs, Subcommittee on Financial Institutions Supervision, Regulation and Insurance, "Statement of Witness Appearing Anonymously Under the Federal Witness Protection Program," *Money Laundering: Hearings Before the Subcommittee on Financial Institutions Supervision, Regulation and Insurance of the Committee on Banking, Finance and Urban Affairs*, 101st Cong., 1st sess., 14–15 November 1989 (Washington, D.C.: U.S. Government Printing Office, 1990). DEA officials familiar with this case confirm the accuracy of Mermelstein's account. Cash, interview; head of DEA intelligence group, interview by author, Bogotá, Colombia, 9 March 2000. However, for a critical review of Mer-

melstein's memoir and its author, see Bill Long, "When a Weasel Sings," *Los Angeles Times,* 5 August 1990, 3.

2. Mermelstein, *Man Who Made It Snow,* 123.

3. Freddy, interview.

4. U.S. Drug Enforcement Administration, Intelligence Division, *The Drug Trade in Colombia: A Threat Assessment* (South America/Caribbean Strategic Intelligence Unit, Office of International Intelligence), DEA-02006, March 2002, http://www.dea.gov/pubs/intel/02006/indexp.html (accessed 13 November 2002).

5. Richard L. Daft and Karl E. Weick, "Toward a Model of Organizations as Interpretation Systems," *Academy of Management Review* 9, no. 2 (1984): 284–95; March and Olsen, "Uncertainty of the Past"; and Weick, *Sensemaking in Organizations.* My discussion of sensemaking also draws on Brown and Duguid, "Organizational Learning and Communities-of-Practice," and Scott, *Seeing Like a State.*

6. Scott, *Seeing Like a State,* 313; and Detienne and Vernant, *Cunning Intelligence in Greek Culture and Society,* 3, 20, 44.

7. Detienne and Vernant, *Cunning Intelligence in Greek Culture and Society,* 20.

8. Arturo, interview.

9. K. Hawkeye Gross, *Drug Smuggling: The Forbidden Book* (Boulder, Colo.: Paladin Press, 1992), 54.

10. Arturo, interview.

11. Mermelstein, *Man Who Made It Snow,* 59–61.

12. Freddy, interview.

13. Third superceding indictment, *United States of America v. Michael Abbell, William Moran, Luis Grajales, Eddy Martinez, Ramon Martinez, J. L. Pereira-Salas, et al.,* Case No. 93 470-CR-WMH (n.d.), 9, 17–18; Mermelstein, *Man Who Made It Snow,* 59; Reyes, *Made in Miami,* 180–81.

14. Scott, *Seeing Like a State,* 316, 319–20; Nussbaum, *Fragility of Goodness,* 95.

15. Ernesto (pseudonym), former coca paste processor, interview by author, Bogotá, Colombia, 4 April 2000 (my translation).

16. Dick Butte, *El sueño de la tierra propia: Un reportaje gráfico sobre una familia de colonos colombianos cultivadores de coca* (Bogotá: El Áncora Editores, 1990), 103 (my translation).

17. Jim McGee, "Drug Smuggling Industry Is Built on Franchises," *Washington Post,* 26 March 1995, A1.

18. U.S. Congress, Senate, Permanent Subcommittee on Investigations of the Committee on Governmental Affairs, testimony of Diego Viafara Salinas, *Hearings on the Structure of International Trafficking Organizations,* 101st Cong., 1st sess., 12–13 September 1989 (Washington, D.C.: U.S. Government Printing Office, 1989), 71–74. See also Carlos Medina Gallego, *Autodefensas, paramilitares y narcotráfico en Colombia: Origen, desarrollo y consolidación; El caso "Puerto Boyacá* (Bogotá: Editorial Documentos Periodísticos, 1990); and Robin Kirk, *More Terrible than Death: Violence, Drugs, and America's War in Colombia* (New York: Public Affairs, 2004).

19. For discussion of organizational memories, see Argyris and Schön, *Organizational Learning II,* 16; Levitt and March, "Organizational Learning," 327; and Simon, *Administrative Behavior,* 218. For a discussion of knowledge-laden routines, see Eden, *Whole World on Fire,* 3.

20. Head of DEA intelligence group, interview by author, Bogotá, Colombia, 9 March 2000; Jon Nordheimer, "U.S. Details Workings of Vast Drug Ring," *New York Times,* 19 November 1986.

21. *El Tiempo,* "Los secretos del manual de vuelo de los Rodríguez," 8 June 1997, 12A; Farah, "Colombian Drug Lords Ran Empire Behind Bars."

22. U.S. and Colombian officials, interviews by author; Pallomari, testimony, vol. 35

(16 July 1997), 37–38; Ron Chepesiuk, *The Bullet or the Bribe: Taking Down Colombia's Cali Drug Cartel* (Westport, Conn.: Praeger, 2003), 243–44.

23. Cash, interview.

24. Gross, *Drug Smuggling*, 43.

25. Although organizational sociologists emphasize the learning benefits of legally sanctioned networks, scholars of illicit networks have been slow to recognize this function, even as they highlight the "flexibility" of criminal enterprises. See Joel M. Podolny and Karen L. Page, "Network Forms of Organization," *Annual Review of Sociology* 24 (1998): 62; Mark S. Granovetter, "The Strength of Weak Ties," *American Journal of Sociology* 78, no. 6 (1973): 1360–80; and Powell, "Neither Market nor Hierarchy."

26. Peter A. Lupsha, "Transnational Organized Crime versus the Nation-State," *Transnational Organized Crime* 2, no. 1 (1996): 34.

27. Various Colombian and U.S. officials, Bogotá and Washington, D.C., interviews by author; *Cambio*, "'Made in' Colombia," 24 July 2000, 36–37; Rosso José Serrano Cadena, with Santiago Gamboa. *Jaque mate: De cómo la policía le ganó la partida a "el ajedrecista" y a los cartels del narcotráfico* (Bogotá: Editorial Norma, 1999), 50–51; Zabludoff, "Colombian Narcotics Organizations as Business Enterprises," 29.

28. Arturo, interview.

29. For a discussion of the role problems can play in stimulating organizational search, see Argyris and Schön, *Organizational Learning II;* Cyert and March, *Behavioral Theory of the Firm;* Garvin, *Learning in Action;* James G. March and Johan P. Olsen, *Rediscovering Institutions: The Organizational Basis of Politics* (New York: Free Press, 1989); and Weick, *Sensemaking in Organizations.*

30. Mermelstein, *Man Who Made It Snow*, 118; DEA group supervisor, interview by author, Bogotá, Colombia, 15 June 2000.

31. Discovery is a set of procedures in the U.S. legal system that allows parties in a civil or criminal dispute to access information that may be used against them in court proceedings. These procedures are designed to help disputants prepare for trial, encourage pretrial settlement, and expose insubstantial claims that should not proceed to trial.

32. Various U.S. and Colombian officials, interviews; Edward J. Kacerosky, "Search Warrant Affidavit of Special Agent Edward Kacerosky," Case No. 93-470-CR-WMH (1 and 5 September 1994), 36, 53, 67–68; Jim McGee and Brian Duffy, *Main Justice: The Men and Women Who Enforce the Nation's Criminal Laws and Guard Its Liberties* (New York: Touchstone, 1997), 65–66; third superceding indictment, *U.S. v. Abbell et al.*, 36–38.

33. Cash, interview.

34. Various U.S. and Colombian officials, interviews. See also Berkeley Rice, *Trafficking: The Boom and Bust of the Air America Cocaine Ring* (New York: Charles Scribner's Sons, 1989), 83; John Kerry, *New War: The Web of Crime That Threatens America's Security* (New York: Simon and Schuster, 1997), 78; U.S. Congress, Senate, "Prepared Statement of the Acting Administrator, Francis M. Mullen, Jr.," *DEA Oversight and Authorization, Hearing Before the Subcommittee on Security and Terrorism of the Committee in the Judiciary*, U.S. Senate, 98th Cong., 1st sess., 23 February 1983 (Washington: U.S. Government Printing Office, 1983), 25, 27; Serrano Cadena, with Gamboa, *Jaque mate*, 154; House Subcommittee, "Statement of Witness Appearing Anonymously" (Mermelstein), 10.

35. Néstor, interview.

36. See Lave and Wenger, *Situated Learning;* Nicolini, Gherardi, and Yanow, *Knowing in Organizations;* Brown and Duguid, "Organizational Learning and Communities-of-Practice"; Orlikowski, "Knowing in Practice"; and Orr, *Talking About Machines.* These scholars draw heavily on Pierre Bourdieu's *Logic of Practice*, particularly Book I, chapter 3, "Structures, Habitus, and Practices," 52–65.

37. Néstor, interview. For a seminal analysis of how friendship networks influence the diffusion of information among job seekers in legal markets, see Granovetter, "Strength of Weak Ties."

38. Arturo, interview.

39. Senior advisor to President Andrés Pastrana for crime and terrorism control, interview by author, Bogotá, Colombia (8 June 2000) (my translation).

40. Germán Castro Caycedo, *En secreto* (Bogotá: Planeta Colombiana Editorial, 1996), 284.

41. Homero, interview.

42. The classic example of "efficiency" or "productive" learning is found in airplane manufacturing, where, beginning in the 1930s, economists discovered that the costs of airplane manufacturing fell predictably with increased production volumes. Many scholars view these production increases as proxies for the accumulation of greater skills and knowledge through task repetition. This phenomenon—labeled the "learning" or "experience" curve—was subsequently found in a number of manufacturing industries and other tasks involving repetition, although learning rates varied considerably across industries, products, and time. For the seminal study of airplane manufacturing, see Theodore P. Wright, "Factors Affecting the Costs of Airplanes," *Journal of Aeronautical Science* 4, no. 4 (1936): 122–28. For more on learning curves, see Garvin, *Learning in Action;* Levitt and March, "Organizational Learning"; and Louise E. Yelle, "The Learning Curve: Historical Review and Comprehensive Survey," *Decision Sciences* 10 (1979): 302–28.

43. Karl E. Weick and Frances Westley, "Organizational Learning: Affirming an Oxymoron," in *Handbook of Organization Studies,* ed. Stewart Clegg, Cynthia Hardy, and Walter R. Nord (Thousand Oaks, Calif.: Sage Publications, 1996), 441.

44. Tetlock, "Learning in U.S. and Soviet Foreign Policy," 22–23.

45. Mermelstein, *Man Who Made It Snow,* 142.

46. Homero, interview.

47. Néstor, interview.

48. U.S. Drug Enforcement Administration, *The Illicit Drug Situation in Colombia* (Washington, D.C.: DEA Intelligence Division, Publications Unit, November 1993), 16.

49. U.S. Government Accountability Office, *Drug Control: Agencies Need to Plan for Likely Declines in Drug Interdiction Assets, and Develop Better Performance Measures for Transit Zone Operations,* GAO-06-200 (November 2005), 22; Office of National Drug Control Policy, *2002 Annual Assessment of Cocaine Movement,* ONDCP-03-01 (March 2003).

50. Senior policy analyst, Office of National Drug Control Policy, interview by author, Washington, D.C., 19 July 1999.

51. U.S. Drug Enforcement Administration, Strategic Intelligence Section, *U.S. Drug Threat Assessment:1993,* DEA-93042 (September 1993), 16–17; U.S. Drug Enforcement Administration, National Narcotics Intelligence Consumers Committee, *The NNICC Report 1993: The Supply of Illicit Drugs to the United States,* DEA-94066 (August 1994), 7.

52. *CM&,* "El submarino construido en Bogotá contenía tecnología de punta," 7 September 2000, http://www.cmi.com.co/2000/Septiembre/Pais2597.html (accessed 16 October 2000) (my translation); *El Tiempo,* "Submarino Made in Faca," 8 September 2000, http://www.eltiempo.com/08-09-2000/judi_0.html (accessed 10 September 2000).

53. DEA, *Drug Trade in Colombia,* 11.

54. Cash, interview.

55. Pallomari, testimony, vol. 36 (17 July 1997), 5850.

56. Various U.S. and Colombian officials, interviews; Arturo, interview.

57. Kacerosky, "Search Warrant Affidavit"; McGee and Duffy, *Main Justice,* 65–66, 147.

58. For a discussion of how legally sanctioned organizations engage in such "deuterolearning," see Argyris and Schön, *Organizational Learning II;* and Gregory Bateson, *Steps to an Ecology of Mind* (New York: Ballantine Books, 1972).

59. "David," black market peso broker, *Frontline: Drug Wars* (aired 9–10 October 2000), http://www.pbs.org/wgbh/pages/frontline/shows/drugs/interviews/david.html (accessed 5 March 2001).

60. Jay Mathews, "White Powder Attracts Prospectors in California Gold Rush of '82," *Washington Post,* 24 October 1982; David McClintick, *Swordfish: A True Story of Ambition, Savagery, and Betrayal* (New York: Pantheon Books, 1993), 246.

61. During a trip to Colombia in 1994, a fellow Peace Corps volunteer and I were given the opportunity to engage in a peso-laundering transaction while sipping coffee at a restaurant in Cali. Though momentarily tempted, I declined the offer, in part because my wiser companion advised me that a record of the transaction would appear on my passport.

62. Michael Isikoff, "Federal Sting Exposes Drug Cartels' Money-Laundering Methods," *Washington Post,* 24 October 1988; Brooke A. Masters, "N.Y. Bank Guilty in Laundering Case," *Washington Post,* 28 November 2002; Catherine Wilson, "Feds: Insurance Helps Launder Drug Money," *Washington Post,* 6 December 2002; and U.S. Department of State, Bureau of International Narcotics and Law Enforcement Affairs, *International Narcotics Control Strategy Report 2003* (March 2004), http://www.state.gov/g/inl/rls/nrcrpt/2003/vol2/html/29920.htm (accessed 8 March 2004). See also Jack A. Blum, "Offshore Money," in *Transnational Crime in the Americas,* ed. Tom Farer (New York: Routledge, 1999), 57–84; and R. Thomas Naylor, *Wages of Crime: Black Markets, Illegal Finance, and the Underworld Economy* (Ithaca: Cornell University Press, 2002).

63. DEA group supervisor, Miami Division, interview by author, Miami, Florida, 15 February 2000.

64. State Department, Bureau of International Narcotics and Law Enforcement Affairs, *International Narcotics Control Strategy Report 2003.*

Chapter 3

1. *Cambio,* "La Pesca," 21 February 2000, http://www.revistacambio.com/20000221/Portada_01.asp (accessed 25 February 2000); U.S. Internal Revenue Service, *FY2000 National Operations Annual Report,* http://www.treasury.gov/irs/ci/annual_report/annualreport2000.doc (accessed 20 February 2003); Sharon Harvey Rosenberg, "Having Cracked Down on Banking Practices That Allowed Money Laundering, Government Targets Businesses Big and Small," *Miami Business Review,* 3 March 2000.

2. U.S. Drug Enforcement Administration, "Training Opportunities," http://www.dea.gov/programs/trainingp.htm (accessed 28 February 2003).

3. See the following publications by the DEA: *DEA Agents Manual,* "Guidelines for DEA Foreign Activities," 200; "International Training," *DEA Training Manual* (Washington, D.C., February 1988); "Training Opportunities," http://www.dea.gov/programs/trainingp.htm; and see U.S. General Accounting Office, *Drug Control: DEA's Strategies and Operations in the 1990s,* GGD-99-108, 21 July 1999.

4. Scott, *Seeing Like a State,* 319–20; Nussbaum, *Fragility of Goodness,* 95–97.

5. The DEA has produced a number of training manuals for special agents and intelligence analysts, including the *Drug Enforcement Handbook* (Washington, D.C.: U.S. Government Printing Office, 1987) and *Intelligence Collection and Analytical Methods* (Washington, D.C.: U.S. Government Printing Office, 1987). Recent counterdrug law enforcement textbooks include Michael D. Lyman, *Practical Drug Enforcement,* 2d ed. (Boca Raton, Fla.: CRC Press, 2002), and George S. Steffen and Samuel M. Candelaria, *Drug Interdiction: Partnerships, Legal Principles, and Investigative Methodologies for Law Enforcement* (Boca Raton, Fla.: CRC Press, 2002).

6. Scott, *Seeing Like a State,* 322.

7. For descriptive treatments of undercover operations, see U.S. Drug Enforcement Administration, *Drug Enforcement Handbook* (Washington, D.C.), 93–115; Carmine J. Motto and Dale L. June, *Undercover,* 2d ed. (Boca Raton, Fla.: CRC Press, 2000), 7; and Lyman, *Practical Drug Enforcement,* 25.

8. For a theoretical discussion of practice-based learning, see Orlikowski, "Knowing

in Practice"; Brown and Duguid, "Organizational Learning and Communities-of-Practice"; Edward Hutchins, "Organizing Work by Adaptation," *Organization Science* 2, no. 1 (1991), reprinted in *Cognition Within and Between Organizations*, ed. James R. Meindl, Charles Stubbart, and Joseph F. Porac (Thousand Oaks, Calif.: Sage Publications, 1996); Lave and Wenger, *Situated Learning;* and Orr, *Talking About Machines.*

9. My analysis of sensemaking draws heavily on Karl E. Weick's *Sensemaking in Organizations.* Although Weick does not consider drug enforcement in his analysis, the basic idea of sensemaking as a social process through which actors extract cues to retrospectively construct plausible interpretations of events applies to criminal investigations. For interesting, if nontheoretical, descriptions of different investigations targeting Colombian trafficking networks, see Samantha Phillips, "The Story of 'Operation Zorro II' and Some Practical Suggestions," *United States Attorneys' Bulletin* 45, no. 6 (November 1997); McClintick, *Swordfish;* and Ann Woolner, *Washed in Gold: The Story Behind the Biggest Money-Laundering Investigation in U.S. History* (New York: Simon and Schuster, 1994).

10. Robert H. Waterman, *Adhocracy: The Power to Change* (Memphis: Whittle Direct Books, 1990), 41, cited in Weick, *Sensemaking in Organizations,* 4.

11. Few officials made the case more dramatically than President George H. W. Bush during his remarks before an international gathering of law enforcers in 1989: "I'm here today to talk about war: first, to see cocaine trafficking for what it is—an attack aimed at enslaving and exploiting the weak; second, to confront what's become a world war. . . . As commanding officers, you know the havoc of which we speak. You see it every day on the streets of your cities and in the mountain villages, in the haunted eyes and the broken dreams of a generation of youth, of children who have fallen victim to a seductive, nightmarish new form of dependency and slavery . . . cocaine users can no longer claim noncombatant status. There is blood on their hands. . . . Your business, then—our business—is to pursue these outlaws to the ends of the Earth, to create a world without refuge, to leave no sanctuary, in your countries or in mind. And I've said it before: The war on drugs is no metaphor. We've been slower to recognize that it is also a world war, leaving no nation unscathed." George H. W. Bush, Remarks at the International Drug Enforcement Conference in Miami, Florida, 27 April 1989, http://bushlibrary.tamu.edu/research/papers/1989/89042700.html (accessed 8 March 2006).

12. DEA resident agent-in-charge, Ventura Office, Los Angeles Field Division, interview by author, Los Angeles, California, 29 April 2003.

13. Ibid.

14. Head of Judicial Police Unit, Department of Administrative Security, Bogotá, Colombia, interview by author, 2 June 2000 (my translation).

15. Head of Special Financial Investigations Unit, Department of Administrative Security, Bogotá, Colombia, interview by author, 2 May 2000 (my translation).

16. Ethan A. Nadelmann, *Cops Across Borders: The Internationalization of U.S. Criminal Law Enforcement* (University Park: Pennsylvania State University Press, 1993), 215.

17. For additional discussion, and copious examples, of the legal and ethical problems associated with using criminal informants in criminal investigations, see Gary T. Marx, *Undercover: Police Surveillance in America* (Berkeley and Los Angeles: University of California Press, 1988), 12, 61, 65–66; and Nadelmann, *Cops Across Borders,* 207–25. For a recent audit of the DEA's confidential source program, which found numerous problems in how the agency manages its approximately four thousand informants, see U.S. Department of Justice, Office of the Inspector General, Audit Division, *Executive Summary: The Drug Enforcement Administration's Payments to Confidential Sources* (July 2005), http://www.usdoj.gov/oig/reports/DEA/a05/final.pdf (accessed 9 December 2005).

18. Naylor, "Mafias, Myths, and Markets," 22; Elaine Shannon, "New Kings of Coke," *Time* magazine, 1 July 1991, 29–33.

19. See House Subcommittee "Statement of Witness Appearing Anonymously" (Mermelstein), 17, 31. See also Naylor, "Mafias, Myths, and Markets," 21–23.

20. Arturo, interview.

21. Homero, interview.

22. Néstor, interview.

23. Nadelmann, *Cops Across Borders*, 53, 96, 226.

24. Conspiracy investigations target high-level drug violators, such as organization leaders, cell managers, and money launderers. As discussed in Chapter 1, these figures represent elusive targets for law enforcers because they insulate themselves from direct participation in drug deals through human buffers or intermediaries and loose coupling between network nodes. Under conspiracy statutes, prosecutors seek to demonstrate a series (i.e., three or more instances) of drug-trafficking or money-laundering offenses between five or more organizers or supervisors who have received substantial income or resources from these violations, even when they never actually handle the drugs or proceeds themselves, and even when they direct their operations from outside the United States. For discussion of these statutes, see Howard Abadinsky, *Organized Crime*, 5th ed. (Chicago: Nelson Hall, 1997), 435, 458–63; U.S. General Accounting Office, *Investigations of Major Drug Trafficking Organizations: Report to the Honorable Joseph R. Biden, Jr. United States Senate*, GGD-84-36, 5 March 1984 (Washington, D.C.: U.S. General Accounting Office, 1984), 24n1; and Jill Jonnes, *Hep-Cats, Narcs, and Pipe Dreams: A History of America's Romance with Drugs* (Baltimore: Johns Hopkins University Press, 1996), 349.

25. Nathan M. Adams, "Cocaine Takes Over," *Reader's Digest*, 7 May 1975, 85; Edward Hudson, "Major Drug Raid Under Way Here," *New York Times*, 6 October 1974, 1; Arnold H. Lubasch, "Twelve Colombians Convicted in Drug Traffic," *New York Times*, 27 January 1976, 21; *New York Times*, "Seven Colombian Aliens Get Fifteen Years in Cocaine Case," 1 August 1976, 20; Richard Smitten, *The Godmother: The True Story of the Hunt for the Most Bloodthirsty Female Criminal of Our Time* (New York: Pocket Books, 1990), 48–60.

26. Robert J. Nieves, *Colombian Cocaine Cartels: Lessons from the Front* (Washington, D.C.: National Strategy Information Center, 1997), 5.

27. James Q. Wilson, *The Investigators: Managing FBI and Narcotics Agents* (New York: Basic Books, 1978); U.S. General Accounting Office, *Gains Made in Controlling Illegal Drugs, Yet the Drug Trade Flourishes*, GGD-80-4, 25 October 1979 (Washington, D.C.: U.S. General Accounting Office, 1979), 85–86; GAO, *Investigations of Major Drug Trafficking Organizations*, 24–25.

28. U.S. Congress, Senate, Committee on Government Operations, *Federal Narcotics Enforcement, Interim Report of the Permanent Subcommittee on Investigations of the Senate Committee on Government Operations*, 94th Cong., 2d sess., S. Rep. 94-1039 (1976). For more on the Jackson committee hearings, see Patricia Rachal, *Federal Narcotics Enforcement: Reorganization and Reform* (Boston: Auburn House, 1982), 138–40.

29. Robert M. Stutman and Richard Esposito, *Dead on Delivery: Inside the Drug Wars, Straight from the Street* (New York: Warner Books, 1992), 107.

30. Slaughter, *New World Order*, 55–56; David L. Westrate, "The Role of Law Enforcement," in *Drugs and Foreign Policy: A Critical Review*, ed. Raphael F. Perl (Boulder, Colo.: Westview Press, 1994), 79–99; and the following DEA publications: DEA *Agents Manual*, "Guidelines for DEA Foreign Activities," 200; "International Training," DEA *Training Manual* (Washington, D.C.: February 1988); and "Training Opportunities," http://www.dea.gov/programs/trainingp.htm (accessed 28 February 2003). See also U.S. General Accounting Office, *Drug Control: DEA's Strategies and Operations in the 1990s*, GGD-99-108, 21 July 1999.

31. Westrate, "Role of Law Enforcement"; U.S. Drug Enforcement Administration, *A Tradition of Excellence: The History of the DEA*, http://www.usdoj.gov/dea/deamuseum/1975_1980.htm (accessed 4 April 2002); McClintick, *Swordfish*, 33–36.

32. Westrate, "Role of Law Enforcement," 86.

33. DEA resident agent in charge, Los Angeles Field Division, interview.

34. See March, "Exploration and Exploitation in Organizational Learning."

Chapter 4

1. For a similar observation in a general discussion of policymaking, see Feldman, *Order Without Design*, 4–5.

2. Reyes, *Made in Miami*, 163–72.

3. Gordon H. McCormick, "Terrorist Decision Making," *Annual Review of Political Science* 6 (2003): 484. While McCormick is concerned with strategic decision making between terrorists and counterterrorists, his insight applies to drug traffickers and law enforcers and other competitive interactions between states and clandestine nonstate actors.

4. One exception to this occurs when law enforcers have so effectively penetrated trafficking groups, through the use of human informants or electronic surveillance, that they discover criminal activities while they are still in the planning stages. A second exception occurs when law enforcers trick people into committing criminal acts, as during the preplanned undercover operations discussed in the preceding chapter. In both cases, however, law enforcers have already identified and targeted specific groups or perpetrators, suggesting that narco-narc interaction is already under way. My concern here is with the initial stages of competitive adaptation, when law enforcers are still seeking targets that will help direct their activities.

5. Pino Arlacchi, *Mafia Business: The Mafia Ethic and the Spirit of Capitalism*, trans. Martin Ryle (London: Verso, 1986), 197.

6. Special agent, Department of Administrative Security (Colombia), Bogotá, Colombia, interview by author, 6 June 2000 (my translation).

7. DEA official, interview by author, Bogotá, Colombia, 5 June 2000.

8. DEA special agent, interview by author, Bogotá, Colombia, 15 March 2000.

9. Ibid.

10. McCormick, "Terrorist Decision Making," 484.

11. For a similar argument in a very different context, see Gernot Grabher and David Stark, "Organizing Diversity: Evolutionary Theory, Network Analysis, and Post-Socialism," in *Restructuring Networks in Post-Socialism: Legacies, Linkages, and Localities*, ed. Gernot Grabher and David Stark (New York: Oxford University Press, 1997), 4.

12. Freddy, interview.

13. Levitt and March, "Organizational Learning," 328–29.

14. Cash, interview.

15. In February 2004 the DEA reported that the precise number of NADDIS records was 5,742,960. However, the number of NADDIS records changes on a daily basis. U.S. DEA, Office of Administration, Investigative Records Unit (in response to Freedom of Information Act request by the author, 13 February 2004).

16. DEA, *DEA Agents Manual*, chapter 62, "Investigative Reporting System," 63.

17. Steven W. Casteel, deputy chief inspector, DEA, quoted in IDC/Avante, "Drug Enforcement Administration" (1996), http://www.cioview.com/dea.pdf (accessed 18 April 2003).

18. DEA special agent, Los Angeles Field Division, interview by author, Los Angeles, California, 24 April 2003.

19. U.S. Congress, House Subcommittee of the Committee on Appropriations, *Departments of Commerce, Justice, and State, the Judiciary, and Related Agencies Appropriations for 2003, Hearings Before a Subcommittee of the Committee on Appropriations*, 107th Cong., 2d sess., 20 March 2002 (Washington, D.C.: U.S. Government Printing Office, 2002), 341.

20. McClintick, *Swordfish*, 245–48.

21. Timothy S. Robinson and Alfred E. Lewis, "Drug Agent Allegedly Sold Secret Information," *Washington Post*, 28 August 1977, D1; and *Washington Post*, "Va. Man Guilty in Plot to Sell Drug Unit's Data," 15 March 1978, C5.

22. Pallomari, testimony, vol. 39 (23 July 1997), 6321.

23. *Washington Post,* "Crime and Justice," 3 December 2003; *Drug War Chronicle,* "Newsbrief: This Week's Corrupt Cops Story," Issue 328, 12 March 2004, http://stopthe drugwar.org/chronicle/328/fbi.shtml (accessed 12 March 2004).

24. Michael Isikoff, "Missing: A Laptop of DEA Informants," *Newsweek,* 7 June 2004, 12.

25. Of course, I cannot discount the possibility that Freddy knew more than he was telling me. However, in the informed consent protocol that he completed prior to our interview, and throughout the interview itself, I stressed to Freddy, as I did to all my trafficker informants, that I was only interested in general aspects of his criminal experience. Specifically, I asked Freddy not to share any details (names, dates, addresses) that could expose him (and, by extension, me) to potential legal—or extralegal—recrimination. I also emphasized that I did not wish to discuss anything that made him feel uneasy—and we did not. In carefully laying out these ground rules for our voluntary discussions, I believe that Freddy and my other informants felt reasonably comfortable talking with me in general terms about their criminal careers. In any event, the discrepancy between Freddy's knowledge of the inner workings of his maritime smuggling cell, and his lack of insight when addressing the larger network, was striking.

26. DEA resident agent-in-charge, Los Angeles Field Division, interview. For discussion of information, asymmetries in organizations and the principal-agent dilemma, see Terry M. Moe, "The New Economics of Organization," American Political Science Review 28, no. 4 (1984): 739–777.

27. Stutman and Esposito, *Dead on Delivery,* 107–10.

28. McGee and Duffy, *Main Justice,* 37.

29. Néstor, interview.

30. Andreas, *Border Games,* 144–45.

31. For discussion of these reorganizations, see Jonnes, *Hep-Cats, Narcs, and Pipe Dreams;* Michael Massing, *The Fix* (Berkeley and Los Angeles: University of California Press, 1998); and Rachal, *Federal Narcotics Enforcement.*

32. Official, Intelligence Center, Colombian National Police, interview by author, Bogotá, Colombia, 14 June 2000.

33. See, for example, Argyris and Schön, *Organizational Learning II,* 187; and Hedberg, "How Organizations Learn and Unlearn."

34. DEA group supervisor, Miami Division, interview.

35. Official, Department of National Planning, Bogotá, Colombia, interview by author, 27 June 2000 (my translation).

36. When targets of drug-trafficking investigations change their phones repeatedly, police officials can apply for "roving" wiretaps, which allow them to intercept calls made on any telecommunications "instrument" the suspect uses. However, to obtain court approval for these more encompassing—and, from a civil liberties perspective, more invasive—electronic surveillance orders, law enforcers must prove to the court that the telephones are being "dropped" so frequently by targets that it is preventing interception of their communications. For a discussion of these and other issues related to electronic surveillance, see *United States Attorneys' Bulletin* 45, no. 5, "Electronic Investigative Techniques" issue (September 1997), http://www.usdoj.gov/usao/eousa/foia_reading_room/ usab4505.pdf (accessed 13 March 2003).

37. DEA official, interview by author, Bogotá, Colombia, 13 April 2000.

38. U.S. Constitution, Fourth Amendment, "Search and Seizure."

39. Michael R. Sklaire, "Electronic Surveillance Guide," *United States Attorneys' Bulletin* 45, no. 5, "Electronic Investigative Techniques" issue (September 1997): 20, http:// www.usdoj.gov/usao/eousa/foia_reading_room/usab4505.pdf (accessed 13 March 2003).

40. U.S. Department of Justice, Office of the Inspector General, Evaluation and Inspections Division, "Review of the Drug Enforcement Administration's Disciplinary System," *Report Number I-2004-002* (January 2004), http://www.usdoj.gov/oig/inspection/DEA/ 0402/final.pdf (accessed 25 May 2004), 2.

41. Nicholas Dorn and Nigel South, "Drug Markets and Law Enforcement," *British Journal of Criminology* 30, no. 2 (1990): 172.

42. Official, Department of National Planning, Bogotá, interview.

43. House Subcommittee, "Statement of Witness Appearing Anonymously" (Mermelstein), 31–32; Michael Levine, *Deep Cover: The Inside Story of How DEA Infighting, Incompetence, and Subterfuge Lost Us the Biggest Battle of the Drug War* (New York: Delacorte Press, 1990).

44. DEA special agent, telephone interview by author, 27 January 2000.

45. Alma Guillermoprieto, *The Heart That Bleeds: Latin America Now* (New York: Knopf, 1994), 326.

Chapter 5

1. U.S. Congress, Senate, Subcommittee on International Operations and Terrorism, "Prepared Statement of Larry C. Johnson, former Deputy Director, Office of Counterterrorism, Department of State," *Al Qaeda International, Hearing Before the Subcommittee on International Operations and Terrorism, Committee on Foreign Relations,* 107th Cong., 1st sess., 18 December 2001 (Washington, D.C.: U.S. Government Printing Office, 2002), 17.

2. Russell, Banker, and Miller, "Out-Inventing the Terrorist," 7–8.

3. Fernando Cubides, "Los paramilitares y su estrategia," in *Reconocer la guerra para construir la paz,* ed. Malcolm Deas and María Victoria Llorente (Bogotá: Ediciones Uniandes, 1999), 160; Richani, *Systems of Violence,* 55, 107.

4. National Commission on Terrorist Attacks upon the United States, *The 9/11 Commission Report: Final Report of the National Commission on Terrorist Attacks upon the United States* (New York: W.W. Norton, 2004) (hereafter *9/11 Commission Report*), 61, 68, 240; National Commission on Terrorist Attacks upon the United States, *Overview of the Enemy,* Staff Statement No. 15, http://www.9-11commission.gov/hearings/hearing12/staff_state ment_15.pdf (accessed 16 June 2004), 5; Kim Cragin, "Hizballah, the Party of God," in Jackson et al., *Aptitude for Destruction,* 48; James J. F. Forest, "Training Camps and Other Centers of Learning," in Forest, *Teaching Terror,* 69–109.

5. Daniel Byman, *Deadly Connections: States That Sponsor Terrorism* (New York: Cambridge University Press, 2005), 206; Rohan Gunaratna, *Inside Al Qaeda: Global Network of Terror* (New York: Columbia University Press, 2002), 71–73; and Stern, *Terror in the Name of God,* 260–61. See also *9/11 Commission Report,* 67; and U.S. Congress, Joint Intelligence Committee, testimony of George J. Tenet, "Written Statement for the Record of the Director of Central Intelligence Before the Joint Inquiry Committee," *Joint Investigation: Hearing Before the Joint Intelligence Committee,* 107th Cong., 2d sess., 17 October 2002, http://intelli gence.senate.gov/0210hrg/021017/tenet.pdf (accessed 26 December 2003), 7.

6. "Testimony of Stephen Gaudin," *United States of America v. Usama bin Laden, et al.,* U.S. District Court, Southern District of New York, 7 March 2001, http://news.findlaw .com/hdocs/docs/binladen/binladen030701tt.pdf (accessed 3 June 2004), 1997–98, 2003.

7. National Commission on Terrorist Attacks upon the United States, *Outline of the 9/11 Plot,* Staff Statement No. 16, http://www.9-11commission.gov/hearings/hearing12/ staff_statement_16.pdf (accessed 16 June 2004), 2, 4, 9; *9/11 Commission Report,* 145–46, 154.

8. "Testimony of L'Houssaine Kherchtou," *United States of America v. Usama bin Laden, et al.,* U.S. District Court, Southern District of New York, 26 February 2001, http:// cryptome.org/usa-v-ubl-10.htm (accessed 7 June 2004); "Testimony of Ahmed Ressam," *United States of America v. Mokhtar Haouari,* U.S. District Court, Southern District of New York, 3 July 2001, http://news.findlaw.com/hdocs/docs/haouari/ushaouari70301rassamtt .pdf (accessed 4 June 2004).

9. Cloonan, interview.

10. Byman, *Deadly Connections*, 207; Sageman, *Understanding Terror Networks*, 121; Stern, *Terror in the Name of God*, 260.

11. To be sure, terrorist manuals are nothing new. In the late nineteenth century anarchists sought to codify their knowledge in published handbooks. Perhaps the best-known how-to terrorism manual, the *Science of Revolutionary Warfare*, written in 1884, contained detailed instructions for preparing and using a variety of bombs, poisons, and incendiary materials. See Johann Most, *Science of Revolutionary Warfare: A Handbook of Instruction Regarding the Use and Manufacture of Nitroglycerine, Dynamite, Gun-Cotton, Fulminating Mercury, Bombs, Arsons, Poisons, etc.*, English translation (El Dorado, Ariz.: Desert Publications, 1978). See also McCormick, "Terrorist Decision Making," 479; and Ann Larabee, "A Brief History of Terrorism in the United States," in *Technology and Terrorism*, ed. David Clarke (New Brunswick, N.J.: Transaction Publishers, 2004), 32.

12. Dave Foreman and Bill Haywood, eds., *Ecodefense: A Field Guide to Monkey Wrenching*, 3d ed. (Chico, Calif.: Abbzug Press, 1993); "Appendix: Examples of Training Manuals for Terrorism and Guerrilla Warfare," in *The Making of a Terrorist: Recruitment, Training, and Root Causes*, vol. 2, *Training*, ed. James J. F. Forest (Westport, Conn.: Praeger Security International, 2006), 311–33; Hoffman, *Inside Terrorism*, 203; Jessica Stern, "The Protean Enemy," *Foreign Affairs* 82, no. 4 (2003), http://www.foreignaffairs.org/20030701faessay15403/jessica-stern/the-protean-enemy.html (accessed 25 July 2003).

13. Personal communication with munitions expert, grade E-4, U.S. military, 9 January 2006.

14. David E. Smith, "The Training of Terrorist Organizations," CSC Report, 1995, http://www.globalsecurity.org/military/library/report/1995/SDE.htm (accessed 24 July 2003). See also Forest, "Training Camps and Other Centers of Learning," 100.

15. Eamon Collins, with Mick McGovern, *Killing Rage* (London: Granta Books, 1997), 66.

16. Tony Geraghty, *The Irish War: The Hidden Conflict Between the IRA and British Intelligence* (Baltimore: Johns Hopkins University Press, 2000), 82–83.

17. Cloonan, interview. See also Daniel Benjamin and Steven Simon, *The Age of Sacred Terror* (New York: Random House, 2002), 123; Peter L. Bergen, *Holy War, Inc.: Inside the Secret World of Osama bin Laden* (New York: Free Press, 2001), 127–33; and Gunaratna, *Inside Al Qaeda*, 70–71.

18. *Declaration of Jihad Against the Country's Tyrants*, http://www.usdoj.gov/ag/trainingmanual.htm (accessed 1 October 2002).

19. Gunaratna, *Inside Al Qaeda*, 70.

20. Stephen Ulph, "A Guide to Jihad on the Web," *Terrorism Focus* 2, no. 7 (31 March 2005), http://jamestown.org/terrorism/news/article.php?articleid=2369531 (accessed 19 June 2006).

21. In his study of Operation Enduring Freedom, Stephen Biddle, then a U.S. Army War College professor, identified similar adaptations by Al Qaeda and Taliban fighters in Afghanistan. In other words, Islamic mujaheddin and American "crusaders" appear to be drawing comparable lessons from their military engagements, if for very different objectives. See Stephen Biddle, *Afghanistan and the Future of Warfare: Implications for Army and Defense Policy* (Carlisle, Pa.: Strategic Studies Institute, November 2002); and Ben Venzke and Aimee Ibrahim, *Al-Qaeda's Advice for Mujahideen in Iraq: Lessons Learned in Afghanistan* (Alexandria, Va.: IntelCenter/Tempest Publishing, April 2003).

22. Jason Burke, "Al Qaeda Launches Online Terrorist Manual," *The Observer* (London), 18 January 2004, http://www.guardian.co.uk/alqaida/story/0,12469,1125879,00.html (accessed 27 May 2004); Paul Eedle and Roula Khalaf, "Discontent and Indifference of Saudi Public Aid Recruitment," *Financial Times*, 31 May 2004; Mark Huband, "Web Sends Call for Jihad Round the Globe in Moments," *Financial Times*, 17 June 2004; Gretchen Peters, "Al Qaeda Publishes Magazine on the Net," *South China Morning Post*, 13 February 2004; Lawrence Wright, "The Terror Web," *New Yorker*, 2 August 2004, 50.

23. SITE Institute, "The Sixth Issue of 'The Vanguards of Kharasan'—A Periodical from the Afghanistan Mujahideen," 7 June 2006, http://siteinstitute.org/ (accessed 13 June 2006); SITE Institute, "The Afghanistan Mujahideen Publish the First Issue of a Periodic Media Magazine: 'The Vanguards of the Kharasan,'" 8 September 2005, http://siteinstitute.org/ (accessed 13 June 2006).

24. Marc Sageman, former CIA case officer and clinical assistant professor, University of Pennsylvania, Philadelphia, interview by author, 3 January 2005.

25. Nic Robertson, "Tapes Show Al Qaeda Trained for Urban Jihad on West," CNN news broadcast, 21 August 2002, http://www.cnn.com/2002/US/08/20/terror.tape.main/index.html (accessed 23 August 2002).

26. J. Bowyer Bell, The IRA, 1968–2000: Analysis of a Secret Army (London: Frank Cass, 2000), 181.

27. 9/11 Commission Report, 167.

28. Fred Burton, "Beware of 'Kramer': Tradecraft and the New Jihadists," Stratfor Weekly, 18 January 2006, http://www.stratfor.com/products/premium/read_article.php?id=261022 (accessed 7 February 2006).

29. Declaration of Jihad Against the Country's Tyrants, "Twelfth Lesson: Espionage (2) Information-Gathering Using Covert Methods," http://www.usdoj.gov/ag/manualpart1_4.pdf (accessed 20 August 2003).

30. Ibid., "Second Lesson: Necessary Qualifications and Characteristics for the Organization's Member," http://www.usdoj.gov/ag/manualpart1_1.pdf (accessed 30 July 2003).

31. Patrick Seale, Abu Nidal: A Gun for Hire (New York: Random House, 1992), 20–25.

32. Collins, Killing Rage, 65.

33. Alistair Horne, A Savage War of Peace: Algeria 1954–1962 (New York: Viking, 1978), 134.

34. For more on cosmic war and religious extremism, see Mark Juergensmeyer, Terror in the Mind of God: The Global Rise of Religious Violence, 3d ed. (Berkeley and Los Angeles: University of California Press, 2003).

35. Anonymous, [Michael Scheuer], Through Our Enemies' Eyes: Osama Bin Laden, Radical Islam, and the Future of America (Washington, D.C.: Brassey's, 2002), 107–8.

36. Michael Slackman and Scott Shane, "Terrorists Trained by Zarqawi Went Abroad, Jordan Says," New York Times, 11 June 2006, http://www.nytimes.com/2006/06/11/world/middleeast/11jordan.html (accessed 12 June 2006).

37. Not all extremist groups fit this transnational pattern. Some guerrilla insurgencies and terrorist organizations, including the Revolutionary Armed Forces of Colombia and the United Self-Defense Groups of Colombia, are subnational actors that direct their political violence against domestic opponents.

38. Paul R. Pillar, Terrorism and U.S. Foreign Policy (Washington, D.C.: Brookings Institution Press, 2001), 48; Daniel Byman, "Should Hezbollah Be Next?" Foreign Affairs 82, no. 6 (2003): 54–66; and Cragin, "Hizballah, the Party of God," 50.

39. Magnus Ranstorp, "Hizbollah's Command Leadership," Terrorism and Political Violence 36, no. 3 (1994): 304.

40. John Arquilla, David Ronfeldt, and Michele Zanini, "Networks, Netwar, and Information-Age Terrorism," in Ian O. Lesser et al., Countering the New Terrorism, (Santa Monica, Calif.: RAND Corporation, 1999), 60–61.

41. Shaul Mishal and Avraham Sela, The Palestinian Hamas (New York: Columbia University Press, 2000), 159–61.

42. Mark Turner, "The Management of Violence in a Conflict Organization: The Case of the Abu Sayyaf," Public Organization Review 3 (2003): 387–401; David Tucker, "What's New About the New Terrorism and How Dangerous Is It?" Terrorism and Political Violence 13, no. 3 (2001): 1–14.

43. Jerrold M. Post, Ehud Sprinzak, and Laurita M. Denny, "The Terrorists in Their

Own Words: Interviews with Thirty-five Incarcerated Middle Eastern Terrorists," *Terrorism and Political Violence* 15, no. 1 (2003): 178.

44. This admittedly dated description of Al Qaeda is based largely, but not entirely, on the courtroom testimony of Jamal al-Fadl during the East African embassy bombing trial of four Al Qaeda associates in Manhattan in 2001. See "Direct Testimony of Jamal Ahmed Al-Fadl," *United States of America v. Usama Bin Laden, et al.*, U.S. District Court, Southern District of New York, 6 February 2001, http://news.findlaw.com/hdocs/docs/binladen/binladen2060itt.pdf (accessed 2 June 2004); and 9/11 Commission, *Overview of the Enemy*, 2–3.

45. 9/11 Commission, *Outline of the 9/11 Plot*, 18.

46. Gunaratna, *Inside Al Qaeda*, 82; Bruce Hoffman, "Rethinking Terrorism and Counterterrorism Since 9/11," *Studies in Conflict and Terrorism* 25 (2002): 308; 9/11 Commission, *Outline of the 9/11 Plot*, 15–16; Sageman, *Understanding Terror Networks*, 159.

47. *Declaration of Jihad Against the Country's Tyrants*, "Fifth Lesson: Means of Communication and Transportation," http://www.usdoj.gov/ag/manualpart1_2.pdf (accessed 4 August 2003).

48. Cragin, "Hizballah, the Party of God," 53.

49. Cloonan, interview.

50. 9/11 Commission, *Outline of the 9/11 Plot*; Sageman, *Understanding Terror Networks*, 167.

51. Former deputy director, CIA Counterterrorist Center, interview by author, Washington, D.C., 27 September 2004.

52. "The Threat of Eco-Terrorism," statement of James F. Jarboe, Domestic Terrorism Section Chief, FBI Counterterrorism Division, Before the House Resources Committee, Subcommittee on Forests and Forest Health, 12 February 2002, http://www.fbi.gov/congress/congress02/jarboe021202.htm (accessed 10 May 2004).

53. Horacio R. Trujillo, "The Radical Environmentalist Movement," in Jackson et al., *Aptitude for Destruction*, 163.

54. *Bite Back Magazine* 1 (n.d.), "News from the Frontline," http://www.directaction.info/library_jon.htm (accessed 15 June 2005). Curtin's interview is also cited in Trujillo, "Radical Environmentalist Movement," 163.

55. Hoffman, *Inside Terrorism*, 179.

56. Ibid.; Russell, Banker, and Miller, "Out-Inventing the Terrorist," 23.

57. Smith, "Training of Terrorist Organizations."

58. Brian A. Jackson, "Provisional Irish Republican Army," in Jackson et al., *Aptitude for Destruction*, 132.

59. Ibid., 132–33.

60. Major, intelligence unit, Israeli Defense Forces, Rosh Hanikra border post, Israel, briefing to group, 6 June 2005. According to another source, a former political advisor to the UN peacekeeping force in Lebanon, Hizballah "has studied asymmetrical warfare. . . . They watch for two months to note every detail of their enemy. They review their operations—what they did wrong, how the enemy responded. And they have flexible tactics, without a large hierarchical command structure." See Steven Erlanger and Richard A. Oppel Jr., "The Militia: A Disciplined Hezbollah Surprises Israel with Its Training, Tactics, and Weapons," *New York Times*, 7 August 2006, http://www.nytimes.com/2006/08/07/world/middleeast/07hezbollah.html (accessed 7 August 2006).

61. CIA, unclassified memorandum, 14 June 2002.

62. Cloonan, interview.

63. Gregory L. Vistica and Daniel Klaidman, "Inside the FBI and CIA's Joint Battle to Roll Up Osama bin Laden's International Network," *Newsweek*, 19 October 1998, 46.

64. U.S. Congress, Senate Subcommittee on International Operations and Terrorism, "Testimony of J. T. Caruso, Acting Assistant Director, CounterTerrorism Division, Federal

Bureau of Investigation," *Al Qaeda International, Hearing Before the Subcommittee on International Operations and Terrorism, Committee on Foreign Relations,* 107th Cong., 1st sess., 18 December 2001, http://www.fbi.gov/congress/congress01/carus0121801.htm (accessed 2 June 2004).

65. Alan Cullison and Andrew Higgins, "How Al Qaeda Agent Scouted Attack Sites in Israel and Egypt," *Wall Street Journal,* 16 January 2002, A1.

66. Cloonan, interview.

67. Sageman, *Understanding Terror Networks.*

68. Bruce Hoffman, "Terrorism Trends and Prospects," in Lesser et al., *Countering the New Terrorism,* 34n70.

69. Katherine Graham, "Safeguarding Our Freedoms as We Cover Terrorist Acts," *Washington Post,* 20 April 1986; Scott Shane, "A History of Publishing, and Not Publishing, Secrets," *New York Times,* 2 July 2006.

70. U.S. Congress, Senate Select Committee on Intelligence and U.S. House Permanent Select Committee on Intelligence, "Prepared Testimony of Paul Wolfowitz," *Joint Investigation, Hearings Before the U.S. Senate Select Committee on Intelligence and the U. S. House Permanent Select Committee on Intelligence,* 107th Cong., 2d sess., 19 September 2002, http://intelligence.senate.gov/020919/wolfowitz.pdf (accessed 13 October 2006).

71. Don Van Natta Jr. and Desmond Butler, "How Tiny Swiss Cellphone Chips Helped Track Global Terror Web," *New York Times,* 4 March 2004, http://www.nytimes.com/2004/03/04/international/Europe/04PHON.html (accessed 4 March 2004).

72. For a discussion of how Khalid Shaikh Mohammed learned from the unsuccessful Oplan Bojinka plot, which sought to destroy twelve U.S. airliners as they flew over the Pacific Ocean in early 1995, to plan the 9/11 attacks, see Rohan Gunaratna, "Al Qaeda's Lose and Learn Doctrine: The Trajectory from Oplan Bojinka to 9/11," in Forest, *Teaching Terror,* 171–88.

73. 9/11 Commission, *Outline of the 9/11 Plot,* 12–16.

74. Walter Enders and Todd Sandler, "The Effectiveness of Antiterrorism Policies: A Vector-Autoregression-Intervention Analysis," *American Political Science Review* 87, no. 4 (1993): 829–44.

75. Gregory A. Raymond, "The Evolving Strategies of Political Terrorism," in Kegley, *New Global Terrorism,* 83.

76. Hoffman, *Inside Terrorism,* 178, 180–81. For a similar, if less lucid, analysis regarding IRA ingenuity in improvising explosives and detonation devices, see Richard Clutterbuck, "Trends in Terrorist Weaponry" in *Technology and Terrorism,* ed. Paul Wilkinson (London: Frank Cass, 1993), 130–39.

77. Jackson points out that this technological chase was bounded by the technology available to IRA engineers. He also notes that as the IRA's "devices became more sophisticated and used increasingly specialized components, they also provided ways for the authorities to track them down." Jackson, "Provisional Irish Republican Army," 100–101.

78. Technical Intelligence Sergeant, "Threats of IEDs in Israel," briefing at Combat Engineers, Special Operations Unit, Israeli Defense Forces, Sirkin Air Force Base, Israel, 7 June 2005.

79. Ibid.

80. Bruce Hoffman, "Insurgency and Counterinsurgency in Iraq," *Studies in Conflict and Terrorism* 29 (2006): 107; Horne, *Savage War of Peace.*

81. Department of Defense, "DoD News Briefing—Mr. Di Rita and Gen. Abizaid," 16 July 2003, http://www.defenselink.mil/transcripts/2003/tr20030716-0401.html (accessed 16 June 2006). See also Hoffman, "Insurgency and Counterinsurgency in Iraq," 107.

82. See, for example, Stephen J. Hedges, "U.S. Battles Low-Tech Threat," *Chicago Tribune,* 2 October 2004, 1; Eric Schmitt, "Insurgents in Iraq Using Roadside Bombs More Effectively, U.S. General Says," *New York Times,* 16 December 2004; David S. Cloud, "Iraqi

Rebels Refine Bomb Skills, Pushing Toll of G.I.'s Higher," *New York Times*, 22 June 2005, http://www.nytimes.com/2005/06/22/international/middleeast/22bomb.html (accessed 24 June 2005); Scott Johnson and Melinda Liu, "The Enemy Spies," *Newsweek*, 27 June 2005, http://www.msnbc.msn.com/id/8272786/site/newsweek (accessed 27 June 2006); David S. Cloud, "Insurgents Using Bigger, More Lethal Bombs, U.S. Officers Say," *New York Times*, 4 August 2005.

83. Anthony H. Cordesman, *Iraq's Evolving Insurgency: The Nature of Attacks and Patterns and Cycles in the Conflict*, (Washington, D.C.: Center for Strategic and International Studies, 3 February 2006), http://www.csis.org/media/csis/pubs/060203_iraqicombat trends.pdf (accessed 15 June 2006), 19–29; Daniel Benjamin and Steven Simon, *The Next Attack: The Failure of the War on Terror and a Strategy for Getting It Right* (New York: Times Books, 2005), 42; Forest, "Introduction," 21–22; Ahmed S. Hashim, *Insurgency and Counter-Insurgency in Iraq* (Ithaca: Cornell University Press, 2006), 191–92; Hoffman, "Insurgency and Counterinsurgency in Iraq," 115; and George Packer, *The Assassin's Gate: America in Iraq* (New York: Farrar, Straus and Giroux, 2005), 299, 372.

Chapter 6

1. Of course, some critics argue that allocating US$40 billion a year in federal expenditures for homeland security is woefully inadequate, and that the U.S. government should not only spend more money but distribute these funds more wisely, avoiding the parochial tendencies of congressional earmarks and special interest groups. See, for example, Stephen E. Flynn, *America the Vulnerable: How Our Government Is Failing to Protect Us from Terrorism* (New York: HarperCollins, 2004).

2. The Special Operations Command (SOCOM), the Defense Department entity responsible for planning and executing combat operations against terrorist networks, received US$5 billion in appropriations in fiscal year 2003. To support SOCOM's expanded role as the lead counterterrorism command in the U.S. military, its funding grew to US$6.7 billion in the administration's 2004 budget request, an increase of 34 percent. Since then SOCOM has continued to grow as it evolves from a "supporting" to a "supported" counterterrorism command. During fiscal year 2006, more than fourteen hundred Special Forces soldiers were added to the command. The president's budget request for fiscal year 2007 includes additional outlays for approximately four thousand more soldiers. See David S. Cloud and Joel Brinkley, "Broad Ripples of Iraq War in Budgets of Two Agencies," *New York Times*, 7 February 2006, http://www.nytimes.com/2006/02/07/poli tics/07security.html (accessed 7 February 2005); U.S. Congress, Senate Subcommittee on Emerging Threats and Capabilities, "Statement of General Bryan D. Brown, Commander, U.S. Special Operations Command," *Defense Authorization Request for Fiscal Year 2006, Hearings Before the Committee on Armed Services, Subcommittee on Emerging Threats and Capabilities*, 109th Cong., 1st sess., 22 April 2005, http://armed-services.senate.gov/sta temnt/2005/April/Brown%2004-22-05.pdf (accessed 19 December 2005); U.S. Congress, Senate Committee on Armed Services, "Statement of Lt. General Bryan D. Brown, Deputy Commander, U.S. Special Operations Command," *Department of Defense Authorization for Appropriations for Fiscal Year 2004, Hearings Before the Committee on Armed Services*, 108th Cong., 1st sess., 9 April 2003, 172; Andrew Feickert, "U.S. Special Operations Forces (SOF): Background and Issues for Congress," *Congressional Research Service Report for Congress*, 28 September 2004, http://www.fas.org/man/crs/RS21048.pdf (accessed 20 December 2005); Jennifer D. Kibbe, "The Rise of the Shadow Warriors," *Foreign Affairs* 83, no. 2 (2004): 110; U.S. Office of Management and Budget, "Winning the War on Terror," *Fiscal Year 2005 Budget of the U.S. Government*, 2 February 2004, http://www.gpoaccess.gov/ usbudget/fy05/pdf/budget/winning.pdf (accessed 4 June 2004); U.S. Office of Management and Budget, "Department of Defense," *Budget of the United States Government Fiscal*

Year 2007, 6 February 2006, http://www.whitehouse.gov/omb/budget/fy2007/pdf/bud get/defense.pdf (accessed 7 February 2006).

3. U.S. Office of Management and Budget, *2003 Report to Congress on Combating Terrorism*, http://www.fas.org/irp/threat/omb_terror_03.pdf (accessed 23 December 2003).

4. Nadelmann, *Cops Across Borders*, 157.

5. U.S. General Accounting Office, *Combating Terrorism: Interagency Framework and Agency Programs to Address the Overseas Threat*, GAO-03-165, May 2003; Federal Bureau of Investigation, *War on Terrorism: Counterterrorism* http://www.fbi.gov/terrorinfo/counterror ism/waronterrorhome.htm (accessed 4 September 2003).

6. Ibid.; Office of the Press Secretary, Executive Office of the President, "Fact Sheet: Making America Safer by Strengthening Our Intelligence Capabilities," 2 August 2004, http://www.whitehouse.gov/news/releases/2004/08/20040802-7.html (accessed 29 June 2006); Risen, *State of War*, 39; James Risen and David Johnston, "Bush Has Widened Authority of C.I.A. to Kill Terrorists," *New York Times*, 15 December 2002; and U.S. Joint Intelligence Committee, testimony of Tenet, "Written Statement for the Record."

7. GAO, *Combating Terrorism*, 156; Gary Berntsen and Ralph Pezzullo, *Jawbreaker: The Attack on Bin Laden and Al Qaeda; A Personal Account by the CIA's Key Field Commander* (New York: Crown Publishers, 2005); Dana Priest, *The Mission: Waging War and Keeping Peace with America's Military* (New York: W. W. Norton, 2003), 147; Gary C. Schroen, *First In: An Insider's Account of How the CIA Spearheaded the War on Terror in Afghanistan* (New York: Presidio Press, 2005); Kevin Whitelaw and Mark Mazzetti, "War in the Shadows," *U.S. News and World Report*, 11 November 2002, 48.

8. Mark Mazzetti and Philip Smucker, "On the Ground," *U.S. News and World Report*, 25 February 2002. See also Dexter Filkins, "FBI and Military Unite in Pakistan to Hunt Al Qaeda," *New York Times*, 14 July 2002, 1; Gordon T. Lee, "Hard-Shelled, SOF-Centered: The Synergy of Might and Mind," *Rand Review* (summer 2002): 40–41; Dana Priest, "'Team 555' Shaped a New Way of War," *Washington Post*, 3 April 2002, A1; James Risen and Eric Lichtblau, "Bush Lets U.S. Spy on Callers Without Courts," *New York Times*, 16 December 2005.

9. Donald H. Rumsfeld, "Remarks at the International Institute for Strategic Studies," Department of Defense, news transcript, 5 June 2004, http://www.defenselink.mil/ transcripts/2004/tr20040605-secdef0816.html (accessed 7 June 2004); Senate Select Committee on Intelligence, testimony of Tenet, "Worldwide Threat 2004"; Josh Meyer, Eric Lichtblau, and Bob Drogin, "Gains and Gaps in Sept. 11 Inquiry," *Los Angeles Times*, 10 March 2002.

10. Some of the more controversial interrogation techniques designed to "simulate" torture include "water boarding" (involving the near drowning of detainees), sleep deprivation, light and noise bombardment, physical stress positions, and the selective treatment of pain medication. See Risen, *State of War*, 32–33; James Risen, David Johnston, and Neil A. Lewis, "Harsh C.I.A. Methods Cited in Top Qaeda Interrogations," *New York Times*, 13 May 2004, http://www.nytimes.com/2004/05/13/politics/13DETA.html (accessed 13 May 2004); Dana Priest, "CIA Holds Terror Suspects in Secret Prisons," *Washington Post*, 2 November 2005; Deborah Sontag, "Secret Justice: Terror Suspect's Path from Streets to Brig," *New York Times*, 25 April 2004, http://www.nytimes.com/2004/04/25/national/ 25PADI.html (accessed 13 May 2004); 9/11 Commission, *Outline of the 9/11 Plot*.

11. Ron Suskind, *The One Percent Doctrine* (New York: Simon and Schuster, 2006), 216–19.

12. Frank Anderson, former chief, Near East and South Asia Division, CIA, interview by author, Washington, D.C., 16 November 2004; Cloonan, interview; W. Patrick Lang, former chief, Defense Humint Service, Defense Intelligence Agency and the Office of the Secretary of Defense, interview by author, Washington, D.C., 25 October 2004.

13. Cloonan, interview.

14. U.S. Congress, House of Representatives, Subcommittee on Financial Institutions Supervision, Regulations and Insurance, "Anonymous Witness Appearing Under the Federal Witness Protection Program," *Money Laundering Hearings Before the Subcommittee on Financial Institutions Supervision, Regulations and Insurance,* 101st Cong., 1st sess., 14 November 1989. See also Naylor, "Mafias, Myths, and Markets."

15. These interpretations are often couched in network terms, one of the primary analytic concepts in this study. There is a lot of discussion these days about the "new Al Qaeda," the "Al Qaeda network," and the "global Salafi jihad network" (emphasis on the singular), suggesting that such enterprises can be understood as a single entity. My own analysis, by contrast, highlights the plurality of network forms of organization that permeate the diffuse, highly diverse world of Islamic extremism.

16. *Declaration of Jihad Against the Country's Tyrants,* "Ninth Lesson: Security Plan," http://www.usdoj.gov/ag/manualpart1_3.pdf (accessed 30 June 2006); "Interview: Michael Scheuer," *Frontline: The Dark Side* (11 January 2006), http://www.pbs.org/wgbh/pages/frontline/darkside/interviews/scheuer.html (accessed 21 June 2006).

17. Risen, *State of War,* 33; Horne, *Savage War of Peace,* 205; and Jane Mayer, "Outsourcing Torture: The Secret History of America's Extraordinary Rendition Program," *New Yorker,* 14 February 2005.

18. Risen, *State of War,* 32–33. For the 9/11 Commission's disclaimer about using coerced confessions from Khalid Shaikh Mohammed, Abu Zubaydah, and other Al Qaeda detainees in its report, see *9/11 Commission Report,* 146.

19. Sontag, "Secret Justice"; Linda Greenhouse, "Justices Decline Terrorism Case of a U.S. Citizen," *New York Times,* 4 April 2006.

20. Michael Isikoff, "Iraq and Al Qaeda," *Newsweek,* 4 July 2004; Dana Priest, "Al Qaeda-Iraq Link Recanted," *Washington Post,* 1 August 2004; Douglas Jehl, "Qaeda-Iraq Link U.S. Cited Is Tied to Coercion Claim," *New York Times,* 9 December 2005; and Mayer, "Outsourcing Torture."

21. Peter Andreas, "Redrawing the Line: Borders and Security in the Twenty-first Century," *International Security* 28, no. 2 (2003): 92.

22. Flynn, *America the Vulnerable,* 140.

23. Donald F. Kettl, *System Under Stress: Homeland Security and American Politics* (Washington, D.C.: CQ Press, 2004), 49.

24. U.S. Congress, Senate Committee on Homeland Security and Governmental Affairs, "Statement Of Richard A. Falkenrath, Visiting Fellow, the Brookings Institution," *The Department of Homeland Security: The Road Ahead, Hearings Before the Committee on Homeland Security and Governmental Affairs,* 109th Cong., 1st sess., 26 January 2005, http://hsgac.senate.gov/_files/HSGACFalkenrathStatement.pdf (accessed 19 July 2005), 1–2.

25. Department of Homeland Security, Office of Inspector General, *Review of the Status of Department of Homeland Security Efforts to Address Its Major Management Challenges,* March 2004, 3, http://www.dhs.gov/interweb/assetlibrary/OIG_DHSManagementChallenges0304.pdf (accessed 25 March 2004).

26. U.S. Congress, Senate Committee on Homeland Security and Governmental Affairs, "Statement of Secretary Michael Chertoff, U.S. Department of Homeland Security," *Department of Homeland Security: Second Stage Review, Hearings Before the Committee on Homeland Security and Governmental Affairs,* 109th Cong., 1st sess., 14 July 2005, http://hsgac.senate.gov/_files/071405Chertoff.pdf (accessed 19 July 2005); U.S. Senate, "Statement of Richard A. Falkenrath"; Flynn, *America the Vulnerable;* and John Mintz, "Infighting Cited at Homeland Security," *Washington Post,* 2 February 2005.

27. Mintz, "Infighting Cited at Homeland Security"; James Jay Carafano and David Heyman, "DHS 2.0: Rethinking the Department of Homeland Security," *Heritage Special Report,* SR-02, 13 December 2004, 12; and Government Accountability Office, *Homeland*

Security: Overview of Department of Homeland Security Management Challenges, GAO-05-573T (Washington, D.C., 20 April 2005), http://www.gao.gov/cgi-bin/getrpt?GAO-05-573T (accessed 20 April 2005), 7.

28. Flynn, *America the Vulnerable*, 143.

29. Hedberg, "How Organizations Learn and Unlearn"; Kathleen Carley, "Organizational Learning and Personnel Turnover," *Organization Science* 3, no. 1 (1992), reprinted in Cohen and Sproull, *Organizational Learning*, 233–34.

30. Eric Lipton, "Former Antiterror Officials Find Industry Pays Better," *New York Times*, 18 June 2006, http://www.nytimes.com/2006/06/18/washington/18lobby.html (accessed 19 June 2006); and *New York Times*, "Tracking the Turnover," (no date available), http://graphics.nytimes.com/packages/pdf/national/20060618_LOBBYLIST2.pdf (accessed 19 June 2006).

31. Levitt and March, "Organizational Learning."

32. Levitt and March, "Organizational Learning," 334.

33. March, Sproull, and Tamuz, "Learning from Samples of One or Fewer"; Levitt and March, "Organizational Learning," 333–34.

34. Department of Homeland Security, *Top Officials Exercise Series: TOPOFF 2, After Action Summary Report* (Washington, D.C., 19 December 2003), http://www.dhs.gov/interweb/assetlibrary/T2_Report_Final_Public.doc (accessed 27 July 2005); Department of Homeland Security, *TOPOFF 3 Frequently Asked Questions*, http://www.dhs.gov/dhspublic/interapp/editorial/editorial_0603.xml (accessed 4 April 2005).

35. Marc Santora, "Two States Are 'Attacked' in a Major Terrorism Drill," *New York Times*, 5 April 2005, http://www.nytimes.com/2005/04/05/nyregion/05top.html (accessed 5 April 2005); Edward Walsh and John Mintz, "Huge Homeland Security Drill Planned," *Washington Post*, 5 May 2003, http://www.washingtonpost.com/ac2/wp-dyn/A13847-2003May4 (accessed 8 October 2004).

36. Jonathan Cleck, program manager, Office for Domestic Preparedness, Department of Homeland Security, interview by author, Washington, D.C., 4 December 2004.

37. Scott, *Seeing Like a State*, 314.

38. DHS, *TOPOFF 3*; Jacob N. Shapiro and Rudolph Darken, "Homeland Security: A New Strategic Paradigm?" in *Strategy in the Contemporary World*, ed. John Baylis et al. (New York: Oxford University Press, forthcoming).

39. Shapiro and Darken, "Homeland Security."

40. Todd R. LaPorte and Paula M. Consolini, "Working in Practice but Not in Theory: Theoretical Challenges of 'High-Reliability Organizations,'" *Journal of Public Administration Research and Theory* 1, no. 1 (1991): 19.

41. Quoted in Thom Shanker and James Risen, "Rumsfeld Weighs New Covert Acts by Military Units," *New York Times*, 12 August 2002, http://www.nytimes.com/2002/08/12/international/asia/12INTE.html (accessed 12 August 2002).

42. Risen, *State of War*, 32.

43. Cloonan, interview.

44. See U.S. Congress, Senate Select Committee on Intelligence, testimony of Eleanor Hill, staff director, Joint Inquiry Staff, *Counterterrorism Information Sharing with Other Federal Agencies and with State and Local Governments and the Private Sector, Hearings Before the Senate Select Committee on Intelligence*, 107th Cong., 2d sess., 1 October 2002, http://intelligence.senate.gov/0210hrg/021001/hill.pdf (accessed 24 December 2003); Senator Richard C. Shelby, Vice Chairman, Senate Select Committee on Intelligence, "September 11 and the Imperative of Reform in the U.S. Intelligence Community," in Senate Select Committee on Intelligence and House Permanent Select Committee on Intelligence, *Joint Inquiry into Intelligence Community Activities Before and After the Terrorist Attacks of September 11, 2001*, S. Rep. 107-351/H. Rep. 107-792, 107th Cong., 2d sess., December 2002, http://www.fas.org/irp/congress/2002_rpt/911rept.pdf (accessed 24 December 2003);

David Tucker, *Skirmishes at the Edge of Empire: The United States and International Terrorism* (Westport, Conn.: Praeger, 1997); and U.S. Department of Justice, Office of the Inspector General, *A Review of the FBI's Handling of Intelligence Information Related to the September 11 Attacks,* November 2004, redacted and unclassified version (released publicly June 2005), http://www.usdoj.gov/oig/special/0506/final.pdf (accessed 10 June 2005).

45. Senate Select Committee on Intelligence and House Permanent Select Committee on Intelligence, *Joint Inquiry into Intelligence Community Activities Before and After the Terrorist Attacks of September 11;* National Commission on Terrorist Attacks upon the United States, *Three 9/11 Hijackers: Identification, Watchlisting, and Tracking,* Staff Statement No. 2, http://www.9-11commission.gov/staff_statements/staff_statement_2.pdf (accessed 11 May 2004); *9/11 Commission Report;* Department of Justice, Inspector General, *Review of the FBI's Handling of Intelligence Information Related to the September 11 Attacks,* 289.

46. Senate Select Committee on Intelligence and House Permanent Select Committee on Intelligence, *Joint Inquiry into Intelligence Community Activities Before and After the Terrorist Attacks of September 11,* 12–16; *9/11 Commission Report;* Department of Justice, Inspector General, *Review of the FBI's Handling of Intelligence Information Related to the September 11 Attacks.*

47. National Commission on Terrorist Attacks upon the United States, *Reforming Law Enforcement, Counterterrorism, and Intelligence Collection in the United States,* Staff Statement No. 12, http://www.9-11commission.gov/hearings/hearing10/staff_statement_12.pdf (accessed 11 May 2004).

48. Risen and Lichtblau, "Bush Lets U.S. Spy on Callers Without Courts"; see Risen, *State of War,* 44–58.

49. Dana Priest, "CIA Puts Harsh Tactics on Hold," *Washington Post,* 27 June 2004; Risen, Johnston, and Lewis, "Harsh C.I.A. Methods Cited in Top Qaeda Interrogations"; Sontag, "Secret Justice"; Michael Slackman, "A Dangerous Calculus: What's Wrong with Torturing a Qaeda Higher Up?" *New York Times,* 16 May 2004, http://www.nytimes.com/2004/05/16/weekinreview/16slac.html (accessed 19 May 2004); 9/11 Commission, *Outline of the 9/11 Plot.*

50. Risen, *State of War,* 55.

51. Former deputy director, CIA Counterterrorist Center, interview.

52. Ibid.

53. Arquilla and Ronfeldt, *Networks and Netwars,* 15.

54. GAO, *Combating Terrorism,* 61–62, 200; White House, "Organization of the National Security Council System," National Security Presidential Directive No. 1, 13 February 2001, http://www.fas.org/irp/offdocs/nspd/nspd-1.htm (accessed 8 June 2004); Department of Justice, Office of the Attorney General, "Prepared Remarks of Attorney General John Ashcroft"; and U.S. Senate, testimony of Eleanor Hill, 7–8.

55. Tucker, *Skirmishes at the Edge of Empire,* 36–39, 125–29. See also the memoirs of Duane Clarridge, a former high-level CIA official who served in the working group. Duane R. Clarridge, with Digby Diehl, *A Spy for All Seasons: My Life in the CIA* (New York: Scribner, 1997), 324.

56. For discussion of the CSG, see Coll, *Ghost Wars,* 389; Pillar, *Terrorism and U.S. Foreign Policy,* 124; White House, Office of the Press Secretary, "Combating Terrorism: Presidential Decision Directive 62," fact sheet, 22 May 1998, http://www.fas.org/irp/offdocs/pdd-62.htm (accessed 8 June 2004).

57. U.S. Senate, testimony of Eleanor Hill, 8.

58. Priest, *The Mission,* 155.

59. Lee, "Hard-Shelled, SOF-Centered."

60. Tucker, *Skirmishes at the Edge of Empire,* 39–42.

61. Coll, *Ghost Wars,* 394–95.

62. Priest, "CIA Puts Harsh Tactics on Hold"; David Johnston, "The Interrogators:

Uncertainty About Interrogation Rules Seen as Slowing the Hunt for Information on Terrorists," *New York Times*, 28 June 2004, http://www.nytimes.com/2004/06/28/politics/28CIA.html (accessed 29 June 2004).

63. For discussion and research on rational choice theory from an institutionalist perspective, see Robert H. Bates et al., *Analytic Narratives* (Princeton: Princeton University Press, 1998); Barbara Geddes, *Politician's Dilemma: Building State Capacity in Latin America* (Berkeley and Los Angeles: University of California Press, 1994); and Elinor Ostrom, *Governing the Commons: The Evolution of Institutions for Collective Action* (New York: Cambridge University Press, 1990).

64. Michael D. Cohen, James G. March, and Johan P. Olsen, "A Garbage Can Model of Organizational Choice," *Administrative Science Quarterly* 17, no. 1 (1972): 1–25; John W. Kingdon, *Agendas, Alternatives, and Public Policies*, 2d ed. (New York: HarperCollins, 1995); Martha Feldman and Anne Khademian, "Models for Decision-Making and Policy Formulation," in *Integrating Environmental Considerations in Policy Formulation: Lessons from Policy-Based SEA Experience*, ed. Kulsum Ahmed and Ernesto Sanchez-Triana (Washington, D.C.: World Bank, forthcoming).

65. Former senior intelligence executive, CIA, interview by author, Washington, D.C., 13 January 2005.

66. Department of Justice, Inspector General, *Review of the FBI's Handling of Intelligence Information Related to the September 11 Attacks*, 223, 308–9.

67. Ibid., 223n159.

68. See ibid., 321; 9/11 Commission, *Reforming Law Enforcement, Counterterrorism, and Intelligence Collection in the United States*.

69. Trial attorney, Counter-terrorism Section, Criminal Division, Department of Justice, interview by author, Washington, D.C., 1 January 2005.

70. Michael A. Turner, *Why Secret Intelligence Fails* (Dulles, Va.: Potomac Books, 2005), 95.

71. Ibid., 94; Markle Foundation Task Force, *Creating a Trusted Network for Homeland Security* (New York: Markle Foundation, 2003), http://www.markle.org/downloadable_assets/nstf_report2_full_report.pdf (accessed 1 April 2005); U.S. Senate, testimony of Eleanor Hill, 6; National Commission on Terrorist Attacks upon the United States, *Law Enforcement, Counterterrorism, and Intelligence Collection in the United States Prior to 9-11*, Staff Statement No. 9, http://www.9-11commission.gov/hearings/hearing10/staff_statement_9.pdf (accessed 13 May 2004), 10; U.S. Congress, Senate Select Committee on Intelligence and House Permanent Select Committee on Intelligence, testimony of Michael E. Rolince, FBI special agent-in-charge, Washington field office, "Prepared Remarks of Michael E. Rolince before the Senate Select Committee on Intelligence and the House Permanent Select Committee on Intelligence," 107th Cong., 2d sess., 20 September 2002, http://intelligence.senate.gov/0209hrg/020920/rolince.pdf (accessed 1 January 2004), 4–5; and Shelby, "September 11 and the Imperative of Reform," 47–48n51.

72. Former CIA senior intelligence executive, interview.

73. For discussion of one effort to reduce the use of ORCON on terrorism threat intelligence, see "Statement of Russell E. Travers to the National Commission on Terrorist Attacks upon The United States," seventh public hearing of the National Commission on Terrorist Attacks upon the United States, 26 January 2004, http://www.9-11commission.gov/hearings/hearing7/witness_travers.htm (accessed 5 April 2005).

74. Former deputy director, CIA Counterterrorist Center, interview.

75. Karen Guttieri, "Unlearning War: U.S. Military Experience with Stability Operations," in *Organizational Learning in the Global Context*, ed. M. Leann Brown, Michael Kenney, and Michael Zarkin (London: Ashgate, 2006), 228.

76. Stephen Biddle, associate research professor of national security studies, Strategic Studies Institute, U.S Army War College, Carlisle Barracks, Pa., interview by author, 18

October 2004. See also Biddle, *Afghanistan and the Future of Warfare;* and Stephen Biddle, "Afghanistan and the Future of Warfare," *Foreign Affairs* 83, no. 2 (2003).

77. Biddle, interview.

78. Coll, *Ghost Wars,* 498.

79. Seymour M. Hersh, *Chain of Command: The Road from 9/11 to Abu Ghraib* (New York: HarperCollins, 2004), 123–25; Seymour M. Hersh, "Escape and Evasion," *New Yorker,* 12 November 2001, http://www.newyorker.com/printable/?fact/011112fa_FACT (accessed 18 June 2003).

80. Clarke, *Against All Enemies,* 199; 9/11 Commission, *Reforming Law Enforcement, Counterterrorism, and Intelligence Collection in the United States,* 7.

81. 9/11 Commission, *Reforming Law Enforcement, Counterterrorism, and Intelligence Collection in the United States,* 9.

82. Benjamin and Simon, *Age of Sacred Terror,* 281; Clarke, *Against All Enemies,* 200.

83. Seymour M. Hersh, "Moving Targets," *New Yorker,* 15 December 2003, 54. Also see Hersh, *Chain of Command,* 262–63.

84. Robin Moore, *The Hunt for Bin Laden: Task Force Dagger* (New York: Random House, 2003), 246.

85. Berntsen and Pezzullo, *Jawbreaker,* 307–8.

86. Larry C. Johnson, former deputy director of the Office of Counterterrorism, U.S. Department of State, and CEO of Berg Associates, interview by author, Washington, D.C., 28 September 2004.

87. Whitelaw and Mazzetti, "War in the Shadows."

88. Johnson, interview.

Conclusion

1. DEA special agent-in-charge, interview by author, Bogotá, Colombia, 12 June 1997.

2. *9/11 Commission Report,* 215–53. Also see Terry McDermott, *Perfect Soldiers: The Hijackers; Who They Were, Why They Did It* (New York: HarperCollins, 2005), 174.

3. Freddy, interview.

4. Serrano Cadena, with Gamboa, *Jaque mate,* 95–96.

5. Raymond Bonner and Don Van Natta Jr., "Regional Terrorist Groups Pose Growing Threat, Experts Warn," *New York Times,* 8 February 2004, http://www.nytimes.com/2004/02/08/international/asia/08TERR.html (accessed 13 February 2004); and Forest, "Training Camps and Other Centers of Learning."

6. Jerry Markon, "Jihad Trial Witness Says Paintball Was Training Drill," *Washington Post,* 12 February 2004, A16; Tom Jackman, "Two in Virginia Jihad Sentenced to Prison Terms," *Washington Post,* 10 April 2004, B1.

7. Sageman, *Understanding Terror Networks,* 53–54, 179.

8. Quoted in Judith Miller, "Qaeda Videos Seem to Show Chemical Tests," *New York Times,* 19 August 2002, http://www.nytimes.com/2002/08/19/international/asia/19CHEM.html (accessed 19 August 2002); Robertson, "Tapes Show Al Qaeda Trained for Urban Jihad on West," CNN news broadcast, 21 August 2002.

9. C. J. Chivers, "Instruction and Methods from Al Qaeda Took Root in North Iraq with Islamic Fighters," *New York Times,* 27 April 2003, 26.

10. Steve Coll and Susan B. Glasser, "Terrorists Turn to the Web as Base of Operations," *Washington Post,* 7 August 2005, http://www.washingtonpost.com/wp-dyn/content/article/2005/08/05/AR2005080501113 8_pf.html (accessed 12 August 2005). Also see Ulph, "Guide to Jihad on the Web."

11. While this discussion board post has generated some concern in the counterterrorism community, it is unclear whether users have actually been able to use the information contained in the post to start their own training camps, or even whether any training

camps, as described by the anonymous author, have been held. For discussion of the post, see Stephen Ulph, "Secret Camps Offer Operational Courses in Jihad Tactics," *Terrorism Focus* 3, no. 12 (28 March 2006): 5–6. For information on the message board that contained the post, see Internet Haganah, "'Top Ten' Salafyist forums (16 May 2006)," http://haganah.org.il/hmedia/16may06-salafy_forums.html (accessed 5 July 2006); and Internet Haganah, "Abualbokhary Is Back," http://internet-haganah.co.il/harchives/005665.html (accessed 11 July 2006).

12. Coll and Glasser, "Terrorists Turn to Web"; Gabriel Weimann, *Terror on the Internet: The New Arena, the New Challenges* (Washington, D.C.: U.S. Institute of Peace Press, 2006); Scott Atran, "The 'Virtual Hand' of Jihad," *Terrorism Monitor* 3, no. 10 (19 May 2005): 8–11; Wright, "Terror Web"; and Evan Kohlmann, "Al Qaeda and the Internet," *Washington Post*, 8 August 2005, http://www.washingtonpost.com/wp-dyn/content/discussion/2005/08/05/DI2005080501262_pf.html (accessed 14 December 2005).

13. To be sure, counter-netwar is not without its critics, particularly among officials immersed in the day-to-day realities of bureaucratic governance, where the need for accountability often trumps other concerns. For discussion of counter-netwar, see Arquilla and Ronfeldt, *Networks and Netwars;* Robert J. Bunker, ed., *Networks, Terrorism and Global Insurgency* (New York: Routledge, 2005); Arthur Cebrowski and John Garstka, "Network-Centric Warfare," *Proceedings of the United States Naval Institute* 24, no. 1 (1998): 28–35; and John P. Sullivan, "Terrorism Early Warning Groups: Regional Intelligence to Combat Terrorism," in *Homeland Security and Terrorism: Readings and Implications,* ed. Russell D. Howard, James J. F. Forest, and Joanne C. Moore (New York: McGraw-Hill, 2006), 235–45. See also the 9/11 Commission's and the Markle Foundation Task Force's respective recommendations for reforming the intelligence community: *9/11 Commission Report,* 400, 418; and Markle Foundation Task Force, *Creating a Trusted Network for Homeland Security.*

14. Jane Mayer, "The Hidden Power: The Legal Mind Behind the White House's War on Terror," *New Yorker,* 3 July 2006, 44–55; Josh Meyer, "CIA Expands Use of Drones in Terror War," *Los Angeles Times,* 29 January 2006; and Risen, *State of War.*

15. Some proponents of counter-netwar, including Arquilla and Ronfeldt, concede that enforcement networks should retain some of the features of government hierarchies, including bureaucratic accountability. Unfortunately, they fail to recognize that the public sector's need for accountability, transparency, and the rule of law impedes the government's ability to mimic the flat network structures of their illicit adversaries. Arquilla and Ronfeldt, "What Next for Networks and Netwar?" in Arquilla and Ronfeldt, *Networks and Netwars,* 327–28.

16. Quoted in Sam Vincent Meddis, "Colombia's Cocaine Chain," *USA Today,* 24 July 1995.

17. UN, Office of Drugs and Crime, *World Drug Report 2006,* vol. 1, *Analysis,* 17.

18. Quoted in Douglas Farah, "Colombian Drug Cartels Exploit Tech Advantage," *Washington Post,* 15 November 1999.

19. U.S. Congress, House of Representatives, Government Reform Committee, Subcommittee on Criminal Justice, Drug Policy, and Human Resources, testimony of Robert B. Charles, Assistant Secretary of State for International Narcotics and Law Enforcement Affairs, Before the House Government Reform Committee, Subcommittee on Criminal Justice, Drug Policy, and Human Resources, *U.S. Policy and the Andean Counterdrug Initiative (ACI),* 108th Cong., 2d sess., 2 March 2004, http://www.state.gov/g/inl/rls/rm/30077pf.htm (accessed 8 March 2004).

20. Significantly, these figures do not include fatalities in Afghanistan, Chechnya, and Iraq, where Islamic militants were fighting in guerrilla insurgencies. See Fred Burton, "Al Qaeda in 2006: Devolution and Adaptation," *Stratfor Weekly,* 3 January 2006, http://www.stratfor.com/products/premium/read_article.php?id=260353 (accessed 7 February 2006).

21. Susan Schmidt and Douglas Farah, "Al Qaeda's New Leaders," *Washington Post*, 29 October 2002; Craig Whitlock, "Terror Probes Find the Hands, but Not the Brains," *Washington Post*, 11 July 2005; Robert Windrem, "The Frightening Evolution of al-Qaida: Decentralization Has Led to Deadly Staying Power," *NBC Dateline*, 24 June 2005, http://www.msnbc.msn.com/id/8307333 (accessed 15 July 2005).

22. Ahmed Rashid, "Afghanistan: On the Brink," *New York Review of Books*, 22 June 2006, http://www.nybooks.com/articles/19098 (accessed 22 June 2006).

23. Scott Johnson and Melinda Liu, "The Enemy Spies," *Newsweek*, 27 June 2005, http://www.msnbc.msn.com/id/8272786/site/newsweek (accessed 27 June 2006); Douglas Jehl, "Iraq May Be Prime Place for Training of Militants, C.I.A. Report Concludes," *New York Times*, 22 June 2005, http://www.nytimes.com/2005/06/22/international/middleeast/22intel.html (accessed 22 June 2005); U.S. Department of State, Office of the Coordinator for Counterterrorism, *Country Reports on Terrorism 2004*, Department of State Publication 11248 (April 2005), http://www.state.gov/documents/organization/45313.pdf (accessed 2 May 2005), 7; Benjamin and Simon, *Next Attack*, 42.

24. Porter J. Goss, "DCI's Global Intelligence Challenges Briefing, Global Intelligence Challenges 2005: Meeting Long-Term Challenges with a Long-Term Strategy," *Current and Projected National Security Threats to the United States, Hearings Before the U.S. Senate Select Committee on Intelligence*, 109th Cong., 2d sess., 16 February 2005, http://intelligence.senate.gov/0502hrg/050216/goss.pdf (accessed 18 February 2005), 3.

25. Jehl, "Iraq May Be Prime Place for Training of Militants."

26. MacCoun and Reuter, *Drug War Heresies*, 24, 34–35.

27. Levitt and March, "Organizational Learning," 319–40; James G. March and Johan P. Olsen, "The Institutional Dynamics of International Political Orders," *International Organization* 52, no. 4 (1998): 943–69; March, "Exploration and Exploitation in Organizational Learning."

28. See State Department, Bureau for International Narcotics and Law Enforcement Affairs, *International Narcotics Control Strategy Report 2006*, vol. 1.

29. Paul R. Pillar, "Intelligence," in *Attacking Terrorism: Elements of a Grand Strategy*, ed. Audrey Kurth Cronin and James M. Ludes (Washington, D.C.: Georgetown University Press, 2004), 116.

30. Ignatieff, *Lesser Evil*.

31. March, "Exploration and Exploitation in Organizational Learning."

Selected Bibliography

Abadinsky, Howard. *The Criminal Elite: Professional and Organized Crime*. Westport, Conn.: Greenwood Press, 1983.

———. *Organized Crime*, 5th ed. Chicago: Nelson Hall, 1997.

Adler, Patricia A. *Wheeling and Dealing: An Ethnography of an Upper-Level Drug Dealing and Smuggling Community*. 2d ed. New York: Columbia University Press, 1993.

Albanese, Jay. *Organized Crime in America*. 3d edition. Cincinnati: Anderson, 1996.

Andreas, Peter. *Border Games: Policing the U.S.-Mexico Divide*. Ithaca: Cornell University Press, 2000.

———. "Redrawing the Line: Borders and Security in the Twenty-first Century." *International Security* 28, no. 2 (2003): 78–111.

Andreas, Peter, and Richard Price. "From War-fighting to Crime-fighting: Transforming the American National Security State." *International Studies Review* 3, no. 3 (2001): 31–52.

Anonymous [Michael Scheuer]. *Through Our Enemies' Eyes: Osama Bin Laden, Radical Islam, and the Future of America*. Washington, D.C.: Brassey's, 2002.

Argyris, Chris, and Donald A. Schön. *Organizational Learning II: Theory, Method, and Practice*. Reading, Mass.: Addison-Wesley, 1996.

Arias, Enrique Desmond. *Drugs and Democracy in Rio de Janeiro: Trafficking, Social Networks, and Public Security*. Chapel Hill: University of North Carolina Press, 2006.

Arlacchi, Pino. *Mafia Business: The Mafia Ethic and the Spirit of Capitalism*. Trans. Martin Ryle. London: Verso, 1986.

Arquilla, John, and David Ronfeldt, eds. *Networks and Netwars: The Future of Terror, Crime, and Militancy*. Washington, D.C.: RAND Corporation, 2001.

Arquilla, John, David Ronfeldt, and Michele Zanini. "Networks, Netwar, and Information-Age Terrorism." In Ian O. Lesser et al., *Countering the New Terrorism*, 39–84. Santa Monica, Calif.: RAND Corporation, 1999.

Atran, Scott. "The 'Virtual Hand' of Jihad." *Terrorism Monitor*, 19 May 2005, 8–11.

Axelrod, Robert. "Schema Theory: An Information Processing Model of Perception and Cognition." *American Political Science Review* 67, no. 4 (1973): 1248–66.

———. *The Complexity of Cooperation: Agent-Based Models of Competition and Cooperation*. Princeton: Princeton University Press, 1997.

Axelrod, Robert, and Michael D. Cohen. *Harnessing Complexity: Organizational Implications for a Scientific Frontier*. New York: Free Press, 1999.

Baker, Wayne E., and Robert R. Faulkner. "The Social Organization of Conspiracy: Illegal Networks in the Heavy Electrical Equipment Industry." *American Sociological Review* 58 (December 1993): 837–60.

Bagley, Bruce M. "Globalisation and Latin American and Caribbean Organised Crime." *Global Crime* 6, no. 1 (2004): 32–53.

Bates, Robert H., Avner Greif, Margaret Levi, Jean-Laurent Rosenthal, and Barry R. Weingast. *Analytic Narratives*. Princeton: Princeton University Press, 1998.

Bateson, Gregory. *Steps to an Ecology of Mind*. New York: Ballantine Books, 1972.

Bell, J. Bowyer. *The IRA, 1968–2000: Analysis of a Secret Army*. London: Frank Cass, 2000.

Benjamin, Daniel, and Steven Simon. *The Age of Sacred Terror*. New York: Random House, 2002.

———. *The Next Attack: The Failure of the War on Terror and a Strategy for Getting It Right*. New York: Times Books, 2005.

Bennett, Andrew, and Alexander L. George. "Case Studies and Process Tracing in History and Political Science: Similar Strokes for Different Foci." In *Bridges and Boundaries: Historians, Political Scientists, and the Study of International Relations*, ed. Colin Elman and Miriam Fendius Elman, 137–66. Cambridge: MIT Press, 2001.

Berenbaum, Michael. *Witness to the Holocaust*. New York: HarperCollins, 1997.

Berenbaum, Michael, and Abraham J. Peck, eds. *The Holocaust and History: The Known, the Unknown, the Disputed, and the Reexamined*. Bloomington: Indiana University Press, 1998.

Bergen, Peter L. *Holy War, Inc.: Inside the Secret World of Osama bin Laden*. New York: Free Press, 2001.

Bernard, H. Russell. *Research Methods in Anthropology: Qualitative and Quantitative Approaches*. 2d ed. Walnut Creek, Calif.: Altamira, 1995.

Berntsen, Gary, and Ralph Pezzullo. *Jawbreaker: The Attack on Bin Laden and Al Qaeda; A Personal Account by the CIA's Key Field Commander*. New York: Crown Publishers, 2005.

Bertram, Eva, Morris Blachman, Kenneth Sharpe, and Peter Andreas. *Drug War Politics: The Price of Denial*. Berkeley and Los Angeles: University of California Press, 1996.

Betancourt Echeverry, Darío. *Mediadores, rebuscadores, traquetos y narcos: Valle del Cauca, 1890–1997*. Bogotá: Ediciones Antropos, 1998.

Biddle, Stephen. *Afghanistan and the Future of Warfare: Implications for Army and Defense Policy*. Carlisle, Pa.: Strategic Studies Institute, November 2002.

———. "Afghanistan and the Future of Warfare." *Foreign Affairs* 83, no. 2 (2003).

Bite Back Magazine 1. "News from the Frontline." N.d. http://www.directaction.info/library_jon.htm (accessed 15 June 2005).

Block, Alan A. "The Snowman Cometh: Coke in Progressive New York." *Criminology* 17, no. 1 (1979): 75–99.

Bloom, Mia. *Dying to Kill: The Allure of Suicide Terror*. New York: Columbia University Press, 2005.

Blum, Jack A. "Offshore Money." In *Transnational Crime in the Americas*, ed. Tom Farer, 57–84. New York: Routledge, 1999.

Bourdieu, Pierre. *The Logic of Practice*. Trans. Richard Nice. Cambridge, UK: Polity Press, 1990.

Bowden, Mark. *Killing Pablo: The Hunt for the World's Greatest Outlaw.* New York: Atlantic Monthly Press, 2001.

Breslauer, George W., and Philip E. Tetlock, eds. *Learning in U.S. and Soviet Foreign Policy.* Boulder, Colo.: Westview Press, 1991.

Brown, John Seely, and Paul Duguid. "Organizational Learning and Communities-of-Practice: Toward a Unified View of Working, Learning, and Innovation." *Organization Science* 2, no. 1 (1991): 40–57.

Bunker, Robert J., ed. *Networks, Terrorism, and Global Insurgency.* New York: Routledge, 2005.

Burt, Ronald S. *Structural Holes: The Social Structure of Competition.* Cambridge: Harvard University Press, 1992.

Burton, Fred. "Al Qaeda in 2006: Devolution and Adaptation." *Stratfor Weekly,* 3 January 2006. http://www.stratfor.com/products/premium/read_article .php?id = 260353 (accessed 7 February 2006).

———. "Beware of 'Kramer': Tradecraft and the New Jihadists." *Stratfor Weekly,* 18 January 2006. http://www.stratfor.com/products/premium/read_article .php?id = 261022 (accessed 7 February 2006).

Butte, Dick. *El sueño de la tierra propia: Un reportaje gráfico sobre una familia de colonos colombianos cultivadores de coca.* Bogotá: El Áncora Editores, 1990.

Byman, Daniel. "Should Hezbollah Be Next?" *Foreign Affairs* 82, no. 6 (2003): 54–66.

———. *Deadly Connections: States That Sponsor Terrorism.* New York: Cambridge University Press, 2005.

Carafano, James Jay, and David Heyman. "DHS 2.0: Rethinking the Department of Homeland Security." *Heritage Special Report,* SR-02. Washington, D.C.: Heritage Foundation and Center for Strategic and International Studies, 13 December 2004.

Carley, Kathleen. "Organizational Learning and Personnel Turnover." *Organization Science* 3, no. 1 (1992). Reprinted in *Organizational Learning,* ed. Michael D. Cohen and Lee S. Sproull (Thousand Oaks, Calif.: Sage Publications, 1996), 230–66.

Castro Caycedo, Germán. *En secreto.* Bogotá: Planeta Colombiana Editorial, 1996.

Caulkins, Jonathan P., Mark A. R. Kleiman, and Peter Reuter. "Lessons of the 'War' on Drugs for the 'War' on Terrorism." In *Countering Terrorism: Dimensions of Preparedness,* ed. Arnold M. Howitt and Robyn L. Pangi, 73–93. Cambridge: MIT Press, 2003.

Cebrowski, Arthur, and John Garstka. "Network-Centric Warfare." *Proceedings of the United States Naval Institute* 24, no. 1 (1998): 28–35.

Chepesiuk, Ron. *The Bullet or the Bribe: Taking Down Colombia's Cali Drug Cartel.* Westport, Conn.: Praeger, 2003.

Chernick, Marc W. "Economic Resources and Internal Armed Conflicts: Lessons from the Colombian Case." In *Rethinking the Economics of War: The Intersection of Need, Creed, and Greed,* ed. Cynthia J. Arnson and I. William Zartman, 178–205. Washington, D.C. and Baltimore: Woodrow Wilson International Center for Scholars and Johns Hopkins University Press, 2005.

Clarke, Richard A. *Against All Enemies: Inside America's War on Terror.* New York: Free Press, 2004.

Clarridge, Duane R., with Digby Diehl. *A Spy for All Seasons: My Life in the CIA.* New York: Scribner, 1997.

Clawson, Patrick L., and Rensselaer W. Lee III. *The Andean Cocaine Industry.* New York: St. Martin's Press, 1996.

Clutterbuck, Richard. "Trends in Terrorist Weaponry." In *Technology and Terrorism*, ed. Paul Wilkinson, 130–39. London: Frank Cass, 1993.

Cohen, Michael D., and Paul Bacdayan. "Organizational Routines Are Stored as Procedural Memory: Evidence from a Laboratory Study." *Organization Science* 5, no. 4 (1994). Reprinted in *Cognition Within and Between Organizations*, ed. James R. Meindl, Charles Stubbart, and Joseph F. Porac (Thousand Oaks, Calif.: Sage Publications, 1996), 403–29.

Cohen, Michael D., James G. March, and Johan P. Olsen. "A Garbage Can Model of Organizational Choice." *Administrative Science Quarterly* 17, no. 1 (1972): 1–25.

Cohen, Michael D., and Lee S. Sproull, eds. *Organizational Learning.* Thousand Oaks, Calif.: Sage Publications, 1996.

Coll, Steve. *Ghost Wars: The Secret History of the CIA, Afghanistan, and bin Laden, from the Soviet Invasion to September 10, 2001.* New York: Penguin Books, 2004.

Collins, Eamon, with Mick McGovern. *Killing Rage.* London: Granta, 1997.

Cook, Scott D. N., and Dvora Yanow. "Culture and Organizational Learning." *Journal of Management Inquiry* 2, no. 4 (1993). Reprinted in *Organizational Learning*, ed. Michael D. Cohen and Lee S. Sproull (Thousand Oaks, Calif.: Sage Publications, 1996), 430–59.

Cordesman, Anthony H. *Iraq's Evolving Insurgency: The Nature of Attacks and Patterns and Cycles in the Conflict.* Washington, D.C.: Center for Strategic and International Studies, 3 February 2006. http://www.csis.org/media/csis/pubs/060203_iraqicombattrends.pdf (accessed 15 June 2006).

Cragin, Kim. "Hizballah, the Party of God." In Brian A. Jackson et al., *Aptitude for Destruction*, vol. 2, *Case Studies of Organizational Learning in Five Terrorist Groups*, 37–55. Santa Monica, Calif.: RAND Corporation, 2005.

Cressey, Donald R. "Methodological Problems in the Study of Organized Crime as a Social Problem." *Annals of the American Academy of Political and Social Science* 374 (November 1967): 101–12.

Cubides, Fernando. "Los paramilitares y su estrategia." In *Reconocer la guerra para construir la paz*, ed. Malcolm Deas and María Victoria Llorente, 151–99. Bogotá: Ediciones Uniandes, 1999.

Cyert, Richard M., and James G. March. *A Behavioral Theory of the Firm.* Englewood Cliffs, N.J.: Prentice-Hall, 1963.

Daft, Richard L., and Karl E. Weick. "Toward a Model of Organizations as Interpretation Systems." *Academy of Management Review* 9, no. 2 (1984): 284–95.

Detienne, Marcel, and Jean-Pierre Vernant. *Cunning Intelligence in Greek Culture and Society.* Trans. Janet Lloyd. Sussex, UK: Harvester Press, 1978.

Deutsch, Karl W. *The Nerves of Government: Models of Political Communication and Control.* New York: Free Press, 1966.

DiMaggio, Paul J., and Walter W. Powell. "The Iron Cage Revisited: Institutional

Isomorphism and Collective Rationality in Organizational Fields." *American Sociological Review* 48 (April 1983): 147–60.

Dodgson, Mark. "Organizational Learning: A Review of Some Literatures." *Organization Studies* 14, no. 3 (1993): 375–94.

Dorn, Nicholas, and Nigel South. "Drug Markets and Law Enforcement." *British Journal of Criminology* 30, no. 2 (1990): 171–88.

Eden, Lynn. *Whole World on Fire: Organizations, Knowledge, and Nuclear Weapons Devastation.* Ithaca: Cornell University Press, 2004.

Eilstrup-Sangiovanni, Mette. "Changing Patterns of Security Cooperation: From Interstate Cooperation to Transgovernmental Networks." Paper presented at the Networked Politics Workshop hosted by the Munk Center for International Studies, University of Toronto, 11–13 May 2006.

Enders, Walter, and Todd Sandler. "The Effectiveness of Antiterrorism Policies: A Vector-Autoregression-Intervention Analysis." *American Political Science Review* 87, no. 4 (1993): 829–44.

Epstein, Joshua M., and Robert Axtell. *Growing Artificial Societies: Social Science from the Bottom Up.* Washington, D.C.: Brookings Institution Press, 1996.

Etheridge, Lloyd S. *Can Governments Learn? American Foreign Policy and Central American Revolutions.* New York: Pergamon Press, 1985.

Evans, Peter B. *Embedded Autonomy: States and Industrial Transformation.* Princeton: Princeton University Press, 1995.

Farah, Douglas. "Colombian Drug Lords Ran Empire Behind Bars." *Washington Post,* 26 December 1996, A37.

Feickert, Andrew. "U.S. Special Operations Forces (SOF): Background and Issues for Congress." *Congressional Research Service Report for Congress,* 28 September 2004. http://www.fas.org/man/crs/RS21048.pdf (accessed 20 December 2005).

Feldman, Martha S. *Order Without Design: Information Production and Policy Making.* Stanford: Stanford University Press, 1989.

———. "Organizational Routines as a Source of Continuous Change." *Organization Science* 11, no. 6 (2000): 611–29.

Feldman, Martha S., Jeannine Bell, and Michele Tracy Berger. *Gaining Access: A Practical and Theoretical Guide for Qualitative Researchers.* Walnut Creek, Calif.: Altamira, 2003.

Feldman, Martha S., and Anne Khademian. "Models for Decision-Making and Policy Formulation." In *Integrating Environmental Considerations in Policy Formulation: Lessons from Policy-Based SEA Experience,* ed. Kulsum Ahmed and Ernesto Sanchez-Triana. Washington, D.C.: World Bank, forthcoming.

Finckenauer, James O., and Elin Waring. *Russian Mafia in America: Immigration, Culture, and Crime.* Boston: Northeastern University Press, 1998.

Fiol, C. Marlene, and Marjorie A. Lyles. "Organizational Learning." *Academy of Management Review* 10, no. 4 (1985): 803–13.

Flynn, Stephen E. *America the Vulnerable: How Our Government Is Failing to Protect Us from Terrorism.* New York: HarperCollins, 2004.

Foreman, Dave, and Bill Haywood, eds. *Ecodefense: A Field Guide to Monkey Wrenching.* 3d ed. Chico, Calif.: Abbzug Press, 1993.

Forest, James J. F. "Introduction." In *Teaching Terror: Strategic and Tactical Learn-*

ing in the Terrorist World, ed. James J. F. Forest, 1–30. Lanham, Md.: Rowman & Littlefield, 2006.

———. "Training Camps and Other Centers of Learning." In *Teaching Terror: Strategic and Tactical Learning in the Terrorist World*, ed. James J. F. Forest, 69–109. Lanham, Md.: Rowman & Littlefield, 2006.

Fuentes, Joseph R. "The Life of a Cell." Ph.D. diss., City University of New York, Criminal Justice Department, 1998.

García Márquez, Gabriel. *News of a Kidnapping*. Trans. Edith Grossman. New York: Penguin Books, 1996.

Garvin, David A. *Learning in Action: A Guide to Putting the Learning Organization to Work*. Boston: Harvard Business School Press, 2000.

Garzón Saboyá, Edgar Alfredo. "Aspectos legales y praxis del narcotráfico y lavado de dinero." In *Drogas ilícitas en Colombia: Su impacto económico, politico y social*. Francisco E. Thoumi et al., 347–408. Bogotá: Planeta Colombiana Editorial, 1997.

Geddes, Barbara. *Politician's Dilemma: Building State Capacity in Latin America*. Berkeley and Los Angeles: University of California Press, 1994.

Geertz, Clifford. "Thick Description: Toward an Interpretive Theory of Culture." In *The Interpretation of Cultures: Selected Essays by Clifford Geertz*, 3–30. New York: Basic Books, 1973.

George, Alexander L. "Case Studies and Theory Development: The Method of Structured, Focused Comparisons." In *Diplomacy: New Approaches in History, Theory, and Policy*, ed. Paul Gordon Lauren, 43–68. New York: Free Press, 1979.

George, Alexander L., and Timothy J. McKeown. "Case Studies and Theories of Organizational Decision-Making." In *Advances in Information Processing in Organizations*, vol. 2, ed. Robert F. Coulam and Richard A. Smith, 21–58. Greenwich, Conn.: JAI, 1985.

Geraghty, Tony. *The Irish War: The Hidden Conflict Between the IRA and British Intelligence*. Baltimore: Johns Hopkins University Press, 2000.

Gould, Stephen Jay. *A Wonderful Life: The Burgess Shale and the Nature of History*. New York: W. W. Norton, 1989.

Grabher, Gernot, and David Stark. "Organizing Diversity: Evolutionary Theory, Network Analysis, and Post-Socialism." In *Restructuring Networks in Post-Socialism: Legacies, Linkages, and Localities*, ed. Gernot Grabher and David Stark, 1–32. New York: Oxford University Press, 1997.

Grahn, Lance. *The Political Economy of Smuggling: Regional Informal Economies in Early Bourbon New Granada*. Boulder, Colo.: Westview Press, 1997.

Granovetter, Mark S. "The Strength of Weak Ties." *American Journal of Sociology* 78, no. 6 (1973): 1360–80.

———. "Economic Action and Social Structure: The Problem of Embeddedness." *American Journal of Sociology* 91, no. 3 (1985): 481–510.

Gross, K. Hawkeye. *Drug Smuggling: The Forbidden Book*. Boulder, Colo.: Paladin Press, 1992.

Guillermoprieto, Alma. *The Heart That Bleeds: Latin America Now*. New York: Knopf, 1994.

Gunaratna, Rohan. *Inside Al Qaeda: Global Network of Terror*. New York: Columbia University Press, 2002.

———. "Al Qaeda's Lose and Learn Doctrine: The Trajectory from Oplan Bojinka to 9/11." In *Teaching Terror: Strategic and Tactical Learning in the Terrorist World,* ed. James J. F. Forest, 171–88. Lanham, Md.: Rowman & Littlefield, 2006.

Guttieri, Karen. "Unlearning War: U.S. Military Experience with Stability Operations." In *Organizational Learning in the Global Context,* ed. M. Leann Brown, Michael Kenney, and Michael Zarkin, 217–35. London: Ashgate, 2006.

Haas, Ernst. *When Knowledge Is Power: Three Models of Change in International Organizations.* Berkeley and Los Angeles: University of California Press, 1990.

Hall, Peter A. "Policy Paradigms, Social Learning, and the State." *Comparative Politics* 25 (April 1993): 275–96.

Hannan, Michael T., and John Freeman. "The Population Ecology of Organizations." *American Journal of Sociology* 82, no. 5 (1977): 929–64.

Hashim, Ahmed S. *Insurgency and Counter-Insurgency in Iraq.* Ithaca: Cornell University Press, 2006.

Heckmann, Friedrich. "Illegal Migration: What Can We Know and What Can We Explain? The Case of Germany." *International Migration Review* 38, no. 3 (2004): 1103–25.

Hedberg, Bo. "How Organizations Learn and Unlearn." In *Handbook of Organizational Design,* vol. 1, *Adapting Organizations to their Environments,* ed. Paul C. Nystrom and William H. Starbuck, 3–27. New York: Oxford University Press, 1981.

Hersh, Seymour M. "Escape and Evasion." *New Yorker,* 12 November 2001. http://www.newyorker.com/printable/?fact/011112fa_FACT (accessed 18 June 2003).

———. "Moving Targets," *New Yorker,* 15 December 2003, 48–55.

———. *Chain of Command: The Road from 9/11 to Abu Ghraib.* New York: HarperCollins, 2004.

Heyman, Edward, and Edward Mickolus. "Observations on Why Violence Spreads." *International Studies Quarterly* 24, no. 2 (1980): 299–305.

———. "Imitation by Terrorists: Quantitative Approaches to the Study of Diffusion Patterns in Transnational Terrorism." In *Behavioral and Quantitative Perspectives on Terrorism,* ed. Yonah Alexander and John M. Gleason, 175–228. New York: Pergamon Press, 1981.

Hoffman, Bruce. *Inside Terrorism.* New York: Columbia University Press, 1998.

———. "Terrorism Trends and Prospects." In Ian O. Lesser et al., *Countering the New Terrorism,* 7–38. Santa Monica, Calif.: RAND Corporation, 1999.

———. "Rethinking Terrorism and Counterterrorism Since 9/11." *Studies in Conflict and Terrorism* 25 (2002): 303–16.

———. "Insurgency and Counterinsurgency in Iraq." *Studies in Conflict and Terrorism* 29 (2006): 103–21.

Holland, John H. *Hidden Order: How Adaptation Builds Complexity.* Cambridge, Mass.: Perseus Books, 1995.

Horne, Alistair. *A Savage War of Peace: Algeria 1954–1962.* New York: Viking, 1978.

Huber, George P. "Organizational Learning: The Contributing Processes and the Literatures." *Organization Science* 2, no. 1 (1991): 88–115.

Hutchins, Edward. "Organizing Work by Adaptation." *Organization Science* 2, no. 1 (1991). Reprinted in *Cognition Within and Between Organizations*, ed. James R. Meindl, Charles Stubbart, and Joseph F. Porac (Thousand Oaks, Calif.: Sage Publications, 1996), 368–404.

Ignatieff, Michael. *The Lesser Evil: Political Ethics in an Age of Terror*. Princeton: Princeton University Press, 2005.

Jaber, Hala. *Hizballah: Born with a Vengeance*. New York: Columbia University Press, 1997.

Jackson, Brian A. "Provisional Irish Republican Army." In Brian A. Jackson et al., *Aptitude for Destruction*, vol. 2, *Case Studies of Organizational Learning in Five Terrorist Groups*, 93–140. Santa Monica, Calif.: RAND Corporation, 2005.

Jackson, Brian A., John C. Baker, Kim Cragin, John Parachini, Horacio R. Trujillo, and Peter Chalk. *Aptitude for Destruction*. Vol. 2, *Case Studies of Organizational Learning in Five Terrorist Groups*. Santa Monica, Calif.: RAND Corporation, 2005.

Jenkins, Brian M. "International Terrorism: The Other World War." In *The New Global Terrorism: Characteristics, Causes, Control*, ed. Charles W. Kegley Jr., 15–26. Upper Saddle River, N.J.: Prentice-Hall, 2003.

Jervis, Robert. *Perception and Misperception in International Politics*. Princeton: Princeton University Press, 1976.

———. *System Effects: Complexity in Political and Social Life*. Princeton: Princeton University Press, 1997.

Jonnes, Jill. *Hep-Cats, Narcs, and Pipe Dreams: A History of America's Romance with Illegal Drugs*. Baltimore: Johns Hopkins University Press, 1996.

Juergensmeyer, Mark. *Terror in the Mind of God: The Global Rise of Religious Violence*. 3d ed. Berkeley and Los Angeles: University of California Press, 2003.

Kappeler, Victor E., Mark Blumberg, and Gary W. Potter. *The Mythology of Crime and Criminal Justice*. Prospect Heights, Ill.: Waveland Press, 1993.

Keck, Margaret E., and Kathryn Sikkink. *Activists Beyond Borders: Advocacy Networks in International Politics*. Ithaca: Cornell University Press, 1998.

Kegley, Charles W., Jr., ed. *The New Global Terrorism: Characteristics, Causes, Control*. Upper Saddle River, N.J.: Prentice-Hall, 2003.

Kerry, John. *New War: The Web of Crime That Threatens America's Security*. New York: Simon and Schuster, 1997.

Kettl, Donald F. *System Under Stress: Homeland Security and American Politics*. Washington, D.C.: CQ Press, 2004.

Khong, Yuen Foong. *Analogies at War: Korea, Munich, Dien Bien Phu, and the Vietnam Decisions of 1965*. Princeton: Princeton University Press, 1992.

Kibbe, Jennifer D. "The Rise of the Shadow Warriors." *Foreign Affairs* 83, no. 2 (2004): 102–15.

Kim, Daniel H. "The Link Between Individual and Organizational Learning." *Sloan Management Review* 35, no. 1 (1993): 37–50.

King, Gary, Robert O. Keohane, and Sidney Verba. *Designing Social Inquiry: Scien-*

tific Inference in Qualitative Research. Princeton: Princeton University Press, 1994.

Kingdon, John W. *Agendas, Alternatives, and Public Policies.* 2d ed. New York: HarperCollins, 1995.

Kirk, Robin. *More Terrible than Death: Violence, Drugs, and America's War in Colombia.* New York: Public Affairs, 2004.

Klerks, Peter. "The Network Paradigm Applied to Criminal Organisations: Theoretical Nitpicking or a Relevant Doctrine for Investigators? Recent Developments in the Netherlands." *Connections* 24, no. 3 (2001): 53–65.

Krauthausen, Ciro, and Luis Fernando Sarmiento. *Cocaína y Co.: Un mercado ilegal por dentro.* Bogotá: Tercer Mundo, 1991.

LaPorte, Todd R., and Paula M. Consolini. "Working in Practice but Not in Theory: Theoretical Challenges of 'High-Reliability Organizations.'" *Journal of Public Administration Research and Theory* 1, no. 1 (1991): 19–47.

Larabee, Ann. "A Brief History of Terrorism in the United States." In *Technology and Terrorism,* ed. David Clarke, 19–40. New Brunswick, N.J.: Transaction Publishers, 2004.

Lave, Jean, and Etienne Wenger. *Situated Learning: Legitimate Peripheral Participation.* New York: Cambridge University Press, 1991.

Lee, Gordon T. "Hard-Shelled, SOF-Centered: The Synergy of Might and Mind." *Rand Review* (summer 2002): 40–41.

Lee, Rensselaer W. *The White Labyrinth: Cocaine and Political Power.* New Brunswick, N.J.: Transaction Publishers, 1989.

Levine, Michael. *Deep Cover: The Inside Story of How DEA Infighting, Incompetence, and Subterfuge Lost Us the Biggest Battle of the Drug War.* New York: Delacorte Press, 1990.

Levitt, Barbara, and James G. March. "Organizational Learning." *Annual Review of Sociology* 14 (1988): 319–40.

Levy, Jack S. "Learning and Foreign Policy: Sweeping a Conceptual Minefield." *International Organization* 48, no. 2 (1994): 279–312.

Lowenthal, Abraham. *The Dominican Intervention.* Cambridge: Harvard University Press, 1972.

Lupsha, Peter A. "Networks Versus Networking." In *Career Criminals,* ed. Gordon P. Waldo, 59–87. Beverly Hills: Sage Publications, 1983.

————. "Transnational Organized Crime Versus the Nation-State." *Transnational Organized Crime* 2, no. 1 (1996): 21–48.

Lyman, Michael D. *Practical Drug Enforcement.* 2d ed. Boca Raton, Fla.: CRC Press, 2002.

MacCoun, Robert J., and Peter Reuter. *Drug War Heresies: Learning from Other Vices, Times, and Places.* New York: Cambridge University Press, 2001.

March, James G. "Exploration and Exploitation in Organizational Learning." *Organization Science* 2, no. 1 (1991): 71–87.

March, James G., and Johan P. Olsen. "The Uncertainty of the Past: Organizational Learning Under Ambiguity." *European Journal of Political Research* 3 (1975): 147–71.

————. *Rediscovering Institutions: The Organizational Basis of Politics.* New York: Free Press, 1989.

———. "The Institutional Dynamics of International Political Orders." *International Organization* 52, no. 4 (1998): 943–69.

March, James G., and Herbert A. Simon. *Organizations*. New York: John Wiley & Sons, 1958.

March, James G., Lee S. Sproull, and Michal Tamuz. "Learning from Samples of One or Fewer." *Organization Science* 2 (1991): 1–13.

Markle Foundation Task Force. *Creating a Trusted Network for Homeland Security*. New York: Markle Foundation, 2003. http://www.markle.org/download able_assets/nstf_report2_full_report.pdf (accessed 1 April 2005).

Marx, Gary T. *Undercover: Police Surveillance in America*. Berkeley and Los Angeles: University of California Press, 1988.

Massing, Michael. *The Fix*. Berkeley and Los Angeles: University of California Press, 1998.

Mastrofski, Stephen, and Gary Potter. "Controlling Organized Crime: A Critique of Law Enforcement Policy." *Criminal Justice Policy Review* 2, no. 3 (1987): 269–301.

May, Ernest R. *"Lessons"of the Past*. New York: Oxford University Press, 1973.

Mayer, Jane. "Outsourcing Torture: The Secret History of America's Extraordinary Rendition Program." *New Yorker*, 14 February 2005.

———. "The Hidden Power: The Legal Mind Behind the White House's War on Terror." *New Yorker*, 3 July 2006, 44–55.

McClintick, David. *Swordfish: A True Story of Ambition, Savagery, and Betrayal*. New York: Pantheon Books, 1993.

McCormick, Gordon H. "Terrorist Decision Making." *Annual Review of Political Science* 6 (2003): 473–507.

McDermott, Terry. *Perfect Soldiers: The Hijackers; Who They Were, Why They Did It*. New York: HarperCollins, 2005.

McGee, Jim, and Brian Duffy. *Main Justice: The Men and Women Who Enforce the Nation's Criminal Laws and Guard Its Liberties*. New York: Touchstone, 1997.

McGloin, Jean Marie. "Policy and Intervention Considerations of a Network Analysis of Street Gangs." *Criminology and Public Policy* 4, no. 3 (2005): 607–36.

McIllwain, Jeffrey Scott. "An Equal Opportunity Employer: Opium Smuggling Networks in and Around San Diego During the Early Twentieth Century." *Transnational Organized Crime* 2, no. 4 (1998): 31–54.

———. "Organized Crime: A Social Network Approach." *Crime, Law, and Social Change* 32, no. 4 (1999): 301–23.

Medina Gallego, Carlos. *Autodefensas, paramilitares y narcotráfico en Colombia: Origen, desarrollo y consolidación; El caso "Puerto Boyacá*. Bogotá: Editorial Documentos Periodísticos, 1990.

Mermelstein, Max, as told to Robin Moore and Richard Smitten. *The Man Who Made It Snow*. New York: Simon and Schuster, 1990.

Meyer, Kathryn, and Terry Parssinen. *Webs of Smoke: Smugglers, Warlords, Spies, and the History of the International Drug Trade*. Lanham, Md.: Rowman & Littlefield, 1998.

Midlarsky, Manus I., Martha Crenshaw, and Fumihiko Yoshida. "Why Violence

Spreads: The Contagion of International Terrorism." *International Studies Quarterly* 24, no. 2 (1980): 262–98.

Mishal, Shaul, and Avraham Sela. *The Palestinian Hamas.* New York: Columbia University Press, 2000.

Moe, Terry M. "The New Economics of Organization." American Political Science Review 28, no. 4 (1984): 739–777.

Moore, Robin. *The Hunt for Bin Laden: Task Force Dagger.* New York: Random House, 2003.

Morselli, Carlo. "Structuring Mr. Nice: Entrepreneurial Opportunities and Brokerage Positioning in the Cannabis Trade." *Crime, Law, and Social Change* 35, no. 3 (2001): 203–44.

Most, Johann. *Science of Revolutionary Warfare: A Handbook of Instruction Regarding the Use and Manufacture of Nitroglycerine, Dynamite, Gun-Cotton, Fulminating Mercury, Bombs, Arsons, Poisons, etc.* English translation. El Dorado, Ariz.: Desert Publications, 1978.

Motto, Carmine J., and Dale L. June. *Undercover.* 2d ed. Boca Raton, Fla.: CRC Press, 2000.

Nadelmann, Ethan A. *Cops Across Borders: The Internationalization of U.S. Criminal Law Enforcement.* University Park: Pennsylvania State University Press, 1993.

Natarajan, Mangai. "Understanding the Structure of a Drug Trafficking Organization: A Conversational Analysis." In *Illegal Drug Markets: From Research to Prevention Policy,* ed. Mangai Natarajan and Mike Hough, 273–98. Monsey, N.J.: Criminal Justice Press, 2000.

National Commission on Terrorist Attacks upon the United States. *The 9/11 Commission Report: Final Report of the National Commission on Terrorist Attacks upon the United States.* New York: W. W. Norton, 2004.

——. *Three 9/11 Hijackers: Identification, Watchlisting, and Tracking.* Staff Statement No. 2. http://www.9-11commission.gov/staff_statements/staff_statement_2.pdf (accessed 11 May 2004).

——. *Law Enforcement, Counterterrorism, and Intelligence Collection in the United States Prior to 9-11.* Staff Statement No. 9. http://www.9-11commission.gov/hearings/hearing10/staff_statement_9.pdf (accessed 13 May 2004).

——. *Reforming Law Enforcement, Counterterrorism, and Intelligence Collection in the United States.* Staff Statement No. 12. http://www.9-11commission.gov/hearings/hearing10/staff_statement_12.pdf (accessed 11 May 2004).

——. *Overview of the Enemy.* Staff Statement No. 15. http://www.9-11commission.gov/hearings/hearing12/staff_statement_15.pdf (accessed 16 June 2004).

——. *Outline of the 9/11 Plot.* Staff Statement No. 16. http://www.9-11commission.gov/hearings/hearing12/staff_statement_16.pdf (accessed 16 June 2004).

Naylor, R. Thomas. "Mafias, Myths, and Markets: On the Theory and Practice of Enterprise Crime." *Transnational Organized Crime* 3, no. 3 (1997): 1–45.

——. *Wages of Crime: Black Markets, Illegal Finance, and the Underworld Economy.* Ithaca: Cornell University Press, 2002.

Nicolini, Davide, Silvia Gherardi, and Dvora Yanow, eds. *Knowing in Organizations: A Practice-Based Approach.* Armonk, N.Y.: M. E. Sharpe, 2003.

Nieves, Robert J. *Colombian Cocaine Cartels: Lessons from the Front*. Washington, D.C.: National Strategy Information Center, 1997.

Nonaka, Ikujiro, and Hirotaka Takeuchi. *The Knowledge-Creating Company: How Japanese Companies Create the Dynamics of Innovation*. New York: Oxford University Press, 1995.

Nussbaum, Martha C. *The Fragility of Goodness: Luck and Ethics in Greek Tragedy and Philosophy*. Cambridge: Cambridge University Press, 1986.

Nye, Joseph S. "Nuclear Learning and U.S.-Soviet Security Regimes." *International Organization* 41, no. 3 (1987): 371–402.

Orlikowski, Wanda J. "Knowing in Practice: Enacting a Collective Capability in Distributed Organizing." *Organization Science* 13, no. 3 (2002): 249–73.

Orr, Julian E. *Talking About Machines: An Ethnography of a Modern Job*. Ithaca: Cornell University Press, 1996.

Ostrom, Elinor. *Governing the Commons: The Evolution of Institutions for Collective Action*. New York: Cambridge University Press, 1990.

Packer, George. *The Assassin's Gate: America in Iraq*. New York: Farrar, Straus and Giroux, 2005.

Pallomari, Guillermo. Direct testimony. Trial transcript, *United States of America vs. Michael Abbell, William Moran, Luis Grajales, Eddy Martinez, Ramon Martinez, J.L. Pereira-Salas, et al.*, U.S. District Court, Southern District of Florida, Miami Division, Case No. 93 470-CR-WMH, vols. 36–40 (17, 21, 22, 23, 28 July 1997) and vol. 43 (31 July 1997).

Pape, Robert A. *Dying to Win: The Strategic Logic of Suicide Terrorism*. New York: Random House, 2005.

Parachini, John. "Aum Shinrikyo." In Brian A. Jackson et al., *Aptitude for Destruction*, vol. 2, *Case Studies of Organizational Learning in Five Terrorist Groups*, 11–35. Santa Monica, Calif.: RAND Corporation, 2005.

Phillips, Samantha. "The Story of 'Operation Zorro II' and Some Practical Suggestions." *United States Attorneys' Bulletin* 45, no. 6 (1997). http://www.usdoj .gov/usao/eousa/foia_reading_room/usab4506.pdf (accessed 16 August 2006).

Pillar, Paul R. *Terrorism and U.S. Foreign Policy*. Washington, D.C.: Brookings Institution Press, 2001.

———. "Intelligence." In *Attacking Terrorism: Elements of a Grand Strategy*, ed. Audrey Kurth Cronin and James M. Ludes, 115–39. Washington, D.C.: Georgetown University Press, 2004.

Podolny, Joel M., and Karen L. Page. "Network Forms of Organization." *Annual Review of Sociology* 24 (1998): 57–76.

Polanyi, Michael. *Knowing and Being: Essays by Michael Polanyi*. Edited by Marjorie Grene. Chicago: University of Chicago Press, 1969.

Posen, Barry. *Sources of Military Doctrine: France, Britain, and Germany Between the World Wars*. Ithaca: Cornell University Press, 1984.

Post, Jerrold M., Ehud Sprinzak, and Laurita M. Denny. "The Terrorists in Their Own Words: Interviews with Thirty-five Incarcerated Middle Eastern Terrorists." *Terrorism and Political Violence* 15, no. 1 (2003): 171–84.

Powell, Walter W. "Neither Market nor Hierarchy: Network Forms of Organization." In *Research in Organizational Behavior*, vol. 12, ed. Barry M. Staw and L. L. Cummings, 295–336. Greenwich, Conn.: JAI, 1990.

Priest, Dana. *The Mission: Waging War and Keeping Peace with America's Military*. New York: W. W. Norton, 2003.

Rachal, Patricia. *Federal Narcotics Enforcement: Reorganization and Reform*. Boston: Auburn House, 1982.

Ranstorp, Magnus. "Hizbollah's Command Leadership." *Terrorism and Political Violence* 36, no. 3 (1994): 303–39.

Rashid, Ahmed. "Afghanistan: On the Brink." *New York Review of Books*, 22 June 2006. http://www.nybooks.com/articles/19098 (accessed 22 June 2006).

Rasmussen, David W., and Bruce L. Benson. *The Economic Anatomy of a Drug War: Criminal Justice in the Commons*. Lanham, Md.: Rowman & Littlefield, 1994.

Raymond, Gregory A. "The Evolving Strategies of Political Terrorism." In *The New Global Terrorism: Characteristics, Causes, Control*, ed. Charles W. Kegley Jr., 71–83. Upper Saddle River, N.J.: Prentice-Hall, 2003.

Redlick, Amy Sands. "The Transnational Flow of Information as a Cause of Terrorism." In *Terrorism: Theory and Practice*, ed. Yonah Alexander, David Carlton, and Paul Wilkinson, 73–95. Boulder, Colo.: Westview Press, 1979.

Reiter, Dan. *Crucible of Beliefs: Learning, Alliances, and World Wars*. Ithaca: Cornell University Press, 1996.

Reuter, Peter, Gordon Crawford, and Jonathan Cave. *Sealing the Borders: The Effects of Increased Military Participation in Drug Interdiction*. Santa Monica, Calif.: RAND Corporation, 1988.

Reyes, Gerardo. *Made in Miami: Vidas de narcos, santos, seductores, caudillos y soplones*. Bogotá: Planeta Colombiana Editorial, 1999.

Rice, Berkeley. *Trafficking: The Boom and Bust of the Air America Cocaine Ring*. New York: Charles Scribner's Sons, 1989.

Richani, Nazih. *Systems of Violence: The Political Economy of War and Peace in Colombia*. Albany: State University of New York Press, 2002.

Richardson, Louise. *What Terrorists Want: Understanding the Enemy, Containing the Threat* (New York: Random House, 2006).

Risen, James. *State of War: The Secret History of the CIA and the Bush Administration*. New York: Free Press, 2006.

Risen, James, David Johnston, and Neil A. Lewis. "Harsh C.I.A. Methods Cited in Top Qaeda Interrogations." *New York Times*, 13 May 2004. http://www.nytimes.com/2004/05/13/politics/13DETA.html.

Rosenau, James N. *Turbulence in World Politics: A Theory of Change and Continuity*. Princeton: Princeton University Press, 1990.

Rubin, Barry, and Judith Colp Rubin, eds. *Anti-American Terrorism and the Middle East: A Documentary Reader*. New York: Oxford University Press, 2002.

Russell, Charles A., Leon J. Banker Jr., and Bowman H. Miller. "Out-Inventing the Terrorist." In *Terrorism: Theory and Practice*, ed. Yonah Alexander, David Carlton, and Paul Wilkinson, 3–42. Boulder, Colo.: Westview Press, 1979.

Sagan, Scott D. *The Limits of Safety: Organizations, Accidents, and Nuclear Weapons*. Princeton: Princeton University Press, 1993.

Sageman, Marc. *Understanding Terror Networks*. Philadelphia: University of Pennsylvania Press, 2004.

Schacter, Daniel L. ed. *Memory Distortion: How Minds, Brains, and Societies Reconstruct the Past.* Cambridge: Harvard University Press, 1995.

———. *The Seven Sins of Memory: How the Mind Forgets and Remembers.* Boston: Houghton Mifflin, 2001.

Schein, Edgar H. "Organizational Culture." *American Psychologist* 45, no. 2 (1990): 109–19.

Schmid, Alex P., and Albert J. Jongman. *Political Terrorism: A New Guide to Actors, Authors, Concepts, Data Bases, Theories, and Literature.* Exp. and updated ed. New Brunswick, N.J.: Transaction Publishers, 1988.

Schroen, Gary C. *First In: An Insider's Account of How the CIA Spearheaded the War on Terror in Afghanistan.* New York: Presidio, 2005.

Scott, James C. *Seeing Like a State: How Certain Schemes to Improve the Human Condition Have Failed.* New Haven: Yale University Press, 1998.

Scott, Richard W. *Organizations: Rational, Natural, and Open Systems.* 4th ed. Upper Saddle River, N.J.: Prentice-Hall, 1998.

Seale, Patrick. *Abu Nidal: A Gun for Hire.* New York: Random House, 1992.

Senge, Peter M. *The Fifth Discipline: The Art and Practice of the Learning Organization.* New York: Doubleday, 1990.

Serrano Cadena, Rosso José, with Santiago Gamboa. *Jaque mate: De cómo la policía le ganó la partida a "el ajedrecista" y a los cartels del narcotráfico.* Bogotá: Grupo Editorial Norma, 1999.

Shapiro, Jacob N., and Rudolph Darken. "Homeland Security: A New Strategic Paradigm?" In *Strategy in the Contemporary World,* ed. John Baylis, Eliot Cohen, Colin Gray, and James Wirtz. New York: Oxford University Press, forthcoming.

Simon, Herbert A. *Administrative Behavior: A Study of Decision-Making Processes in Administrative Organizations.* New York: Macmillan, 1947.

———. "A Behavioral Model of Rational Choice." *Quarterly Journal of Economics* 69 (1955): 99–118.

Sklaire, Michael R. "Electronic Surveillance Guide." *United States Attorneys' Bulletin* 45, no. 5 (1997): 20. http://www.usdoj.gov/usao/eousa/foia_reading_room/usab4505.pdf (accessed 13 March 2003).

Slaughter, Anne Marie. *A New World Order.* Princeton: Princeton University Press, 2004.

Smith, David E. "The Training of Terrorist Organizations." CSC Report, 1995. http://www.globalsecurity.org/military/library/report/1995/SDE.htm (accessed 24 July 2003).

Smitten, Richard. *The Godmother: The True Story of the Hunt for the Most Bloodthirsty Female Criminal of Our Time.* New York: Pocket Books, 1990.

Sontag, Deborah. "Secret Justice: Terror Suspect's Path from Streets to Brig." *New York Times,* 25 April 2004. http://www.nytimes.com/2004/04/25/national/25PADI.html (accessed 13 May 2004).

Sparrow, Malcolm K. "The Application of Network Analysis to Criminal Intelligence: An Assessment of the Prospects." *Social Networks* 13 (1991): 251–74.

Stacey, Ralph D. *Complex Responsive Processes in Organizations: Learning and Knowledge Creation.* New York: Routledge, 2001.

Steffen, George S., and Samuel M. Candelaria. *Drug Interdiction: Partnerships,*

Legal Principles, and Investigative Methodologies for Law Enforcement. Boca Raton, Fla.: CRC Press, 2002.

Stein, Janice Gross. "Political Learning by Doing: Gorbachev as Uncommitted Thinker and Motivated Learner." *International Organization* 48, no. 2 (1994): 155–83.

Steinbruner, John D. *The Cybernetic Theory of Decision: New Dimensions of Political Analysis.* Princeton: Princeton University Press, 1974.

Stern, Jessica. *The Ultimate Terrorists.* Cambridge: Harvard University Press, 1999.

———. *Terror in the Name of God: Why Religious Militants Kill.* New York: Ecco, 2003.

———. "The Protean Enemy." *Foreign Affairs* 82, no. 4 (2003). http://www .foreignaffairs.org/20030701faessay15403/jessica-stern/the-protean-enemy .html (accessed 25 July 2003).

Stutman, Robert M., and Richard Esposito. *Dead on Delivery: Inside the Drug Wars, Straight from the Street.* New York: Warner Books, 1992.

Sullivan, John P. "Terrorism Early Warning Groups: Regional Intelligence to Combat Terrorism." In *Homeland Security and Terrorism: Readings and Implications,* ed. Russell D. Howard, James J. F. Forest, and Joanne C. Moore, 235–45. New York: McGraw-Hill, 2006.

Suskind, Ron. *The One Percent Doctrine.* New York: Simon and Schuster, 2006.

Tetlock, Philip E. "Learning in U.S. and Soviet Foreign Policy: In Search of an Elusive Concept." In *Learning in U.S. and Soviet Foreign Policy,* ed. George W. Breslauer and Philip E. Tetlock, 20–61. Boulder, Colo.: Westview Press, 1991.

Thoumi, Francisco E. *Political Economy and Illegal Drugs in Colombia.* Boulder, Colo.: Lynne Rienner, 1995.

———. *Illegal Drugs, Economy, and Society in the Andes.* Washington, D.C.: Woodrow Wilson Center, 2003.

Tilly, Charles. "War Making and State Making as Organized Crime." In *Bringing the State Back In,* ed. Peter B. Evans, Dietrich Rueschemeyer, and Theda Skocpol, 169–91. New York: Cambridge University Press, 1985.

Trujillo, Horacio R. "The Radical Environmentalist Movement." In Brian A. Jackson et al., *Aptitude for Destruction,* vol. 2, *Case Studies of Organizational Learning in Five Terrorist Groups,* 141–75. Santa Monica, Calif.: RAND Corporation, 2005.

Tucker, David. *Skirmishes at the Edge of Empire: The United States and International Terrorism.* Westport, Conn.: Praeger, 1997.

———. "What's New About the New Terrorism and How Dangerous Is It?" *Terrorism and Political Violence* 13, no. 3 (2001): 1–14.

Turner, Mark. "The Management of Violence in a Conflict Organization: The Case of the Abu Sayyaf." *Public Organization Review* 3 (2003): 387–401.

Turner, Michael A. *Why Secret Intelligence Fails.* Dulles, Va.: Potomac Books, 2005.

Ulph, Stephen. "A New Journal for Algerian Jihad." *Terrorism Monitor* 2, no. 15 (29 July 2004): 3–5.

———. "New Magazine for al-Qaeda in Iraq." *Terrorism Focus* 2, no. 5 (3 March 2005): 3–4.

———. "A Guide to Jihad on the Web." *Terrorism Focus* 2, no. 7 (31 March 2005). http://jamestown.org/terrorism/news/article.php?articleid = 2369531 (accessed 19 June 2006).

———. "The *Voice of the Caucasus*—A New Jihadi Magazine." *Terrorism Focus* 2, no. 8 (28 April 2005): 1–2.

———. "Secret Camps Offer Operational Courses in Jihad Tactics." *Terrorism Focus* 3, no. 12 (28 March 2006): 5–6.

United Nations, Office of Drugs and Crime. *World Drug Report 2006*. Vol. 1, *Analysis*. http://www.unodc.org/pdf/WDR_2006/wdr2006_volume1.pdf (accessed 11 July 2006).

U.S. Congress. House of Representatives. "Statement of Witness Appearing Anonymously Under the Federal Witness Protection Program." *Money Laundering: Hearings Before the Subcommittee on Financial Institutions Supervision, Regulation and Insurance of the Committee on Banking, Finance and Urban Affairs*, 101st Cong., 1st sess., 14–15 November 1989. Washington, D.C.: U.S. Government Printing Office, 1990.

U.S. Congress. Joint Intelligence Committee. Testimony of George J. Tenet, "Written Statement for the Record of the Director of Central Intelligence Before the Joint Inquiry Committee." *Joint Investigation: Hearing Before the Joint Intelligence Committee*, 107th Cong., 2d sess., 17 October 2002. http://intelligence.senate.gov/0210hrg/021017/tenet.pdf (accessed 26 December 2003).

U.S. Congress. Senate. Select Committee on Intelligence. Testimony of George J. Tenet, "The Worldwide Threat 2004: Challenges in a Changing Global Context." *Current and Projected National Security Threats to the United States: Hearing Before the United States Senate Select Committee on Intelligence*, 108th Cong., 2d sess., 24 February 2004. http://intelligence.senate .gov/0402hrg/040224/tenet.pdf (accessed 26 February 2004).

U.S. Congress. Senate Select Committee on Intelligence and U.S. House Permanent Select Committee on Intelligence. *Joint Inquiry into Intelligence Community Activities Before and After the Terrorist Attacks of September 11, 2001*, S. Rep. 107-351/H. Rep. 107-792, 107th Cong., 2d sess., December 2002. http://www.fas.org/irp/congress/2002_rpt/911rept.pdf (accessed 24 December 2003).

U.S. Department of Justice, National Drug Intelligence Center. *National Drug Threat Assessment 2006*. Johnstown, Pa., January 2006. http://www.usdoj .gov/ndic/pubs11/18862/18862p.pdf (accessed 11 July 2006).

U.S. Department of Justice, Office of the Attorney General. "Prepared Remarks of Attorney General John Ashcroft." Speech given at the Organized Crime and Drug Enforcement Task Force Twentieth Anniversary Conference, Washington, D.C., 30 July 2002. http://www.usdoj.gov/ag/speeches/2002/073002ocdetfremarks.htm (accessed 24 June 2003).

U.S. Department of Justice, Office of the Inspector General. *A Review of the FBI's Handling of Intelligence Information Related to the September 11 Attacks* (November 2004), redacted and unclassified version (released publicly June 2005). http://www.usdoj.gov/oig/special/0506/final.pdf (accessed 10 June 2005).

U.S. Department of State, Bureau for International Narcotics and Law Enforcement Affairs. *International Narcotics Control Strategy Report 2003* (March 2004). http://www.state.gov/g/inl/rls/nrcrpt/2003/vol2/html/29920.htm (accessed 8 March 2004).

———. *International Narcotics Control Strategy Report 2006,* vol. 1, *Drug and Chemical Control* (March 2006). http://www.state.gov/p/inl/rls/nrcrpt/2006/vol1/.

U.S. Drug Enforcement Administration. *Intelligence Collection and Analytical Methods.* Washington, D.C.: U.S. Government Printing Office, 1987.

———. Intelligence Division. *U.S. Drug Threat Assessment:1993.* DEA-93042. Washington, D.C.: DEA Intelligence Division, Publications Unit, September 1993.

———. *The Illicit Drug Situation in Colombia.* Washington, D.C.: DEA Intelligence Division, Publications Unit, November 1993.

———. *The Drug Trade in Colombia: A Threat Assessment.* South America/Caribbean Strategic Intelligence Unit, Office of International Intelligence. DEA-02006, March 2002. http://www.dea.gov/pubs/intel/02006/indexp.html (accessed 13 November 2002).

U.S. General Accounting Office. *Investigations of Major Drug Trafficking Organizations: Report to the Honorable Joseph R. Biden, Jr. United States Senate.* GGD-84-36, 5 March 1984. Washington, D.C.: U.S. General Accounting Office, 1984.

———. *Drug Control: DEA's Strategies and Operations in the 1990s.* GGD-99-108, 21 July 1999. Washington, D.C.: U.S. General Accounting Office, 1999.

———. *Combating Terrorism: Interagency Framework and Agency Programs to Address the Overseas Threat.* GAO-03-165, May 2003. Washington, D.C.: U.S. General Accounting Office, 2003.

Vargas Meza, Ricardo. *Drogas, máscaras y juegos: Narcotráfico y conflicto armado en Colombia.* Bogotá: Tercer Mundo, 1999.

Vaughan, Diane. *The Challenger Launch Decision: Risky Technology, Culture, and Deviance at NASA.* Chicago: University of Chicago Press, 1996.

———. "The Dark Side of Organizations: Mistake, Misconduct, and Disaster." *Annual Review of Sociology* 25 (1999): 271–305.

Venzke, Ben, and Aimee Ibrahim. *Al-Qaeda's Advice for Mujahideen in Iraq: Lessons Learned in Afghanistan.* Alexandria, Va.: IntelCenter/Tempest Publishing, April 2003.

Weick, Karl E. *The Social Psychology of Organizing.* 2d ed. New York: Random House, 1979.

———. *Sensemaking in Organizations.* Thousand Oaks, Calif.: Sage Publications, 1995.

Weick, Karl E., and Frances Westley. "Organizational Learning: Affirming an Oxymoron." In *Handbook of Organization Studies,* ed. Stewart Clegg, Cynthia Hardy, and Walter R. Nord, 440–58. Thousand Oaks, Calif.: Sage Publications, 1996.

Weimann, Gabriel. *Terror on the Internet: The New Arena, the New Challenges.* Washington, D.C.: U.S. Institute of Peace Press, 2006.

Westrate, David L. "The Role of Law Enforcement." In *Drugs and Foreign Policy:*

A Critical Review, ed. Raphael F. Perl, 79–99. Boulder, Colo: Westview Press, 1994.

Whitelaw, Kevin, and Mark Mazzetti. "War in the Shadows." *U.S. News and World Report,* 11 November 2002, 48.

Williams, Phil. "Organizing Transnational Crime: Networks, Markets, and Hierarchies." *Transnational Organized Crime* 4, nos. 3–4 (1998): 57–87.

————. "Transnational Criminal Networks." In *Networks and Netwars: The Future of Terror, Crime, and Militancy,* ed. John Arquilla and David Ronfeldt, 61–97. Santa Monica, Calif.: RAND Corporation, 2001.

Wilson, James Q. *The Investigators: Managing FBI and Narcotics Agents.* New York: Basic Books, 1978.

Woolner, Ann. *Washed in Gold: The Story Behind the Biggest Money-Laundering Investigation in U.S. History.* New York: Simon and Schuster, 1994.

Wright, Lawrence. "The Terror Web." *New Yorker,* 2 August 2004.

Wright, Theodore P. "Factors Affecting the Costs of Airplanes." *Journal of Aeronautical Science* 4, no. 4 (1936): 122–28.

Yelle, Louise E. "The Learning Curve: Historical Review and Comprehensive Survey." *Decision Sciences* 10 (1979): 302–28.

Zabludoff, Sidney. "Colombian Narcotics Organizations as Business Enterprises." *Transnational Organized Crime* 3, no. 2 (1997): 20–49.

Zaitch, Damián. *Trafficking Cocaine: Colombian Drug Entrepreneurs in the Netherlands.* The Hague: Kluwer Law International, 2002.

————. "The Ambiguity of Violence, Secrecy, and Trust Among Colombian Drug Entrepreneurs." *Journal of Drug Issues* 35, no. 1 (2005): 201–28.

Zhang, Sheldon, and Ko-Lin Chin. "Enter the Dragon: Inside Chinese Human Smuggling Organizations." *Criminology* 40, no. 4 (2002): 737–67.